Walking In The Footsteps Of
JESUS

The Sunday Lectionary
YEAR A

REFLECTIONS

Msgr. Raphael A. Owusu Peprah

Walking In The Footsteps Of
JESUS
THE SUNDAY LECTIONARY
YEAR A
REFLECTIONS
Copyright @ 2025 Raphael A. Owusu Peprah

Printed in the United States of America

ISBN: 979-8-9987459-1-1

Cover Design by Elizabeth Lawless and Sheila Weidman

Unless otherwise stated, Scripture texts in this book are taken from the Good News Bible, Second Edition C. 1994.

The nihil obstat (Latin, "nothing stands in the way") and imprimatur (Latin, "let it be printed") are declarations that a book or pamphlet is free of doctrinal or moral error. No implication is contained therein that those who have granted the nihil obstat or imprimatur agree with the contents, opinions or statements expressed.

Nihil Obstat is granted by Rev. Peter Naah, S.T.L.

Imprimatur is granted by Most Rev. Gabriel Justice Anokye, Archbishop of Kumasi, Ghana.

Msgr. Raphael A. Owusu Peprah
St. Luke Catholic Church
2304 Salem Road, Virginia Beach, VA 23456

DEDICATION

Dedicated with thanks to
my older brother Raphael Anthony Owusu,
and parishioners Joseph A. Malfitano and Donald Jellig,
demonstrably, men of faith, love, and generosity.

REFLECTIONS – What People Are Saying

I have been reading your homilies for quite some time, always learning as I do. It seems that in almost all of them, you fit in somewhere that we should love and take care of one another, no matter their standing in society, ethnicity, religion, or anything else. Sometimes it's an easy fit, and sometimes it slides in where I don't expect it to, but I feel that is your mission... to call us to be our best selves in our relations with others, as Jesus called us to do. Today, Third Sunday of Easter, Year B, you wrapped that up in five minutes or less! When you said that those in the Middle East need to know Jesus, the way of peace, I think it clicked for lots of people sitting in front of you! It was palpable!!

You were so yourself doing that... so relaxed, yet so sure. Obviously, you made my day, but I think you reached so many this morning! Good on you. You did an amazing job!

Thank you!

Sheila Weidman

It is truly a closer walk with Jesus whenever I read each reflection in your series – Walking in the Footsteps of JESUS. They have afforded me a channel of growth in the Lord. Thank you for your spiritual insight and the valuable wisdom you share with many others.

Mercy Ampofo

This collection of scholarly and inspirational homilies has been a work forged in love of and for God and for the parishioners that Monsignor Raphael Owusu Peprah has served, both past and present. This compilation of works has helped those who have heard them and those who have read them to understand more fully God's plan for us and has drawn us closer ever more in love with Him. Each of these homilies posits the big questions for us to reflect on and to discover God's will for each of us. By reading and contemplating Monsignor Peprah's words, we better understand God's words.

Catherine Rogers, PhD, and William Brown, PhD

In his book of Reflections for Cycle A readings, Msgr. Raphael Peprah gracefully blends history, theology, and practical insights to aid and encourage the reader in his or her personal Walk. Msgr. Raphael's pastoral heart and concern for his flock are evident on every page. The questions at the end of each reflection enable the reader to evaluate his or her own progress in the spiritual life and to take action steps to grow closer to the Lord. I can attest to the fact that Msgr. Raphael has poured his heart into this work, and his aim is eternal - to lead everyone to Walk in the Footsteps of our Lord and Saviour Jesus Christ.

Regina Gomez

My sincere gratitude to Monsignor Raphael Owusu Peprah for this inspiring collection of homilies and I vouch their impact on understanding God's plan and will for Christians, especially young women and men. This is a special apostolate, to be a leader in the faith, and may the Lord guide you to accomplish the task.

Priscilla Jamoni, PhD

TABLE OF CONTENTS

FOREWORD

With a plethora of published reflections on the Liturgy of the Word in our Christian world, one may wonder why Msgr. Raphael Owusu Peprah's book should be singled out for special attention. The answer to this query is that beyond being a Lectionary, the book, "Walking in the Footsteps of JESUS – the Sunday Lectionary Year A," powerfully seeks to make the Faithful internalize the messages of Scriptural readings selected for each Sunday during the celebration of the Holy Eucharist. In the Roman Catholic tradition, Scriptural readings at Mass are bundled in three Cycles, namely, Year A, Year B, and Year C. This book is Year A.

Msgr. Peprah demonstrates that he is a successful product of the Liturgical Movement which emerged in the 19th Century and was aimed at making the liturgy more meaningful to the Faithful in the modern Christian life. Pope Pius XII in his encyclical, *Mediator Dei*, endorsed the aim of the Liturgical Movement, stressing the importance of the liturgy and the need for the Faithful to exemplify what they hear at Mass in their day-to-day life situations. Msgr. Peprah seeks to achieve this objective with his series of Walking in the Footsteps of JESUS.

As someone who has listened to many of Msgr. Peprah's homilies at Mass, I can attest to the quality and incisive nature of his preaching. At one of his homilies, which I remember vividly, he, in a typical posture of a teacher of eschatological things, taught and brought home forcefully to the packed St. Peter's Cathedral Basilica in Kumasi the need for all to accept that all things earthly are ephemeral – they will come to an end – and, therefore, there was no need for people to cling to earthly glory or riches. He counseled those in whose hand wealth had accumulated to place their surplus at the service of the needy. Similarly, he urged those who wallow in worldly poverty not to pursue earthly riches or curse themselves or others for their predicament for theirs is the Kingdom of Heaven. The refrain that punctuated the key points of his well-crafted homily was, "All This Shall Pass," and that everyone should rather maintain a gaze on the Heavenly glory that Our Father has reserved for us. At the end of the Mass, many were heard saying they had been touched by the sermon.

Msgr. Peprah's communication style coupled with the real-life examples he gives during his homilies always capture his audience's attention and this has enabled him to become what can be described as "master of the pulpit." It is with this incisive quality that Monsignor has provided in this book an endurable teaching that cannot help but become a prolific source the Faithful can avail themselves of for many years to come. It is a treasure that the Faithful who are determined to gain deeper understanding of God's Word can rely on as a viable compendium and a supplement to what they hear from their pastors every Sunday.

The book is not merely informative in outlook; it also pushes for witnessing to the Gospel message. I find the semi-interactive annotations and prayer at the end of each homily in the book very useful as they kick the reader back to re-affirm his or her understandings.

A major defect in our Christian practice is that while we earnestly attend Mass and hear the Word of God, we invariably fail to adequately showcase the "witnessing" aspect of our Christian duty. I become gratified that Msgr. Peprah makes a bold attempt to step into the shoes of St. Charles Borromeo and says, "Be sure that you first preach by the way you live. If you do not, people will notice that you say one thing but live otherwise." In this era when the Supreme Pontiff is urging Catholics to pay attention to the core purpose of our calling, Msgr. Peprah's book becomes relevant because he establishes a strong link between anthropology and theology and opines validly that prayer or spiritual life is not the only worthwhile activity towards the "universales salutatis sacramentum."

A Christian's life must portray the value of what he or she says or proclaims as the Truth. The Christian must perform his or her faith. As Pope Benedict XVI teaches in *Spe Salvi facti sumus*, the Christian message was not only "informative" but "performative." That means the Gospel is not merely a communication of things that can be known - it is one that can make things happen or change in real life situations. In effect, we must witness to what the Gospel says, and this is a perspective that runs through the length and breadth of the book.

Putting a whole year's homilies in one book provides Catholics with an ever-present voice of an authentic preacher and the value is, indeed, immeasurable. Msgr. Peprah has published other books and, looking at his vocational pathways, he does not give any indication that he is done yet. He epitomizes Natalie Goldberg's saying that "Writing is elemental. Once you have tasted its essential life, you cannot turn from it without some denial and depression." We can expect to benefit again from his gift as a writer to add the other Cycles, Year B and Year C. He has taken the road less travelled but given his great determination, he surely will make a huge difference with his talent. While we make the effort to patronize the book, let us also pray for Msgr. Peprah in all his efforts to feed the minds of the Faithful with worthwhile publications such as this book. I cannot but congratulate him.

Sir Fosuaba A. Mensah Banahene
President, Forum of Papal Knights and Dames, Ghana

INTRODUCTION

"I may truly think and say this most assuredly: Lord I am nothing. I can do nothing by myself that is good. I am in all things broken and ever tend to nothing. Unless I am assisted and interiorly instructed by You, I become wholly tepid and relaxed. But You, O Lord, are unchanging and endure unto eternity. You are ever good, just and holy, doing all things well, justly, holily, and wisely.

But I am changing, having failed so many times, and am more inclined to go back, than to go forward. But, if You please, when You stretch out Your helping hand, it quickly becomes better. For You alone, far beyond the help of any man, can assist me and so strengthen me. Nothing so changes my demeanor and converts my heart, as the rest I find in You alone.

He who is too secure in time of peace is often too dejected in time of war. If you could just remember yourself as humble and little, and if you could keep your spirit ordered, you would not fall so easily into danger and offense. It is wise to remember: when you make your plans in the fervor of summertime, how will it be when the light is withdrawn?"

Thomas A' Kempis
Imitation of Christ, Book III, Chapters 7 and 40.

Welcome friends, neighbors, and travelers.

We attend Mass to be in communion with Jesus Christ and honor his sacrifice to save us, and we begin with the Living Word of God—the Scriptures that are always speaking to us in new and meaningful ways, although the words remain the same. There is comfort in that repetition, in the familiarity of knowing the passages you hear are the same message millions have heard over the past several centuries. It brings us together in unity and harmony in a way few things in this world can.

After the reading, the homily provides a time of reflection on God's Word and the message he is sending out to his people. For many, the homily provides clarity and guidance that may not be found in reading the Scriptures alone. It also provides topics for reflection and discussion within the family and the community. Revelations inspired by these homilies have frequently been shared with Pastors, the individuals sharing with joy how the message affected them and their lives.

In the coming pages, you are invited on a journey to walk through the personalized messages of Monsignor Raphael Owusu Peprah as he helps us to understand the Scriptures in our present day. Taking his devotion a step further than the timed homilies during each Mass, he has provided more detailed and in-depth reflections on the Scriptures throughout the entire year. With present day scenarios, real-world events, and thought-provoking questions, he encourages us to look beyond materialism, power, wealth, and position to see God present in every aspect of our lives, most especially in our neighbors. His words—reflective of the gifts and fruits of the Holy Spirit that ground us in our humanity, ethics, and morals—provide a roadmap to opening our hearts and minds to our Lord's desires for love of God and our neighbor, as He so loves us that He gave His beloved son in sacrifice to redeem us.

The world is full of opportunities for us to make a difference in the lives of so many, both known and unknown to us. The complete homilies that follow will light the flame of the Holy Spirit in your heart to reach out with kindness, compassion, and empathy to our lesser brothers and sisters. Each account will deepen in you the good we can do in helping each other by reflecting on God's message to us in our current world and to the future we are creating.

God knows what we need, and He knows where we are going. He is with us every day, encouraging, loving, and forgiving, showing mercy and charity to those who seek him. Join him and Monsignor Peprah on this path toward selflessness and spirituality: in reflection on God's message to you and in action to fulfill that message. Trust in the Lord's message, shared through Monsignor's wisdom and experiences, to align you more closely to Christ, the Saints, the Church, and the community. As you do so, you will find the Holy Spirit strengthening you in the fruits and gifts with which you have been blessed while lifting your soul in hope and promise to keep the light from above shining on our beautiful and blessed world.

God bless you and all those close to you on this journey.
Julia Neuweiler

Ghanaian "Akan Adinkra" Symbol

Adinkra Symbols depict concepts and proverbs among the Akan people of Ghana and the Ivory Coast.

GYE NYAME
"Except God"
Symbol of the Omnipotence of God

ACKNOWLEDGEMENTS

God's Plan of Salvation is about His love for a world He created and the events in human history designed by Him to bring about salvation. The course of salvation is recorded in the Holy Bible beginning from creation and will end at the second coming of Jesus Christ, the Messiah through whom God's salvation plan reaches its climax.

In the Old Testament is the ultimate evidence of God's salvation rooted in Israel's deliverance from Egypt as narrated in the Book of Exodus. The Historical Books in the Old Testament record God's intervention to settle the people of Israel on the Promised Land. The concept of salvation is basically about humankind being liberated from sin and spiritual death through repentance as narrated in the Prophetic Books. This notion of universal dispensation of salvation is central to the New Testament showing Jesus Christ as "Son of God" and source of salvation, and John the Baptist as His herald. Believing in Jesus Christ who shed His blood on the Cross as the "new sacrificial lamb" or "Passover Lamb," saves one from sin and spiritual death. Jesus, the Messiah, is the ultimate restorer of the good relationship that existed between God and our first parents, Adam and Eve. At the end of His life on earth, Jesus Christ commissioned His disciples to make all peoples of the world into "the family of God," with the supreme directive to love God and neighbor.

This book is intended primarily for Christians who thirst to understand the Scriptural passages used in the Sunday Lectionary. It is also a guide for priests, religious, catechists, and Sunday School teachers in preparing homilies for the Liturgical Seasons, Solemnities, and Holy Days. Furthermore, the chapters can be read as separate meditational segments which is how the lay faithful will find the book very useful. My fervent hope is that readers will endeavor to walk in the footsteps of Jesus. The Word of God is not abstract theory; it must reflect how we live in today's world.

Preparations to publish Year B and Year C are in progress. I am grateful for the amazing interest and tremendous support of Marilyn Bucich and Tom Byrnes (Holy Name of Jesus Church, Brooklyn). Across the Atlantic, between Ghana and New York, the couple and I burned the midnight oil working together. We discussed each reflection searching for the clarity intended and they made valuable suggestions.

My profound gratitude to Sir Peter Fosuaba Banahene for generously accepting to write the Foreword and David Atigah for writing the blurb.

Many thanks to the parishioners of the Saint Peter's Cathedral Basilica, Kumasi, Ghana, whose copious thirst for understanding the Word of God motivated me to start writing the Sunday reflections.

The computer has become the biggest library in the world. The "Wikimedia Foundation" and other numerous contributors, researchers, and authors have again made the computer the greatest source of shared knowledge. My indebtedness to such organizations and contributors is hereby acknowledged.

I thank Ann Watkins (Cardiff, Wales, UK), Sr. Jacquelyn Cramer, BVM, Catherine Rogers, and William Brown for their special interest in the book and their invaluable suggestions.

I want also to thank the parishioners of St. Luke Catholic Church, Virginia Beach, Virginia, USA, particularly the staff, both present and retired, Deacon Lito Magsombol, Patty Trail, Ginny James, Rosemarie Rivera, Jean Malbas, Melissa Paulmino, Hilda Paulino and Zeta Castillo.

My profound gratitude goes to Sheila Weidman, Julia Neuweiler, and Regina Gomez, for editing the manuscript, including the publisher, Elizabeth Lawless.

The Peace of the Lord be with you.
Msgr. Raphael A. Owusu Peprah

THE LECTIONARY

The Lectionary is a book of Scriptural readings selected from the Holy Bible that are read during the celebration of the Holy Mass every day of the year and at special occasions. There are two different types like The *Evangeliary* or Book of the Gospels, a liturgical book containing parts from the four Canonical Gospels, and *The Epistolary*, a book containing readings from the New Testament Epistles.

The use of a Lectionary for the celebration of liturgies on Sabbath days had developed in many Jewish religious communities. The Lectionary contained extracts from The Old Testament, comprising the Torah, the prophetic books, and history books such as The Book of Judges and the first and second Books of Kings. The Early Christians adopted the Jewish practice of including extracts from the Old Testament on the Sabbath, and over the centuries, added portions from the Evangelists (the Gospels) and the letters of the Apostles (the Epistles). By the third and fourth centuries different local churches had developed their own Lectionaries usually on a one-year basis.

After the Second Vatican Council (1962-1965), a common Lectionary was produced with readings for Sundays and major feasts recurring in a three-year cycle and readings in a two-year cycle for the weekdays. There are four readings on Sundays and major feasts: one from the Old Testament (though during the Easter Season certain books of the New Testament are used), one from the Psalms which ideally is sung, one from the Epistles, and one from the Gospels. Three extracts are read on weekdays: one from the Old Testament or the Epistles, one from the Psalms both of which recur in a two-year cycle, and a passage taken from the Gospel which recur after a single year. There are also selected readings in the Lectionary for other occasions such as the celebration of the Sacraments, anniversaries, and funerals.

19

Although, originally developed as the Roman Catholic Mass Lectionary, its use is basically interdenominational today. It is used principally by the major or mainline Christian churches mainly due to the avid commitment to ecumenism that allows these groupings to be part of the common Lectionary. Furthermore, the essence of ecumenism has brought churches together to strive for uniformity especially since they use the same Scripture as the basis of their faith. Like the Bible, the Lectionary replicates "Salvation History" in a chronological order designed as Seasons in the Year, emphasizing its linkage with Jesus' birth (Incarnation), life, death, and resurrection. It presents Jesus Christ as the living Lord and Savior, who makes us "sons and daughters" of God the Father through the power of the Holy Spirit in the ritual of baptism, recognized by all the major churches. The readings together with the Responsorial Psalms, are usually purposely selected to reflect the theme of the day or occasion.

The Sunday Lectionary

The Sunday Lectionary's three-year cycle is designated as A, B, and C. Cycle A or Year A begins on the First Sunday of Advent. The following year, Cycle B or Year B also begins on the First Sunday of Advent. Cycle C or Year C will follow Cycle B and begin on the First Sunday of Advent after which the cycle will revert to Cycle A or Year A. Traditionally, the yearly cycle begins on the First Day of Advent, usually the Sunday between November 27 and December 3 inclusive.

One of the three Synoptic Gospels is read in its entirety each year. The Gospels are read corresponding to the years:

- Year A: The Gospel According to Matthew

- Year B: The Gospel According to Mark

- Year C: The Gospel According to Luke

The Gospels of Matthew, Mark, Luke, and John are called "canonical" Gospels, officially approved by Christians as books that give "accurate and authoritative" account of the life, ministry, death, resurrection, and ascension of Jesus Christ of Nazareth.

The first three Gospels are also referred to as the "Synoptic Gospels." The word "synoptic" is from two Greek words meaning "see together." The Synoptic Gospels are so-called because they are presumed to have developed from a single source and generally bear the same features, content, and have identical wording.

Many Scripture scholars are of the opinion that the Gospel of Mark was written first and used as a reference manuscript by Matthew and Luke. This hypothetical source is referred to the "Marcan Priority," making the Gospel of Mark the "primary source" of much of the information about Jesus' ministry contained in the Gospels of Matthew and Luke.

The materials common to the Gospels of Matthew and Luke but not found in Mark's Gospel are believed to have come from another source which scholars refer to as the "Q Source." It is made up of a collection of stories and sayings by Jesus transmitted by Christian oral tradition. The theory proposing that the two gospels evolved around two sources is known as the "two-source hypothesis" (or 2SH). 'Q' is the first letter of Quelle, the German word for "source." The information about Jesus in the "Q Source" was not in the hands of Mark. It means Matthew and Luke wrote independently but relied on two sources. The "Q Source" was written in Greek which included the "Lord's Prayer" and the "Magnificat." The document does not give the exact times or places for the sayings. Thus, although the same words are used in the Greek language, both authors provide different times and places for the sayings. The materials unique to Luke's account are said to be derived from the "L Source." Similarly, the materials special to Matthew were derived from the "M Source" that originated from Matthew's own Jewish-Christian community perhaps in Roman Syria nearing the end of the first century A.D.

All this notwithstanding, each of the Synoptic Gospels has its unique approach to how the life of Jesus and his teachings are narrated. Thus, it is when they are read separately that their distinguishing features can be appreciated.

The Gospel of John differs from the Synoptic Gospels in many ways. First, many important events in the Synoptic Gospels are absent in John's Gospel such as the temptation of Jesus, the transfiguration of Jesus, the Sermon on the Mount, Jesus casting out demons, and a detailed account of the Last Supper. Many scholars suggest that the Gospel of John contains no parables, and they do not consider the narrative regarding "The Vine and the Branches" (John 15:1-8) as a parable. Second, the Gospel of John has materials not found in the Synoptic Gospels, such as the resurrection of Lazarus and Jesus' long farewell discourse. Third, Jesus' ministry in the Gospel of John extends over a period of three or four years with multiple visits to Jerusalem. The Synoptic Gospels seem to have about one year of Jesus' ministry and only a first and last visit to Jerusalem. Fourth, John seems to be more reflective in his presentation than the others. For example, the Gospel of John begins with a long prologue which presents the divine nature of Jesus. Fifth, the Gospel of John contains long dialogues with individuals like Nicodemus and the Samaritan woman. The Gospel also has extended discourses such as the Bread of Life Discourse and the Farewell Discourse. Sixth, the author uses symbols and attaches theological meanings to them more than is found in the Synoptic Gospels such as the use of light and darkness or water and Spirit. The Gospel of John is read throughout the Season of Easter each year and during the seasons of Advent, Christmas, and Lent where suitable.

The Weekday Lectionary

The Weekday Lectionary is a two-year cycle of Scriptural readings for the weekday Masses referred to as Cycle I and Cycle II with odd-numbered years as Cycle I and even-numbered years as Cycle II. There are three readings each day: the first reading can be taken from the Old Testament, the Acts of the Apostles, the Epistles, and The Book of Revelation. The second reading is a Responsorial Psalm, and the third reading is from one of the Gospels in such a manner that excerpts from all the four Gospels are read every year. However, the first readings and the Psalms are arranged in a two-year Cycle. Generally, the Sunday readings are longer than the weekday readings. In addition, the three-year cycle of Sunday readings and the two-year cycle of weekday readings are arranged such that they cover the entire Bible in a three-year period. Again, the Gospel of John is read during the Easter Season. Furthermore, in the Roman Catholic Lectionary, there are readings selected for feasts of major saints, feasts in honor of the Blessed Virgin Mary, Masses celebrating the Sacraments, funerals, and for various occasions.

The Current Year

This year is Cycle A or Year A. The Year begins on the First Sunday of Advent and primarily uses The Gospel According to Matthew.

The Gospel According to Matthew

The Gospel According to Matthew, also known as The Gospel of Matthew or simply Matthew, is the first book of the New Testament. The Gospel of Matthew is one of the four Canonical Gospels and one of the Synoptic Gospels.

The Gospel of Matthew was written for a Jewish Community. The "Q" and the "M" sources are very particular about Jewish Law. Again, the "M" manuscript does not give explanations for Jewish names and customs with the presumption that they would be known or understood by the Jewish audience.

Another significant factor is how Matthew writes about Jesus' origins. While Luke traces Jesus' ancestry to Adam, indicating that Adam is the father of humanity, Matthew's line of lineage goes back only to Abraham, father of the Jews. Furthermore, the "M" Source is extremely strict with keeping the Jewish Law, suggesting that there was already an organized strict Jewish community or sect (in Roman Syria) who upheld the Gospel of Matthew. The Gospel of Matthew is therefore an account of the life and ministry of Jesus, the Messiah of Israel, to the chosen people of God. However, the Messiah is rejected by the chosen people of Israel whose leadership plans to kill him. The people of Israel become the non-believing Jews. The message of Jesus is now directed instead to the Gentiles: "Go, then, to all peoples everywhere and make them my disciples" (Matthew 28:19).

It is suggested that the Jewish Christian Community rejected in Israel settled in Syria probably in Antioch or one of the eastern Mediterranean coastal cities near Galilee or Judea. While Jews observed the Law to the letter and still awaited the Messiah, the Jewish Christians of Antioch preached about "obedience to law" which would be done by following the message of Jesus the Messiah. The sheer numbers of the Gentiles made Christianity a Gentile religion distancing itself from Judaism.

Authorship

Like the other Canonical Gospels, the author of the Gospel of Matthew is not named in the book. One early mention of the author as the Apostle Matthew, the tax-collector, starts with an Early Christian Bishop called Papias of Hierapolis (ca. 100-140). He suggested that "Matthew collected the oracles ("logia" – sayings of or about Jesus) in the Hebrew language" and his disciples, "each one interpreted or 'translated' them as best he could'" into Greek. This may suggest that the Gospel of Matthew was originally a Hebrew testament which was later translated into Greek. However, many scholars opine that the Gospel of Matthew passes for an excellent original Greek text which was not the direct translation from another language. All the same, towards the end of the second century, the Apostle Matthew or Matthew the tax-collector was accepted as the author of the Gospel of Matthew, hence, the title, The Gospel According to Matthew.

Many Biblical scholars today disagree that the Gospel of Matthew was written by the Apostle Matthew. They cite for example that the Gospel of Matthew, like the other synoptic Gospels, relied heavily on the Gospel of Mark ("Marcan Priority") and the "Q source." When Matthew relies on Mark, the "sequence is the same and the actual words in the original Greek are almost identical." The scholars intimate further that "it seems unlikely that an eyewitness of Jesus' ministry, such as Matthew, would need to rely on others for information about it." Scholars therefore contend that the Gospel of Matthew was written between 80 and 90 A.D. by a highly educated Jew. This was the first century when Christianity as a new religion faced mounting opposition and persecution. The author was "intimately familiar with the technical aspects of Jewish law" and sought to defend the new religion as the fulfillment of the Old Testament. There is an excellent parallel between Mathew's story of the "killing of the Innocents" by Herod and the killing of male-born Jews in Egypt by the Pharaoh. The "flight to Egypt" meant that like Moses, Jesus came out of Egypt to save Israel. Again, with the genealogy story Jesus is the son of Joseph just as Joseph was the son of Jacob in the Old Testament.

Literary Characteristics and Theology

Many Biblical scholars agree that the author of the Gospel of Matthew was familiar with the Zoroastrian religion which originated in Persia (modern day Iran). It preached a monotheistic God and was founded by Zoroaster, who lived, it is estimated, between 1500 and 1000 B.C. Zoroastrianism was the official religion of the Persian Empire (559-331 B.C.) which at its summit comprised modern day Iran, Egypt, Turkey, and some areas of Afghanistan and Pakistan. Zoroastrianism is described as probably the oldest of the monotheistic revealed religions whose influence on human history has been more than Jewish, Christian, and Muslim beliefs (Mary Boyce d. 2006). Its theology has influenced these monotheistic religions especially regarding "God and Satan, the Soul, Heaven and Hell, the Virgin Birth of the Savior, the Resurrection, Final Judgment," and so on.

It is suggested that the author of the Gospel of Matthew makes Christianity the fulfillment of Zoroastrianism by adopting some of its beliefs into Christianity. Some of them are the miraculous events surrounding the Virgin Birth, the Magi, and the Passion. The birth of Zoroaster was believed to have been prophesied, and when he was born the forces of evil wanted to kill him. The Magi were priests of the Zoroastrian religion who visited the Child Jesus. They gave him expensive gifts to indicate their acknowledgement of the supremacy of the birth of the true Messiah of Israel. It is believed when Zoroaster died the dead came out of their graves walking into Jerusalem. He rose from the dead when an earthquake removed the stone of his tomb, and an angel sat on it.

Less than 200,000 Zoroastrians are in the world today found in North America, the United Kingdom, Australia, India, and Iran. Their fewer numbers are attributed to the fact that the religion is ethnic in character and conversion from the outside is strictly forbidden.

The Author of the Gospel of Matthew maintains the same general plan of the Synoptic Gospels – the ministry of John the Baptist and the inauguration of Jesus' ministry and temptation; Jesus' ministry (teaching and healing) in Galilee; the journey to Jerusalem and the events on the way; the events of Jesus' last week in Jerusalem, an incident in the Temple culminating in his crucifixion on the day of the Passover holiday; and Jesus' resurrection and appearances. Matthew, Mark, and Luke agree that although Jesus' ministry started in Galilee, it is Jerusalem, the Holy City, which becomes the center of his redemptive activity. The Messiah is the "Suffering Servant" who is rejected and experiences excruciating suffering and death on the cross.

In addition to following the Synoptic Plan, Matthew begins his Gospel with the genealogy of Jesus. The word "genealogy" (in Greek, "Genesis") is used "deliberately echoing the first words of the Old Testament in Greek." Matthew traces Jesus' ancestry from Abraham to David and to Joseph "who married Mary, the mother of Jesus, who was called the Messiah" (Matthew 1:16). Furthermore, Mathew provides short expositions about the miraculous virgin birth, the visit by the Magi, the killing of innocent children, the flight to Egypt, and the journey back to Nazareth.

Like the Gospels of Mark, Luke, John, and the Acts of the Apostles, Matthew is very particular about the closing section of his Gospel. Jesus appears to the "eleven disciples," assures them of his authority from the Father, and gives the "Great Commission." He tells them his message is Universal: "Go, then, to all peoples everywhere and make them my disciples: baptize them in the name of the Father, the Son, and the Holy Spirit, and teach them to obey everything I have commanded you. And I will be with you always, to the end of the age" (Matthew 28:16-20). Thus, Matthew leaves a measured and profound spirituality for the disciples of Jesus who would "labor in the vineyard of the Lord, looking forward to the end of the day." (Saint Augustine).

The person described as "sitting in the customs office" (Matthew 9:9), is Matthew, the tax-collector at Capharnaum who collected taxes for Herod Antipas. He is the same person referred to as Levi in Mark 2:14 and Luke 5:27. Biblical scholars suggest that Levi was his original name. Due to his trade, he was despised by his fellow Jews. When he accepted to follow Jesus, he organized a party and invited his fellow tax-collectors and "sinners." The Pharisees frowned at this, but Jesus said, "I have come not to call the just but sinners" (Matthew 9:13).

Matthew is named as one of the Apostles (Matthew 10:3) and one of the witnesses of the resurrection. As an apostle he witnessed the Ascension then joined the believers in the Upper Room with Mary, the mother of Jesus, and the other brethren (Acts. 1:12-14). Not much is said about Matthew after the Upper Room experience. Legend has it that he was a missionary to Persia and the Kingdom of the Parthians, Macedonia, and Syria. The Latin Church celebrates his feast on September 1 and the Orthodox Church on November 16.

THE CHURCH'S LITURGICAL YEAR

Ordinary Time

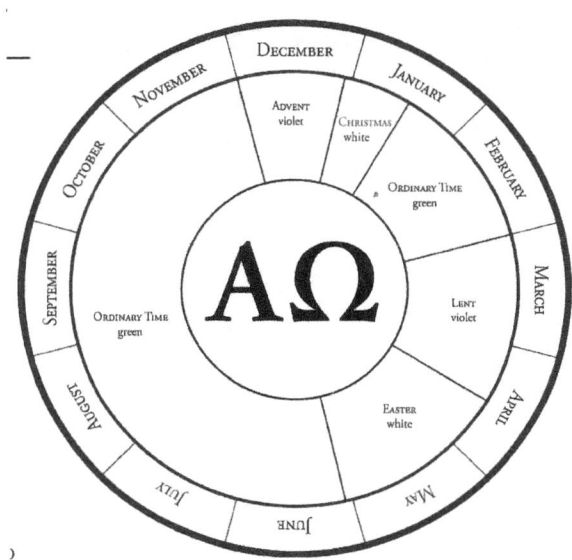

2022 J.S. Paluch Company Catholic Calendar

God's Plan of Salvation or Salvation History is about God's special concern for the world and the events in human history designed by Him to bring about salvation. The process of salvation is recorded in the Holy Bible beginning from Creation and the fall of Adam. It will end in the second coming of Jesus Christ, the archetypal Messiah, through whom God's Salvation Plan reaches its climax.

In the Old Testament, the ultimate evidence of God's salvation is seen in Israel's deliverance from Egypt as narrated in the Book of Exodus. The Historical Books of the Old Testament are records of God's intervention to settle the people of Israel. Subsequently, the concept of salvation is basically about humankind receiving salvation as clearly shown in the Prophetic Books. This notion of salvation is central to the New Testament which portrays Jesus Christ as the source of salvation. Believing in Jesus, one is saved from sin and death. Jesus is the ultimate restorer of the relationship that existed between God and our first parents, Adam and Eve.

The Church's Liturgical Year, also known as the Church Year or the Church's Liturgical Calendar, repeats the ageless mysteries of God's plan for our salvation. Within the year, the Church remembers and celebrates the various events in the life of our Lord Jesus Christ. The Church takes us through lessons of faith, hope and love, and encourages us to reflect deeply on the history of our salvation. We learn that our deliverance is based on God's unconditional love, and this understanding must totally influence our daily living.

The Church's Liturgical Year is made up of three parts, the Christmas Cycle, the Paschal Cycle, and the Yearly Cycle or the Ordinary Time. Each cycle has several events, feasts, and memorials for honoring particular saints. There are liturgical colors identified with each season or occasion. The events of the church year are reflected in the colors used in the church such as the altar and vestments used by the clergy and other ministers during the celebration of the liturgy. Furthermore, in each cycle, portions of the Scriptures are selected and read from the Lectionary to signify the mood of the season.

In the Roman rite of the Catholic Church, the Liturgical Year commences with the Cycle of Christmas comprising the Season of Advent and the Season of Christmas. The Season of Advent begins on the First Sunday of Advent and ends on the Eve of Christmas, December 24. The Season of Advent prepares Christians for the birth of Jesus Christ and his second coming. The Season of Christmas, also known as Christmastide, begins on the evening of December 24 and continues to the Feast of the Baptism of the Lord. The Paschal Cycle follows and consists of both the Season of Lent and the Easter Season. The Season of Lent begins on Ash Wednesday and ends officially on Holy Saturday. The Easter

Triduum, which recalls Jesus' Last Supper with his apostles, crucifixion on Good Friday, burial, and resurrection on Easter Sunday, are however celebrated or commemorated with special liturgies. It starts with the evening of Holy Thursday when the Mass of the Lord's Supper is celebrated and ends on Easter Sunday. The Easter Season begins on Easter Sunday and ends on Pentecost Sunday when the Church celebrates the descent of the Holy Spirit upon the disciples of Jesus and a small group of others who were present shortly after the Ascension. The weeks after Pentecost Sunday are commonly referred to as the Cycle of Ordinary Time or Ordinary Year.

Liturgical Colors

Violet and purple are the colors generally worn during Advent season signifying penance, sacrifice, and submission or surrender. Appropriate colors like white and red are used on feast days and holy days. On the Third Sunday of Advent, "Gaudete Sunday," rose or pink color is used to express joy in anticipation of Christmas. The color for the Christmas and Easter seasons is white signifying the birth and resurrection of Jesus respectively. White is the color for funerals to signify resurrection. In some cultures, however, violet may be used to express sorrow for the loss of a person. During Lent and Holy Week, the color violet and purple are used to signify the mood of the season. On "Laetare Sunday," Fourth Sunday of Lent, rose or pink color is used to anticipate the joy of Easter. Palm Sunday and Good Friday colors are red depicting the Passion of Jesus. During "Ordinary Time," the color used is green representing life, hope, and expectation.

THE CHRISTMAS CYCLE

The Christmas Cycle begins on the First Sunday of Advent, the four Sundays before Christmas Day, and ends with the Feast of the Baptism of the Lord. The Christmas Cycle, therefore, comprises Two Seasons—the Season of Advent and the Season of Christmas—with some major feasts commemorating certain events in the life of Jesus. Known as the Feasts of the Lord Jesus Christ, they include:

- The Nativity of the Lord celebrated on December 25.

- The Epiphany of the Lord celebrated on January 6 or the Sunday between January 2 and January 8.

- The Baptism of the Lord celebrated on the Sunday after January 6.

- The Holy Family of Jesus, Mary, and Joseph celebrated on Sunday in the Octave of Christmas.

- The Solemnity of Mary, Mother of God, celebrated on the first day of January.

The Season of Advent

THE SEASON OF ADVENT

Advent is the beginning of the Church's Liturgical Year. The Season of Advent is the period between the First Sunday of Advent and Christmas Eve or the four-week period before Christmas. In the Church's calendar, therefore, "New Year's Day" is the First Sunday of Advent.

Meaning of Advent

The word "Advent" derives from the Latin word "adventus," which means an "arrival" or a "coming." It is a period of preparation for the coming or arrival of the Lord Jesus Christ, our brother in our humanity and our God in his divinity.

The "coming" of the Lord Jesus Christ has three meanings:

First, it refers to the birth of Jesus as a historical fact. The promise God made at various periods in the Old Testament about the birth of the Messiah was fulfilled over 2000 years ago by the birth of Jesus, a descendant of Abraham and David (Matthew 1:1-17) and the true Son of God the Father (Matthew 16:16; John 3:16). Therefore, during the Season of Advent, Christians prepare to celebrate the birthday of Jesus.

Second, Advent celebrates the reality of Jesus' existence among us. Jesus comes again mystically at Christmas to "dwell among us" (John 1:14). One of his many attributes is "Emmanuel," meaning, "God is with us" (Matthew 1:23). The meaning of his name "Jesus" as announced by the Angel Gabriel is that "he will save his people from their sins" (Matthew 1:21).

Third, Advent looks forward to the second coming of Jesus, which will be another historical event. Jesus' birth fulfilled the Old Testament expectation of the Messiah (Luke 3:15) and his second coming (Acts 1:10-11; 1 Thessalonians

3:13; Philemon 1:6) will fulfill the New Testament expectation of the end of human history when Jesus will come again in glory. The second coming is described as the "Parousia" or the "Day of the Lord," or "Judgment Day."

During the first two weeks of the Season of Advent, the Lectionary puts particular emphasis on the second coming of Jesus when the righteous will be rewarded with a New Heaven where God's people will live in peace and harmony symbolized by the Prophet Isaiah's vision of "the wolf and the lamb living together and leopards co-existing with young goats" (Isaiah 11:6).

Personalities in Advent

The Season of Advent calls attention to certain important personalities in the Bible: David, Isaiah, John the Baptist, and the Blessed Virgin Mary. The first readings of the first and fourth Sundays of Advent are about God's promise to David of an everlasting kingdom. The readings prepare us to expect another important king from the lineage of David, who, like David, would be born in Bethlehem.

The next significant figure is Isaiah, whose prophecy dominates the readings of Cycles A and B. During Cycle C, however, Isaiah gives way to other prophets who share their thoughts concerning God's promise of salvation. These prophets are Jeremiah, Baruch, Zephaniah, and Micah.

John the Baptist is another remarkable figure in Advent whom we read about in the Gospels of the second and third Sundays of Advent. John the Baptist is the "last voice" in the wilderness, calling upon people to prepare for the Lord's arrival through repentance.

The greatest attention during the Season of Advent is, of course, given to the Blessed Virgin Mary, whose response of "Yes" to God's invitation to give birth to Jesus made her the "Ark of the New Covenant." The Virgin Mary closes the Old Testament saga and begins the New Testament chronicle of salvation history.

The evangelists also play a significant role in the New Testament. They are remembered as saints who have given us the "Good News" and call us to faith in Jesus. The Gospel of Matthew is used during Cycle A. The Gospel of Mark is used in Cycle B, and the Gospel of Luke is used for Cycle C. The Gospel of John is not given a specific year, but portions are used over the three-year cycle. For example, the Gospel of John is used on the third Sunday of Cycle B, specifically for his detailed story on John the Baptist. In a similar vein, the Gospel of Luke is used during the fourth Sunday of Advent Cycle B.

Themes of Advent

Another essential aspect of Advent is that the Sundays come with unique themes derived from the Gospel readings. The First Sundays of Advent highlight the second coming of Jesus (the Parousia) or Judgment Day, reiterating the theme of the previous Sunday, the Feast of Christ the King. Jesus who is the King of the Universe, will return to end human history and establish a new kingdom. The Second and Third Sundays of Advent focus on John the Baptist's ascetic life, mission, and message. The Fourth Sundays of Advent noticeably underline the Christmas story, stressing the extraordinary roles of the Virgin Mary and Joseph in God's plan of salvation for humanity.

Human Death and the Second Coming

Jesus had said that the day of his return was known only to the Father (Matthew 24:36). However, the Early Christians believed that Jesus' second coming would occur during their lifetime. Hence, they had "to be ready and prepared at all times." In Rome, for example, Christians who died were buried in the Catacombs, and it was hoped that at the "last trumpet" announcing the return of Jesus Christ, they would rise to meet the Lord (Matthew 23: 29-31).

The fact of the matter is that no one knows when the second coming of Jesus will take place. It might not happen in our own lifetime either. All the same, each of the Early Christians experienced the Lord's Day in the sense that they experienced physical death.

The reality of life, though, is that death seems imminent to each individual and looms over us all the time. It is even more terrifying knowing that death can occur unexpectedly. Therefore, each day must be a day of complete preparedness, exactly as John the Baptist preached.

The Joy of Advent

The second readings of all the Sundays of Advent, except for the Fourth Sundays that highlight Jesus himself, draw a lot of attention to the presence of Jesus in our everyday life. They prescribe a way of life for Christians to live in love and harmony with one another to adequately prepare to meet Jesus when he appears (1 Thessalonians 33:12-13; Philemon 1:9-11, 4:5). This is the joy of Advent: precisely that the love of God and neighbor can overcome the fear of death, adequately disposing us to meet the Lord Jesus Christ both at Christmas and during his second appearance, because we are living by his commandments. The second readings are mainly from Saint Paul's letters, with one reading each from the letters of James, Peter, and Hebrews.

Penance in Advent

The disposition required during the Season of Advent comes from profound inward reflection. Advent is therefore the antecedent penitential period for the joy of Christmas, just as the Season of Lent prepares us for the joy of Easter. The Roman Rite omits the "Gloria in Excelsis" except for feast days and other important occasions in the diocese or archdiocese. It also omits the Alleluia usually sung before the Gospel Readings during other seasons of the year.

Certain practices remind us about the importance of penance in Advent. The liturgical color is violet or purple, which symbolizes repentance. The use of decorations is limited until the joyful day of Christmas. Rose color may be used on the Third Sunday of Advent, usually termed Gaudete Sunday, (Rejoicing Sunday). Showing acts of charity and fasting are recommended to all Catholics. They are expected to pray, read the Bible and meditate on it, and learn more about the Church. They are also required to attend Mass frequently and go to Confession, the Sacrament of Reconciliation. Advent wreaths are encouraged to be mounted in churches and homes.

The Advent Wreath

The Advent Wreath was a pre-Christian practice that was embraced by Christianity. In Europe, people collected green leaves and lit candles as symbols of hope for the Spring Season. During Advent, starting in Germany, the practice was adopted by both Catholics and Protestants to show that Christmas would soon arrive. The Advent Wreath has four candles attached to it, each candle representing a week in Advent. One candle is lit during the first week and an additional candle is lit in each subsequent week. Candles for weeks one, two, and four are purple; the candle for the third week, Gaudete Sunday, is pink or rose. In the United States, the middle of the wreath holds a white candle representing Christ, which is to be lit on Christmas Eve.

The Advent Wreath depicts living in spiritual darkness and waiting for Jesus to light both the world and especially our individual hearts at Christmas. If mounted in the house, it helps people to slow down and meditate on the meaning of the coming of Jesus and about life in general. Again, in the home, the family can light the candles during their morning devotion, before dinner, or anytime that the family is praying together. If asked, a priest may bless the wreath in the home, or families could bring their wreaths to the altar on the First Day of Advent for blessing.

Liturgical Colors

Traditionally, violet and purple are colors used during the Season of Advent symbolizing penance, sacrifice, and submission. On feast days and holy days appropriate colors like white and red are used. On "Gaudete Sunday," the Third Sunday of Advent, rose or pink color is used to express joy in anticipation of Christmas.

Conclusion

During every Advent Season, we must show our determination to prepare ourselves spiritually and wait in joy for the Lord's birth or second appearance. Let us regularly take part in the Eucharistic celebration, fast, pray, read and meditate on the Holy Scriptures. Above all, let us see the Lord Jesus Christ arriving each day in the person of the poor, the needy, the sick and dying, the beggar, refugee, migrant and the suffering, as well as in the person of abundant wealth. By showing such great concern for each other, the joy of Advent will certainly illuminate our hearts.

Prayer
Father, refresh your people with a new vision of Advent. May the Season remind us of what love really means and give us the grace to live it by showing love to all persons who represent the presence of Jesus Christ. Your people need your grace also to eschew greediness, pride, and injustice so that we can adequately prepare for the coming of your Son, our Lord and Savior Jesus Christ, who, with you and the Holy Spirit, live as God forever and ever. Amen.

FIRST SUNDAY OF ADVENT

Isaiah 2:1-5; Romans 13:11-14; Matthew 24:37-44

VIGILANCE AND EARNEST LIFE

Today the Church begins another Calendar Year or Liturgical Year. The Gregorian Calendar, named after Pope Gregory XIII, who promulgated it in October 1582, is used internationally and begins on January 1. It was an improved version of the Julian calendar produced by Julius Caesar in 45 B.C. There are other calendars pertaining to other religions and cultures throughout the world. The Church's Calendar Year or Liturgical Year is mainly about public Christian religious worship used among Christian Churches and begins with the First Sunday of Advent.

Human beings cherish the practice of celebrating the milestones in human life beginning from conception. A celebration occurs for each milestone in life, from birth into adulthood: baptisms, confirmations, first holy communion, graduations, marriages, anniversaries, and deaths.

The first moment of joy is a hint from the mom-to-be that her body's normal rhythm is changing because of a pregnancy. The couple and their families prepare for the birth of the child with excitement. Relatives and friends, typically female, organize a baby shower for the mom-to-be, sending congratulatory messages and cards to her as well as gifts for the child. The in-laws are anxiously expecting a grandchild, and the entire family is excited awaiting a new arrival.

The Church follows the same sequence in the life of Jesus Christ. Duly commemorating each aspect of Jesus' life during the year, the Church keeps tradition and observes the celebrations with solemn service, elaborate ritual, and earnest devotion. The celebration of the Annunciation is a joyous occasion, announcing the ancient prophecy's fulfillment of the birth of a Savior (Luke 1:26-38). We celebrate the Visitation of Mary to Elizabeth that revealed the mystery concerning Mary as Mother of God and the "Song of Praise" by Mary (Luke 1:39-56). We celebrate Jesus' birth as God living among us ("Emmanuel"), and we join the angels in their song praising God and announcing salvation to the world (Luke 2:13-14). We celebrate Jesus' baptism and confirmation thereafter by a voice from the Father and the appearing of the Holy Spirit in the form of a dove. We celebrate other notable events like The Transfiguration, Triumphant Entrance into Jerusalem (Palm Sunday), The Passion and Death of the Lord (Good Friday), Resurrection of the Lord, and Ascension of the Lord. The totality of the phases of Jesus' life gives meaning to the life of Christians, leaving a tremendous impact.

The word "Advent" is derived from the Latin word *adventus,* meaning "coming." In ancient times, it was a period when worshippers brought out the images of their gods or deities to signify the spirits coming to live among them or to bless them. Advent also meant expecting a king's arrival to a city or to his inauguration. The people prepared with fervent spirits and eagerly waited for his arrival.

The Season of Advent, which is a four-week period at the beginning of the Christian calendar, is to prepare for the "coming of the Lord" in three different ways:

First, it is the celebration of the physical birth or the birthday of Jesus Christ in Bethlehem over 2000 years ago. Christians celebrate the "mother of all mysteries" when God became a human being (incarnation) and lived on earth as Light to guide humanity's journey on earth to God (John 1:14).

Second, it is the coming of the Lord as "Emmanuel" (God living with us). Hence, we all prepare our hearts and minds to receive him and allow him to speak to us and direct our lives. Jesus is present and his message is full of life. He speaks to the person who cannot show love or work for peace; cannot forgive and reconcile; struggles to show respect to a partner in marriage; cannot develop genuine camaraderie in the community; cannot quit a bad habit; slights other people because of status, ethnicity, prejudice, and language.

Third, the Church's usage of "coming" relates to the Greek word "Parousia" which refers to the second coming of Jesus Christ at the End of Time. It means that after the Lord's coming to earth as man, another period of hopeful waiting has started. This moment will be fulfilled when Jesus Christ returns, just as the Apostles saw him rising into the sky (Act 1:10-11).

The theme for the First and Second Sundays of Advent is about the "Parousia." The readings of the liturgy are clear exhortations for thoughtful vigilance and thorough preparedness for Jesus' coming at the End of Time. With the example of the era of Noah and his preparedness for the flood —in contrast to others in their merrymaking, eating and drinking, marrying and giving in marriage, doing regular brisk businesses, and oblivious to Noah's warnings—Jesus warned his followers, then and today, about complacency and reliance on worldly interests, power, and sinful lifestyles. He stressed the urgent need to stay awake and in readiness, like a householder who would be vigilant to keep any intruder off his property. Indeed, Jesus emphasizes that the person who is well prepared and ready while working in the field or grinding at the mill with a friend would by whisked away to meet the Lord and the unprepared left behind.

In today's first reading, the Prophet Isaiah talks about the "Day of the Lord" when people from all corners of the world who have accepted God's sovereign rule will march on to the mountain of the Lord to meet him. This is a day we must prepare and hope for, represented by how we live our lives in the present: becoming women and men of peace, ending hatred and warfare, building bridges, fostering reconciliation with one another, and accepting each other as sisters and brothers. Isaiah acknowledges universal salvation that goes beyond the borders of Israel to include all those ready to abide by God's laws which do not tell people to train for war but urge everyone to walk in the light of the Lord.

Echoing the sentiments of the first and Gospel readings of today, the Apostle Paul tells us in the second reading that now is the time to change. He laments a world in darkness because of wars, suspicions, hatred, and wickedness. We must throw off these manifestations of darkness, accept the Lord Jesus, and conduct ourselves properly as true Christians waiting for his return. Remaining under such circumstances is tantamount to sleeping at night: daylight may appear suddenly, catching one off guard. Once again, preparedness for the coming of Jesus Christ, both at Christmas and at the End Time, links with transformation of the heart that leads to a way of life worthy of a true Christian.

Advent is a period of preparation that combines joy and penance. We are joyful to celebrate Jesus' birth that reminds us he is still living among us, showing the proper way to live our lives. But we also prepare with contrite hearts because we cannot live up to our expectations and we do not know the time the world will end, nor the time of our own individual deaths. Our sins create major stumbling blocks to any meaningful association with Jesus. Advent, therefore, is a period of spiritual reflection, discernment, and purification to particularly experience Jesus among us. This will also show our readiness to meet him during his second coming. He asks us to change if selfishness, greed, and pride enslave us or if anger, impatience, lying, corruption, and untoward habits take control of us. Indeed, each one of us has something that is not right—something that needs prompt correction.

The Church, which has the mandate that empowers her priests to forgive us our sins, grants us the privilege with a singular opportunity to approach Jesus and make amends for our failures in the Sacrament of Reconciliation.

The Peace of the Lord be with you.

Prayer
Father, you have given us this moment of immeasurable grace to prepare our hearts and minds to meet your Son both at his birth and second coming. Wash away any stain of sin and lead us towards a deeper experience of the profound presence of your Son in our lives. Amen.

SECOND SUNDAY OF ADVENT

Isaiah 11:1-10; Romans 15:4-9; Matthew 3:1-12

TREAT EACH OTHER LIKE THE MESSIAH IS AMONG YOU

Today the second candle of the Advent Wreath is lit alongside the first. The Second Sunday of Advent reminds us once again about the two-fold theme of the Season of Advent: the celebration of Jesus' birth in Bethlehem on Christmas Day as Emmanuel (God-with-us), and the preparation for his second coming at the end of the world as King and Judge. Traditionally, the First and Second Sundays of Advent underscore the theme of the End Times. In the first reading, the Prophet Isaiah surprises us as he presents some strange and unlikely realities in our human world, just as he told his eighth century B.C. audience. Isaiah writes:

> *"Wolves and sheep will live together in peace,*
> *and leopards will lie down with young goats.*
> *Calves and lion cubs will feed together,*
> *and little children will take care of them.*
> *Cows and bears will eat together,*
> *and their calves and cubs will lie down in peace.*
> *Lions will eat straw as cattle do.*
> *Even a baby will not be harmed*
> *if it plays near a poisonous snake."*

Is the Prophet saying that on that day, "the Day of the Lord," a baby will play by the cobra's den, and lay his hand on the hideout of a poisonous snake?

Growing up, my senior brothers, cousins, and I would travel to our uncles' cocoa farms to plant and harvest cocoa. These were trips we always looked forward to during the long break from school and I continued to do so even in the years close to my ordination.

As the saying goes, "The sun does not shine every day!" And certainly not in those rural areas.

There was one thing, however, I dreaded most about the farms. Snakes! Many times, they crossed our paths into the forests. In the village, we learned a hired worker died from a snake bite because the farms were far away from the hospital. Another person nearly lost his sight when a spitting snake spat into his eyes. Even today, I look the other way or immediately switch off my television set or cell phone whenever a snake appears on screen. Again, I shake when they appear in my dreams because I think about them whenever I am walking along the narrow sidewalk to the rectory at night! Once, I saw a long and big greenish object at the rectory doorsteps and shouted as I thought it was a snake. When it did not move, I discovered it was a snakeskin placed there by a parishioner who knew I feared snakes!

In the real world of the calf and lion, the cow and bear, and the baby and a snake, friendly relations do not happen. Likewise, in the human world, we see some people who do not relate well due to hatred, prejudice, nationalism, selfishness, cruelty, disrespect, racism, machinations of thought, dictatorship, and corruption. Again, around us, hate speeches are on the increase and civil wars are fought with many human lives in peril. There is apparent lack of self-sacrifice and compassion. For example, someone shows kindness and generosity to the other expecting to be reciprocated. Kindness, love, generosity, and compassion are not seen by many as Divine command.

We understand the images and descriptions from the Prophet Isaiah as pictures of what Jesus' second coming would be like when the spirit of the Lord manifests itself in a new world, particularly regarding human relationships. Indeed, the spirit of the Lord will discern among men and women as "a spirit of wisdom and understanding, a spirit of counsel and strength, a spirit of knowledge and of the fear of the Lord" (First reading). The first reading concludes that God will raise up the ideal Davidic king, who will manifest the spirit of the Lord. Through him, change will come into the whole world. God will establish peace on earth and end hatred and violence and bring enemies to the table to smoke the peace pipe.

The Gospel reading presents John the Baptist preaching about repentance and preparation for the Messiah, the Davidic king, described as the "Day of the Lord," which he said was imminent. A new beginning had dawned, John the Baptist said, and warned the people to change their ways to meet the Lord. He said he was unworthy of loosening the Messiah's sandals. In the new dispensation, the Messiah would be a Good Shepherd seeking the lost sheep or the prodigal sons and daughters. He would heal wounds of division and bless the poor and the needy. All nations would learn about his integrity, justice, boundless love, and faithfulness. All would see the true nature of God as loving, and that absolute compliance to his will would ensure absolute peace and harmony on earth.

This era of true peace and idyllic harmony is symbolized by another vision of Isaiah when countries of the world would reshape swords, spears, and other weapons of mass destruction into agricultural tools and ornaments. In Somalia thousands of detonated landmines that had been scattered in the country during their civil war, and the remaining husks, were melted into ornaments that sold in New York, USA.

In the second reading, Saint Paul gives credence to Isaiah's vision, saying that people aligned with different entrenched ideologies, cultures, and religious beliefs must come together, "welcome one another," and praise the Lord with one voice.

This is a message of hope that God is preparing us to experience when his Son, Jesus Christ is born at Christmas, a moment of God's gratuitous grace to humanity. God will absorb all his sons and daughters into his love and make us agents of love, healing, forgiveness, and comfort wherever we find ourselves: in church, home, street, market, office, and on the bus.

Our preparation starts with absolute conversion, a total detachment from our former ways of life, and complete surrender to God's will. The message of John the Baptist echoes in the desert: "make straight your paths." It becomes the mantra of Jesus at the start of his mission: *"turn away from your sins, because the Kingdom of Heaven is near"* (Matthew 4:17), a message delegated to the Apostles to preach to all nations (Matthew 28:19-20).

Advent is therefore a period of total confrontation with oneself and boldly embracing a pragmatic response that becomes the blueprint for a new way of life, a new way of thinking, a complete change of heart ("metanoia" in Greek), centered on Jesus Christ, who is with us.

In the prologue of his book, *Holy Moments: A Handbook for the Rest of Your Life* (2022), the prolific Catholic writer, Matthew Kelly, shares the story of a woman who sought counsel from an Abbot in a monastery. With tears streaming down her face, the woman shares her problems and anxieties with the Abbot. After a long silence, she asks, "What advice do you have for me, Father Abbot?"

The venerable Abbot is silent for a moment and says softly, "Treat every person you ever meet like the second coming of Jesus in disguise."

This is the same advice given to the Abbot when he sought counsel with an elder priest in another monastery. The Abbot visited a revered Hermit to seek guidance in solving problems with his monks who were unfriendly to him and to each other in the monastery, and even impatient to visitors. The Abbot asked, "What wisdom do you have for me and confreres? How do we rejuvenate the monastery? How can we best serve the people who come to visit?"

"I will answer your questions with one answer," the Hermit said. "Go back and tell the brothers... the Messiah is among you."

From that time, the monks treated each other with love, renewed kindness, and profound respect as they perceived each other as the Messiah! They "praised and encouraged each other; compassion and forgiveness returned to their hearts, and they were kind to each other." There was tremendous change and improvement, and many visitors returned to the monastery to meet the welcoming monks.

During the second week of Advent, let us reflect on peace in the world and ensure we promote peace wherever we are.

How are you concerned about your relationship with God and other people?

Are you ready to make amends with your partner, family members, and friends, to correct all wrongs and thus become an instrument of peace?

Do you feel in yourself you are bearing good fruits? Otherwise, what do you think you must cut off to enable you to bear a hundredfold good fruit?

Endeavor to "treat every person you ever meet like the second coming of Jesus in disguise" because "the Messiah is among you."

The Peace of the Lord be with you.

Prayer
Father, let each of us see the Messiah disguised in one another and to understand that through our generous acts of love and compassion to each "Messiah," we will bring peace and harmony to our homes, communities, and workplaces to take away pain and hatred in the world. Amen.

THIRD SUNDAY OF ADVENT

Isaiah 35:1-6a, 10; James 5:7-10; Matthew 11:2-11

REJOICE AND BE GLAD

We read from Saint Luke's Gospel in the translation by the Good News Bible, "The Law of Moses and the writings of the Prophets were in effect up to the time of John the Baptist; since then, the Good News about the Kingdom of God is being told, and everyone forces their way in" (Luke 16:16). The Old Testament presents the message about the Law of Moses and the writings of the Prophets. The Law of Moses or The Law comprises the first five books of the Hebrew Bible, also known as the Pentateuch ("five books" in Greek) or the Torah, ascribed to Moses as the author. The writings of the Prophets are the books written by the Prophets, which like the Law, were accepted as inspired by God. The Septuagint, meaning the number 70 (LXX in Latin), is the Greek translation of books from the Hebrew Bible. The number 70 signifies the number of scholars who did the translation. Jesus summarized the Law and the Prophets as "Love of God and love of neighbor" (Matthew 4:17).

Interpretation of the text from Luke 16:16 suggests that John the Baptist was the last prophet of the Old Testament. But the text says that until John the Baptist appeared, teachings were from the Law and the Prophets, and since then, a new Law—the Good News, which is about the Kingdom of God—is being launched. From the wilderness of Judah, John the Baptist unveils a new mission dressed as a hermit, wearing "a garment of camel's hair and leather belt around his waist; and his food was locusts and wild honey" (Matthew 3:4). Many people accepted his message of repentance and change of heart, and he baptized them in the Jordan River.

John the Baptist had disciples. One disciple was Andrew, the brother of Simon Peter. He and another disciple heard John's reference to Jesus as "the Lamb of God." Andrew then left John to follow Jesus (John 1:35-40). The first century Romano-Jewish historian, Josephus, wrote that the main reason behind the killing of John was that King Herod feared the significant influence John had over the people and how John could easily have received tremendous support in a rebellion.

Theologians opine that the Gospel of today shows the conciliatory or peacemaking gesture to avoid disagreement between the disciples of John and Jesus. All the Evangelists show how John himself attested he was only a herald of the Messiah. He said he was baptizing with water, but the one coming, "who is greater," would baptize with the Holy Spirit. "I am not good enough even to untie his sandals," John said. The Messiah, he added, would separate the wheat from the worthless chaff and burn the chaff in a fire that could never be extinguished (Luke 3:15-17). John insisted that sincerity, honesty, justice, and moral uprightness were the best ways to escape God's wrath. Indeed, he fearlessly opposed King Herod marrying Herodias, formerly the wife of his half-brother. The king ordered John to be imprisoned and later beheaded.

John's role in Salvation History as the forerunner of the Messiah becomes clearer from prison. He sends his disciples to Jesus with the question, "Are you the one John said was going to come, or should we expect someone else?' If Jesus, whom he had baptized (Matthew 3:13-17), was the Messiah, then it was proper for his disciples to accept that the end of John's mission was imminent, but he had prepared the way for Jesus to come.

Jesus sends the disciples of John back with the message about the new mission of the Messiah. The Lord's anointed (Messiah) will not incite a rebellion against any worldly regime (Luke 20:20-26). He will not execute divine retribution. Rather, his vision and mission will be as the Prophet Isaiah prophesied: to bring good news to the poor, proclaim liberty to captives, sight to the blind, and freedom to the oppressed (Luke 4:18-19).

It will be a time of joy and great optimism for those who are morally upright and "do not lose faith." He will be both the "Gate" of the pen and the "Good Shepherd" whose protection will give life and the joy of life, "life in all its fullness" (John 10:7-16). The joy will come to anyone who, like the farmer in the water-scarce land of Palestine, waits patiently for the rains to water the crops (first reading).

The message of the Messiah is also one of hope, reminiscent of Isaiah's words to the people exiled in Babylon. God would bring them back safely to Israel just as he rescued their ancestors from slavery in Egypt. He would make their lives better. Their lands would be productive, the weak strengthened, and the sick cured. The returnees will rejoice, and their "sorrow and sighing shall flee away."

Again, the Messiah represents divine love on earth, bringing wholeness to people. It liberates them from a different type of slavery, that of sin, which distances humanity from God and from one another. It is about a relational harmony with God and neighbor, blessing those who are humble of heart, and spreading joy to those seeking love, justice, and peace. Indeed, it is about people who live close to God and live by God's values to transform their lives.

When the disciples of John left, Jesus testified John had performed the important task of preaching repentance to prepare for his coming. In all this, we see how tolerance and understanding between the disciples of John and Jesus played out. Their coming together was a prominent sign of how we can settle our differences, whether social, political, or religious, to bring about the joy, peace, and harmony which the Messiah represents.

The Third Sunday of Advent is traditionally called "Gaudete Sunday," derived from the entrance antiphon of the Holy Mass, beginning with the words "Rejoice in the Lord always" (Latin: Gaudate in Domino Semper). In the readings of today, the word "rejoice" and its synonyms, such as joy, hope, be glad and celebrate, appear several times. Other texts of the Mass also use these words to reflect the joyous anticipation of the Lord's coming. The sense of joy comes from the fact that we are already halfway to the birth of the Lord. Again, it echoes the joy expressed by the Angels in the first Christmas song of joy to the world.

Ministers of the liturgy wear rose-colored vestments to replace the traditional Advent violet-colored vestments. The pink or rose-colored candle, the third candle in the Advent wreath, is lit today along with the two previously lighted candles representing the First and Second Sundays of Advent. The Season of Advent continues as a period of reflection to reject sin, renew our knowledge of Jesus, welcome him into our lives, and experience him personally.

Many years after Isaiah and John the Baptist, the call to lament about the state of sin in society and in private lives still resounds. A great number of people live without the fear of the Lord. Others doubt God's existence. Many regard the conscience as a purely personal affair, defining their own values and personal choices about life. So many people selfishly blind themselves to love and goodness. We see hatred and ethnic tensions resulting in violence and an increase in refugees and homelessness. Politicians tell their constituents that the state of economy in their countries is bad and that they need victory one more time in the next election to make things better for all. However, when they come to power, things do not change to better the lives of ordinary people. There is often little difference between times of high inflation and low inflation. The only discernible difference is that conditions continue to get worse, and life becomes tougher and more unbearable for the citizenry. We need contrition, repentance, and a change of heart to bring about the peace and happiness we need in ourselves and in the world.

How do we find joy today with so much darkness around us? We reflect on the Advent Wreath and know that the Lord

Jesus is near. Speaking through his Church, he invites everyone to renew their confidence in his saving mission.

Each of us must prepare by repenting of our sins. The greatest act of remorse for one's previous ungodly life is to acknowledge him immediately as Lord and Savior. This can be shown by our readiness to share with the needy, act justly, show love and concern for our neighbor, and to be content with our lot (Luke 3:8, 10-14). We are challenged to plan immediate resolutions and firmly stand by them.

Do you "see" those parts of your life which you have to work on to enable you to walk in the footsteps of Jesus?

Do you pray for courage and strength to amend these ways and return to the life Jesus wants you to live?

How can others see your love for God in the life you lead at home, church, and workplace?

The Peace of the Lord be with you.

Prayer
Father, give us the grace and courage to deal with whatever needs correction in our lives. While patiently waiting for the coming of your Son, let our lives mirror the joy and hope you bring us. Amen.

FOURTH SUNDAY OF ADVENT

Isaiah 7:10-14; Romans 1:1-7; Matthew 1:18-24

THE DAWN OF THE GOOD NEWS: A SIGN FULFILLED

A girl in her early twenties, and in her final year at the university, demands plastic surgery on her face because the procedure will enhance her beauty and boost her marketability in the corporate world. To do the beautification procedure immediately, the young lady insists her mother must come up with the money now.

A man gets a call from the local police station. His son is in custody. He was involved in armed robbery in a bank that led to shootings and the death of three passersby.

A man searches the wallet of his teenage son and discovers small packets of cocaine!

A bright and talented young man is holding a banner in front of a large group of activists. His parents are in a state of disbelief, horrified as they recognize their only child on television's prime time news. They hear for the first time that their son is engaged in a secret society planning to cause protests across the country.

There is a shooting at a shopping mall in a busy commercial area and several people are killed or wounded.

A bomb detonates at a railway station, causing mayhem, killing and maiming hundreds of innocent commuters.

Political and civil wars continue to be waged unabated in many places throughout the world.

Swindling in the corporate world, political scandals, corruption, religious scandals, and similar troubles are widespread around the world.

The proliferation of disturbing stories fills our world each day! The list is endless: abortions, divorces, couples living together outside of marriage, and drug peddling. The world today wallows in darkness and despair. But these realities in the world should not foster more despondency; they should heighten our consciousness with the message that our disillusioned world needs conversion and redemption! The readings of the Fourth Sunday of Advent highlight hope for the world.

The first reading takes place in the eighth century B.C., during the time of the Prophet Isaiah. Kings who denounced the true God and followed false gods have led the Southern Kingdom (Judah). King Ahaz made images of Baal throughout the kingdom. He burned incense, sacrificed animals, and even gave "his own sons as burned offerings to idols" (2 Chronicles 28:1-4). Ahaz was unfaithful to God, and this led to moral decadence and political weakness. Syria and the Northern Kingdom (Israel) threatened an invasion to subdue the nation of Judah and its capital, Jerusalem, when Ahaz refused to join forces with them against Assyria. Ahaz and the people were frightened about the impending attack and "trembled like trees shaking in the wind" (Isaiah 7: 2).

The Prophet Isaiah warned against any such coalition and urged Ahaz to trust in God's plan to save his people. The King turned down Isaiah's counsel and requested help from Assyria, a decision that marked the beginning of the end of all the surrounding kingdoms. Despite all this, God gave Ahaz the chance to repent, worship, and serve the true God. He sent Isaiah to inform him that the two kings would fail. God asked Ahaz to ask for a sign to prove what God was saying, an offer which any of us would take advantage of regarding our future.

But Ahaz was not raised by his father Jotham or his grandfather Uzziah to believe in and worship the God of Israel; all of them abandoned the faith of Israel and completely refused to worship him. So, at God's request, Ahaz responded arrogantly: "I will not ask, nor will I test the Lord" (Isaiah 7:12). For the sake of the salvation of the people, God himself pronounced a sign: a virgin is with child and will soon give birth to a Son who will be called Emmanuel, a name which means "God-with-us."

Isaiah offered Ahaz the chance to ask for a sign to prove that God was real, but he completely declined God's invitation. Like Ahaz, we often refuse God's invitation to know, worship and serve him. Instead, we succumb to the enticements of the world that include status, pleasure, power, and wealth, while thinking that they define and give meaning to life. We refuse to identify with a divine reality influencing our lives. We doubt our faith bequeathed to us by our parents, grandparents, the Church, family, and culture because of the despair and failures that overwhelm us in life.

How are parents today inculcating the sense of God in their children? Failing to do so will certainly leave them struggling with their faith as grownups, leading them to make unpleasant and destructive decisions in later life. Many parents are struggling to understand their children, who face many challenges posed by the world today.

The sign to Ahaz signifies the future Messiah, who would turn a darkened world of despair into a perfect one (Acts 10:34-35). For Christians, therefore, the birth of Jesus Christ fulfilled the promise of a Messiah (Acts 10:42-43). Saint Paul echoes the universal character of God's revelation in Jesus Christ as "a mystery kept secret for endless ages" (Romans 16:25-27).

In his Gospel, Saint Luke writes about the Angel Gabriel's visit to the Virgin Mary. The Angel promised Mary that she would give birth to the Savior of the World. In today's Gospel, Matthew writes about a pregnancy having occurred and a birth to be expected soon. The sign God pronounced for the salvation of his people arrives as promised.

The fourth and last Advent Candle is lit today, along with the first three. Some traditions call it the Angel's Candle to recall the hosts of Angels rejoicing at Jesus' birth. The Fourth Sunday of Advent shows that the celebration of Jesus' birth is near. We reflect on God-made-man (Incarnation).

We do not find the meaning of Christmas in how we decorate our houses, streets, and offices, nor in the sumptuous meals for the people we plan to invite. Christmas is about our salvation. It is about how we lift ourselves and others from sin and chaos in our world. It is about inviting the child Jesus and his message into our homes and into our lives.

Look at the baby Jesus lying in the manger and recognize him as God's Son. He comes to us as a child and begins his mission of loving us. He promises to be with us always (Matthew 28:20). Embrace him in your heart and mind. He wants you to hold him as your own child. He wants to become part of your family. He is the Word that became human (Incarnation) and is dwelling among us (John 1:14). He is the Light of God to subdue the surrounding darkness (John 1:5).

Christmas is also about Mary and Joseph, who believed in the unknown, the message announced by the angel, and the hope that all things are possible with God. Like Joseph and Mary, we must trust, obey, and be faithful to God.

God wants to touch the lives of the young men and women I mentioned at the beginning of the homily. Indeed, God wants to touch each one of us and has designed a salvation plan for the world whose foundational stone is Jesus Christ, his Son soon to be born.

How have you prepared since the beginning of Advent to meet the child Jesus in readiness to accept him as your Lord and Savior?

As we move close to Christmas, apart from planning an ambiance of joy and camaraderie with decorations and delightful cuisines at home and work, are you also building a sense of warm spirituality around them?

The Peace of the Lord be with you.

Prayer
Father, we are ready to welcome your Son at Christmas. Give us grace to embrace him totally and allow him to direct our lives. Amen.

The Season of Christmas

PRELUDE: THE GOSPEL OR THE GOOD NEWS OF CHRISTMAS

The New Testament is about the Gospel or the Good News. It is about Jesus Christ and his message of salvation for humanity. Salvation is a gift from God offered through Jesus Christ, the Messiah promised by God to the People of Israel in the Old Testament. It is about knowing Jesus as the Son of God, embracing him as Lord and Savior who forgives our sins in baptism, and claiming sonship with God. It is about accepting his teachings and allowing the Holy Spirit to help us live by them. The Good News gives meaning to our lives. It defines our purpose in life. It transforms us into the People of God.

Christmas commemorates the birth of Jesus Christ. The Season of Christmas unveils the Good News announced by the Angel Gabriel (Luke 1:26-38); the song of the angels at Christmas (Luke 2:8-16); the Sermon on the Mount (Matthew 5-7"); the Resurrection (Matthew 28:5-6); and the descent of the Holy Spirit (Acts 2:1-4).

As we prepare this week for the celebration of the birth of Jesus Christ, the Church does something remarkable. The Church wants us to acknowledge the roles played by the women and men chosen by God to make God's Salvation Plan happen—Mary, Joseph, Elizabeth and Zachariah. These people were living their normal lives when God touched and transformed them. They allowed God to dwell in them and to direct them. They developed a special relationship with God.

Indeed, the celebration of Christmas is to allow Jesus, our Lord and Savior, to step into our lives, transform us, and lead us through a completely distinct path.

Can you develop a special relationship with Jesus Christ, who is to be born tomorrow night? Can you see Christmas as a time for renewing your faith and hope in God expressed by deepening your love of God and neighbor?

Until now, you may not have allowed Jesus Christ to touch your life completely. If you allow him, many lives will also change, and people will show generosity and will cross over ethnic and racial barriers to build peace and harmony in the world.

Tomorrow, the song of the angels will echo in the heavens and throughout the world:

"Glory to God in the highest heaven, and peace on earth to those with whom he is pleased." (Luke 2:14)

Make a delightful journey to the manger and join in the joyful song—The Song of all Seasons. Merry Christmas!

Prayer
Father, your people are on their knees around the crib in churches and in their homes adoring the baby Jesus. Allow the peaceful aura around the crib to engulf them every day of their lives. Amen.

THE NATIVITY OF OUR LORD
(Midnight Mass)

Isaiah 9:2-7; Titus 2:11-14; Luke 2:1-14

A CHILD IS BORN TO US

During the day, an astonishing state of panic, confusion, and frustration marked the rush of crowds into the ancient, modest town of Bethlehem. Frazzled and weary after long hours on rugged roads under the scorching sun, travelers sought food and accommodation in the little town. Even more disconcerting were the unfriendly, hostile, and infuriating innkeepers who took advantage of the stressed visitors and sought to charge ridiculous rates once visitors started pouring into the village in great numbers. The owners screamed, pointing fingers at the exhausted visitors to move elsewhere, such as low-class houses or shepherds' sheds, down another rough road.

According to the Gospel of Luke, Joseph and his wife Mary started the journey to Bethlehem from where they lived in Nazareth. The Roman Emperor Caesar Augustus had requested a census of the Roman Empire, including all of Palestine. It was required that everyone go to their ancestral home to be registered (Luke 2:1-7). Well known among the indigenes, the design and purpose of the census consolidated power and enforced effective ways of collecting more taxes for Rome. Thus, while the crowds thronged into Bethlehem, everybody complained about the Roman decree and the inconveniences their journeys caused.

Many travelers arrived late and could not procure rooms at the few available decent inns. A good number could not afford the expensive hostels, and Joseph and Mary bedded down in an animal shed. Apparently, the shepherds had camped out elsewhere deep in the fields with their animals, seemingly oblivious to the bustling in the town. One of the shepherds' wives who remained in the camp that night saw Mary's situation as critical. She gave the desperate couple the best of the sheds.

The hustle and bustle of the day slowly abated by midnight. There was peace and quiet in the town and countryside. A deep darkness blanketed the land. Strangely, foxes were not howling from distant reach. This gladdened the hearts of the shepherds. Their animals were safe. The desert snakes quieted their rattles. The crickets were silent. In the camp, the sheep ceased to bleat. The goats stopped any activity. In the night's calm, the shepherds and their animals dozed off.

Far away in the skies, the stars glittered and twinkled. The eldest of the shepherds, who often offered to keep watch, observed an unusual star. It seemed the nearest, the biggest, and the brightest. Instinctively, he blinked his eyes several times to clear his vision. He was feeling worried. In his many years of keeping watch, he had never seen a star quite like this one. He stood up. He looked to the left and then to the right. The shepherds were sound asleep. He gazed up again. It was astonishing. He wondered about what he might witness on that silent night.

Suddenly, the star beamed a bright ray directly towards their sheds a mile or so away from their main camp. The frightened shepherd shook his companions. They sprang to their feet, each rubbing his face with his palm. Immediately, an unfamiliar voice, pleasing and piercing, spoke: "Do not be afraid. Listen, I bring you news of great joy, a joy to be shared by the whole people. Today, in the town of Bethlehem, a savior has been born to you. He is Christ the Lord!"

The speechless shepherds became more afraid. Their eyes pierced the darkness that engulfed them, searching for the source of the angelic voices. Still befuddled, the shepherds heard hosts of voices singing the praises of the Almighty God: *Glory to God in the highest heaven and peace to people who enjoy his favor.* The shepherds heard the entire earth echo the song of praise and blessing.

The modest men hurried to their camp and immersed themselves in the star's light around the shed. They saw the wife who'd stayed in the camp. She beckoned them to enter. Quietly, they shuffled into the hut, some absently pressing their ewes to their chests. They found a newborn babe sleeping peacefully in one manger in the stable. They praised God and congratulated the couple. Mary smiled shyly, gracefully, and with warmth. She remembered her role in God's salvation plan. She had contemplated it many times since she received the Angel Gabriel's salutation. She silently sang the Magnificat in her heart. Gradually, the mysteries were unfolding and becoming more real and meaningful to her. She meditated on the name that she would give to her son, Jesus, who is the "Emmanuel" meaning God-with-us.

The shepherds withdrew for the time being to allow the family to rest. They were full of joy and aware something mysterious was being revealed. They were experiencing the divine. So full of gratitude for the miracle they witnessed, they shared their story and sang the song of the angels with zeal and zest: "Glory to God in the highest, and peace to his people on Earth." In fact, "all who heard it were amazed" and some hurried to the stable to see for themselves.

The song of the Angels has become the song and prayer of all who hear the story, and the shepherds' song has become that of eternity. The Angels sang it all the time (Isaiah 6:3). Over two thousand years ago, after the Law and the Prophets expected the birth of Jesus and it came true, the people sang. All creation that has ever existed was waiting for this hope, while all in nature have been ready to embrace this amazing moment.

Tonight, God's people celebrate the solemn festival of Christmas. The story of Jesus' birth is retold and re-staged worldwide. The song of the angels echoes in the heavens, on earth, in churches, and in homes at every corner of the earth. Come and join in the song of all seasons: "Glory to God in the highest, and peace to His people on Earth."

Indeed, there is a place for each one of us around the manger and in his kingdom.

As you listen to the many hymns this Season, reflect on the words, repeating them as your prayer to the newborn the King, our Lord and Savior. It is said that when you sing a prayerful song, you pray twice. Which is your favorite religious Christmas song? If you do not have a singing voice, hum a song in the shower and imagine the baby Jesus smiling as he listens to you.

Remember the reason for the season, the Birth of our Lord and Savior Jesus Christ.

Keep Jesus Christ at Christmas. Say Merry Christmas to all.

The Peace of the Lord be with you.

Prayer
Father, let your light direct all people to the newborn King to join the angels of heaven and the whole of creation in singing:
Glory to God in the Highest and Peace to His people on Earth.

THE NATIVITY OF THE LORD
(Christmas Day)

Isaiah 52:7-10; Hebrews 1:1-6; John 1:1-18

BEING A GIFT TO ANOTHER

The greatest miracle of the Christian Faith is that "the Word became a human being and, full of grace and truth, lived among us" (John 1:14). The manifestation of this miracle, referred to as "Incarnation," is celebrated on December 25 as Christmas Day. In the dawn of this day, Jesus the Son of God, was born on earth to begin his life as a human being, except for sin. It was a completely new life for God to live among his own creatures as he did soon after creation. At that moment, God sanctified human life and all manner of life in the world until sin became known. Indeed, the Incarnation (God becoming man in Jesus) is a great gift from God the Father to the world to save it from sin. (John 3 :16-17).

The Christmas story, therefore, is one of redemption, closing the distance between God and humanity. It is also a story of stewardship and fellowship. God has shared his life with us, and we in turn are called to share our lives with one another. This is precisely what is expected of us by our Creator.

Thus, we journey towards God the Father in Heaven with Jesus Christ leading the way, the Holy Spirit binding God's people together in love, and the Church keeping us as one family. The most important thing required of us is that we are united in love, giving our love as gift to one another as a demonstration of our love for God.

Christmas has become a universal festival. Throughout the world bells are ringing, Christmas carols are being sung, and frantic last-minute decorations preparations carried out in our homes, streets, workplaces, and churches to celebrate the Christmas Season. Dioramas of how Jesus was born are created with figurines of the infant Jesus, Mary, Joseph, shepherds and their animals, the Magi, and stars. The dramatization of the birth of Jesus is made by both adults and children to portray the religious meaning of Christmas. Churches celebrate Christmas Eve with candlelight and midnight Mass or other services.

Some Christmas traditions include Christmas trees, Santa Claus, and frantic Christmas shopping for decorative items and gifts to loved ones. The day after Thanksgiving in America known as "Black Friday" (replicated worldwide) has become an important commercialized shopping day to begin Christmas purchases. Many people send Christmas cards and electronically "e-cards" with messages of goodwill and love to family members and friends, a moment for charitable and volunteer work when people reach out to the poor and needy in the society.

A comment by someone goes something like this:

If I have a beautifully decorated house both indoors and outdoors but I have no love for my family, then I have nothing. If I have a gorgeous Christmas tree with lots of beautifully wrapped presents under it but have no love for my family, then I have nothing. If I have a sumptuous meal spread on my table but have no love for my family, then I have nothing.

Therefore, to those who hurt us, let us offer the gift of forgiveness; to those who slight us, the gift of tolerance; to those who disrespect us, the gift of our respect, and to those in need, the gift of our love.

The Peace of Christmas be with you.

Prayer
Father, Jesus, your Son has become one of us to live among us as your greatest gift to us. With the power of the Holy Spirit, teach my people to be gifts to one another, forgiving, and loving one another. Amen.

THE FEAST OF THE HOLY FAMILY OF JESUS, MARY, AND JOSEPH
(Sunday in the Octave of Christmas)

Sirach 3:2-6, 12-14; Colossians 3:12-22; Matthew 2:13-15, 19-23

THE FAMILY IS A DOMESTIC CHURCH

In the Catholic Church, some Lutheran and some Anglican churches, the Sunday in the Octave of Christmas is dedicated to the Holy Family comprising the Child Jesus, the Blessed Virgin Mary, and his foster Father, Joseph. When Christmas falls on a Sunday, the Feast of the Holy Family is shifted to December 30. The Holy Family in art form gained recognition from the 1490s and many religious, secular institutions, and churches are named in honor of the Holy Family.

Between the years 1662-63, Marie-Barbe d'Ailleboust, a French social worker among the indigenous peoples in Canada, founded the Confrérie de la Sainte-Famille ("Confraternity of the Holy Family") in Montreal. She dedicated her life entirely to charity and piety. It is said the natives gave her a name which translates to "She who takes pity on us in our wretchedness." The Association was later established in Quebec where the devotion to the Holy Family was promoted by Monsignor François de Montmorency Laval (1623-1708). When he became the first bishop of the Diocese of Quebec and Canada, he established the Feast of the Holy Family in the Diocese of Quebec in 1665. He published *The Little Book* in 1675 as a guide to living a virtuous life based on the life of the Holy Family. The Feast was promulgated by Pope Leo XIII in the Roman Catholic Church (the Latin or Western Rite). This was to promote a wider participation of the devotion to the Holy Family, support family values that were floundering at the time, and offer intercessory prayers to the Holy Family to guide families to emulate the virtuous life of the Holy Family. It portrayed the Holy Family to the world as the model for all Christian families and marriages. It demonstrated the value and sanctity of the family unit as a domestic church. It also called for prayerful moments for the married with the Holy Family and urged couples to seek grace from the Holy Family in their families.

Saint Chrysostom noted Christian families must make their homes "family churches" by praying, reading the scriptures, and attending Mass together, especially on Sundays and Holy Days of Obligation. This, he added, would encourage families to live and conduct themselves like the Holy Family, united in prayer, and bonded in respect, tolerance, and love.

Indeed, the first and second alternative readings from Ecclesiasticus/Sirach and Colossians respectively remind us that families must remain a united "family of God" in the Holy Spirit with each person performing his or her task. The reading from Sirach is part of its traditional wisdom teachings regarding how order and harmony can lead to a successful and happy family. After a short comment on parental responsibilities in the family as divinely oriented, Sirach reflects on the duties of children towards their parents, particularly when parents are elderly. Bringing comfort to one's parents, showing kindness towards them, and being considerate to them in their later years, Sirach continues, will ensure God's blessings on the children.

The Letter to the Colossians re-emphasizes the notion that marriage and family life are divinely ordained, and partners in marriage are "God's chosen ones." Saint Paul means to say that marriage is now transformed into a sacrament by Jesus Christ, and partners in marriage must reflect the nature of God possessing "heartfelt compassion, kindness, humility, gentleness, and patience." Again, they must live "bearing with one another and forgiving one another." The second reading ends with one of the most quoted verses in scripture: "Wives must respect their husbands and husbands love their wives."

There is not much written about Jesus, Mary, and Joseph, as a family in the New Testament except the stories about the birth of Jesus, his circumcision, presentation, the flight to Egypt, return of the family to Nazareth, and the "finding of Jesus in the Temple" in Jerusalem. All the same, much is learned from the scanty literature about the Holy Family.

Today's Gospel readings narrate the ceremony of purification by Joseph and Mary forty days after her son's birth as prescribed by the Law of Moses, eighty days for a female baby (Leviticus 12). In our liturgical calendar, this will fall on February 2, when the Church celebrates the Feast of the Presentation of the Lord. The Church teaches that Jesus, the Son of God, and Mary, Full of Grace, submitted to the purification ceremonies, including baptism, not because they needed to be purified from sin or uncleanliness per se but to fulfill the Law of Moses. The rite of purification comprised "a one-year-old lamb for burned offering and pigeon or turtledove for a sin offering." If the woman could not afford that, she presented "two doves or two pigeons, one for a burned offering and the other for a sin offering."

Mary and Joseph practiced their traditional family values and observed their religious obligations, which they were taught by their families and society. Their dedication to the Lord, faithful devotion to the treasured wisdom of the community (Luke 2:39), patience, and parental duties paved the way for the child Jesus to grow up to be full of the wisdom of their ancestors (Luke 2:24).

Joseph is described as "a man who always did what was right" (Matthew 1:19). He was obedient, submissive, and respectful. He obeyed God's instruction and took Mary as a wife in difficult circumstances (Matthew 1:24). In 1870, Pope Pius IX proclaimed Saint Joseph as patron of the Universal Church. He is also patron of a happy death due to the belief that he died in the arms of Jesus and Mary.

Mary was a thoughtful woman who reflected deeply on the events in her life and was very patient as each chapter of her life unfolded (Luke 2:19). She was humble and accepted

God's will (Luke 1:34). She was dignified in her simplicity, and those who encountered her received inner joy and peace (Luke 1:41).

Mary and Joseph lived exemplary lives worthy of emulation by all Christian families. Despite the direct divine influence in their lives, they come to us as ordinary human people who faced the challenges of everyday life and were confronted with hard decisions to make. They obeyed the ruling Roman authority and traveled on a donkey over rugged terrain and dusty paths to their ancestral home to register their names. They had difficulty finding decent accommodation and finally had to occupy the shed of animals. They faced an unpleasant and unsanitary environment and had a stable as Jesus' bed. They traveled as refugees to Egypt, a foreign land, to seek protection. They feared to lose Jesus at the age of twelve during a trip to Jerusalem for the Passover Feast (Luke 2:48). They worried about their teenage son's direct response to them when questioned about being away from them for three days (Luke 2:49). Finally, there was Mary's bitter journey with family and friends to the hills of Calvary at the crucifixion of her son (John 19:25-27). During moments of sorrow and predicament in life, each person or family must look to the family of Nazareth and believe in God's presence at every stage of our daily lives.

We are born into families that ought to nurture us. However, not all families are good environments for children, particularly when modern definition of marriage and family are a far cry from indigenous and Christian traditional definitions. A family can contribute to the sound moral upbringing of a child or the deterioration of a child's moral behavior. The family is, therefore, a very important institution in society. Good families are made, not born, it is said. They are built through hard work, sacrifice, respect, dedication, and faith. Good families are created by men and women who are patient, show signs of love, offer forgiveness, and share their joys and sorrows. When our homes are peaceful and loving, our children will be raised as loving, peaceful, and compassionate people. Like Jesus, they will grow and become "strong, filled with wisdom; and the favor of God" will be upon them.

We must frequently meditate on the hardships that Joseph and Mary endured.

Pray to Saint Joseph and the Blessed Virgin Mary for courage and strength to deal with your challenges.

As you look at the Nativity Scene in the house or at church, do you welcome them into your life? Do you make your home the embodiment of love with concern for others and the fear of God?

The Peace of the Lord be upon you.

Prayer
Father, unite in constant affection all families especially young couples. Show them the value of family life and let them emulate the life of the Holy Family united in love. Amen.

SOLEMNITY OF MARY, THE HOLY MOTHER OF GOD
(January 1)

Numbers 6:22-27; Galatians 4:4-7; Luke 2:16-21

MARY, MODEL FOR CHRISTIANS

The Feast of Mary, Mother of God, commemorates the divine motherhood of the Blessed Virgin Mary, the mother of Jesus. The feast is celebrated on the first day of January, the Octave Day of the Nativity of the Lord (Christmas Day). Although the divine maternity of Mary has been questioned and debated at various stages in the history of the Christian Church, the doctrine has always been seen as a great divine gift to the Church and the world. Over the years, the feast has become a popular pious devotion to Mary, marked by prayers, music, and visual arts.

The earliest usage of the term "Mary, Mother of God," goes back to the writings of the Early Christian Fathers. For example, Irenaeus (A.D. 189) wrote, "The Virgin Mary, being obedient to God's Word, received from the Angel the glad tidings that she would bear God's Son." Ephraim the Syrian (A.D. 351) wrote, "Though still a virgin she carried a child in her womb .... and became the 'Mother of God.'"

The virgin birth of Jesus was defended as a Marian doctrine during the first Ecumenical Council of Nicaea in A.D. 325. The Council decreed that Mary, who conceived miraculously by the action of the Holy Spirit, remains a virgin. In the Quran, an entire chapter is dedicated to Mary presenting her in Islam as the Virgin Mother of Jesus. Again, in Islam, Jesus is recognized as one of the great prophets though not as Son of God.

The dogma or doctrine recognizing Mary as Mother of God is based on a syllogistic argument or logic fervently accepted by logicians over the millennia, and even beyond the birth of Jesus (Isaiah 7:14). It states that since Mary is Jesus' mother and Jesus is God, then she is the "Mother of God" (*Mater Dei* in Latin) or the "God-bearer" (Theotokos in Greek). The logic obviously is not suggesting that the title Mother of God means Mary is the source of Jesus' divinity or that Mary is older than Jesus. It is the belief in the Incarnation when God the Son becomes human through Mary that makes her "Mother of God." This is the work of God.

Like the people of the time, Mary was deeply rooted in the hope of Israel's future Messiah. She surrendered herself to God's will and plan as the "Ark of God's New Covenant" bearing the Son of God, the Savior of the world. Her obedience and humility to God's Word therefore makes her the perfect model for Christians. Through her positive response, the world can now establish a deeper union with the incarnate God.

At the Second Vatican Council and in the encyclical of Pope John Paul (*Redemptoris mater*), Mary is also referred to as the "Mother of the Church." The Catholic Church also teaches that Mary, as Mother of God, was assumed into heaven, body and soul, at the end of her earthly life.

The Marian doctrine stating that Mary is Mother of God was finally decided by the Council of Ephesus in A.D. 431, which examined the long-time debate about Jesus' divine and human natures. At the heart of this discussion was whether Mary merited the title "Mother of God."

Richard Nestorius, Patriarch of Constantinople from A.D. 428 to 431, had opined that Mary was only the mother of Jesus' human nature, but not his divine nature. This view was rejected at the Council of Ephesus in A.D. 431 and again at the Council of Chalcedon in A.D. 451. Both Councils affirmed Jesus was "fully God and fully human" and that these natures were united in one person, Jesus Christ. It was therefore erroneous that Nestorius (*Nestorianism*) would separate the human and divine natures of Jesus Christ.

The exact date when the feast day of Mary's divine maternity was established is not certain. In the Eastern Church, the Day of the Theotokos was celebrated either before or after Christmas Day. In 1751, Pope Benedict XIV allowed the churches in Portugal to celebrate the feast on the first Sunday of May. The feast was extended to other countries, and by 1914, it was celebrated on October 11. The feast became universal in 1931.

In 1968, Pope Paul VI chose the first day of January for the feast of Mary, Mother of God, connecting it to Jesus' birth. Since Mary is referred to as "Queen of Peace," the Holy Father designated the day also as World Day of Peace to usher in the New Year and to ask for the intercession of Mary for peace in the world. Pope Paul VI declared, "The purpose of the celebration is to honor the role of Mary in the mystery of salvation." It was also to "renew the adoration rightfully to be shown to the newborn Prince of Peace," as the "priceless gift of peace" to the world. Thus, the Feast of Mary, Mother of God, honors Mary chosen to give birth to the Son of God. Furthermore, as Christmas honors Jesus as Prince of Peace, it also honors Mary as Queen of Peace.During Advent Season, we are urged to "beat swords into plowshares," and work diligently for peace among all peoples. We are asked to dream of a new world where the wolf will play with the lamb, the leopard will lie down with babies, the desert lands will bloom with luscious greenery, the blind will see, the deaf hear, the mute speak, and the lame leap like a strong stag.

As we begin a New Year, we must not wilt nor waver in our faith in the *Emmanuel* ("God-is-with-us"). Let us respond favorably to God's call to develop a relationship with him, and a positive connection with all peoples of the world. Indeed, we are called to grow as people who can be trusted with the grace of God, like Mary, Mother of God and the Queen of Peace. We are called to ponder and reflect on the Word of God throughout the New Year. When we do this, we become people of peace. We are called to open ourselves to others with love and kindness, honesty and fairness, forgiveness and tolerance, and patience and understanding.

These virtues must emanate from our hearts where *Emmanuel* has made a dwelling. We are called to be truthful with one another and contribute to bringing about peace in the world, stopping hatred, and preventing war. We must give care to the sick, sustenance to the poor and needy, the hungry and desperate, the migrant and refugee, the aged, the lonely, and prisoners.

We honor the Blessed Virgin Mary, Mother of God and Queen of Peace, on New Year's Day and ask for her intercession to become instruments of peace.

May the Lord gracefully usher all peoples of the world into a Blessed New Year, and I send you a blessing from the Book of Numbers (6:24-26):

> *The Lord bless you and keep you;*
> *the Lord make his face shine on you,*
> *and be gracious to you;*
> *the Lord turn his face toward you*
> *and give you peace"*
> *(New International Version, NIV).*

The prayer, *Under Thy Protection,* is the oldest known prayer to Mary, Mother of God, dating to A.D. 250:

> *"Under Thy protection, we seek refuge,*
> *Oh, Mother of God;*
> *Despise not our petitions in our needs,*
> *But deliver us always from all dangers,*
> *Virgin Glorious and Blessed. Amen."*

THE FEAST OF THE EPIPHANY OF THE LORD
(January 6 or Sunday between January 2 and 8)

Isaiah 60:1-6; Ephesians 3:2-3a, 5-6; Matthew 2:1-12

JESUS, THE LIGHT OF THE WORLD

The Feasts of Christmas, Epiphany of the Lord, and Baptism of the Lord are a trilogy of celebrations referred to as the Manifestation Feasts. Other events depicting the manifestation of the Triune God in the figure of Jesus include the message of the angels to the shepherds on the night Jesus was born (Luke 2:8-15), the Presentation in the Temple (Luke 2:22-38), the Wedding at Cana (John 2:1-12), Jesus' first visitation to Nazareth (Luke 4:20-21), and the Transfiguration (Luke 9:28-36). John the Baptist also revealed the identity of Jesus as the Messiah to some of his disciples: "There is the Lamb of God!" (John 1:36). Saint Chrysostom observed that the meeting between the Three Kings, King Herod, and Herod's court officials regarding the date of the birth of a king was a manifestation of the Lord to the Jewish people except that "his own did not receive him" (John 1:11).

The Catholic, Orthodox, and Anglican Churches observe the Feast of Epiphany, also known as Three Kings Day. The day commemorates the visit of the Magi, also variously known as the Three Wise Men, the Three Kings, and the Three Astronomers. They represent the Gentile world visiting the Messiah born for the entire world.

The Latin Rite (Western Christianity) celebrates the Feast of Epiphany on January 6 or the Sunday between January 2 and 8. The day is marked by Christmas carols and nativity scenes in churches, homes, and streets, portraying the visit of the three kings. Christian art depicting the Magi's visit on Christmas cards shows various cultural portrayals throughout the world. Epiphany is the traditional day in some areas for baptisms and the blessing of homes and compounds. Traditionally, many peoples exchange Christmas gifts. In Italy, gifts are connected customarily with the older woman, Befana (from the word Epiphany) and in Spain it is linked to the Magi. In the Scandinavian countries, gift exchange came to be associated with St. Nicholas, a fourth century saint who threw gifts into homes.

A medieval legend gives the names of the Magi as Caspar (or Gaspar), Melchor, and Balthazar. Other traditions give different names to the Magi while artists have portrayed them as coming from three different parts of the world. Caspar is usually presented as an Oriental man, and a young African or Moor depicts Balthazar. In the movie Ben-Hur (1959), Balthazar, as an old man, went back to Palestine to look for the adult Jesus.

In the Gospel of Matthew, these dignitaries used their knowledge in astronomy, mystical insight, and wisdom to travel "from the East to Jerusalem" following a bright star to pay homage to the infant Jesus (Matthew 2:1-2). They were the first to worship the infant Jesus as "King of the Jews." In a divine dream, they received the revelation not to report back to King Herod the Great, which led the king to order the murder of innocent infants. Herod had a frenzied fear of losing power and would kill anyone he saw as a threat, including his own family members. He hoped that by killing the infants, Jesus, too, would die (Matthew 2:12, 16-18). Prior to the gory massacre, the Holy Family fled to Egypt after an angel had warned Joseph about Herod's malicious intent to kill the infant Jesus. The Feast of the Holy Innocents, observed in the Western and Eastern churches on December 28 and December 29, respectively, commemorates the killing of infants in Bethlehem by King Herod the Great. Ironically, while the Jewish people still expected the Messiah, God had revealed the Savior of the world to people of Gentile origins.

There is a belief that Saint Matthew used some familiar stories from the ancient monotheistic Zoroastrian religion, founded by Zoroaster in Persia about the sixth century B.C. The religion might have influenced Christianity through Judaism and influenced Islam. Zoroastrianism survives till today as one of the world's oldest religions.

Originally, the word *magos* referred to one belonging to the Persian priestly class. Over the years, it was associated with scientific studies and astronomy fortunetelling. A theory suggests that the Magi in Matthew's Gospel were Zoroastrian astronomer-priests or missionaries who traveled from the East, the cradle of Zoroastrianism, to pay homage to the infant Jesus. Their visit and gifts showed they recognized Jesus as the true Messiah and not Zoroaster. They knelt to worship the child Jesus, and offered gifts associated with royalty. It is said their three gifts represented the Zoroastrian motto of "Good Thoughts, Good Words, and Good Deeds." The readers of Matthew's Gospel were to understand that Christianity was superior to a rival Zoroastrian religion, whose priests visited Jesus and acknowledged him as the Messiah.

The Magi brought Jesus gifts of gold, frankincense, and myrrh, whose spiritual symbolisms are very significant: gold as a symbol to adorn royalty, frankincense used for temple worship depicting Jesus' priesthood, and myrrh, a spice or balm for preparing bodies for burial, representing Jesus' burial. Myrrh also became chrism, a combination of myrrh as an herb mixed with olive oil, to anoint kings (1 Samuel 10:1). Thus, the gifts portray Jesus as a king, priest, and savior.

The word *epiphany* originates from the Greek word *epiphaneia* which means manifestation, or revelation, or appearance. In ancient times, the word was associated with a king visiting one of his provinces or vassal states. Epiphany in Christianity is the revelation or appearance of God (Incarnation) in the person of Jesus Christ, the Son of God; "The Word became a human being, and full of grace and truth, lived among us" (John 1:14). Epiphany reveals him as the "source of life" through whom every life and everything in the universe came into existence (John 1:3-4). He is "the

Lamb of God, who takes away the sin of the world" (John 1:29).

The Eastern Church, where the feast originated in the late second century, celebrates Epiphany as the Baptism of Jesus. Until the recorded first Christmas date of December 25, 336 A.D., Jesus' baptism received more prominence than his birthday. At Jesus' baptism, John the Baptist proclaimed Jesus as "Son of God" when he saw the Spirit come down upon Jesus (John 1:32-34) and when the Holy Spirit appeared as a dove and God said "You are my own dear Son. I am pleased with you" (Luke 3:21-22). The feast is also known as *theophany* from the Greek word meaning "shining forth" or "divine manifestation."

Jesus is the primordial "Light of God" present at the creation of the world that shines in the world and shines on everyone (John 1:4-5, 9). The story of Creation states that darkness existed until God created light. The Gospel of John says that "From the very beginning" of creation, "the Word already existed; the Word was with God, and the Word was God." It was "through him God made all things," the "source of life" which "brought light to humanity" and darkness has never subdued the light (John 1:1-5). Epiphany reveals Jesus as the "Word of God" and "Light of the world."

The first reading from the Prophet Isaiah presents divine brightness exuding from the newborn to the ends of the earth. Like the Magi, the disciples of Jesus would become torch bearers of the light of Christ, carrying the message of salvation to all peoples baptized into the Body of Christ (Matthew 28:19).

As Epiphany celebrates the gift of God's Son to the world, it also enables us to learn from his life. Jesus gives meaning to each life, and his presence and love bring comfort. He shows that the ultimate essence of human life is to know God, love him, and serve him through others while showing them love and mercy (Matthew 5:7, 9). The light of Christ will subdue the darkness of anger, hatred, prejudice, racism, intolerance, jealousy, and pride in our hearts (Galatians

5:19-21). The light of Christ will nurture the seed of love that will grow and bear fruits of the Holy Spirit: love, joy, peace, patience, kindness, goodness, faithfulness, gentleness, and self-control (Galatians 5:22-26).

Do you realize it is best to follow the light as you journey through life?

With determination, the Magi followed the star to Jesus. With similar resolve, let us look for the star and follow it to Jesus.

Whenever we spot a church, we see the star that will bring us to Jesus.

Whenever the priest raises the consecrated host at Mass and each time we go before the Blessed Sacrament at adoration, the Light of Christ engulfs us; we worship him as Savior of the world.

The Peace of the Lord be with you.

Prayer
Father, all of us rejoice today about the Star that led the Magi to Jesus, your Son. When the Star leads us to Jesus, deepen our friendship with him throughout the New Year, enkindling in us the spirit of love, charity, and kindness. Amen.

THE FEAST OF THE BAPTISM OF THE LORD
(First Sunday of the Year)

Isaiah 42:1-4, 6-7; Acts 10:34-38; Matthew 3:13-17

CALLED TO PUBLIC MINISTRY

The Feast of the Baptism of the Lord commemorates the baptism of Jesus in the River Jordan by John the Baptist. Originally, Epiphany combined the three important feasts: the Visit of the Magi, the Baptism of the Lord, and the Wedding at Cana. In 1955, Pope Pius XII separated Epiphany and the Baptism of the Lord because the story of the Magi had eclipsed it. Catholics, Anglicans, Lutherans, and some Methodist parishes commemorate the Baptism of the Lord. In the liturgical calendar, the feast concludes the Christmas Season; the following day, the Church's Season of Ordinary Time begins, which breaks during the Season of Lent.

The Feast of the Baptism of the Lord is about Jesus appearing along the banks of the River Jordan to be baptized by John the Baptist. Praying after baptism might have been part of the ritual for John's baptism. Jesus was praying when the sky opened, and a dove hovered over him to signify the descent of the Holy Spirit. A voice followed, "This is my own dear Son, with whom I am pleased" (Matthew 3:17) This incident is a clear manifestation of the doctrine of the Holy Trinity: Jesus is being baptized, the Holy Spirit hovers around Jesus in the form of a dove, and the Father's voice confirms Jesus' identity as the Beloved Son.

The Synoptic Gospels of Matthew, Mark, and Luke record the baptism of Jesus; the Gospel of John only alludes to it. The Evangelists are sending the message about Jesus Christ as the Son of God in whom the Spirit of the Lord dwells. He is called to inaugurate God's Salvation Plan to save the world. John the Baptist serves as Jesus' messenger who preaches about repentance, forgiveness of sins through baptism, and the imminent arrival of the "one far greater," who "must increase and I decrease" (John 3:30).

Scripture scholars suggest that by stepping into the river to receive baptism, Jesus was identifying with sinful humanity to wash away the sins of the world with the flowing waters of the Jordan River. His emergence from the water marked a rebirth and renewal for those receiving baptism, culminating in their resurrection with him after his own resurrection. Again, at the baptism, his identity defined his mission. He was in the world as Son of God and beloved of the Father to serve and give up his life to save souls (Matthew 20:28). He was identifying with the people in their miseries, weaknesses, and limitations to save them (Hebrews 5:1-4).

As we celebrate the baptism of the Lord, we must note the reference to the Holy Spirit in the Gospels and his presence in the life of the Church and in our own lives. The dove imagery has become a symbol for the Holy Spirit in Christianity and in Christian art. The Holy Spirit came down upon the Virgin Mary, who conceived the Son of God (Luke 1:35). John the Baptist proclaimed that the man upon whom the Spirit appeared like a dove was the Son of God (John 1:32-33). On Pentecost Day, the Holy Spirit filled the disciples of Jesus (Acts 2:4). The Holy Spirit, who opened the heavens to make Jesus visible, filled Saint Stephen (Act 7:55), and this vision emboldened Stephen to forgive those who were stoning him (Act 7:60). Peter and John placed their hands on believers to receive the Holy Spirit (Acts 8:17), a symbolism and legacy in the Church as the Sacrament of Confirmation.

The Lord's baptism is seen by many Fathers of the Church and medieval scholastics as the institution of the Sacrament of Baptism. Therefore, the baptism of the Lord reminded us that the "baptismal garment is an outward symbol of the brightness and glory of Christ, in which we are wrapped—even swaddled—on our baptismal day and every day of discipleship" (Brink and Colloton, *Living the Word*, 2018). Like Jesus, we receive the gift of the Holy Spirit during baptism. If we were prepared adequately for our baptism, or if our parents gave us good Christian teaching from the time, we received baptism as infants, the Sacrament of Confirmation should make us experience an inner spiritual transformation into the likeness of Jesus.

The Feast of the Baptism of the Lord begins Jesus' public ministry. The voice from heaven, "You are my Beloved Son; with you I am well pleased," was God's blessing for Jesus to start his public evangelization. As we celebrate the feast, we are being anointed again as children of God chosen before our birth. God selected us for a mission on earth, blessed us and sent us forth for public evangelization (Jeremiah 1:4-10). We are disciples at home, at church, on the streets, and in workplaces. Each day, the power of Holy Spirit reminds us of our calling by Jesus to help the poor, the broken-hearted, and those in grief (Isaiah 61:1-4). This was the passage quoted by Jesus in his hometown to let his people know about his mission (Luke 4:18). It is a call to discipleship extended to all of us.

Again, in the minds of the evangelists, Jesus is the Son of God in whom the Spirit of God dwells. He came to inaugurate God's salvation plan for all peoples who will gather to a banquet (first reading). The Church always gathers for the Eucharistic banquet within our various communities anticipating the grand banquet at the end of time when all those baptized in Jesus who have lived for the faith will be assembled. Until this time, our lives must be entwined with the Eucharist, which is Jesus in us and among us. This is a call to holiness, which is how we manifest Jesus in our lives wherever we may find ourselves. Indeed, at the heavenly banquet, one's invitation card or dinner dress is simply the assessment of oneself to see if the heart is ready to meet the Lord. Hence, in baptism, God claims us for his Son to become "One Body," a community which is the Church.

The preparation for baptism of an adult is purging oneself to be received into the Body of Christ, the Church. With an infant baptism, the parents bring their child into the Body of

Christ. The practice of baptizing babies in the Sistine Chapel on the Feast of the Baptism of the Lord was started by Saint Pope John Paul II to emphasize the importance of infant baptism. In his homily at the baptism of children on the feast day in 2018, Pope Francis quoted Pope Benedict XVI saying, "God desired to save us by going to the bottom of this abyss himself so that every person, even those who have fallen so low that they can no longer perceive heaven, may find God's hand to cling to and rise from the darkness to see again the light for which he or she was made." Later in the square, Pope Francis said, "The Lord is always there, not to punish us, but with his hand outstretched to help us rise up" (Cindy Wooden, Catholic News Service, January 9, 2023).

By our baptism, our human nature joins with the divine. We are born again into the Lord and empowered for a public ministry. This mission starts in the home (the domestic church) and brings us to the church, and to the streets of our villages and towns, and our countries. Our spiritual birth takes place at baptism, where the Spirit inspires us to think, act, forgive, and love like Jesus. Those around us must see and experience God's Spirit present within us, as well as God's love flowing through us. When the people around us see we are truly God's children by our love and deeds, they will adore and glorify God through us. If we received baptism as infants, we need to revitalize the gift of the Holy Spirit that implanted in us and marked us as children of God.

Do you perceive your baptism as you being brought into the sheepfold of Jesus?

How often do you think of your responsibilities as a follower of Jesus?

Have you been faithful to the promises you made to God at your baptism?

If you ever step off the path that Jesus wishes you to follow, remember that you are only one footstep away from returning to the journey he has planned for you.

The Peace of the Risen Lord be with you.

Prayer
Father, all of us, both infants and adults, are grateful to you for your gift of baptism. Assist us to live as true members of the Body of Christ. Amen.

The Paschal Cycle

(Ash Wednesday to Pentecost)

INTRODUCTION

In the Church's Liturgical Calendar, the Paschal Cycle, composed of the Season of Lent and the Season of Easter, is the period between Ash Wednesday and Pentecost Sunday.

THE SEASON OF LENT

The Season of Lent is a forty-day period in the Liturgical Calendar from Ash Wednesday to Holy Saturday at the Easter Vigil Service. In the Orthodox Church (Eastern Christianity), this period is referred to as the "Great Lent" to distinguish it from the Season of Advent known as the "Winter Lent." The Early Christians commemorated Easter Sunday or the Resurrection of the Lord as the mother of all Sundays or the mother of all feasts.

Like the Season of Advent during which people prepare for Christmas, Lent is a time of preparation for Holy Week or Passion Week and Easter. During the Lenten period, Christians commemorate the events in the life of Jesus Christ leading to his crucifixion and resurrection. It is a time of deep personal reflection, an opportunity to reconcile with God, and an occasion to practice the seven-corporal works of mercy which are acts of charity or compassion to alleviate people's physical needs. The seven-corporal works of mercy are to feed the hungry, give drink to the thirsty, give clothes to those who lack them, shelter the homeless (including refugees), care for the sick, visit the imprisoned, and provide decent burial to those who cannot afford one.

Forty Days

Between Ash Wednesday which falls within February 4 and March 10, and Easter Sunday which falls on a Sunday between March and April (approximately within the

Northern Hemisphere's Spring), there are forty-six days. All the same, Lent is regarded as forty days simply because Sundays within the Lenten period are not counted as part of the forty days of the Lenten Season. Sundays during this time are referred to as Sundays of Lent. The historical or traditional explanation is that fasting was not deemed proper on a Sunday, the Day of the Lord, when Christians commemorated the Resurrection of Jesus Christ. A Sunday was therefore not regarded as an appropriate day for penance.

The guideline determining the date for Easter Sunday for any given year is that Easter Sunday is the first Sunday after the full moon which follows the Spring Equinox. The spring equinox usually falls on March 20 or March 21. The date Lenten Season begins – that is, the date upon which Ash Wednesday occurs – is forty days before Easter Sunday, not counting Sundays.

Initially, three days were set aside to prepare for Holy Week. Over the years, however, the forty-day period was instituted as more adequate for prayer, fasting, and meditation on the suffering and death of Jesus Christ. The figure "forty" is also symbolic as it reminds us of certain biblical events: Moses spent forty days and forty nights on the Mountain of the Lord without food or water (Exodus 34:38); during the days of Noah, God made it rain for forty days and forty nights (Genesis 7:17); the people of Israel wandered through the wilderness for forty years to prepare to enter into the Promised Land; the prophet Jonah urged the people of Nineveh to fast for forty days before receiving God's grace and forgiveness (Jonah 3:4); the Prophet Elijah journeyed in the desert for forty days and forty nights to the Mountain of the Lord (1 Kings 19:8). For Christians, the number forty connotes an even a deeper meaning in relation to the story of Jesus. He fasted for forty days and forty nights in the desert to prepare for his mission (Matthew 4:1-2), and this seemed to have greatly influenced the adoption of forty days for Lent.

It is significant therefore that before the commemoration of the greatest feast in the calendar of the Church, Christians must use forty days and forty nights to prepare by praying, fasting, and reflection on the suffering and death of the Savior.

Origin of Lent

Lent is an English word derived from the ancient Anglo-Saxon name for March, "lencten." The name remained because the Lenten Season would usually fall in the month of March. The name is also associated with the "Season of Spring" in Old German language. The Spring Season comes after winter when snow melts and plants spring up and animals in hibernation come out with renewed vigor. The same spirit of change or renewal of life is expected of us after the winter's long darkness gives way to longer and brighter days.

The observance of Lent originated in the fourth century. It was a period when converts or initiates who had received strict instructions for entry into the faith fasted in preparation for the Sacrament of Baptism on Easter Eve. It was also a time of preparation for Easter Sunday, the commemoration of the Resurrection of Jesus Christ.

Near the end of the fourth century, instructions were given throughout the six weeks of Lent for three hours each day. Lent was therefore the final hurdle after the various stages of initiation. Thus, within the last couple of weeks prior to their baptism, catechumens or converts were expected to observe times for prayer, fasting, and self-examination. This was an opportunity for them to reflect deeply on past life and God's salvation plan which they had accepted and affirmed their resolution to live as true followers of Jesus. The Lenten Season was also a period when those who had separated from the Church prepared to rejoin the community of believers.

With the great influx of members into the Church, especially following the acceptance of Christianity as the state religion of Rome in the fourth century, the Season of Lent assumed a new character. Those who accompanied converts to profess the faith publicly, were likewise requested to renew their commitment to faith in Jesus Christ. Furthermore, over the years, since the newly baptized were received into a "community of faith," the Lenten fast and practices became obligatory for all Christians. Thus, today, during the Season of Lent, Christians are required to observe fasting and prayer, as well as to practice charity and ask for forgiveness for their failure to live up to the commandments of the Risen Christ.

Traditions in Lent

The forty days of Lent are traditionally marked by fasting, penitential prayer, abstinence, charity, and other acts of penance. In ancient times, Christians observed a very rigid schedule of fasting. In certain places all animal products were strictly forbidden and only fish and birds were permitted to be eaten. Other areas did not allow one to eat fruits and eggs. Some people ate only bread while others refused food the entire day; others ate one meal a day. In some places, people abstained from food until three o'clock in the afternoon.

In the Eastern Orthodox Church, people continue to this day to abstain from meat products just as in ancient times. Their meals are usually vegetarian during Lent. These and similar practices are meant to "refocus on spirituality in a culture that is increasingly secular" (Dennis Bratcher).

In the West (Roman Rite), however, Christians have eagerly relaxed the previously strict and purposefully spiritual exercises that emphasized self-control and self-discipline. The common practice today is to deny oneself things one likes, such as chocolate, sweets, alcohol, meat, and other types of food or an activity, such as the theatre, and devote the time or donate the money that would be spent to charity. In other words, what one would have used on excesses is converted to money that the poor can use to buy food. Others may decide on a Lenten discipline and do volunteer work or perform some kind of Lenten devotion.

Again, in the Roman Rite, persons above the age of maturity, generally above eighteen years and below sixty years, must fast during Lent (Canon 1251). Although Canon Law requires that Ash Wednesday, Fridays throughout the year, and certain other days are days of abstinence from meat, Bishops' Conferences are permitted to set the days of fasting and abstinence (Canon 1253). Thus, in many countries, fasting and abstinence are required on Ash Wednesday and Fridays within the Lenten Season.

Many modern Protestants and Anglicans regard the observation of Lent as a choice than an obligation as in the Roman Catholic Church or other Eastern Rites. Ash Wednesday is however a day of fasting in the Anglican Church as indicated in the Anglican Book of Common Prayer. In this regard, Christians may choose to concentrate on performing penitential activities other than fasting such as performing charitable acts, providing poor people with food and clothing, and giving money to charitable organizations.

The Liturgy in Season of Lent

Customarily, preparation for baptism is at the final stages during the period of Lent. Baptism means the convert has entered a covenant with God and accepted the salvation sought through the death and resurrection of Jesus Christ. This makes the account of the history of salvation read at the Easter Vigil very significant. Consequently, the covenants of the Old Testament are recounted to instruct the convert and remind others about the stages of God's plan of salvation culminating in the Risen Christ. As close as possible, the second readings during Lent complement the Old Testament and the Gospel readings.

The parts of the Gospel of John, traditionally associated with faith and baptism, are used on Sundays of Lent except for the second Sunday. The Gospel reading for First Sunday of Lent recounts Jesus' temptation episode in the desert (Matthew 4:1-11); the Second Sunday of Lent is about the

Transfiguration of the Lord (Matthew 17:1-9); the Third
Sunday of Lent relates the story of Jesus at the Well meeting
the Samaritan woman (John 4:5-42); the Fourth Sunday of
Lent is about the healing of the blind Bartimaeus (John
9:1-11); and the Fifth Sunday of Lent narrates the Death and
Resurrection of Lazarus (John 11:1-45)

The last three Sunday readings are specific to Year A.
However, like the first two Sundays, they may be used in all
the Cycles (A, B, and C), when catechumens are to be
baptized. What is proper to Year C is the story of the Woman
Caught in Adultery (John 8:1-11).

In the Roman Rite, the Anglican Eucharist, and the
Lutheran Service, the "Gloria in Excelsis Deo" is not sung
nor recited during Lent, the Gloria is omitted from Ash
Wednesday until Easter Vigil. Exceptions are made on major
feast days when the Gloria is sung or recited to reflect the
joyful character of the Mass of the day, but the penitential
nature of the season is not reduced. Another example is Holy
Thursday when the Gloria is sung or recited. Similarly,
throughout the period of Lent, the Alleluia is not used but
replaced by a Lenten or Gospel acclamation usually with an
alternate prayer such as "Praise and glory to you, Lord Jesus."

The Scrutinies

What is known in theological parlance as the *Great
Commission* was Jesus' instruction to his disciples:

*"Go, then, to all peoples everywhere and make them my disciples:
baptize them in the name of the Father, and the Son, and the
Holy Spirit, and teach them to obey everything I have
commanded you." (Matthew 28:19-20)*

Since the eve of Christianity, baptism or Christian
initiation, has been regarded as the first response by
anyone who hears and accepts the Faith bequeathed to the
Church by Jesus through the disciples who obeyed the

command to spread the message guided by the Holy Spirit. Baptism is the first of the Holy Sacraments and most Christian denominations accept each other's baptism if they use the invocation of the Holy Trinitarian formula: *"I baptize you in the name of the Father, and the Son, and the Holy Spirit."* The element of water in the sacred rite of baptism symbolizes the cleansing of one's sins, the beginning of a new life in Jesus, and initiation into the Christian faith.

Baptism is one of the ancient purification rituals practiced in all cultures and religions. Christian baptism has its roots in Judaism performed by immersion in water as was performed by John the Baptist. It was a form of spiritual purification symbolized by repentance, forgiveness of sins, and a new way of life. Hence, in the Early Church, baptism was a public affirmation of the Faith, admission into the Christian community, and a profound commitment to abide by the teachings of Jesus. The immersion in water or the pouring of water demonstrated the person's participation in the death and resurrection of Jesus, a spiritual rebirth. As an outward or visible sign of God's grace, baptism also conferred the Holy Spirit on the baptized just as Jesus received the anointing of the Holy Spirit during his baptism.

Infants in the Catholic Church are baptized into the faith of their parents, immersed into the Catholic community, and freed from original sin. An adult seeking baptism for the first time, a Protestant who joins the Catholic Church, and baptized infants who become of age, are catechized through the Order of Christian Initiation of Adults (OCIA).

Scrutinies are three special Purification and Enlightenment Rites celebrated when the OCIA is nearing its end for the people to be baptized at the Easter Vigil. Scrutinies are celebrated in the third, fourth, and fifth weeks of the Lenten Season. They also remind the faithful present to review their faith. Cheryl Hadley writes that the scrutinies "are about seeing sin in its right aspect and coming to understand the way we fall victim to it. They are also about the transformative healing possible for us through

Christ, as He offers Himself to us" (The Catholic Company, 2022).

Lenten Colors

The altar linens and priests' chasubles are violet during Lent in the Roman Catholic and Anglican Traditions. During holy days and feasts, the linens and vestments resume their proper colors, usually white or red. The colors of Lent are symbols of Jesus' suffering that end on Calvary with his crucifixion. In addition, Lenten colors symbolize the pain and suffering of humanity and the world under the reign of sin. Purple, which is a royal color, may be used in Lent. Purple is in anticipation of the suffering and death of Jesus that will culminate in his resurrection on Easter Sunday. Grey is also a favorite color in Lent especially on Ash Wednesday. It is the biblically symbolic color of mourning and repentance. The traditional color for Good Friday is red signifying God's love and blood shed on Calvary. It also signifies both the death of Jesus and the death of the world through sin. White vestments are used during the Vigil service and on Easter Sunday: Christ, Light of the world, has overcome darkness and evil. Church decorations during Lent are considerably restrained. The practice of placing flowers in the sanctuary is avoided in many places. The mood in the church must be one of penitence and reflection.

Holy Days in Lent

Within the Season of Lent there are many holy days. The first is Ash Wednesday which begins the Lenten Season in Western Christianity. In the Eastern Orthodox Church, the season begins on "Clean Monday" or "Ash Monday." Ash Wednesday falls on the seventh Wednesday before Easter Sunday. The name "Ash Wednesday" is derived from the ancient practice of marking the foreheads or heads of Christians with ashes. The practice stemmed from the ancient

Near Eastern tradition of throwing ashes over one's head as a sign of repentance before God. In the Early Church, ashes were given only to those who made public confessions and wished to be reconciled to God and the community of faith. Over the years, the practice of marking the foreheads was extended to the whole congregation. The priest or minister (or lay person) marks the foreheads of worshippers in the form of a cross with smudged black ashes formed from burned palm leaves from the previous year's Palm Sunday celebration. The palm leaves are burned, blessed, and mixed with olive oil or water as a fixative. The mark in the shape of a cross is expected to remain until sundown. Those marked walk through the streets acknowledging they are saved by the death and resurrection of Jesus. The marking on the foreheads with ashes comes with instruction for the receiver:

"Remember, man, that you are dust. And unto dust you shall return." (Genesis 3:19)

Or

Turn away from sin and be faithful to the Gospel.

Or

Repent, and hear the Good News.

Ash Wednesday in the Roman Catholic Tradition is marked by prayer, fasting, abstinence, (especially from meat), and almsgiving. The Church encourages these acts to enable the Faithful to better emulate Jesus' sacrifice and spend more time to relate to God.

Ash Wednesday is also a day of repentance when we reflect and grieve over our failures and inability to please God all the time. The act of marking people's foreheads is sacramental but not a sacrament. However, Catholics revere the practice, and churches are usually packed on Ash

101

Wednesday. The modest act places the Christian humbly before God to consider the consequences of sin.

The last Wednesday of Lent, Wednesday of Holy Week, is referred to as "Spy Wednesday," the day Judas Iscariot was supposed to have spied on Jesus before betraying him the following day. The Thursday of Holy Week is known as "Maundy Thursday," when Christians commemorate the Lord's Supper or the Last Supper when Jesus celebrated the Passover with his apostles the night before he was crucified. At the Last Supper, Jesus instituted the Eucharist and the office of Priesthood. On Good Friday, Christians remember the Lord's scourging, crucifixion, and burial. Traditionally considered as a shameful death, the crucifixion of Jesus was his sacrifice to atone for the sin of the world. The Easter Vigil celebration on Holy Saturday concludes Holy Week and the Season of Lent. Easter Sunday is the climax of God's Salvation Plan to save the world. It is a joyful Sunday; Jesus rises from the death, a renaissance for humankind, the true meaning of life or existence finds its fulfillment in Jesus, and where he has gone, we too shall be after our own resurrection.

Reflections on Lent

In its chapter on the Liturgical Year, the Constitution on the Sacred Liturgy (109) stresses reflecting on the significance of baptism as well as the maintenance of a penitential spirit during the Season of Lent. Within a period of forty days, we are expected to look critically at what continues to foster our sinfulness. In this regard, therefore, Lent is a period of private penance. It is our passage through the desert with Jesus, reflecting on our lives in relation to his. We also identify with the sufferings of Jesus from his trial to his death. Within the silent setting of our personal stay in the desert, we are required to delve into our innermost selves to discover what we are before God: proud, jealous, over-ambitious, judgmental, and uncharitable. Indeed, from all

102

angles of our introspection and self-examination, we may become totally dismayed at our own tattered selves before God who has always loved us and expects us to love him and one another in return.

Again, to our greatest surprise, we realize that even our own physical bodies appear unhealthy due to overindulgence in things not suitable for the body, including possibly our eating and drinking habits. Thus, in the desert, one should recognize the need to make changes to save both body and soul. In fact, fasting or the apparent physical pain of hunger makes one appreciative of Jesus' pain both in the desert while he fasted and during his journey of pain to Mount Calvary and suffering on the cross. Furthermore, physical pain identifies us with the sufferings of the poor who seem to live in a state of perpetual fasting. Such experiences and familiarity with the poor, sick, marginalized, and powerless in society must humble us as Christians to really care about others.

The spiritual exercises during Lenten Season – fasting, abstinence, charity, introspection, and prayer – are also the supplications of the sinner. They place the sinner at the gates of heaven where he or she wallows in sin while singing a prayer for help as in Psalm 86. That is to say that at the threshold of heaven one becomes absolutely disposed to the superfluous grace of God. The repentant sinner strikes the breast, stoops, or prostrates acknowledging his or her inadequacies, weakness, and guilt before God. Thus, with ashes on the forehead on Ash Wednesday, the penitent goes before God with true humility to pray, "Lord, be merciful to me a sinner." Then, completely forgiven and graced by God's gentle beckoning, one gladly steps forward into the arms of a generous Father (Psalm 86: 20). In the presence of God the Father, one is finally privileged to remain in the house of the Lord forever (Psalm 23:6). The redeemed now come to the Father to place their needs, fears, failures, and hopes into the hands of God, ready to allow God's transforming grace to work in our lives. It is with this joy and enthusiasm that we enter the Easter Season. In a joyous procession behind the Paschal Light representing the Risen Lord, we sing: "The Lord is Risen indeed. Alleluia! Alleluia!"

THE SEASON OF EASTER

The Season of Easter is the second part of the Paschal Cycle which is a seven-week season or period from Easter Sunday to Pentecost Sunday. The Season of Easter starts directly after the Paschal or Easter Triduum – the three days of Holy Thursday, Good Friday, and Easter Vigil – recognized as the most significant event in Christianity. Easter Season is a period of joy and continues to celebrate the resurrection of Jesus, his appearances, and the work of the apostles in spreading the Word of God. Hence, subsequent Sundays from Easter Sunday are referred to as "Sundays of Easter," and not "Sundays after Easter." The Church celebrates the end of the Paschal Season on Pentecost Sunday when she is officially inaugurated, and missionary activity is continued with the presence of the Holy Spirit.

The Season of Lent

ASH WEDNESDAY

Joel 2:12-18; 2 Corinthians 5:20-6:2; Matthew 6:1-6, 16-17

MADE FROM THE SOIL: YOU ARE LIKE DUST!

In the world today, cremation is common practice. My first funeral Mass for a cremated body was years ago at the Holy Name of Jesus Catholic Church, Brooklyn, New York. Before Mass, I sought permission from the family to look inside an urn with beautifully decorative designs. I opened the container, and of course, it was the ashes of a cremated human being. I was overwhelmed and deeply humbled.

Ash! Dust! A human body reduced to mere ashes which when blown by air is a faint wisp of breeze that swiftly is gone with the wind!

Our Christian belief is that God fashioned the human being from the soil. God breathed the breath of life into the man and his woman companion, and together they became living beings (Genesis 2:7). However, sin separated them from their Creator, altering their destiny: they and their descendants "would work hard and sweat to make the soil produce anything, until you go back to the soil from which you were formed" (Genesis 3:19).

In the Catholic and some Christian churches— Anglicans, Episcopalians, Lutherans, United Methodists, and Presbyterians—priests, deacons, ministers, and other lay ministers make a smudge of ash from burned palm fronds of the previous year's Palm Sunday celebration, mixed with water or oil. The one who smears the moistened ash on your forehead in the form of a cross reminds you that the substance or element of your being is nothing but ordinary soil, and eventually, you will return to soil. The practice in the Early Church was to sprinkle ashes over Christians, which changed to ashes smeared on the forehead at the dawn of the Middle Ages. The ashes symbolize one's sinful state and his or her pledge to return to God with complete self, while the shape of the cross signifies redemption.

The Church states that at the end of your life on earth, God's breath of life (the Soul), which is eternal, will return to him if you allowed yourself to be guarded by Jesus' two Commandments of Love: "Love the Lord your God with all your heart, with all your soul, and with all your mind," and "Love your neighbor as you love yourself" (Matthew 22:37-39). If you ignored God's Commandment of Love, your soul is denied access to the presence of God.

The day of judgement for you could be soon in coming because "death, a necessary end, will come when it will come" (Shakespeare's Julius Caesar). Besides, Scripture says that the average life span for humanity is 70 years, and 80 years for those who are strong (Psalm 90:10). How old are you? How many more years do you have here on earth? Ash Wednesday is a humble and sobering reminder of human mortality, a symbol of death gaping at us all to suggest that your remains, or my corpse, could soon be ashes in a jug or a frozen body in a coffin!

The Church is telling you today to *Remember that you are dust, and to dust you shall return.*

Therefore, *"Repent, and believe in the Gospel,"* or *"Repent and hear the Good News."*

In the hustle and bustle of everyday life, the Church furthermore urges you to observe a forty-day period of profound introspection; to reflect on the revelation that humanity has received salvation from Jesus Christ—the Son of God, our Lord and Savior—who died on the cross to atone for our own sins and sin inherited from Adam. Indeed, before God, you are acknowledging your imperfections and sinfulness and the urgent need for reconciliation with God.

Ash Wednesday begins the Season of Lent in Western Christianity. It is a forty-day period of repentance, and the three readings of today remind us how fasting, penitential prayer, abstinence, charity or almsgiving, and other acts of penance mark the days. Christians learn simplicity of life and harmonious relationships devoid of rancor, hatred, deeply rooted bigotry, selfishness, and intolerance. We are to emulate Jesus' seclusion in the desert to fast, pray, and reflect on the Word of God and his mission on earth; therefore, we fast, pray, and reflect on the Word of the Lord and our mission on earth. We recognize daily that the same three basic temptations of Jesus confront us, supplied by lack of faith or trust in God, abuse of values, clamor for power, influence, status, illicit wealth, and other worldly materials. We fester selfishness, hatred, bitterness, hostility, and prejudice when we should be focused on with love, compassion, sympathy, and charity.

Since life is relatively short, we need to make reparation for our sins and move towards our Creator. The Prophet Joel tells us—the assembly and all peoples, including children—to grieve from committed sins and to come back with our whole heart to the Lord who is gracious and merciful, tolerant and kind, and slow to punish; we are to tear our hearts and not our clothes, show genuine guilt and repentance, and fast (first reading). Saint Paul said this is the proper time, our "day of salvation" (second reading) to prepare our souls by living like Jesus.

Prayer and meditation during Lent will make our minds focus on Jesus. Fasting will make us feel the pain and grief of the poor, realizing that it is our mission to assist them with love and compassion. Sharing our blessings with those in dire need of life's necessities gives us inner joy from God.

It is said that life is like the sunflower, blossoming only for a few days and then withering away. In its brief life, the sunflower is one of the most colorful flowers. The plant follows the movement of the sun, relying on the sun's rays to brighten its flower. Hence, its name is Sunflower or Sun Follower. In the morning, the sunflower stands facing the east to meet the rising sun; it turns to face the sun across the sky during the day; and turns west to face the setting sun. The sunflower loses its life support at dusk until the sun rises again to give it life and beauty.

Christ is God's Light on earth (John 1:2-5). Just as the sunflower gets its name from following the sun, we derive our names from following Christ. We are called Christians or "Christlike," relying solely on the grace of our Lord and Savior Jesus Christ. Like the sunflower, let us blossom in the Light of Christ. We must live like the sunflower, knowing that our life support is the Light of Christ shining upon us, even in times of troubles and sorrow. God's breath gave us life. Jesus Christ gives us the gift of the Holy Spirit that "produces love, joy, peace, patience, kindness, goodness, faithfulness, humility, and self-control" (Galatians 5:22-23). We must allow the Spirit to direct our lives (Galatians 5:25) through Jesus Christ to bear the fruits of compassionate love, selflessness, sincerity, decency, and justice. What Christians receive from God they are expected to give back; what we give to God goes to the poor and most in need.

Make the sign of the cross on your forehead on Ash Wednesday a meaningful, holy, and sacred symbol as you begin the Season of Lent.

Wherever you go, let others take notice of the sign of the cross with ashes on your forehead to know that they, too, must allow their lives to be directed by the Light of Christ and the Spirit of God (Galatians 5:25).

Let the ashes you receive on your forehead be a sign of your pledge to conversion today and a sincere surrender to God of your entire self (first reading).

Let the ashes you receive remind you about your belief in Jesus as the Resurrection and the Life (John 11:25). Jesus is Life. Death has no power over him. He is the Resurrection. He lives forever. The Easter Story: "He is Risen" (John 16:6).

Do you want to wait till tomorrow before you accept Jesus when you could turn into ashes today?

Will you make an indelible mark on your imagination with the ashes on your forehead from today until you meet your maker?

May the Spirit of the Lord lead us throughout this Season of Lent.
The Peace of the Lord be with you.

Prayer
Father, no miracle is difficult for you. Touch the minds and hearts of each of your people and let them know the real purpose of their lives here on earth. Amen.

FIRST SUNDAY OF LENT

Genesis 2:7-9. 3:1-7; Romans 5:12-19; Matthew 4:1-11

LENT–TIME FOR SELF-EXAMINATION

In the natural world, we observe the expected re-occurrence of a twenty-four-hour rhythm of the earth rotating on its axis. This phenomenon causes the day when many of us work and the night when most of us sleep or rest. The earth's movement around the sun makes one complete elliptical revolution per year, which causes the various seasons. Another example of a natural cycle is that of precipitation and evaporation. The rain and snow shower the earth and return to the atmosphere via the process of evaporation. Each movement and its natural rhythm seem effortless and endless, ongoing and eternal, so to speak.

The Church's Liturgical Year is about Christian yearly religious worship, celebrating the same sequence in the birth and life of Jesus Christ. We observe each moment of his life during the year with a kind of natural rhythm and "a tradition kept and observed with solemn service, ritual, and devotion." The Church reminds us that every event in our faith-related life is an integral part of the cyclical celebration of each aspect of Jesus' life.

The Season of Lent informs us about the wonder of the natural rhythm regarding human life. Our belief is that human beings and all other living creatures fashioned from the soil will return to the soil—an inert matter—after the death of the physical body. God formed the human being, man and woman, out of the soil and breathed life-giving breath into them (Genesis 1:26-28). God designed the human life cycle because of human disobedience (Genesis 3:19). Thus, after some years on earth, averaging seventy or eighty for those who are strong; "life is soon over, and we are gone" (Psalm 90:10), and the body returns to the soil from which it was formed. Like Adam and Eve, "You were made from soil, and you will become soil again" (Gen 3:19b). God's breath of life, the soul, or the extension of God within us, which is an inimitable gift to each person, will return to God depending on how well the person valued and lived the gift of life as God intended it: to experience God, love Him, and serve Him.

The Season of Lent is also an example of the re-occurring rhythm of how Christians must discover the meaning of life, build their faith, and incorporate the faith into their daily lives. It is the spiritual commemoration of Jesus' forty days of fasting in the desert, and for Christians, it is a time of self-examination, conversion, repentance, penance, prayer, and almsgiving. Lent challenges us to ponder profoundly what the Church plainly stated on Ash Wednesday to "remember that you are dust, and to dust you shall return," and therefore we ought to "repent, and believe in the Gospel."

Today's first reading narrates the story of the creation of our first parents, Adam and Eve. It explains how they sinned, symbolic of their weak human nature, and their inclination to exist separated from the Creator, particularly when induced by the evil Satan signified by the snake in the story. The story admonishes us to be aware of the reality that human life has finality and tendency to easily distance ourselves from God. What things do you need to change around you to pave the way for transformation in the Lord? Is fasting merely abstinence from food and drink, or does it lead you closer to God, to open your heart, and be mindful of those who seek meaning in life, love, and help? Lent is therefore a time to think about what we can do both to change ourselves and the lives of those around us: family, co-workers, community, and the Church.

We refer to the First Sunday of Lent, or the Sunday after Ash Wednesday, as Quadragesima (Latin word for "fortieth") Sunday. This portrays the forty days until Good Friday. It is the spiritual commemoration of Jesus' forty days of fasting and prayer in the desert before his public ministry.

Traditionally, the Gospel in the Liturgy of the Word is about Jesus' temptations shortly after completing his fasting, which gave Jesus a stage to prepare for some temptations he would face during his three years of ministry.

Do we realize how the devil always sets the stage for us to be angry or show prejudice, jealousy, and aversion towards others? He offered life's false choices to Jesus, even daring to attack his discerned identity as the Son of God during his fasting, meditation, and praying. What are the alternatives that are being suggested to you by the devil regarding how you must live your life?

Jesus was told to satisfy his hunger by turning stones into loaves of bread after forty days of fasting. The choices the devil suggests to us are things we can do to feed the insatiable hunger for accomplishment, power, status, control, ambition, and wealth. How often do we accuse political, corporate, and religious leaders of corruption, nepotism, and sometimes violence to achieve their selfish ends? Are we not also being diverted from the real meaning of life to seek bodily comforts, self-glory, and self-gratification?

As human, Jesus' greatest weapon to defeat the devil was not his own strength or power but his faith and trust in God. Who always gives power and support to those who trust in him. Jesus is the "Word of God" and the "Source of Life" who in the beginning of creation existed together with God: "And the Word was God" who has graced our lives with divine mercy and infinite love (John 1:1-5). His power over his temptations offers us strength and hope in him to help us overcome the temptations we face every day from the devil and our own fervent desires.

The Gospel reading offers us an example of how Jesus overcame Satan. Saint Thomas Aquinas cites four reasons why Jesus, although the Son of God, allowed himself to be tempted. First, the temptation of Jesus in his human nature encourages us to deal with our own temptations. Our humanity disposes us to temptations, and the acts of fasting and prayer will help us fight back evil. Second, the

114

temptation of Jesus is a warning that no matter how righteous one may be, he or she cannot escape being tempted. Third, the fight against the devil in the desert is an example of how we can resist evil. Our sharpest weapon to fight sin is to be well-versed in the Scriptures and to pray continuously as Jesus said to Satan, "Worship the Lord your God, and serve him only" (Matthew 4:10). And fourth, Jesus always assures us that his mercy and grace are abundantly available. Jesus' temptation in the desert relates to our everyday lives. Therefore, we should have confidence in him.

As we journey through Lent, let us undergo serious self-examination and resolve to do better since our time on earth is finite. We need to work hard to overcome what we seriously identify as our weaknesses.

Which temptations are the hardest for you to conquer? Keep a mental or written list during this Lenten season and ask Jesus to inspire and support your efforts to conquer these hurdles which keep you from him.

What are some plans and strategies that you have implemented in the past or can implement in the future to help overcome the distractions in your life?

Are you joyful that the grace of God will help you overcome the tests of life, especially by trusting in his Word, observing a good prayer life, and practicing charity?

It is a time for you to think seriously about the meaning of life and your relevance in the family and community.

The Peace of the Lord be with you.

Prayer
Father, we lift our hearts to you in thanksgiving for this season. Help us see this season as another special invitation to experience your salvation. Amen.

SECOND SUNDAY OF LENT

Genesis 12:1-4a; 2 Timothy 1:8b-10; Matthew 17:1-9

LENT - JOURNEY TO THE MOUNTAIN TO SEE THE GLORY OF GOD

After spending about a year or two with Jesus, the Apostles had developed some familiarity with him. They knew some of the obvious facts regarding him, such as where his hometown was and who was in his immediate family. Convinced that Jesus was the one whom Moses and the Prophets alluded to (Matthew 1:45), they acknowledged him as "the Son of God" and "the king of Israel" (Matthew 1:49). They confirmed among themselves: "We have found the Messiah" (Matthew 1:41). It seemed their understanding of the personality of Jesus was better than the ordinary folks who saw Jesus as Elijah, Jeremiah, or one of the Prophets. Simon Peter daringly summed up the beliefs of the Apostles concerning Jesus' personality and mission: "You are the Messiah, the Son of the living God" (Matthew 16:16).

Jesus was, however, quick to recognize his disciples' lack of profound understanding of the Messiah's general notion. The well-known Old Testament image of the Messiah was that a shoot would grow from the stump of David (Isaiah 11:1). The "redeemer figure" would establish a new kingdom comprising Israel's tribes. He would deliver Israel from physical bondage, bring the exiles back home (Isaiah 11:11), and rule with "justice and integrity" (Isaiah 11:5). Thus, the people viewed the Messiah not as God or "a Son of God" but a king figure. The expectation of his appearance was a deep-seated belief, one heralding a reign of global peace to improve the state of humanity. Within this expected glorious dispensation, the mother of James and John hoped to gain privileged political positions (Matthew 20: 21).

With this understanding firmly rooted also in the minds of the disciples, Jesus surprised them when he proposed another not well-known Old Testament Messianic concept—the Suffering Messiah—as the true essence of the Messiah. About 700 years before the birth of Jesus, the Prophet Isaiah had preached about a "Suffering Messiah" (Isaiah 52: 13-15; Isaiah 53) which some of the ancient rabbis had interpreted as the symbolic suffering of the nation of Israel; others suggested, however, that this meant the actual suffering of the Messiah.

At the time of Jesus, these concepts of Israel's suffering and a famous Messiah-king were familiar. Jesus' interpretation was undoubtedly a hard pill to swallow (Matthew 17: 23b). Peter reminded Jesus of a celebrated worldly Messiah (Matthew 16:22), but Jesus gave his disciples the true meaning as predicted by Isaiah: a Suffering Messiah. He would be Israel's "guilt offering," known in the Levitical sacrifices as *asham*, meaning one's sins symbolically placed on the lamb before it was sacrificed. Jesus, therefore, was the lamb to bear the afflictions of Israel. He would be sacrificed (Matthew 17:22-23) as "sin offering," (Isaiah 53:7-8), or "the lamb of God who takes away the sin of the world" (John 1:29). He was a spiritual Savior (Matthew 16:24-26), the true interpretation and fulfillment of the Law and the Prophets. Jesus was educating his disciples about his own suffering, death, and resurrection (Matthew 16:21).

A few days after Peter's pronouncement, Jesus invited Peter, James, and John to prayer with him a high mountain. Deep in prayer, his countenance changed; he transformed into a glorified figure with face shining like the sun and his garment appearing as a glistening light.

When the priest raises the Consecrated Bread during Mass today, will you feel transformed, bright as the sun piercing through your heart with love? How will you receive him when he invites you to come to the altar of Grace to take his body and eat or take his blood and drink?

At the Transfiguration, Moses and Elijah appeared and talked with Jesus regarding how he would fulfill the vision of the Suffering Messiah. The disciples at the scene felt completely engulfed in the divine presence, shaken, puzzled, and fearful about this spectacular occurrence. In a bemused state, Peter wished they remained in the aura surrounding them and immediately offered to create three booths for the three of them, referencing the booths used by Israel on the Feast of Tabernacles (Leviticus 23:34-42). Equally overwhelming was the cloud just as God appeared to the Israelites and a powerful voice as divine communication, confirming the divinity of Jesus. It was a voice intended to evoke an insight into the true nature of Jesus.

Do you see the Liturgy of the Word and homily as the powerful voice of God, which must be received with joy and allow to affect your life?

The voice of God was a direct divine instruction to the disciples to show stronger interest in the mystical story of Jesus over the Law and the Prophets. Jesus said he had not come to abolish the Law and the Prophets but to fulfill them by becoming the expression of God's Law. The Law and the Prophets—represented by Moses and Elijah at the transfiguration scene—are now replaced by God's Son, Jesus, who would establish a new covenant (kingdom of God) to include all peoples of the earth (first reading) as Jesus commanded in his *Great Commission* to the apostles (Matthew 28:19-20).

The three Synoptic Gospels Matthew (17:1-13), Mark (9:2-13), and Luke (9:28-36) report the Transfiguration of the Lord. The word transfiguration has its roots in Latin as *trans* (meaning "across") and *figura* (meaning "form" or "shape"). Thus, Jesus' form or shape or appearance changed on the mountain. Officially commemorated on August 6 as The Feast of the Transfiguration, it is regarded as one of the significant events in the life and ministry of Jesus. It unveils the divinity of Jesus as the "Son of God," the second of the Holy Trinity, and shows him as the image and fulfillment of the Old Testament's Messianic figure. Again, this event signifies Jesus' predicted resurrection, and after comforting them, Jesus urges Peter, John, and James to keep it secret until his resurrection.

Last week, we journeyed with Jesus up the mountain for spiritual introspection. This was to enhance our relationship with him through whom we are co-heirs of God's kingdom (Matthew 5:5) in a more personal and practical way. Today, the Church urges us to see Jesus as guilt offering (*asham*), the "Suffering Messiah" who atones for our sins. With this understanding of Jesus, we are encouraged to go mountain climbing today on a pilgrimage with Jesus. On the mountain, we shall have a glimpse of his glory, the same "Morning Star" that manifested itself at his birth, baptism, and Easter morning to overcome the darkness of the world. But our home is not on the mountain yet. We must descend as transformed men and women filled with joy, amazing grace, and powerful spiritual experience to embrace God's will, listen to his beloved Son, and allow the mountain experience to reflect in our everyday life.

Saint Peter writes that the three of them were eyewitnesses to the Transfiguration. They did not depend "on made-up stories" about the divine privilege of witnessing Jesus' greatness and "honor and glory" bestowed on him by God (2 Peter 1:16-18). Certainly, the experience transformed Peter, James, and John, and things become clearer after Jesus' suffering, death, and resurrection. Peter understood suffering as a test to prove one's faith (1 Peter 1: 6-7).

Will you allow the Lenten Season to transform you spiritually?

Will this conversion enhance your faith, love of God, and love of others?

How do you present yourself to others as someone who is truly living a holy life and giving hope to those losing faith because of illness, conflict, despair, personal failure, disappointment, and lack of faith?

The Peace of the Lord be with you.

Prayer
Father, let all people experience the glory of your Son each day. By your grace, help us all listen to Jesus, Your Son, and our Savior. Amen.

THIRD SUNDAY OF LENT

Exodus 17:3-7; Romans 5:1-2. 5-8; John 4:5-42

LENT - JOURNEY TO THE WELL OF LIVING WATER

Foreseeing a probable conflict with the Pharisees, as today's Gospel reading narrates, Jesus left Judea with his apostles and headed towards Galilee through Samaria. During Jesus' time, Samaria was between Galilee to the north, and Judea to the south. They avoided the well-known but long and winding route and instead took the Samaria Road to Jerusalem, passing through towns and villages. Jews usually avoided the Samaria Road because of the hatred between Jews and Samaritans that began with the split of the two kingdoms over 700 years prior.

After King Solomon, the Kingdom of Israel split between his two sons to become the Kingdom of Judah and the Northern Kingdom. When King Omri became king of the Northern Kingdom, he built Samaria as his capital (1 Kings 16:24). Bad governance, corruption, and blatant refusal to obey and follow Yahweh, marred both kingdoms. The people ignored the repeated warnings from prophets about the consequences of their sins against Yahweh. The prophets cautioned imminent attack by foreigners. Assyria conquered the Northern Kingdom (722-721 B.C.) and deported many of the inhabitants of the surrounding areas to Babylon. The Assyrians brought to Israel foreigners from Mesopotamia and Syria and intermarried with those who remained unaffected by the deportation order. Their descendants, half-Jewish and half-Gentile, became known as Samaritans. The newcomers brought their native religions into Samaria, integrating their idol worship into Israel, compromising the Jewish religion (2 Kings 17:22-41). The kingdom of Judea in the south also fell finally to the Babylonian Empire (586 B.C) that led to the destruction of Jerusalem with its walls and Temple. King Cyrus of the Persian Empire (559-530 B.C) ended the Babylonian captivity and started the return of the Jewish exiles to Jerusalem during the time of the Prophet Nehemiah.

The Jews who returned from exile did not accept the Samaritans as genuine Jews. They did not allow them to join in rebuilding Jerusalem and the Temple. The Samaritans also undermined the reconstruction project and wanted the Persian rulers to slow it down (Ezra 4). Later, on Mount Garizim, the Samaritans built a rival temple which was not recognized by the Jews as a suitable worshipping place for Yahweh. Even when Alexander the Great (356-323 B. C) allowed the restoration of the Samaritan Temple on Mount Gerizim, the Jews did not recognize it. The Temple on Mount Garizim was vandalized by the Jews (128 B.C.) in favor of the Temple in Jerusalem. Around the time of Jesus' birth, Samaritan extremists reportedly desecrated the sanctuary of the Temple in Jerusalem with the bones of dead human beings. All this exacerbated the hatred between Jews and Samaritans.

Today's Gospel shows Jesus sitting at the well of Jacob near the town of Sychar while the apostles went to the town for supplies. While there, a Samaritan woman came from the town to draw water. The woman had risked the scorching mid-day heat when most people rested at home or sought shade elsewhere. She immediately recognized a devout looking young Jew who, surprisingly, asked her for water. The conversation that followed was the longest and most detailed between Jesus and any other individual in John's Gospel. Over the centuries, the story has had a tremendous appeal in the Bible and in the Christian religion.

Some cultural taboos, powerful symbolisms, and spiritual revelations show up in the story. A Jew did not engage in a conversation in public with a Samaritan; worse yet was to request a drink from a cup considered unclean by Jews. Jesus revealed himself as the Messiah to a foreigner and said, "I am he, I who am talking with you" (John 4:26). He was not that explicit with Nicodemus, a fellow Jew, about his identity (John 3:1-21). Jesus also referred to himself as "living water," superior and more sustaining than water from Jacob's well, although the well had existed for centuries. Thus, Jesus becomes the "Well of Living Water," the source and provider of water that sustains eternal life and washes away sin to bring about holiness, particularly at the Easter Vigil's baptism of the catechumens.

It was common social practice for women to walk in groups to fetch water in the morning and to catch up with current news in the neighborhood. That the woman went to the well alone under the mid-day's extremely hot weather shows she was a social outcast. It was common knowledge that she had been married to five men and her current companion was not legally married to her. From the lens of society, she lacked morals. However, Jesus saw her heart and, noticing her potential goodness, allowed God's grace upon her home and live righteously. Jesus knows our individual life stories, our true selves: "He told me everything I have done," the woman told the people of her town. We need to accept him to receive life-giving water, grace for transformation, and to right our wrongs.

In the story, Jesus clarified God is Spirit and is not limited to buildings or specific geographical borders. God, as Spirit, is everywhere, to be worshipped anywhere.

The woman's culture restricted her to what she could or could not do. In the story, however, Jesus empowers her to proclaim the Word of God, bringing many people to Jesus. She becomes the first evangelist in John's Gospel. We are called to accept God's Word and become disciples of the Word, particularly by example.

At the Well of Living Water, a female Samaritan of a race with no association with Jews met Jesus who ignored the long-established cultural stereotypes between them. In the Parable of the Good Samaritan, Jesus' main hero is a Samaritan who ignored an ancient old rivalry and xenophobia

123

to assist a victim of a highway robbery while his fellow Jews refused to show mercy. We ought to address the canker of many violent sectarian conflicts rising in the world from religious, ethnical, racial, and partisan affiliations. For example, the rise of Islamic fanatics, the feud between Sunni and Shia Muslims in the Middle East, the persecution of minorities in Rohingya in Myanmar, the hostility between Muslims and Hindus in India and between Muslims and Christians across Africa, and racial tensions in the world are existential issues we must bring to Jesus at the Well of Living Water for healing.

Two weeks ago, we traveled to the desert with Jesus to learn from him how to overcome our temptations. Last week, we joined Peter, James, and John on the holy mountain to witness Jesus transfigured before us. Despite both experiences, we may still feel distanced from Jesus. Today, the Church invites us to another spiritual pilgrimage, this time to the Well of Living Water with the Samaritan woman profoundly transformed after her holy encounter with Jesus.

In the middle of our Lenten Season, the Lord will reform us as we spend a holy hour with him at the well (with the Blessed Sacrament Adoration), sharing our personal experiences to grow our faith. We would never forget our experience of the Lord and not doubt his eternal presence in our lives. (First reading). Indeed, the Lord is our peace, our hope, and the meaning of our existence, whose Spirit fills us with God's gratuitous grace and enduring love (Second reading).

The Peace of Christ be with you.

Prayer
Father, give your people courage and fortitude to return to the path you want them to take in life after their experience of the transfigured Jesus. Amen.

FOURTH SUNDAY OF LENT

1 Samuel 16:1b. 6-7. 10-13a; Ephesians 5:8-14; John 9:1-41

LENT - A JOURNEY INTO THE LIGHT OF CHRIST

In the Latin Rite, Laetare Sunday is the traditional reference for the Fourth Sunday of Lent to signify joy during the somber Season of Lent. It is derived from the first two words of the Introit of the day, "Laetare Jerusalem," translated as "Rejoice Jerusalem." The verse is an invitation to rejoice because we are in the middle of Lent anticipating the joy of Easter when the whole world will sing the Exsultet, a hymn of praise and thanksgiving to God that Jesus Christ is risen: "Rejoice Christ is risen!" The Liturgical vestments for today change from the traditional Lenten violet color to rose-colored or pink to signify joy. Christians are encouraged to finish the Lenten observance of penance, prayer, fasting, and almsgiving because Easter is imminent.

We celebrate with joy the second rite of the three Scrutinies with candidates, called the Elect, taking part in the Christian Initiation of Adults (OCIA) for baptism during the Easter Vigil Mass. The rites assist the Elect to search their souls, purify, and inform the candidates to grow in their spiritual knowledge of the Sacrament of Baptism. The prayer of exorcism at the end of the rite invokes God to fill the Elect with the Spirit of Jesus, purify them from sinful desires, and enlighten them to follow God's Word.

Last week (the first scrutiny), the Elect received Jesus Christ as the Living Water through blessing. Today (the second scrutiny), the Church reveals to the Elect that Jesus

Christ is the Light of the World; and next week (the third scrutiny), the Elect will see Jesus Christ as the Resurrection and the Life. Indeed, the word "scrutinize" means "seeing clearly," and the Elect are urged to recognize and understand that yielding to sin is not a good option in any aspect of life. The Elect discern the importance of God's grace, make the conscious effort to turn away from sin, and joyfully step into the peaceful and saving Light of Christ. Those present at Mass take part in the rites to be reminded of their own baptismal promises and to help them experience continuous conversion.

Today's Gospel is another perspective of John's thorough and thought-provoking narratives, richly laden with significant theological symbolisms. This is characteristic of John's writing that appealed to the Early Christian Church's strong establishment towards the end of the first century. The story of the man born blind highlights the images of "darkness" and "light" from John's "Prologue" (John 1:1-18). The reference to darkness and light shows the blind man's physical and spiritual healing, making him see Jesus as Light in his new life.

On his way to the Synagogue on a Sabbath Day, Jesus saw a blind man begging at the roadside for his daily bread. The disciples asked about the common belief that disability, misfortune, or poverty resulted from a person's sins or the sins of the parents. The blind man's condition, Jesus explained, had nothing to do with his sins or the sins of his parents. It was one instance when God's power become manifest, Jesus told them. Jesus saw an opportunity to provide the evidence of his power to bring light into the life of the blind man. Jesus reiterated his purpose: "While I am in the world, I am the light for the world" (John 9:5).

Customarily, Jews kept lamps on two massive golden lamp stands in the "Treasury." Several lamps were also lit after evening prayer in the streets, especially during festivals when locals and visitors socialized at night. It is opined by some scholars that the diffusion of light from the lamps both in the Temple and outside prompted Jesus to declare, "I am the light of the world," a symbolic expression referring to the Messiah (Isaiah 9:2; Malachi 4:2; Luke 2:32) who would have the singular mission of making his followers sons and daughters of the light (John 12: 36, 46). Again, the Messiah referred to the symbolic "pillar of fire that glows to the honor of God" (Exsultet). As the sun brings light to all parts of the world, so Jesus enlightens the hearts of all people; as the sun produces energy to sustain the solar system, Jesus illuminates God's creation (John 1:9) and keeps it as one unit (Ephesians 2:13). There is the need, therefore, for God's light in the world because "the whole world is under the rule of the Evil One" (1 John 5:19) plunged the world into darkness.

It is also suggested that the quest for water from the Pool of Siloam for healing, particularly during festivals, is why Jesus referred to himself as "living water." He was the better option as "Living Water" and not the Pool of Siloam that was shut down at certain times.

Jesus healed the blind man. The Pharisees accused him of healing on a Sabbath day, which was tantamount to working unlawfully. They also had difficulty accepting that a miracle had occurred. A long interrogation of the man and his parents by the Pharisees takes about half of the story.

The man gained his sight, but the Evangelist was also stressing the man's eyes being opened spiritually to discover a profound understanding of Jesus. In the end, the man praised

Jesus for the new spiritual light he had discovered, saying, "I believe, Lord," and kneeled before Jesus.

In the story, we remember that baptism is our spiritual rebirth, from the darkness of sin without Jesus Christ to a new life in his resurrected Light, where we find a new meaning and purpose in life (John 3:3,14). Baptism, therefore, means a symbolic death to the past and an emerging new life —a fresh beginning—in a new direction based on the life of Jesus Christ. We fully identify with him at baptism and recognize him as the reason of our existence, the one who guides us to our goal, the Father in heaven.

The first reading is about God scrutinizing or looking with sharp eyes into the heart and mind of each son of Jesse to select a suitable person to be king for his people, Israel. Samuel looked at the splendid appearances of the seven strong men, but God's scrutiny was deeper and more thorough, finding favor with a mere kid to be secretly anointed as king. The light of Jesus shines deeper into our minds and hearts to turn every dark spot into a wonderful light. The darkness in the world today is dense, extensive, and startling, pleading for the light of Jesus.

The insightful words of Jesus in the Gospel must touch us profoundly: "I am the Light of the world." The light of Jesus must shine in our lives to overpower the darkness surrounding us. The darkness of racial, religious, partisan tensions; untruth, injustice, prejudice, struggle for power, corruption, and selfishness. For example, we show generosity not paybacks because God commands our affection and compassion towards our neighbors. The world continues to deny a Grand Designer who created the world and his divine plan for humanity. As a result, human beings define their own values and make the conscience an individual matter, not realizing the echo of God's voice in our minds.

Our Lenten journey last week was to drink of the "living water." We see the living water again symbolized by the Pool of Siloam, where Christ washes away the darkness of our lives to bring us into his invigorating light. We feel compelled to wash in the living waters of Christ and emerge facing the horizon to see the rising light of the resurrected Christ.

May the Light of Christ subdue the darkness of the world and heal it. As Saint Paul admonishes, "You were darkness once, but now you are light in the Lord." We must live as children of light who produce "every kind of goodness and righteousness and truth" (second reading).

Is the rite of today's Scrutinies and the light of Jesus inspiring you to search within to see what hides in the dark corners of your life and boldly discard them?

What can you do to bring yourself, family members, friends, neighbors, co-workers, and even strangers out of darkness into the light of Christ?

The Peace of the Lord be with you.

Prayer
Father, Your Son Jesus, Light of the World, shines everywhere to dispel darkness representing sin and evil. May the Light of the world never extinguish but lead us to walk in the footsteps of Jesus. Amen.

VEILING IMAGES AND CROSSES
IN CHURCH

As you enter the church today on the Fifth Sunday of Lent, you notice something is conspicuously different. Veils cover the images in the church except for the Stations of the Cross and stained-glass windows. The veils on crosses and crucifixes come off after the celebration of the Lord's Passion on Good Friday. The other veil-covered images remain so until the start of the Easter Vigil when the Gloria is intoned, or as the vigil Mass is ending. However, the duration of such veiling may differ in other local churches, and in some places, the church removes the images entirely.

An early explanation links the custom of veiling images in the church to Jesus hiding, so to speak, from the rage of the Pharisees who were determined to stone him (John 8:31-59). By veiling the cross, the Church purports Jesus is unseen by the world while preparing for the ultimate end of his mission, we eagerly anticipate his resurrection. A later association occurred relating to a custom in Germany (9th century) when from Ash Wednesday, a large cloth called "Hungertuch" (hunger cloth), hung to separate the main altar from the people.

Statues of saints are covered because the images of Jesus, the Lord, remain covered. Families, referred to as "domestic churches," may cover prominent religious images in their homes to remind their members about the ancient tradition and pass on to their children and grandchildren who will certainly ask questions.

The Church calls on the Faithful to meditate on the Passion story and the liturgies of the Sacred Triduum. The veiled images prepare us for Easter Sunday, the Resurrection of Christ. The veil also symbolically means we have buried our sins, and, at the resurrection, the Light of the Resurrected Christ will remove our veils and shine on us. From this moment, we must allow our lives to be directed by the Spirit of Christ or the Light of Christ and the Commandments of the Lord planted in us by God in fulfillment of the prophecies of Ezekiel (first reading) and Jeremiah (Jeremiah 31:33-34). This new life in the "Spirit or Light of Christ" is confirmed and preached by Saint Paul (second reading) and evidenced by Lazarus' gift of a new life (Gospel reading).

FIFTH SUNDAY OF LENT

Ezekiel 37: 12-14; Romans 8:8-11; John 11: 1-45

LENT—A TIME TO REFLECT ON HOW TO LIVE IN PEACE AND HARMONY

A few years ago, I traveled in a Rwanda Air Boeing 737 to Kigali, Rwanda, where I connected to Nairobi, Kenya. As usual, some passengers were sleeping, some reading, and others chatting. I was reading one of the Airline's publications called *INZOZI* (September-November 2013 edition). The publication featured much about the natural forests of Africa, specifically those in Gabon. The forests of Gabon are part of a long stretch of dense forests that extend from the shores of the Atlantic Ocean deep into the interior, covering the countries of Cameroon, Equatorial Guinea, Congo, and the Democratic Republic of Congo (DR Congo).

It was gratifying reading about Gabon, described in the journal as "so green with forests that cover over 80 percent of its total surface area." Portrayed as the richest treasures in Africa, the forests of Gabon, Cameroon, the Congo and DR Congo are full of life and beauty. In Gabon, for example, one "cannot help but marvel at its beauty" of common scenes showing "huge trees of thirty to fifty meters in height with roots that spread over a diameter of ten meters." The forests are home to many species of flora, enhanced by copious rainfall and steady sunshine. The forests also shelter several kinds of fauna, including exotic birds of the air and many types of wildlife, comprising elephants, gorillas, antelopes, buffaloes, and others. The author of the article concluded with the hope that "ambitious conservation programs in this land of green" would benefit the world's land ecosystem.

Now, I looked through the cabin's window to view what I was reading concerning the forest of Africa. It was a huge stretch of undulating forested land nestled calmly below, with

132

huge and tiny rivers meandering while small and vast lakes rested peacefully, scattered throughout the elegant and welcoming forest.

Peace, serenity, and elegance! Are such words not deceiving in Africa? Do they describe Africa on the ground?

I picked up another magazine I had slipped into my carry-on bag before I started my journey in Accra called *Africawatch* (September 2013 edition). The featured article was mainly about DR Congo. The author lamented the continued fighting between government and rebels and the dangers it continued to pose to the country, destabilizing an enormous mass of the entire region. Countless efforts to bring government and rebel leaders to negotiating talks had been elusive. Sometimes, governments and unyielding rebels tried to start peace settlements after losing many lives and displacing thousands of innocent civilians, but to no avail. *Africawatch* described the major rebel group called M23 as the "reincarnation of older insurgent movements, and just one of dozens of militias in the region." Rebel groups re-organized to fight again in the forests and deserts. At some point, the dangerous and dire situation in the area led to the United Nations sending over 17,000 Peacekeeping Forces to the country.

Because of ethnic disputes, animosities, and mistrust, the conflict had spilled into neighboring Rwanda, Congo, and Uganda. From the 1994 Rwandan genocide to the present, these areas had lost millions of women, men, and children due to political and tribal conflicts.

From the forests, mountains, and deserts of Africa, South America, and Southeast Asia to the highlands and caves of Afghanistan, rebels continued "to destabilize communities and commit grave human right abuses against civilians." They had done this through senseless killings, rape, and burning of towns and villages, and they had also recruited child-soldiers to carry out these atrocities. Elsewhere, ethnic and religious tensions in the Middle East, as well as racial and social exclusion in Europe and North America, continue to have detrimental effects.

As the plane descended into Kigali Airport, Rwanda, I mourned with Mother Africa for losing her millions of innocent sons and daughters over the years because of social, ethnic, and religious conflicts. Africa bears the scars of evil in the world, a chunk of them perpetrated by her own people. I prayed the peace and elegance of nature I observed in the skies would translate to reality on the ground. I remembered the exhortation of the Holy Father, Pope Francis, to participants at an evangelization conference in the Philippines on Friday, October 18, 2013. The Pope urged us to consider ourselves as brothers and sisters in the Lord Jesus and share the Gospel with humility and joy. We must "not get tired of bringing the mercy of the Father to the poor, the sick, the abandoned, the young people and families," the Holy Father lamented. The Pope added that we must "let Jesus be known in the world of politics, business, arts, science, technology and social media. Let the Holy Spirit renew creation and bring forth justice and peace ..."

Certainly, most of today's homilies will be about Jesus raising Lazarus to life. They will tie to the belief in life after death or the resurrection, and rightly so, because the Gospel reading teaches about the resurrection of the dead: "Whoever believes in me, even if he dies, will live," Jesus said. In John's Gospel, the resurrection of Lazarus is seen as the greatest of Jesus' miracles because it anticipated Jesus' resurrection, as well as the resurrection of those who would believe in him. Many of you, my dear people of God, would have expected that I expounded about belief in the resurrection today.

However, it is of utmost importance to reflect on the Evangelist's narrative regarding the life of Lazarus and his family, and Jesus' impact on them. Lazarus and his sisters, Mary and Martha, lived near Bethany, which was a town close to Jerusalem. Jesus stayed with the family when he attended festivals in Jerusalem. Some scripture scholars suggest that perhaps Lazarus was a retired prosperous man whose sisters managed his business and family affairs. The family lived together and felt affection for each other. They were religious, respectable, and generous. Jesus was a friend and loved them. When Lazarus was seriously sick, his sisters sent a message to Jesus: "Master, the one you love is ill." We can picture Martha's somber and disappointing demeanor when she welcomed Jesus: "Lord, if you had been here, my brother would not have died," she lamented. Jesus was deeply touched by the pain of Mary and Martha: "And Jesus wept." The mourners expressed solidarity, sympathy, and support. We, too, must weep with our friends and dear ones when they are afflicted with death, pandemic, poverty, diseases, persecution, racial bias, and stigmatization.

Today, the world faces astonishing pressures in human history that seem to shift human behavior to a dire state that has hit the fabric of society, presenting the entire world with insurmountable tensions and challenges requiring new perspectives about life and ways of doing things. Corrupt governments disregard their responsibilities and marginalize their own people, depriving them of fairness, justice, and equity; the media spreads hate; the proliferation of arms threatens world peace; the war on drugs has woefully failed; different cultures, religious intolerance, and political and religious ideologies have seriously divided the world; and nature is losing its battle with humanity to sustain itself because of the latter's push on land and resources leading to serious global warming. This is the time for humanity to grow together while accepting each other as brothers and sisters, by collaborating on integrated peace treaties to help and protect one another and the environment.

Let us reflect on Pope Francis' prayer for including Jesus in all aspects of our lives.

What little sacrifice can you offer each day to spread the mercy of God to the poor, sick, and vulnerable?

How can you be an instrument of peace and justice to those denied them, particularly in conflict and war-torn areas, and those fighting societal systems that keep them on the fringes of society?

How can you use today's Gospel to reflect on the love Jesus had for Lazarus' family, and subsequently, the love he has for each of us and humanity in general?

Do you realize that peace begins with you? Do you think about what you could do to bring about peace in your own family and with your own circle of friends and acquaintances —even for those you are yet to meet?

Do you care about the environment, including the preservation of the earth given to us to cultivate and guard? (Genesis 2:15)

The Peace of the Lord be with you.

Prayer

Father, always touch the hearts of all people to realize we are brothers and sisters who must live in peace with one another and in harmony with nature. Amen.

PALM SUNDAY OR THE PASSION OF THE LORD

Isaiah 50:4-7; Philippians 2:6-11; Matthew 26:14-27:66 (Year A); Mark 14:1-15:47 or 15:1-39 (Year B); Luke 22:14-23:56 (Year C)

A JOURNEY TO THE CROSS, SYMBOL OF OUR SALVATION

The Christian Feast of Palm Sunday commemorates the **Triumphal Entry of Jesus Christ** into Jerusalem a few days before his death on the cross. Today is also called Passion Sunday. The Latin word *passio* is the noun derived from the verb "patior" or "pati" meaning to "suffer, endure, or resign." Its derivative in English is the word "passion" used to signify the sufferings Jesus Christ, "endured for our sins on the last day of his life" (Edward Sri, 2022). This is called the "Passion of Jesus Christ." The word passion has other meanings denoting intense emotions, resilient desires, or profound attachment to a cause or interest.

The Passion narratives in the Gospels keenly follow Jesus' suffering and agonizing moments from the room of the Last Supper to the Garden of Gethsemane and to his death on the cross on Calvary, the place of crucifixion. Thus, the expression "to meditate on the Passion of Jesus Christ" means to meditate on the narratives regarding the suffering and death of Jesus Christ. The ministers during the liturgy wear red vestments (the color of blood) to symbolize Jesus shedding his blood on the cross as the redemptive sacrifice to save humankind.

The celebration of Passion Sunday begins outside the church, where the priest or deacon blesses palm fronds with holy water and distributes them to the faithful or they are blessed while holding the palm branches. The people proceed with the clergy into the church, waving branches and singing, "Hosanna, our king is coming," and other similar songs. In some countries, the people make long processions through the streets with brass instruments amid singing and jubilation.

Palm Sunday or Passion Sunday falls on the Sixth Sunday of Lent before Resurrection Day (Easter Sunday). It is the last Sunday of Lent and regarded as an anteroom into the mansion of Holy Week. During the week, Christians commemorate and meditate on the last week of Jesus' life: the jubilant entry into Jerusalem; the Washing of the Feet of the Apostles, the Last Supper, and betrayal on Maundy Thursday; the trials before the Sanhedrin and Pontius Pilate; and the torture, crucifixion, death, and burial on Good Friday. All events culminate in Jesus' glorious resurrection on Easter Sunday.

The Canonical Gospels—Matthew, Mark, Luke, and John—recount the triumphant entry, showing how the story marked itself indelibly in the mind of the Early Church. In the Synoptic Gospels, comprising Matthew, Mark, and Luke, a crowd of followers joined Jesus and his disciples from Jericho to Jerusalem (Matthew 20:29). Jericho was a place where pilgrims traveling to celebrate feasts like the Passover and Pentecost gathered to cross the Jordan River (Osborne, 2010). The crowd grew larger via Bethphage and Bethany at the foot of the Mount of Olives because of Jesus' miracles (Matthew 20:34) and his fame in Galilee. Jesus sent two disciples to look for a donkey (and a colt in Matthew) and to inform the owner, "the Master needs it" (Luke 19:34). The owner of the donkey readily obeyed the directive, showing Jesus to be well-known. The Synoptic Gospels show a jubilant crowd accompanying Jesus and acclaiming him Messiah during a triumphant entry into Jerusalem to the amazement of the people in the city (Matthew 21:10-11).

As Jesus entered Jerusalem, the people threw cloaks or capes on the donkey and carpeted the path with them while they waved branches. Matthew's narrative reminded his readers of yore: "Look, your king is coming to you ... humble and riding on a donkey" (Matthew 21:4-5). The Prophet Zechariah predicted 575 years earlier about the Messiah entering the holy city on a donkey (Zechariah 9:9-10).

Do we acknowledge God is the one and true master in our lives and not fame, wealth, or power? Saint Paul advises us (second reading) to set aside private ambitions and racial prejudices to provide for one another like Jesus who served others, "becoming obedient to the point of death," to redeem humankind.

In the Gospel of John, Jesus was the guest of Lazarus, Martha, and Mary in Bethany. The miraculous raising of Lazarus from the dead ultimately convinced many people that Jesus was the Messiah, and they came to Bethany to see him and Lazarus (John 12:12-13). The pilgrims who had traveled to Jerusalem for the Passover heard about Jesus and Lazarus. When they got a hint that Jesus was arriving in Jerusalem, many gathered at the city gate to meet him and join to process into the city. They waved branches and sang the victory song of Psalm 118: "Hosanna to the Son of David; Blessed is he who comes in the name of the Lord."

The Gospels remarkably present the significance of symbolisms in the story. It was customary to spread cloaks, branches of trees, and rushes (a grassy species) along the path of prominent persons, like a king, arriving in a city. Riding on a donkey, Jesus demonstrated a symbol of peace and humility. Jesus is the Prince of Peace who wants his followers to be peaceful.

It was also the practice for people to spread cloaks on the way as a new king walked the steps to receive his throne (2 Kings 9:13). Jesus is the king symbolically entering Jerusalem to receive the throne of David, but he is the king who lays down his life for his subjects and teaches them about love of God and neighbor, and forgiveness.

Again, the cloak was a special garment that kept the owner warm as bedding. Jesus instructed his followers to keep one cloak for themselves. Are we doing enough to help people by sharing our blessings or are we giving away worn-out or outdated things? Do we give from our pantry because we want to create more space for more hoarding?

139

The palm branch was a symbol of joy and bountiful harvest (Leviticus 23:40). The procession with palms also foreshadows the joyous welcome of Jesus at his second coming (*Parousia*) as king and Judge (Revelation 7:9-17). To prepare adequately for this momentous occasion, we must exhibit great faith in God, reconcile with Him, and show that our way of life is beneficial to ourselves, family, friends, and the entire community. Since the fourth century, the palm branch has been used as symbol of joy for the faithful because of Jesus' resurrection, described as his victory over death. The green leaf therefore symbolizes new life in Jesus Christ because of God's saving grace connected to baptism, Christmas, and the Resurrection. Again, the green palm branch reminds us of Zacchaeus's sycamore tree that sheds its bark or exfoliates yearly to symbolize renewal. The sycamore tree can live up to five hundred years, and at each exfoliation, the tree looks young and fresh.

In the Roman Catholic, Anglican, and Lutheran traditions, people fold palm branches into a variety of shapes like the cross and place them in their homes, on private altars, or tucked into Bibles or holy portraits. They signify God's presence, one's connection to God, and devotion to Him. The branches are returned the following year to be burned into ashes for Ash Wednesday, the start of the Season of Lent, when Christians go through fasting, penance, renewal, almsgiving, and show humility before God. We will acknowledge our betrayal of Jesus as we praise him today, like those who cheered him, but later asked for his crucifixion (Luke 23:18). The palm branch taken home will turn brown, reminding us of our failure to keep God's Word but encouraging us to focus and ponder on the renewal of our love for God and neighbor.

Our journey this week will take us to Mount Calvary, to the wooden cross on which hung the Savior of the world. At the foot of the cross a Roman Centurion will acclaim, "Truly this was the Son of God." Jesus will hang on the cross because of his faithfulness to do the will of the Father and his gratuitous love for a sinful people now called his "brethren" (Matthew 28:10; John 20:17), after his blood atones for their sins. On the cross, he will declare that his disciples and all who sought salvation in him are his sisters and brothers with Mary as their mother (John 19:25:27).

The example of Jesus' profound and passionate love to suffer and die for our salvation must be our greatest gift to each other, a light in our hearts to make us recognize and accept one another and pledge to build the world's future together. Caring for one another is our surest solution to the troubles of the world. It is all that our true Master expects us to do. It is not status in society, power and pride, wealth and influence, knowledge and fame; it is not clamoring for properties like vehicles, planes, yachts, and other material things that can become unused or useless, such as we saw during the COVID-19 pandemic. Indeed, the most certain answer is in investing in our common humanity, defined by a mosaic of cultures, colors, shapes, duties, ideas, and vocations. Again, ultimately, it is our collective mission of true respect for one another and responsibility in our separate tasks that can make the world a better and peaceful place for all.

Our journey will end at the Gate of the Sepulcher—the Gate of the Spring of Hope—from where Mary Magdalene ("and the other Mary" in Matthew 28:1) will joyfully announce to the entire world on Easter morning that "The Lord is Risen" (John 20:18).

We are experiencing the Season of Spring when flora and fauna rise gracefully from their slumber in the coldest darkness of winter to a new beginning. Symbolically, it is our emergence through the rugged walkways of our own lives believing that in the Lord Jesus, hope springs eternal.

May God bless us all and give us the hope the world needs now.

The Peace of the Lord be with you.

Prayer
Father, today your people join all believers in praising Your Son, the Messiah. May the branches they carry home always remind them to remain faithful to his Word. Amen.

Holy Week

REFLECTION FOR MONDAY OF HOLY WEEK

Isaiah 42:1-7; John 12:1-11

JOURNEY TO THE EMPTY TOMB: FIRST DAY JESUS' DEEP LOVE FOR HIS FRIENDS

Today, Christians begin the observation of Holy Week, a seven-day commemoration of Jesus' last week spent on earth: his arrest, trial, suffering, crucifixion, and resurrection. As noted on Palm Sunday, Jesus' sacrifice was because of his faithfulness to do God's will and his passionate love to save humanity. As we reflectively follow the events of his life during Holy Week and particularly following his footsteps from Pilate's palace to Calvary, let us allow him to take us with him and nurture the seed of love written in our hearts as part of God's Law.

Jesus and his disciples had traveled from Galilee to Jerusalem in Judea to celebrate the Feast of Passover. It was incumbent on all able-bodied devout Jews to be in Jerusalem for the Feast. Many of them would stay on to celebrate another important feast—the Feast of Pentecost—celebrated on the fiftieth day after Passover. The Jews and converts to Judaism (Acts 2:11) had come from various parts of the two great empires at the time: the Roman Empire and the Parthian Empire (Act 2:9-11). Those in Jerusalem seemed to be "from every country in the world" (Acts 2:5) with fifteen provinces mentioned. Jerusalem, a Roman province, was relatively at the center of the two rival empires.

Passover and Pentecost were the two most celebrated feasts during the time of Jesus. Passover celebrates the day Israel broke free of slavery and oppression in Egypt. Pentecost, also known as Shavuot, is a Greek word meaning "weeks" (hence, the "Feast of Weeks"). It also means "sevens," suggesting that the feast was seven weeks after Passover. Shavuot was originally called the Feast of Ingathering, as a

Jewish wheat harvest festival. Later, it became associated with the day Israel received the Torah from God on Mount Sinai. The word *Pentecost* is the Greek equivalent of Shavuot, which means "fiftieth," celebrating fifty days after Passover Thus, while Passover celebrated the nation's freedom, Shavuot celebrated the giving of the Law of God. It is likely those who were in Jerusalem for the Passover also stayed for the Shavuot before returning to their provinces.

We begin our journey with Jesus and a large crowd heading towards Jerusalem. They include the twelve apostles and the disciples who witnessed his miracles in towns and villages along the route to Jerusalem. Jesus and the apostles arrive in Bethany close to Jerusalem and lodge in the house of Lazarus and his sisters, Martha and Mary.

There, in the house of Lazarus, a remarkable scene occurs! From all over Galilee, Judea, Samaria, and from afar, people traveling for the Passover and Shavuot festivities gather at the house of Lazarus. First, they see Lazarus, buried for four days and raised back to life. Second, the person who performed this amazing miracle is present.

People troop in every single day. They come, see Jesus and Lazarus, and now believe that Jesus is the Messiah. But the Pharisees have a problem! They will not accept the miracle of Lazarus' resurrection from the dead as convincing enough to acclaim Jesus as Messiah.

Their perspective is not surprising! To this day, many people remain unconvinced that God sent Jesus to save the world. Many unbelievers fault Christians for their association with Jesus and their acknowledgement that he is of divine origin, the Son of God.

Today's Gospel reading shows another remarkable event in the house of Lazarus. Customarily, the guests would wash their feet before entering the house after a long journey on foot, particularly on dry terrain. In the house, it was normal to smear the feet of one's guests with oil. After the regular traditional greetings, Martha is in the kitchen, heating and making ready the food she and Mary had prepared for the guests. Jesus and his disciples, including Lazarus, recline at table, as was the custom when ready to have dinner. In the meantime, her younger sister, Mary, sits at the feet of Jesus. She smears the feet of Jesus with expensive, sweet-smelling perfumed oil. She dries Jesus' feet with her thick hair.

This Holy Week, demonstrate your love for Jesus as you show love to your neighbor, especially the poor, elderly, sick, distressed, refugee, and needy.

The Peace of the Lord be with you.

Prayer
Father, we thank you for your gift of faith by which we wholeheartedly believe in your Son, Jesus Christ. Increase the faith of your people, Lord. Amen.

REFLECTION FOR TUESDAY OF HOLY WEEK

Isaiah 49:1-6; John 13:21-33, 36-38

JOURNEY TO THE EMPTY TOMB:
SECOND DAY
FAITH SUSTAINED TO THE END

Today is Holy Tuesday. From the day of his Triumphant Entry into the city of Jerusalem, Jesus remains in the vicinity, commuting between Jerusalem and "the city of Bethany" (Matthew 21:17). He spends his last days preaching, teaching, and confronting the chief priests, elders, and teachers of the Law until his arrest, trial, and crucifixion (Matthew 26:1-4). He has a huge following because he "wasn't like the teachers of the Law; instead, he taught with authority" (Matthew 7:29). We can refer to his manner of preaching and teaching in the Sermon on the Mount as a unique formula that was incredibly compelling: "You have heard that it was said in the past .... But now I tell you" (Matthew 5 -7).

His fame spread everywhere (Mark 1:27-28). His authority, measured by his words as he preached, also showed in his power to perform miracles, with the most astonishing being the rising of Lazarus back to life. Indeed, the crowd following him had started in Galilee through Samaria to Jerusalem in Judea.

Jesus had also done several things that caused the wrath of the authorities. He prophesied the destruction of the city and the demise of its people (Matthew 19:41-44). In 70 A.D. when the Roman army destroyed the Temple and the city of Jerusalem after a five-month siege. Jesus stopped money launderers and the sale of goods in the Temple and drove the perpetrators out. He had several confrontations on a series of issues with the authorities, directing most of his parables at the chief priests, elders, and teachers of the Law. One such parable was the Parable of the Tenants in the Vineyard, which they believed was spoken against them. (Matthew 21:45). Jesus did all this although he knew about their plans to arrest him and kill him. (Matthew 26:1-2).

Today, we read from the Gospel of John about the Last Supper scene where Jesus is celebrating Passover with his apostles. Earlier on, he had washed their feet as a sign of his love and requested them to live together in love, washing each other's feet. Jesus is concerned and saddened that one of those he has always loved would betray him.

There are lessons in today's Gospel to meditate deeply upon. Judas betrayed Jesus, and if this was his kismet or not, it lives in the divine bosom. Having opined thus, we have lessons from his behavior. Judas was part of the twelve apostles who, like the others, "left everything to follow" Jesus. Although he was a devout follower, with all the faculties to preach and heal (Luke 9:1-2), he allowed Satan to exploit his soul with the vices of selfishness and ambition (Luke 22:3-4).

How often do parents not grieve and blame themselves that their children have turned away from the faith after entering college? How often do marriages fall on rocks because of personal interests and lack of respect between partners? Some suggest Judas opened his heart to Satan when he pocketed the team's money and bargained with the authorities to sell Jesus for thirty pieces of silver. As leaders in society, whether civil or religious, we always open our hearts to Satan when we begin to work against the interest of the collective by allowing bigotry, cronyism, and nepotism to take control of us. In the end, "the story of Judas reminds us that nothing good can come from giving up on Jesus" (Colin Smith, 2018) who teaches us love.

The last segment of the Gospel reading for today is an interesting dialogue between Jesus and Peter, when the latter cannot grasp the import of Jesus' message. All the same, he pledges to follow Jesus wherever he would go, only to realize later he could not be truthful to his promise at Jesus' trial. Peter quickly restores himself and embraces the faith to the end, becoming the "Rock" on which the Church would be built.

Are you determined to hold on to the faith to the end despite secular detractions and appeal for wealth, power, and status?

The Peace of the Lord be with you.

Prayer
Father, each day we betray Your Son who has laid down his life for our redemption because of his gratuitous love. Sustain the faith of your people to the end. Amen.

REFLECTION FOR WEDNESDAY OF HOLY WEEK

Isaiah 50:4-9a; Matthew 26:14-25

JOURNEY TO THE EMPTY TOMB: THIRD DAY GOING BACK TO JESUS

We go back in history to the city of Jerusalem during the time of Jesus. Jerusalem was an important political and religious center within the geographical area comprising the provinces of the two rival foreign powers—the Roman Empire and the Parthian Empire (Act 2:9-11). Israel was under the Roman Empire ruled from Rome, and Jerusalem was the social and religious center of Israel because of the Temple where Jews within and outside prayed and offered sacrifices to God. Some archaeological findings propose that Jerusalem, and its surroundings had a population of about 80,000 which soared to over 600,000 during the Feast of Passover and the Feast of Shavuot. The population was diverse—Jews, Romans, Greeks, and other ethnic communities—explaining the high population and cosmopolitan ambience. Jerusalem was at par with other ancient cities such as Rome, Athens, and Alexandria with respect to infrastructures, trade, religious, cultural, and social life.

It is Wednesday of Holy Week, and many events are taking place. Pilgrims—especially diaspora communities whose ancestors settled far and near during the return of the Babylonian exiles—are pouring into the environs of Jerusalem to celebrate the two most important feasts of the Jewish nation: Passover and Shavuot, fifty days apart.

The scene is one of joy for those coming to Jerusalem for the first time in their lives; people reuniting with their families at least since their last Passover visit; booming business for transport owners and other economic activities; hospitality industry looking extremely good with lodgings of all kinds fully booked; streets bustling with varied shops; and shoppers buying and selling to prepare for the Feast of Passover.

Since his triumphal entry into Jerusalem, and close to the end of his life on earth, Jesus has been preoccupied in the city preaching and teaching. He performs miracles such as the one in the Pool of Bethesda involving a man paralyzed for 38 years, and in the Pool of Siloam where he heals the blind Bartimaeus. He interacts with the religious leaders and teachers of the Law, which is almost always contentious, particularly because Jesus has a large following who believe he is the "Christ," the long awaited Messiah. The Jewish leadership plans to kill him. The Roman authorities fear and anticipate a potential revolt led by the seemingly revolutionary Jesus, either within the Jewish setup or against the Roman foreign power. Therefore, intelligence gathering increases and further intensifies each day approaching Passover. The presence of Roman soldiers at strategic areas is conspicuous and extraordinary.

Scholars speculate that most likely Jesus spends Wednesday of Holy Week in Bethany in the quiet, reflecting on the events he knows will happen to him in less than 48 hours.

Wednesday of Holy Week is given different names: Holy Wednesday, Spy Wednesday, and Good Wednesday. The Orthodox Church refers to it as Holy Wednesday or Great Wednesday.

On Spy Wednesday Judas Iscariot, one of the twelve apostles in charge of finances, conspires with the Jewish leadership to expose Jesus. Judas therefore becomes the spy among the disciples and betrays Jesus in the Garden of Gethsemane. The Synoptic Gospels, Matthew, Mark, and Luke, narrate how Judas Iscariot traded Jesus for thirty pieces of silver with the chief priests. All the four Canonical Gospels show Jesus predicting his betrayal as in today's Gospel. In the Gospel of John, Jesus hints to his disciples that one of them was "a devil" and would betray him (John 6:70). After this, the disciples asked Jesus one after the other, "Surely it is not I, Lord?" Note that the response of Judas is different. He does not say Lord: rather he says Rabbi or Teacher. He asked, "Surely it is not I, Rabbi?" It is repeated when Judas giving the "kiss of betrayal" in the Garden of Gethsemane says, "peace be with you Rabbi" (Matthew 26:49). Judas gets thirty pieces of silver for this rare "kiss of betrayal." In Matthew's Gospel, Judas attempts to return the money to the Sanhedrin after learning that Jesus is to be crucified. He commits suicide shortly thereafter.

Human beings always betray one another due to hatred, envy, power, money, favor, and property. And usually, like in Judas' case, for a mere pittance! Because of such betrayals, kingdoms have fallen, friendships have ended, marriages have been broken, and families disintegrated.

I want to commemorate Good or Holy Wednesday and despise Spy Wednesday. I want to spend the day reflecting on Jesus' compassionate love for me. I want to rediscover Jesus again and possess him fully. I want to understand how each day, he invites me to show and give love to all.

Have the most enriching Holy Wednesday.

The Peace of the Lord be with you.

Prayer
Father, we are overwhelmed by Your Son's resolve to embrace our betrayal of him as He who continues to love us and chooses to die for us. Help your people to embrace him and learn from him. Amen.

REFLECTION FOR HOLY THURSDAY: MAUNDY THURSDAY

Exodus 12:1-8, 11-14; 1 Corinthians 11:23-26; John 13:1-15

JOURNEY TO THE EMPTY TOMB: FOURTH DAY WASH ONE ANOTHER'S FEET AND LOVE ONE ANOTHER

During Holy Week, we do not see ourselves as spectators at a sporting event in a heavy packed stadium. Rather, like Saint Peter who followed Jesus step by step, we place ourselves in the scenes of the Scriptures to follow Jesus at every episode of his last week on earth from his Grand Entry into Jerusalem to his crucifixion on Mount Calvary. The highpoint of Holy Week with its profound significance for Christians is the Paschal Triduum referring to the three days from Holy Thursday, to Saturday of the Easter Vigil. In the fourth century Saint Augustine came out with the term "Triduum" (Latin word for three days) to signify the three days of the Passover (Last Supper), crucifixion, and resurrection.

On Holy Thursday, Christians commemorate (indeed take part in) the Last Supper of Jesus with his apostles before his betrayal, arrest, trial, and crucifixion on Good Friday.

The Chrism Mass prefixes the solemn celebration of the Last Supper referred to as the First Holy Mass or Eucharist. The Chrism Mass is officiated by the bishop of the diocese who blesses oils used as Sacred Oils in the celebration of the Sacraments throughout the year. These are the Oil of the Sick, the Oil of Catechumens, and the Oil of the Sacred Chrism. Originally, the blessing of the Oil of Chrism and other oils was part of the Easter Vigil (Holy Saturday) celebration when catechumens were baptized after months of religious instruction. Due to long distances between Cathedrals and

154

parishes, the Chrism Mass moved from Holy Saturday to Holy Thursday, and today, many dioceses celebrate Chrism Mass on Holy Monday or Holy Tuesday. Preceding the blessing of the oils, the bishop invites the priests in the diocese, required to attend the Chrism Mass, to renew their commitment to priestly service to the People of God (all peoples), and in God's Holy Church. The rite of the Renewal of Commitment to Priestly Service also commemorates the anniversary of the institution of the Holy Priesthood by Jesus on Holy Thursday at the Last Supper.

The Church celebrates the Last Super of the Lord (Holy Mass or Eucharist) in the evening. Within the celebration is the enactment of foot-washing, derived from the Gospels when Jesus washed the feet of his apostles. During the last three decades or so, foot-washing on Holy Thursday has gained special attention with recipients including women and the youth. The original rule to choose twelve men to represent the twelve apostle is softened. Pope Francis started washing the feet of prisoners, migrants, and incarcerated youth. Jesus' message about love and service in the community and in the world, particularly towards the less privileged is highlighted.

The Last Super is also in remembrance of Jesus' New Commandment of Love. Rolled into this celebration is the expression Maundy Thursday, another name for Holy Thursday. The word "Maundy" derives from the anglicized Latin word *mandatum*, meaning mandate or commandment. Thus, we celebrate the night Jesus gave his New Commandment: "And now I give you a new commandment: love one another. As I have loved you, so you must love one another. If you have love for one another, then everyone will know that you are my disciples" (John 13:34-35). From this time, Jesus' new Commandment has had a great influence on the course of human history.

The Last Supper was essentially a celebration of the Jewish Passover Feast by Jesus and his apostles. The Passover was a yearly ritual meal of thanksgiving to God for freeing the people of Israel from slavery in Egypt, referred to as the Exodus from Egypt. It was also the celebration of Israel's arrival in the Promised Land.

For Christians, the Passover is replaced by the Last Supper (Eucharist), which celebrates the liberation from slavery out of sin through the death of Jesus Christ. At the Last Supper, Jesus ordained the apostles as the first priests to begin the ministerial priesthood. They were to continue the celebration of the Eucharist; preach the Good News about Jesus as the Lamb of God sacrificed for the sins of the world; and preach the New Commandment of Love to the world. Regrettably, the Holy Institution of the Ministerial Priesthood is at the center of the Church's crisis today due to inappropriate clergy conduct. We need to pray to our Chief Priest, the Lord Jesus Christ, for many devoted priests and ask the intercession of the Blessed Mother Mary to assist each one of her dear children in the priesthood with her grace.

As Savior of the world, Jesus instituted the Eucharist to replace the Passover meal. At each Mass, he offers his body and blood as spiritual food and drink from heaven: "I am telling you the truth: if you do not eat the flesh of the Son of Man and drink his blood, you will not have life in yourselves" (John 6:53-57). The Eucharist is the new and eternal link with God the Father through Jesus Christ and by the power of the Holy Spirit. Saint Thomas Aquinas taught that at the Last Supper, Jesus made the promise to be in the Sacrament (Eucharistic Presence) and to be with those who take part in it as he was with his apostles at the Last Supper.

Jesus and his disciples had received a cheerful welcome into Jerusalem, perhaps the first time some of the disciples had entered the holy city where every Jew wished to visit. The mood was overwhelming, and the disciples were hopeful for a new life in Jerusalem. The Messiah had come at long last! They were his closest friends and optimistic about getting reputable positions in the new kingdom their Master had been talking about for almost three years.

We continue our journey through the Holy Week with the Lord Jesus Christ. In our passionate desire to place ourselves at the scene of the Last Super, we are tiptoeing, one by one, in complete silence and awe, into the hall, our hands folded on our chests! We feel our hearts beating heavily!

A modest hall has been prepared with decorations for the celebration of the annual Jewish Passover. The Apostles sing Psalms in different powerful crescendos: "This is the day the Lord has made," they sing happily. And so, they sing, eat, and drink, celebrating the Passover feast with fraternal joyfulness.

Strangely, none of them had noticed the tightness on Jesus' face and how his demeanor had slightly changed since they entered the hall. Jesus gazes intensely at the wooden ceiling in a contemplative mood, turns his head to the right, and then to the left, penetrating the eyes of each of them. He turns to the two large loaves of bread in front of him, possibly specially prepared by Martha and Mary. He looks at the special chalice filled with wine, possibly provided by the house owner. Until now nobody has touched the loaves and the cup, usually reserved for the Master or the elder of the family to bless. Jesus taps on the table. There is silence. Interminable wait.

"The time has now come, the moment of humiliation and death," Jesus sighs. He stands up. He pulls a large towel. He moves to each disciple. He stoops to wash their feet as a servant would do. Now, they understand why he had asked for more water, a large towel, a basin, and a jug. Now they understand why he had requested them not to wash their feet after their journey from Bethany to Jerusalem. He does something symbolic to show the depth of his love for them. It is also to leave an example of absolute humility, love, and self-sacrifice among his followers. His gesture is about love, unity, and service.

Jesus takes the loaves of bread with reverence. He speaks in sad tones and with greatest emotion: "In a little while I will leave you. But I will be present in the bread as my Body for you. Take and eat."

He takes the cup of wine, and speaking softly, said: I will be present in the wine as my Blood for you. Take and drink."

Jesus says further: "You are my priests, ordained to transform me from ordinary bread and wine into the Eucharist of my Body and Blood for people to eat and drink. You are my friends sent to the ends of the world. To every nation, region, and race. To preach, love, serve, and convey my peace to the world."

In silence, the apostles take the bread and drink from the cup.

"It is time, a time for everything. Let us go," Jesus says somberly.

In the silence of the night, the apostles follow Jesus.

We too follow in their footsteps.

The Peace of the Lord be with you.

Prayer
Father, our hearts jumped within us when we visualized Your Son in the bread and in the wine. His love is powerful, peaceful, attractive, binding the People of God professing one faith. Let all your people allow themselves to be transformed by the Eucharist. Amen.

REFLECTION FOR GOOD FRIDAY

JOURNEY TO THE EMPTY TOMB: THE LORD'S PASSION

AT THE FOOT OF THE CROSS, GAZING AT JESUS CRUCIFIED

Today, Christians throughout the world observe the day Jesus Christ was crucified. It was a harsh punishment carried out by the Romans solders against thousands of people sentenced to death as accused criminals. The Cross, however, becomes significant because of the one person who, on Good Friday, died on a cross for the specific purpose of saving sinners. Thus, in the Catholic Church, it is required that, "on or close to the altar there is to be a cross with a figure of Christ crucified" (General Instruction of the Roman Missal no. 117).

While many Protestants use only a plain or bare cross, suggesting it is wrong to keep Jesus on the cross because of the resurrection, Catholics officially use the crucifix: a cross with an image of Jesus Christ on it. Mary Beth Kremski (2000) writes: "When we know that Jesus is inviting each of us to join him at Calvary, the value of the crucifix becomes obvious." She appreciates the crucifix as "a vivid reminder of the very essence of salvation—my own sinfulness that made such an extreme sacrifice necessary and the incomprehensible love of God incarnate laying down his life for me. In the crucifix, I see the hope of humanity, victory over Satan, the cleansing of sin, and the open door to heaven. I see a school of love, humility, forgiveness of our enemies, and all other virtues." Furthermore, she writes: "When I look at Christ crucified... I hear 'love one another as I have loved you'" (John 15:12).

The crucifix reminds us that because of human obstinacy to remain in sin, the suffering of Jesus is not over. The world

159

is confronted with humanity's evil behaviors and insensitivity to the plights of others. The crucifix also reminds us to endure human suffering as we remember Jesus' suffering. All notwithstanding, the crucifix gives us hope as we anticipate a light at the end of the tunnel because of the resurrection.

Once again, we are not mere spectators in a heavily packed stadium or theater to watch an event. Jesus leads his disciples into the Garden of Gethsemane. He leaves them, and in silence goes into the darkness of the garden to pray. We observe in sadness the tragedy of Judas' "kiss of betrayal" and the subsequent arrest of Jesus. Jesus' response, "I am he," is reminiscent of how God introduced himself to Moses in the burning bush (Exodus 3:14-15).

At Jesus' response, the soldiers draw back and fall to the ground. Jesus is divine, we attest. This shows the power of Jesus! Yet we see him submitting to human ridicule, insult, and humiliation. Jesus has a mission which is almost at its completion, although this moment is the hardest hurdle: "Father, if possible, take this cup of suffering from me" (Matthew 26:39).

Certainly, Jesus will not let power and pride disrupt his almost accomplished divine mission. His passionate love for you and me and his desire to secure both of us make him take up the cross. We must deeply meditate on each segment of the events from the Garden of Gethsemane to Mount Calvary, the place of crucifixion: betrayal by Judas, plot and trial by the Jewish leadership, Peter's weakness in denying his Master, desertion by the friends of Jesus, the verdict by Pilate for Jesus' crucifixion, the cruelty and impudent conduct of the soldiers, the sorrows of a mother and the tears of the other women, and the sad moments of quick burial.

There is always a general feeling of silence and sadness in the world on Good Friday. Certainly, this is a miracle, a sense of the presence of the divine in the world. From the liturgy of last night until Holy Saturday, we observe silence to reflect on Jesus' love, adoring him, asking for forgiveness of our sins, and asking for grace and strength. Jesus' act of love is the reason why today is referred to as the Great Friday or Good Friday, even though the day commemorates his death. We want his great act of love and suffering to always stick in our minds.

Again, we reflect on the mystery of God's Salvation Plan for humanity. Christ has saved us with his blood, and we are precious to him. Let us adore him and listen to him. He brings us back to God, whom the world is losing.

Christians observe Good Friday through fasting, abstinence, and prayer with other major devotional services. The first is the re-enactment of the steps taken by Jesus to the place of crucifixion. We do this with prayerful and reflective processions anytime from late morning to early evening, but more precisely in the afternoon around 3 pm, to coincide with the hour Jesus died on the cross, according to the Gospel narratives. The acting out of this momentous past event by local Christian communities is referred to as "The Stations of the Cross" or "The Way of the Cross."

The practice originated in the 15th century when Christian pilgrims gathered in the old city of Jerusalem to trace the road believed to have been walked by Jesus, forced by the Roman soldiers from the palace of Pontius Pilate, the Roman Governor, to the crucifixion at Golgotha. The current route established in the 18th century is called the Via Dolorosa (Sorrowful Way). In local community churches, paintings and sometimes statues are placed in the church or outside to enable members to replicate the journey to Calvary in a prayerful and reflective manner.

The second service on Good Friday is the proclamation of the Lord's Passion on the day Jesus died. This is done after the priest and deacon have prostrated themselves in front of the altar as a sign of reverence and humility before the cross of Jesus. On this most solemn day, the congregation hears the message of how Jesus suffered and died for the salvation of humanity. We also accept Jesus as our personal Lord and Savior who gives meaning to our lives such that we no longer live for ourselves, but for him who died and was raised for us (2 Corinthians 5:15).

Subsequent services include the Universal Intercessory Prayers for the Church and peace in the world; Veneration of the Cross, whereby each person present approaches a cross mounted in front of the altar to venerate it by touching, kissing, or bowing; the singing of "Behold the wood of the Cross on which hung the Savior of the world," and the Reception of the Holy Communion as the last service during Good Friday.

Today, Jesus brings us with him to the ultimate end of our Lenten journey; at the foot of the cross gazing at Jesus crucified. As we kiss the cross, he allows us to tie up our own crosses in life to his: those of personal weaknesses, failures, despair, addictions, unsuccessful relationships, jealousies, hatred, illnesses, and all the untidy details of our lives. Let us allow all this to be buried with Jesus, "putting to death our human nature with all its passions and desires" (Galatians 5:24). At the resurrection, we must find ourselves transformed to lead a meaningful life controlled by the Spirit of God (Galatians 5:25). Pope Benedict XVI wrote we must "place God in the center of our thoughts, words, and actions," and be "renewed and mastered by faith."

The Peace of the Crucified Lord be with you.

Prayer
Father, we thank you for bringing us to the cross on which Your Son died for us. As we gaze at him suffering for our sake, may we tie all sufferings and hardships with the sufferings of our Lord and Savior. Amen.

REFLECTION ON HOLY SATURDAY

JOURNEY TO THE EMPTY TOMB:
CHRIST IS RISEN
CHRIST OUR LIGHT

The Sacrament of Reconciliation, well-known as Confession, is always a profound, awesome, and humbling experience before the Lord. It is one of the extraordinary moments when we feel closest to God. The Holy Spirit leads us to empty ourselves of our weaknesses, imperfections, failures, challenges, and all the untidy details of our lives to God. After our honesty before God, we sincerely and prayerfully recite the powerful "Act of Contrition." Then the Priest, the representative of Jesus Christ, invokes the equally powerful "Prayer of Absolution," and gives penance. Sometimes, the priest gives guidance and advice, and one feels full of God, resolved to think carefully and prayerfully about the direction of one's life. However, as soon as we step outside the confessional, away from the solemn experience of heavenly presence and grace, we are precipitously engulfed by darkness and challenged again and again by the habits of everyday flaws and faults.

Today is the last day of Holy Week. The liturgy comprises varied services involving symbols and actions unique to Holy Saturday. The ceremonies begin with the faithful outside the church after sunset when darkness falls, depicting a sinful world in total darkness; a world that seems to have lost the sense of the divine and direction designed by God; a world that focuses on human intellect as a substitute for God. Lights in the church are switched off or dimmed. The darkness surrounding the people outside is reminiscent of the time prior to creation when "everything was engulfed in total darkness." A small bonfire (the Easter Vigil fire) flares, reminiscent of the primordial light God commanded to appear to subdue darkness (Genesis 1:2-3). The "Service of Light" or "The Solemn Beginning of the Vigil" (Lucernarium in Latin) is when the bonfire is blessed and the Paschal Candle is also blessed, marked with symbols, and lit from the fire to show that Jesus is the Christ, the new Light in the world, the sun risen to usher in a new day, a new era in God's Salvation Plan.

The deacon or priest takes the Paschal Light and leads a procession of the people to the front door of the church. The minister lifts the candle and proclaims, "The Light of Christ." The people respond, "Thanks be to God." At the middle of the church, the song and response are repeated. The people light their individual candles at this point to show that Jesus is risen to dispel the darkness around us.

At the front of the altar, the minister sings the third time, and the people respond. All lights in the church are switched on. The Paschal Candle is placed in its special candle stand near the altar. The Paschal Candle is incensed. The "Exsultet"—a Hymn of Praise or proclamation—is sung by a deacon, priest, or cantor, proclaiming the Risen Christ to the world as its Light. On this night described as "this most holy of nights" (or the "mother of all holy vigils" by Saint Augustine), churches throughout the world join in singing the "Exsultet," the Easter Proclamation (Praeconium Paschale in Latin), which is echoed by the voices of angels and saints in heaven. The "Exsultet" (Rejoice) is the first word of the original Latin hymn. It is a Song of Praise and Thanksgiving, a rendition of joy recounting God's salvific actions from creation; God's deliverance of Israel from Egypt (Passover Feast); Israel's miraculous passing through the Red Sea, symbolizing the waters of Baptism that washes away sin; God as "the Pillar of Fire" that led the people through their journeys in the desert; salvation through the Passion of Christ and his resurrection symbolizing the Light of Christ dispelling the darkness of sin and death; and the symbolism of the Paschal Candle solemnly pronounced. The Paschal Candle was lit from the primordial fire for the world, and we thank God for the Light that will stay "undiminished," "the

Morning Star who never sets, who lives and reigns for ever and ever. Amen."

The readings that follow the Easter Proclamation recall the events in Salvation History about God's constant love for his creation, culminating in sending his Son who sacrificed his life out of love for his brothers and sisters.

Catechumens are baptized and confirmed into the Christian community, and baptismal vows are renewed by the congregation. We profess faith, trust, and reliance on God through Jesus and by the power of the Holy Spirit. We take part in the one bread and one cup in the Eucharist, as the People of God appreciating Jesus' love, and promising to show love for each other.

Like the Sacrament of Reconciliation, the Vigil Mass is a remarkable moment to experience Jesus our Lord and Savior in a special way. We are grateful to God for a celebration which brings us close to Jesus. Again, like the Sacrament of Reconciliation, we leave this holy place, blessed, and forgiven but are soon challenged by our own human limitations and inadequacies. However, we take solace from the words of Saint Paul reminding us that our baptism in Christ means we were buried with him and rise with him. It means we leave behind our old life to embrace a new one in Jesus Christ who helps us to transcend all human failures. Are you braced for newness of life in the Risen Lord starting from tonight?

As you step out tonight, do not let the wind blow or the rain wash away the blessings you have received. God's grace is enough to fix conflicts in your life and eliminate things around you which sometimes mislead you to think they give you satisfaction but are actually perilous like impulsive anger, pride, envy, greed, hatred, and impatience.

Holy Saturday focuses on the Risen Jesus as the new way of life for us. In his letter to the Corinthians, Paul tells us how to live the way of Jesus: share generously with the needy and strangers, work hard and do not be lazy, show kindness in a cheerful manner, love one another sincerely and warmly, hate evil and hold on to what is good, eagerly show respect and live in peace with everybody, serve the Lord with devotion and let your hope in him keep you happy. Misfortunes in life must teach us patience and the need to always pray (2 Corinthians 12). And now, we must all "place God (Jesus) in the 'center of our thoughts, words and actions,'" and be "renewed and mastered by the faith" (Pope Benedict XVI).

Christ, our Light, is Risen.

The Peace of the Risen Lord be with you.

Prayer
Father, this evening's liturgy has taught us a lot about your plan to protect and save us. Help your people to cherish the new way of life Your Son stands for and live it to the full. Amen.

The Season of Easter

EASTER SUNDAY OF THE RESURRECTION OF THE LORD

Acts 10:34.37-43; Colossians 3:1-4 or 1 Corinthians 5:6-8; John 20:1-9

THE LORD IS RISEN! "EUREKA!"

Archimedes was an ancient Greek philosopher and scientist born about 287 B.C. in the ancient seaport city of Syracuse in Sicily. He was one of the leading scientists in classical antiquity. The most widely known story about Archimedes is how he discovered a method for determining the volume of irregular bodies.

Archimedes was tasked by King Hiero II of Syracuse to measure a golden crown without melting it into a more measurable shape. This was mind-boggling for Archimedes who struggled with the challenge and even ignored the project for some time. One day, he filled a tub almost to the rim to take a bath. He stepped in and lowered himself into the bath. The water level in the tub rose and spilled over the rim onto the floor. What would have become a mess on the floor became a scientific discovery for Archimedes. As he looked at the overflowed water, the answer to his task hit him. He realized the amount of water on the floor ought to be equal to the volume of his own body space.

Excited by the discovery, Archimedes jumped quickly out of the tub and ran naked in the city streets shouting, "Eureka!" "Eureka!" meaning "I have found it!"

Archimedes' discovery has become known as the Archimedes Principle. An object immersed in a liquid exerts an upward force called the buoyant force, The Archimedes principle states that "the upward buoyant force that is exerted on a body immersed in a fluid, whether full or partially, is equal to the weight of the fluid that the body displaces" (Archimedes' principle – Wikipedia). The Archimedes principle is a law of physics related to fluid mechanics useful for determining the volume and density of irregular-shaped solid objects. The insight of a philosopher and scientist looking at a normal everyday life experience contributed to the course of science.

Eureka, as an English word derived from the ancient Greek word "heureka," is used to express the excitement of discovering something novel and valuable or when one solves a very difficult problem with the breakthrough solution.

Today, the Lord Jesus Christ is risen from the dead! The word "eureka" reverberates throughout the whole world.

The Gospel accounts talk about the Empty Tomb and subsequent appearances of Jesus to his disciples. Mary Magdalene arrives at Jesus' tomb and notices the stone blocking the tomb's entrance has been pushed aside. She is concerned and rushes to Simon Peter and "the other disciple," reporting that someone, not part of them, had removed Jesus' body. The two men come to witness the Empty Tomb. They leave the premises worried. Mary Magdalene remains in the garden. She hears sounds like whirring and rattling. Then, close to where she is standing, she hears her name called. Immediately, she recognizes the familiar voice. It is Jesus! He speaks to her. After a brief dialogue, she hurries back to the house and inform the rest of the disciples: "I have found the Lord! Eureka! Eureka!" she cries joyfully.

On another occasion, when the disciples gather in a locked room "for fear of trial," Jesus appears in their midst! They rejoice when they see the Lord (John 20:19-23). Thomas, who earlier openly doubted Jesus' resurrection, is so excited when he encounters Jesus and screams: "My Lord and my God" (John 20:28).

Today is Easter Sunday. Like the disciples, we have discovered the Risen Lord. Eureka! A new way of life opens for us. It is the way of Jesus, and we must be glad to embrace it. It is the feast of Jesus transforming us and making us into a new creation. The Resurrection is the foundation of our Christian faith. We are joyfully celebrating the glorious resurrection of our Lord Jesus Christ and his victory over sin and death.

For Christians, this is the most important feast in the Church. The experience of the resurrection is more important than proving it. The resurrection threw a new light on the suffering and death of Jesus and transformed the disciples. It led them to a very different understanding of what at first seemed a tragedy, a disaster, and a failure. The disciples, who were at first frozen with fear of being arrested, suddenly made a complete turnaround and began boldly to proclaim that Jesus, who died on the cross, was alive and with them in his Spirit.

In today's first reading, Peter, having denied Jesus at trial and now completely transformed, confidently and courageously gives witness to the mystery of the resurrection of the Lord. The Spirit of the Risen Lord gave them unshakable bravery and resolve to proclaim what they believed, ready to die for the truth that they proclaimed.

Easter Sunday highlights not only our faith in the resurrection of Jesus, but we are also called to proclaim joyfully and be witnesses of the same faith in the Risen Lord. Proclamation and witness in our lives are the two central themes running through today's readings. We must live what we proclaim.

We asked ourselves the same questions last night.

How am I going to address the impulsive anger, pride, envy, greed, impatience, and negative tendencies towards other people?

How am I going to show love, tolerance, calmness, and respect for others?

The Lord is risen to transform our lives. Let us rejoice and be glad.

The Peace of the Risen Lord be with you.

Prayer
Father, Your Son is victorious over death. Eureka! By our baptism we too die and resurrect with Jesus, our Lord and Savior. May the rebirth we are experiencing be sustained until he comes again. Amen.

SECOND SUNDAY OF EASTER
(Divine Mercy Sunday)

Acts 2: 42-47; 1 Peter 1:3-9; John 20:19-31

FAITH SUNDAY

The second Sunday of Easter is traditionally called Octave Day of Easter, occurring on the eighth day after Easter Sunday. In the Eastern Orthodox Church, it is called Saint Thomas Sunday because of Thomas' doubt and reluctance to believe in the resurrection story, demanding unquestionable evidence of it, and averring he would believe only when he saw Jesus and touched the scars of his wounds. When Jesus revealed himself again to the apostles with Thomas present, a week after his resurrection, he invited him to place his finger on the nails and spear marks on his body. The phrase "Doubting Thomas" has become an expression referring to a doubtful person seeking proof or evidence of an issue.

More importantly, however, Thomas is remembered today for a doubt that gave expression to a remarkable profession of faith: "My Lord and my God," spoken out of profound affection, sincere contrition, and total surrender to the presence and divinity of Jesus. Although initially disbelieving the resurrection of Jesus, Thomas was first to proclaim publicly the two natures of Christ: human (Lord) and divine (God) after Jesus' resurrection. It was a surprisingly pleasant changing moment for Thomas.

The period of Jesus' arrest, trial, and crucifixion was a harrowing and shocking experience for the disciples. Preceding all this was a toned-down Last Supper or Passover Feast, a despairing moment in the Garden of Gethsemane, and an interminable grueling night in the High Priest's court. On Friday morning, the Roman soldiers scourged Jesus and later in the morning, the trials ended.

Verdict: guilty as charged! He carried a crooked wooden cross on the streets of Jerusalem. He was crucified (John 19:16-18). He died a slow and agonizing death on the cross. He was buried (John 19:38-42). The apostles had their hideout under lock, avoiding the religious leaders and the irate crowd who wanted Jesus crucified. They worried the people might call death sentences on them like their master. Some of them, like Cleopas and his friend, hastily left Jerusalem (Luke 24:1-35); probably Thomas too. They could not fathom Jesus was dead, as happens to us when we suddenly lose our dear ones.

Some days earlier on, Thomas had dared the apostles to show boldness and resolve to follow Jesus to Jerusalem and fight for him, and if worse came to the worse, die with him (John 11:16). Indeed, they believed Jesus would lead an uprising to fight for political independence from the Romans, whereby some of them could gain positions in a new political order. However, to their utmost dismay, they witnessed Jesus die on a cross. They were afraid, shocked, discombobulated, and felt absolutely abandoned. Then, they woke up on Sunday morning to the breaking news that, "The Lord is Risen." Thomas would not accept the testimony of his colleagues until he faced the one whose death and burial he had witnessed.

The Gospel of John presents a series of symbolic events in the upper room on this day after the resurrection of Jesus. The Second Sunday of Easter was an incredibly significant day regarding the beginnings of the Church. The Apostolic Community in the upper room became the Apostolic Church of Jesus Christ. The Holy Spirit would fully confirm this gratuitous grace on Pentecost Sunday with his outpouring of his gifts. This would signify the inaugurating of the Church of Christ so that by baptism all believers would become part of the new "People of God." Through baptism and the outpouring of the Holy Spirit, we assume a new status as sons and daughters of God, heirs of God's new kingdom. Even when we stray away, the Church would have the power to

173

forgive us our sins in the Sacrament of Reconciliation (Matthew 16:19)

Jesus' appearance and Thomas' confession of faith, representing the collective faith of the apostles, empowered them as a solid new community with Peter as temporal head (Matthew 16:18-19). Jesus established his church on the foundation of Peter's confession of faith (Matthew 16:16), replicated by Thomas after the resurrection in today's Gospel reading. It was the day, so to speak, the apostles officially met as one body with Jesus as its spiritual head and spiritual force. Jesus blessed the holy union (the Church) with divine blessing: "Peace be with you." The apostles' confession of faith, proclaiming Jesus as Messiah and Son of God, became the indestructible foundation of the Church (Matthew 16:18-19).

For the Early Church, the confession of Thomas pointed to the very heart of its faith. In this respect, today is also appropriately called "Faith Sunday" when the Church and all believers embrace the resurrection message with the testimony of faith acclaimed by Thomas: "My Lord and my God." We have received baptism believing in the risen Lord and look forward to the day we shall see our Lord and our God face to face in his glory on the condition that we remain faithful and devoted to his Word.

Has there been a moment in your life when you doubted Jesus' divine presence and questioned his resurrection as what gives meaning to your existence?

How often have you shown remorse and moved on with a sincere and unswerving profession of faith, like Thomas?

The second thing that happened in the upper room was Jesus breathing on the apostles to give them the divine gift of the Holy Spirit with the authority to forgive sins. This symbolized a new life reminiscent of God's breath of life transferred into the shape formed from the soil of the earth, turning it into living human beings (Genesis 2:7). God did the same with the animals and birds that he had created from the soil (Genesis 2:19). In the past, priests who baptized babies breathed on them to symbolize God's breath of life to the babies.

Again, upon it's commissioning, the Apostolic Church became a mission ministry with a divine mandate to spread the Good News: "As the Father sent me, so I you." This is the message Jesus emphasized in his subsequent appearances after the resurrection (Matthew 28:19-20) and at his departure from the earth (Acts 1:8-9). By the power invested in him (Matthew 28:18), Jesus blessed his Church to evangelize the world with his Word and promote peace in the world. All of us baptized in Christ have the divine gift of the Spirit, giving us the grace and courage to evangelize by our words and actions.

Is your life a testimony of the Spirit of God dwelling in you?

Furthermore, Jesus epitomizes the love and mercy of God the Father by his obedience to sacrifice himself for the sins of humanity. The apostles represent humanity redeemed from sin who offer salvation—the Good News which must reach the entire world. Today, humanity celebrates God's mercy and love.

It is therefore providential that Pope John Paul II instituted the second Sunday of Easter as Divine Mercy Sunday on April 30, 2000. Predicated on the fact that humanity stands always in need of God's love and mercy, Divine Mercy comes from the heart of Jesus and these graces emanate and flow generously onto us. Robert Stackpole (2000) records the two very important statements about mercy given by Saint Pope John Paul II in his letter, *Dives in Misericordia* (1981) (translated as "Rich in Mercy"): "Mercy is love's second name," and mercy is "the greatest attribute of God." Certainly, both statements reveal "the merciful love of the Father."

Today typically climaxes the novena to the Divine Mercy of Jesus revealed to Saint Maria Faustina Kowalski (1905-1938), a Polish nun associated with the message of Divine Mercy. She was a mystic who received revelations from Jesus in a series of apparitions about the mercy and love of Jesus Christ for sinners. Saint Maria Faustina also stressed the need for a special devotion to Divine Mercy that will "show a childlike trust in God and love of neighbor." At the tomb of Sister Faustina in 1997, Pope John Paul II declared, "There is nothing that man needs more than Divine Mercy" (Fr. Seraphim Michalenko, MIC, 2006).

Let us reflect on God's divine mercy, for "His mercy endures forever" (Responsorial Psalm).

We need a trusting faith in God's mercy and love to heal the wrongs of humanity that cause most of our sufferings. Indeed, Saint John writes in the second reading of today: "And we win the victory over the world by means of our faith." We prove faith when we love God and obey his commandments that are actually "not too hard for us." Again, John writes elsewhere: The command that God has given us is this: "all who love God must love their brother or sister also" (1 John 4:21).

On Divine Mercy Sunday, therefore, let us also reflect on the practice of agape love found in the Early Church as we read in the first reading that each believer showed acts of mercy. The word "mercy" is from the Latin word *misericordia* and Fr. George Kosicki, a Divine Mercy advocate, explained misericordia as "having a pain in your heart for the pains of others, and taking pains to do something about their pain" (Robert Stackpole, 2000).

Let us teach the world that what matters in life is not ourselves but all others, and the capacity to show love, respect, commiseration, and kind-heartedness. These are motivating words that create the need for one to share in the pain of another because of misfortunes and the divine imperative and personal desire to help.

Unfortunately, society teaches our children that they are different because they are brown, white, or dark-skinned. Let us show them there is only one humanity designed by the Creator and designated for friendship and love. Let us teach them that different people can live together in peace and harmony when we obey Jesus' commandment of Love, which is to love God and neighbor. Let us teach them that Jesus is alive in each person, and they must treat every person they meet like they would treat Jesus. Let us teach them God loves them, and love is the meaning of life, especially love that recognizes neighbor and stranger; love that treats the homeless, the physically challenged, the foreigner, the sick, and elderly with mercy and compassion. Let us teach them everything stems from faith, which must never fade away from their hearts. And finally, they must know there is divine presence and divine mercy in the world, a reality that ephemeral things around us like possessions, wealth, power, and status should not blur or encumber us from the commandment of Love.

Saint Maria Faustina further noted that receiving the Sacrament of Penance today, going to Mass, and availing oneself of the Sacrament of the Eucharist, would result in the forgiveness of sins.

Jesus, I Trust in You. Jesus, we Trust in You.

The Peace of the Risen Lord be with you.

Prayer
Father, we are thankful for your great gift of faith. Let the Spirit of Your Son Jesus Christ bring us forgiveness, peace, and confidence in the power of his resurrection. Amen.

THIRD SUNDAY OF EASTER

Acts 2:14, 22-33; 1 Peter 1:17-21; Luke 24: 13-35

OUR ROAD TO EMMAUS

The astonishing events of the weekend begin on Holy Thursday night with a quiet and modest Passover meal. The Gospels and Saint Paul (1 Corinthians 11: 23-26) recount the Last Supper where Jesus predicts his betrayal and foretells Peter's denial of knowing him before the cock crows. He washes the feet of the Apostles and gives them a New Commandment: "love one another as I have loved you." He institutes the Sacraments of the Eucharist and the Priesthood. The ceremony is probably cut short, and Jesus quietly leads them to the Garden of Gethsemane. The guardsmen sent by the Chief Priests and Elders are impolite and harsh. They heckle the apostles and arrest Jesus to face one of the speediest trials in history in the courts of the High Priest, Pontius Pilate, and King Herod. Pontius Pilate condemns Jesus to be crucified at the demand of the people. Jesus carries a ragged cross, staggering on a rugged road to Calvary. He is crucified. He dies and is buried.

The apostles had great and glowing prospects with the thought that Jesus was the Messiah to deliver Israel from political control and economic quandary caused by exorbitant taxes by the Romans (Matthew 24:21). The recently acclaimed Messiah the people welcomed at his triumphal entry into Jerusalem (John 12:13) had suffered a humiliating death. Desperate, frightened, and completely clueless about what to do next for fear of being rounded up by the Jewish authorities, the disciples disband and go their separate ways. Some hide in Jerusalem (John 20:19) while others flee the city. The hard-to-believe stories about Jesus' rising from the dead spread in the city and countryside. Thomas shows signs of disbelief, denial, despair, and cynicism about reports of

Jesus being seen after his death (John 20:25b). In today's Gospel, Cleopas and his friend, also disciples of Jesus, doubting the trending resurrection story are fleeing Jerusalem.

The journey to Emmaus story is powerful and fascinating. Without revealing his identity, Jesus catches up with the two disciples and explains the import of the Scriptures and what Moses and the Prophets had said about the Messiah. The disciples, like the others, had perceived a charismatic leader, political figure, and liberator. Clearly, they had not observed any spiritual or redemptive meaning in Jesus' life and death. Jesus' synopsis of the Scriptures riveted them, and he was invited home. At dinner, Jesus had the opportunity of "celebrating" the "breaking of bread" with them (Luke 24:30). Then, "their eyes were opened, and they recognized him." They stared at each other, and by the time they turned back to their guest, he had disappeared. They turned to each other again marveling at how they felt within them while Jesus spoke to them about the Scriptures on the way to Emmaus.

Like Cleopas and his friend, we must recognize Jesus in the Word. We must not treat any scriptural reading as a normal story, even when read or sung privately. Each reading of the Word of God or Christian song is a chance to meet Jesus, know him intimately, personally, and relate to him intensely. It must always be a special personal encounter to awaken within us a compelling desire to be with him and share our experience of him with others. We must experience the amazing presence of Jesus in the Word of God, burning within us, and giving us a sense of understanding of the Scriptures, inner peace, joy, and refuge. A familiar set of readings is that of the Easter vigil liturgy comprising a chronological presentation of God's salvation history, culminating in the resurrection of Jesus.

The Gospel reading of today urges us to recognize Jesus in the "breaking of bread" and by extension the Sacraments. They are conferred through God's Word and human actions backed by faith and affect what they signify. Received with the proper disposition, the Sacraments bestow God's grace and enhance one's relationship with divine life. The Church regards the seven Sacraments—confirmed by the Fourth Council of the Lateran (1215) and reaffirmed by subsequent Councils of Florence (1439) and Trent (1545-1563)—as instituted by Jesus Christ, bestowed to the Church, and administered through the minister who represents Jesus. The Church holds that the efficacy of a Sacrament comes *ex opera operato*, a Latin phrase, meaning that grace is given irrespective of the "state of grace" or "personal holiness" of the one dispensing it.

The Sacrament of Baptism is a birth to become a child of God, member of the Body of Christ or the People of God. The Sacrament of Confirmation confers the gifts of the Holy Spirit: wisdom, understanding, counsel, fortitude, knowledge, piety, and the fear of the Lord. We are transformed by these divine gifts to bear the fruits of the Spirit, which are love, joy, peace, patience, kindness, goodness, faithfulness, gentleness, and self-control (Galatians 5). The Catholic Tradition quotes other fruits according to the Vulgate version of the Bible listed in Galatians to include charity, faith, modesty, and chastity.

At the celebration of the Holy Eucharist, the forms of bread and wine transform in their "inner reality, though not in appearance," into the Body and Blood of Jesus Christ, a transformation referred to as transubstantiation. This is our spiritual nourishment from Jesus Christ, a source of grace and renewal as we invite him into our lives. The Holy Eucharist is also called the Blessed Sacrament or Holy Communion. Jesus reveals himself in the breaking of the bread. We realize how powerful that one simple act is; breaking the bread is everything for us. This is Jesus, not a mere symbol, but our Lord and Savior in the priest's hands, the person with the authority to take and bless the bread and wine into the actual presence of God and distribute to the faithful. Indeed, the Mass celebrated every day has continued unabated since Holy Thursday at the Last Supper when Jesus instituted both the Holy Eucharist and Holy Orders. In the Early Church, the disciples gathered in homes for the breaking of the bread after hearing scriptural readings in the synagogues.

The Sacrament of Penance or the Sacrament of Reconciliation or Confession is a Sacrament of Spiritual Healing that reunites the baptized with Jesus after he or she succumbs to human weaknesses and sins. Anointing of the Sick is another Sacrament of Healing but administered to any faithful "in danger by reason of illness or old age" (Canon Law no. 1004). When we need physical healing, we ask for the anointing of the sick.

Priesthood or Holy Orders reminds the People of God about the divine in our lives and feeds the faithful with the Word of God and the Body and Blood of Christ. In the Sacrament of marriage or matrimony, couples are "consecrated" to a uniquely new spiritual and physical relationship in which both seek a common goal in life and commit themselves to the upbringing and education of their children.

The Gospel narrates Jesus' appearance to the two disciples as a stranger and how they warmly received him and happily invited him to where they lodged. Jesus comes to us every day as the stranger on the street requesting help; the stranger with an inferior status in society or a reprehensible background; the person with special needs; the destitute or vulnerable child who must be protected; the sick, poor, and needy; the dejected person who needs a smile and a hug; the refugee and migrant who cannot enjoy the comfort of home. Jesus also comes to us as the well-educated, the wealthy, and the generous person.

Another dimension to view the story in today's Gospel is how each person's life is a journey to Emmaus. In one of his addresses, Pope Emeritus Benedict XVI said the fact that no one has discovered the original village of Emmaus means Emmaus is everywhere and that the road that leads to Emmaus is the path of every Christian. The two disciples, like the others, were in a state of despair, betrayal, regret, and defeat. The death of Jesus wrecked their hopes and beliefs. They had banked their hopes and entire lives on a popular revolution led by Jesus, acclaimed to be the Messiah. Jesus had died as a weakling, taunted, scorned, and disgraced.

Many people today are grappling with questions about life's difficulties and challenges without satisfactory answers and seem to have lost life's meaning. We know, literally, that no step or phase in life is smooth for anyone. We face bumpy roads, gaping holes, and winding paths in life. After each phase in life, we must stop to acknowledge Jesus' presence catching up with us. We ought to ask every day what Jesus would do in various situations in our lives, always recognizing his presence. The author of the poem "Footprints in the Sand" (authorship largely disputed but many attributed it to Mary Stevenson in 1936) writes that as we walk with Christ, two sets of footprints will appear in the sand—ours and Christ's. When only one set of footprints appears, he has not deserted us but is carrying us.

Peter's message (first reading) was an article of faith and conversion for the Early Church, possibly like the clarification of the Scriptures by Jesus to Cleopas and his friend. As part of the Early Christian catechism, the message portrayed Jesus as the humble Savior for all peoples. He was not a militant leader to defend an ideology or political liberation. The Old Testament prophecies about the Messiah pointed to Jesus, who manifested God's Salvation Plan for a new Kingdom of God that recognizes reconciliation with God and one another. Peter spoke fearlessly about the new dispensation fulfilled in Christ Jesus. He professed the divine mandate to proclaim the message of Jesus through the outpouring of the Holy Spirit (Acts 1:8). He urged people to accept Jesus and have faith in him as "God with us," one who has saved the world by his death and resurrection. The second reading is an exhortation from Peter to Christians to have faith in the Risen Christ.

Let us see ourselves as the modern-day Peter boldly professing our faith even in despair. Indeed, our personal road to Emmaus ends at the place we hear the Word of God and recognize the Lord in the Eucharist.

Let the Word of God always have meaning for us as we endeavor to live it.

Let us open our palms to receive the one we recognize as Lord and Savior, Jesus Christ, the risen Lord.

The Peace of the Risen Lord be with you.

Prayer
Father, we encounter strangers every day and in many places. Give us the grace to recognize your Son in each and every one of them. Amen.

FOURTH SUNDAY OF EASTER
(Good Shepherd Sunday)

Acts 2:14a, 36-41; 1 Peter 2:20b-25; John 10:1-10

"EGO SUM PASTOR BONUS," I AM THE GOOD SHEPHERD

The Fourth Sunday of Easter is traditionally called Good Shepherd Sunday, derived from the Gospel of John with Jesus saying: "I am the good shepherd, who is willing to die for the sheep."

As keeping domestic animals, particularly sheep, was familiar to pastoral people, the Israelites accorded significant importance to shepherding. The number of sheep defined the social status of the owner, who hired honest and capable shepherds to take care of the sheep. With his staff, the shepherd led the flock to green pastures, interacting with the flock via his sounds and verbal commands. When he rescued an errant sheep, he carried it close to him back to the sheepfold. In this way, the animal became familiar with his smell so it would not wander away again. In their socio-religious life, the Israelites were like a flock led by God as shepherd and protector. The Book of Genesis recounts how the Patriarch Joseph was saved "by the Shepherd, the Protector of Israel" who "is your father's God who helps you" (Genesis 49:24-25).

The God-shepherd image was a revered theme in the writings of the prophets like Isaiah, Jeremiah, Ezekiel, including King David. Psalm 23 portrays a familiar image of a shepherd ascribed to God, which begins with "The Lord is my shepherd." The Psalm speaks about God's caring and protective nature and his never-ending presence in the lives of those who believe in him and follow him. The kings and prophets of Israel were considered shepherds of the people. When, apparently, these people failed in their task of shepherding the people, God declared he would shepherd the people. The Prophet Ezekiel prophesied about God saying:

"I myself will look for my sheep and take care of them in the same way as shepherds take care of their sheep that were scattered and brought together again" (Ezekiel 34:11-12).

Thus, the special relationship between the shepherd and his sheep was the best way to describe how God related to his people.

A story from a Jewish tradition depicts Moses as the first person to be chosen by God to shepherd his people. Moses was raised in royalty in Pharaoh's household in Egypt. As an adult, he killed an Egyptian who assaulted a Hebrew slave. Moses would not compromise his stance on truth, justice, and impartiality. Therefore, he escaped from Egypt and became a shepherd in the desert of Midian. Moses was honest to Jethro, his father-in-law, whose sheep he shepherded with tender loving care. At one time, Moses carried a stray and injured lamb on his shoulders back to the camp to the admiration of Jethro. Moses had trailed the strayed lamb far away to a brook near Horeb, the mountain of God. Watching the lamb drink thirstily, Moses remarked he would have carried the lamb on his shoulders to the brook if he knew it was thirsty. God heard his words about the lamb and declared concerning Moses, "Moses is worthy of being the leader of my people" (The Fellowship: December 12, 2022).

Because of Moses' honesty and goodness in treating another person's sheep caringly, as well as his kindness and concern even for a little vulnerable animal, God called him to shepherd Israel to the Promised Land. From a royal background to being a shepherd had taught him humility, compassion, kindness, wisdom, patience, and strong leadership. After God's revelation in the burning bush (Exodus 3), Moses remained a man of faith, surrendering completely to God, and committing to his call and mission. Indeed, people described him as "a very humble man, more humble than anyone else on the face of the

185

earth" (Numbers 12:13). It is said that in Palestine, the word "shepherd" mirrored goodness, such as generosity, honesty, sincerity, selfless love, and commitment. A committed shepherd would fight raiders or wild animals attacking his flock.

Has your experience of the Lord Jesus Christ taught you humility, compassion, kindness, wisdom, patience, and strong leadership? Is your life providing a vibrant setting for good neighborliness, respect, and the willingness to show love, compassion, and kindness to all manners of persons irrespective of their background?

The same unique association between shepherd and sheep was how the Early Christians saw Jesus and his Church. They identified Jesus as the New Moses who lived humbly and mindfully, becoming the sacrificial lamb for the atonement of human sin (second reading). The analogy of shepherd portrays Jesus as shepherd and his followers as sheep. This shows his total protection to ensure proper care and safety for humanity, who, like sheep, is vulnerable and easily strays from the shepherd without direction. Jesus as Good Shepherd became a well-accepted symbol of faith which featured in Early Christian art in people's homes, churches, catacombs, and tombs. The image of Jesus as the Good Shepherd continues to be prominent in the lives of Christians and in the Church, with churches, schools, hospitals, and other institutions named after Jesus, the Good Shepherd.

Today, we remember Jesus as the Good Shepherd leading and caring for us on our life's journey. Jesus is close to our personal concerns, and we are safe when we recognize his voice, listen to him, and follow in his footsteps. How we know the voice of the Good Shepherd and relate intimately to him is by fostering a spiritual and routine life based on the Word of God, reflecting on its meaning shrouded in Jesus' commandment of Love, and doing good even when met with insults and suffering (second reading). Again, we can build that relationship through daily mass, daily prayers, listening to our pastor's explanations, and trusting ourselves to his care.

We are reminded that Jesus calls us to function as good shepherds, a call to discipleship. This is a mission mandated by the risen Christ, more so in today's world that accepts individualism, consumerism, and untoward practices as norms in society. Our civil leaders must dispense their duties as shepherds who love and serve their countries and communities without self-interest or favor. Religious heads must not harbor doubts about co-workers for their different views or peddle partiality. Coworkers must avoid blatant falsehoods and misinformation about others at work. Parents and children must imitate the good shepherd by showing love and respect in the family. We must be good shepherds to our church communities, showing love and compassion to everyone, especially the poor and the needy. What the Good Shepherd is to his flock is what the clergy ought to be with God's faithful, to preach the Word of God, nourish them with the Sacraments, assist them spiritually, and support them in their temporal needs.

Today is also Vocations Sunday or World Day of Prayer for Vocations. Christians pray for priests, deacons, and men and women in Religious Life, and for more vocations in the Church. Jesus needs shepherds to take care of his flock. Therefore, discerning young men must respond to divine calling with zest and zeal, sincere love, resolve, and commitment. Once ordained, they must awaken each day to the extraordinary role as "in persona Christi" (in the person of Christ) or "alter Christus" (another Christ) to bring about changes in the lives of Christians. The priest must reverently pronounce the words of consecration over typical bread and wine "which earth has given, and human hands have made" and which are changed into the Body and Blood of Jesus Christ. The faithful accept in sublime reverence with "Amen" (it is true) and humbly receive Jesus into their lives as Lord and Savior. Again, the priest, in persona Christi, absolves sins to bring drifting sheep back into the arms of the Good Shepherd. The Church does not ordain priests as shepherds to be gripped by selfish interests. The parishioners and all others must know them as sincere shepherds, trustworthy, compassionate, and respectful. In the last decade or so, however, a

187

triple-tragedy has plagued the Church: the continual dearth of priests; a plethora of scandals involving abuses; and decline in church membership in an ever-increasing secular period.

The Gospel of Year A (Fourth Sunday of Easter) shows another significant image nearly eclipsed by the good shepherd symbol. Two times, Jesus refers to himself as "the gate for the sheep." In the ancient Middle East, sturdy walls and well-secured gates fortified cities against marauders. Similarly, domestic animals remained in pens secured by circles of rocks. At night, the shepherd kept watch at the gate to ward off thieves and wild animals, becoming a gate himself. Shepherds took turns to be "sheep gates" when the enclosure was a communal one. In the morning, each shepherd made familiar sounds or voices to invite his sheep to follow him to the pasture.

The analogy of the gate or door is equally pertinent today, when gates or doors virtually protect all properties, providing safety and ensuring ownership. The "gated community" is in vogue to make residents feel a great sense of security. Jesus is therefore the gate to our "gated community" (the Church) through whom we get access to God; Jesus is the gate who protects against attacks of the Evil One. Jesus, the Chief Shepherd, has transferred the keys of the gate to Peter and his successors (Matthew 16:18-20). The successor of Peter is the Chief Shepherd of the Universal Church, the Bishop is the Shepherd of the diocese, and the Pastor is the Shepherd of the local church. We are safe and secured by trusting ourselves to the care of our shepherds who lead us to God through Jesus Christ.

Take time to pray for your shepherds to be faithful protectors of their flock. Each faithful, when properly formed, will reach the heavenly gate to meet the eternal Good Shepherd.

The Peace of the Risen Lord be with you.

Prayer
Father, priests are ordained as shepherds to form and guide your flock. By word and example, let them bring back to the fold your scattered sheep. Amen.

FIFTH SUNDAY OF EASTER

Acts 6:1-7; 1 Peter 2:4-9; John 14:1-12

ECCLESIAL STRUCTURES FOR UNITY

Today's first reading leads us into some of the historical, social, and theological milieux at the time of the Early Christian Church. In the Gospel reading, Jesus reveals his true nature at the Last Supper before his Passion. Thus, an appropriate title for today's Gospel could be "Jesus, the Way to the Father." In the second reading, Peter calls for strong faith in Jesus, the figurative cornerstone, "a stone, a tested stone, a precious cornerstone of a sure foundation," upon which God would build his people Israel (Isaiah 28:16). Jewish religion leadership rejected Jesus with any historical or prophetic ties to the Messiah. For Christians, however, Jesus is the predicted cornerstone upon which the New People of God would be built in the Spirit of God (Ephesians 2:20-22).

The crucifixion of Jesus was unexpected, a setback to his followers, which made them disperse, some to their former trade (John 21:1-14), others like Cleopas and his friend, to their hometown of Emmaus (Luke 24:13-35), and others to voluntary lockdown (John 20:19). Shortly, another shock wave started with stories about Jesus' resurrection and the physical experience of him by some disciples. A third remarkable episode was the outpouring of the Holy Spirit on Pentecost Day that opened their minds to the Scriptures about the Law and the Prophets (Luke 24:27). On Pentecost Day, Peter inaugurated the Jesus Movement (Acts 2:5-12,42) and started with about 3,000 people by baptism (Acts 2:41). The apostles recalled Jesus' Great Commission (Matthew 28:18-20) and spread the new message everywhere, guided by the Holy Spirit (Acts 8:4, 25).

189

The Movement was mainly a section in Judaism comprising two major social groups with different backgrounds. The first was the Greek-speaking Jews (Hellenists) with leaders like Stephen and Philip. They were Jewish settlers in Jerusalem from the diaspora who had joined the new movement. Brought up outside Israel, Hellenists spoke the Greek language and read the Greek Old Testament referred to as the Septuagint, the Greek translation of the original Hebrew Bible. Although they were staunch devotees of the Law and of the Prophets, they were more tolerant of foreigners and less stringent in their observance of purification rituals and other Jewish traditions and customs.

The second group was the Aramaic speaking native Jews (Hebrews) who had converted into the new movement. These Hebrews observed the daily strict rituals prescribed in the Law and the Prophets and had a history of dissociation with Gentiles to avoid any contagion. For example, the group insisted on circumcision of Gentiles and observance of Jewish traditions and customs (Acts 15:1).

The two groups worshipped in their respective synagogues on the Sabbath but were also devoted to the apostolic teachings and fellowship, the breaking of bread, and prayers, and cared about the daily needs of each other especially the poor and needy. Despite combining their resources and living as a large extended family, disconcerting disputes arose among them that potentially threatened their unity. The tension was much more insidious than the mere day-to-day material allocation for widows and other poor families. The conflict growing from their backgrounds was a litmus test of the survival of the new faith community. After the death of Stephen, most of the Hellenists moved away from Jerusalem, settling in Antioch and its environs, where Gentile membership increased in great numbers (Acts 11:18).

The first reading presents perhaps one of the earliest convocations that brought together the apostles, the community of believers, and some women like Mary, the mother of Jesus, to help solve concerns emerging within a

190

fledgling and growing Christian movement. At the end of their deliberations, they appointed and ordained seven deacons to attend to the physical needs of the group for the apostles to focus on the Word of God and liturgical prayers (Acts 6:4). By instituting the diaconate ministry, the apostles, with Simon Peter as Vicar of Christ, assumed leadership of the new community now called "disciples" (Acts 6:7).

The Early Church built several significant institutions and traditions. From Jerusalem as headquarters, the apostles gave direction to the Church and addressed doctrinal and social concerns like the question of circumcision (Acts 15:1-6), and the Cornelius issue (Acts 10:44-48) from which the apostles passed on various resolutions (Acts 11:22; 13:25; 15:1-2). Fr. Thomas Rosica (Salt and Light Catholic Media Foundation, Canada) has shown how from this time we seem to get into "a clear perception of the diversity of offices and duties in the first apostolic community." Both the Greek and Hebrew speaking groups accepting the decisions of the apostles was an explicit recognition of the authority of the leadership, the humility of the believers, and the respect and honor accorded the apostles and elders. It all reminds us of similar cultural, social, and political conflicts the Church has confronted both internally and externally over the past centuries, as well as the role of the Popes. Peter led a community of believers whose membership was spreading. Jesus had given the leadership mantle to Peter (Matthew 16:18-19; John 21:16). Peter bequeathed this venerable position to his successors, which in the Church's tradition has been the Popes, assisted by the priesthood. The roles of the Papacy and the priesthood are therefore significant. Like the story in the first reading, men and women are today called, trained, and presented for ordination through prayers and imposing of hands to assume various duties and ministries in the Church (1 Timothy 4:14).

It is significant also to appreciate that despite its social differences, the Early Church acknowledged the most important figure in the Church as Jesus Christ and the salvation he accomplished for the world. Baptism had the dual effect of washing away sins and initiating Christians into the mystical body of Christ. Therefore, despite the apparent inevitable cultural and social differences in the Church today, mutual respect must prevail among all cultural groups professing the same faith and baptism.

In today's Gospel reading, John attempts to catechize the young and nascent Church, which required solutions to vital concerns. John, therefore, uses the Last Supper scene to introduce a dialogue between Jesus and the apostles to answer some basic questions of faith which are still pertinent in our time. What would be the reward for being a Christian? Does belief in Jesus and a close relationship with him offer a better hope of securing life after death? Would Christians experience the physical presence of Jesus after this life? Will the Soul enjoy the eternal presence of God? What would be the purpose of the Christian before Jesus' return? Must Christians follow Jesus' commandment of Love? Is he "the Way, the Truth and the Life?" Despite attacks and persecutions from within and outside since its inception into the eve of the third millennia, the Church has survived, always gathering to involve others in settling disputes and theological concerns for the Church to grow.

Let us thank the Lord for our baptism that makes us members of the New People of God. Jesus gives meaning to our existence as "the Way, the Truth, and the Life."

Are people around us recognizing our Catholic faith by how we live among them?

How do we see in ourselves that we practice what we profess?

If we are not walking the way of Jesus, we must reflect on the changes we need to make and pray for the strength to make them.

Do our actions or words invite unity or discord? If we have a complaint like the Hellenists, do we address such concerns to the proper channels or do we spread dissension?

Do we pray for love and peace in our faith community and help those in physical and spiritual need?

The Peace of the Risen Lord be with you.

Prayer
Father, enlighten the hearts and minds of your people to acknowledge all people as your children. Assist Church leaders to use their time, energy, and the gifts you have bestowed on them to grow the Church and assist others in need. Amen.

SIXTH SUNDAY OF EASTER

Acts 8:5-8, 14-17; 1 Peter 3: 15-18; John 14:15-21

GOD'S HOLY SPIRIT LIVING WITHIN US

The readings of today continue to trace the historical, spiritual, and theological progress of the Early Christian Church following the expectations of its head, Jesus Christ. The Gospel emphasizes the assurances of Jesus to the apostles at the Last Super and the phenomenal role of the Holy Spirit as a new reality in the life of the Church: "But when the Holy Spirit comes upon you, you will be filled with power, and you will be witnesses for me in Jerusalem, in all Judea and Samaria, and to the ends of the earth" (Acts 1:8). Thus, beginning as a small community from the "Upper Room" (Acts 1:13), and emboldened by the Holy Spirit, "the believers who were scattered went everywhere, preaching the message" (Acts 8:4). The disciples preached along the Mediterranean Sea and in Rome with zeal and chocked remarkable successes.

Samaria was a territory sandwiched between Galilee and Judea with a long history of deep animosity with the Jews (Third Sunday of Lent). A Jew would normally not ask a Samaritan for water to drink, as shown in the story of Jesus and the Samaritan woman (John 4:9). Samaritans were of mixed origin—descendants of the remnants of the Northern Kingdom tribes who had intermarried with foreign settlers brought into Israel during the Assyrian or Babylonian captivity or exile (597 -538 B.C.). Most Jews considered descendants of the racial intermarriage as "people of mixed blood" or "half-breeds," or not fully Jewish. In addition, because the foreign settlers had brought the worship of their gods to Israel, the Jews considered them to be without legitimate faith. The kingdom of Judea in the South also fell finally to the Babylonian Empire (586 B.C.) that led to the destruction of Jerusalem, and its walls and temple, followed by a massive deportation. The Babylonian Empire fell to the Persian king, Cyrus the Great, in 539 B.C. who permitted the Jews in exile, comprising over 40,000, to return to Judah in 537 B.C as recorded in the historical accounts of the prophets Ezra and Nehemiah. The Persian foreign policy was to use local personages to govern conquered territories and not deport their peoples. The Jews denied the Samaritans to join in rebuilding the temple. The Samaritans could not worship in the temple and so built a "rival" temple to Yahweh on Mount Gerizim. The Jews burned down that Temple in 128 B.C. which exacerbating the soiled relationship between the Jews and Samaritans. The route to Jerusalem from Galilee through Samaria was the shortest, but pious Jews avoided it because of the mistrust, dislike, and attacks by vandals on the road.

The animosity between Jews and Samaritans continued during the time of Jesus. In the Gospel of Matthew, Jesus did not send the apostles to any Samaritan town or village when he first deployed them to evangelize (Matthew 10:5). Luke writes about a Samaritan village denying Jesus and his disciples to pass through the village to Jerusalem. This infuriated James and John, "Sons of Thunder," (Mark 3:17) who asked Jesus to call down fire from heaven to destroy the village (Luke 9:51-54).

The first reading is about the passion and dedication with which Deacon Philip proclaimed the Word of God in Samaria, a successful missionary work accompanied by signs and healings that brought "great rejoicing" to the Church in Jerusalem. The conversion of the Samaritans was incredibly significant to the early growth of the Church. The union of the Gentile communities with the Church in Jerusalem ensured that there was unity, collaboration, and loyalty.

Philip's amazing work in Samaria confirmed the salvific message of Jesus preached by the Church could also reach the Gentiles, paving the way for Peter and John to visit the communities, pray over them, and lay hands over them to receive the Holy Spirit. All this meant that institutions and sacraments were emerging in the Church. Rituals were established for sacraments and people in positions in the churches were recognized as having received authority from God. For example, as deacon (a status conferred by the "imposition of hands"), Philip lacked the "faculty" to confer the gift of the Holy Spirit on the baptized. The Sacrament of Confirmation was the imparting of the gift of the Holy Spirit by the imposition of hands. Philip had to wait for Peter and John from Jerusalem, as the delegation duly consecrated to confer the gift of the Holy Spirit (Acts 8:17).

Sacraments in the Church are outward or visible signs and instruments of God's inward or invisible grace received or stirred up through words and the laying on of hands (Third Sunday of Easter). Their effect, according to Church belief, comes "ex opera operato," that is, "by the very fact of being administered, regardless of the personal spiritual standing of the minister, because Jesus is the author and giver of the sacraments. However, the recipient must be "properly disposed" by showing expression of faith toward receiving the sacraments." For example, the pouring of water in baptism symbolizes the cleansing of sins and a new birth into the Christian Community. The words that accompany baptism testify that the baptized have inwardly received God the Father, God the Son, and God the Holy Spirit (The Trinity). Later in life, especially with an infant's baptism, confirmation becomes a symbolic action where, through the imposition of hands by the Bishop, the Holy Spirit in the person stirs or re-awakens. There are seven Sacraments acknowledged by the Church: Baptism, Eucharist, Confirmation, Priesthood, Reconciliation, Marriage, and the Anointing of the Sick.

Once again, today's readings open a theological window for us to delve into the thinking, wisdom, and rationale behind the Early Church. By this exercise, we will embrace the inspiration to further build and deepen our faith today. In the Gospel, for example, we see an incredibly significant teaching concerning the Trinity and an emphasis on the presence of the Holy Spirit. Fr. Andrew Greeley (died 2013) opined that the readings of today show that the early Christians saw that "God is a community of relationships, that there is so much knowledge and love in God, that the knowledge and love explode into distinct personages."

Among the most favored New Testament verses is John chapter 3 verse 16, which mentions God's love for us expressed in the presence of Jesus in the world. Jesus came to restore the marred relationship between humanity and God. He shows the deep love he as God has for us. He is the Good Shepherd, leading his flock to heavenly pastures. He is the Lamb slain to bring about salvation. He promises believers will not be orphans and will join him in heaven if they keep his Commandment of Love. He promised the gift of the Holy Spirit to guide believers as the "Spirit of Truth," the "Spirit of Life," the "Advocate" to enlighten and invigorate the relationship Christians have with him and the Father.

The Holy Spirit, as the third person in the Triune Godhead, is a gift of the Father who sent his Son into the world. If we live a truly Christian life, the Holy Spirit will dwell in us and enable us to fully experience the Father and the Son in our innermost self. The remarkable result of this singular relationship will be love, which will always lead our lives: "My Father will love those who love me; I too will love them and reveal myself to them" (John 14:21).

Saint Paul reminded us of the fruit of the Spirit: "love, joy, peace, patience, kindness, goodness, faithfulness, humility, and self-control" (Galatians 5:22-23). He further teaches that those who avow and profess love for Jesus Christ must allow the Spirit to direct their lives. They must not succumb to "the desires of human nature" (Galatians 5:16) which show themselves in "immorality, indecency, belief in idols and witchcraft, fighting, anger, jealousy, and exaggerated ambitions" (Galatians 5:19-21).

Saint Paul's clarion call to allow the Holy Spirit to guide us to grow in love are increasingly more relevant and urgent today. The Samaritans and the Jews created the hatred between them about 200 years before Jesus. Sometimes hatred in us goes back many years, but we overtly and covertly revive it in our own generation. The sin of hate continues to divide and break humanity created by God for peace and harmony. Jesus sets a caveat: "Those who accept my commandments and obey them are the ones who love me" (Gospel Reading). Genuine love seems to be too ideal for us since, many times, living it becomes a tremendous challenge. Does it feel impossible to love someone who has hurt you, such as your spouse, son or daughter, close friend, or co-worker?

The Holy Spirit, called "the Paraclete" (from the Latin *Paracletus*) in the Gospel reading, translates variously as "Advocate," "Counselor," "Comforter," or "Companion."

The Holy Spirit helps us to know the truth that we are "a community of relationships" immersed in the knowledge of God's love to bloom into a mosaic of "distinct personages," fitting into each other and living in perfect harmony and peace.

The Holy Spirit is our comforter and companion when life's burdens seem unbearable.

The Holy Spirit gives us the grace to be one another's advocate, counselor, comforter, and companion.

The prayer of Jesus for the Early Church and for the world today is, "Father, I pray that they may all be One" (John 17:21-23).

The Peace of the Risen Lord be with you.

Prayer
Father, Your Son's prayer is for all seasons and times: "Father, I pray that they may all be One." By your Grace let all people come together as brothers and sisters in the Lord Jesus bound by the Holy Spirit. Amen.

SEVENTH SUNDAY OF EASTER

Acts 1:12-14; 1 Peter 4:13-16; John 17:1-11A

UNITY IN PRAYER AND SUFFERING

The period of nine days between Jesus' Ascension and the descent of the Holy Spirit at Pentecost, was a somber and anxious time for a small group of generally simple men and women, "about 120 in all"(Acts 1:15), whose charismatic leader had disappeared in a shocking manner, ridiculed, scourged, and crucified. The community of followers of Jesus was composed of the twelve Apostles, now including Matthias, Jesus' mother Mary, and other men and women, many of them having accompanied Jesus from the time of his baptism, through his journeys, his death, resurrection, and ascension (Acts 1:21-22). In this moment of uncertainty and fear, the disciples were terrified and felt at risk to go out-of-doors. They gathered behind closed doors, devoted themselves to praying (Acts 1:14), and waiting for the arrival of the promised advocate who according to Jesus would strengthen and fire up their faith to promote the urgent message designed by God and destined to change the direction of the world forever.

Luke's account alludes to a group that had gathered with one accord, in a nine-day retreat or novena (nine consecutive days) to pray continuously. This has led to the tradition of observing a novena of prayer and fasting in the days between the Ascension and Pentecost. In addition, the group was preparing for the Jewish feast of Pentecost which required male adults to make a pilgrimage to Jerusalem to participate (Exodus 23:14-17). Again, the disciples might have used the time to study the Scriptures, relating what they read to the life, death, and resurrection of Jesus, and the mission ahead of them. These were times of collaboration and mapping out strategies and protocols for successful evangelization to effect the Great Commission (Matthew 28:19-20). By the tenth day, they seemed to have had sufficient understanding of the Scriptures to enable Peter, a fisherman by trade, whose bravery and command over languages gifted by the Holy Spirit (Acts 2:4), to deliver his first and astonishing speech on Pentecost Day (Acts 2:14-39). Although, Peter's background is little known, some scholars opine he was a skilled fisherman running a relatively huge fishing enterprise. Therefore, it is suggested he might have had some literate background to be asked by Jesus to take care of his Church especially in foreign Rome. He understood being part of Jesus' mission "to restore the kingdom to Israel" (Acts 1:6). His message was one of love and forgiveness, a call to fellow Israelites to recognize Jesus as the fulfillment of God's intention to restore the glorious kingdom of Israel (Zephaniah 3:20). It was the fervent hope of the apostles that after Jesus had established a kingdom, they would govern provinces of the kingdom. Again, this may suggest that at least some of them were educated in some kind of administrative or other endeavors. Jesus might have had a good reason to name James and John "Boanerges, which means 'Men of Thunder.'" (Mark 3:17). Jesus had given the disciples the ability "to understand the Scriptures," starting with the two travelers to Emmaus and his appearance in the Upper Room. Indeed, in the forty days between his resurrection and ascension, Jesus "talked with them (his disciples) about the Kingdom of God" and told them to wait for "the gift the Father had promised" (Acts 1:3), who would empower them to bring the Good News "to the ends of the earth" (Acts 1:8). The question posed by the disciple regarding when Jesus would restore the kingdom to Israel meant that Jesus had earlier talked about establishing the new kingdom of Israel (Acts 1:6) that would comprise all people of the world.

In his Gospel, Saint Luke also underscores the role of Mary, the mother of Jesus, who shares her own experiences of the Holy Spirit when the angel Gabriel appeared to her with a message to be the Mother of God and when she visited

Elizabeth (Luke 1:39-56). In the early days after the ascension, Saint Luke appropriately places Mary among the apostles as a unifying figure on the inauguration of the Church. In many Medieval Artworks, Mary is always at the center with the apostles, showing how she was considered as mother by the apostles (John 19:27).

Suffering comes to the fore in today's second reading as a likely concern during the period of waiting for the Holy Spirit. Reminiscing on the suffering and death of Jesus during their retreat, as well as thinking of the inevitable suffering in their mission of witnessing to message of Jesus, the disciples concluded they were expected to imitate Jesus in his suffering in their daily lives and follow his footsteps by humbly enduring all forms of hardships and suffering. It was a daunting task to preach what they had come to experience in the life of Jesus. Thus, they believed that any afflictions seen in the perspective of sharing the sufferings of Jesus, whose purpose was to show love to others, bring relief to the poor and the needy, and embrace personal pain as a result of mishaps in one's life, would let them receive the rightful compensatory reward when Jesus was revealed in glory during his second coming (Matthew 19:28).

The understanding of Christian suffering and its corresponding reward was communicated to all converts like those that Peter addressed in the second reading. The basis for all this is the Christian belief that our existence here on earth is temporary and that our future home that will bring us everlasting happiness will be found in heaven with the Lord Jesus.

Today in this broken world, everyone called a Christian or a disciple of Jesus, must pray daily, and especially in times of hardships and suffering, to seek the gifts and guidance of the Holy Spirit.

As part of his "Farewell Discourse," at the Last Supper, Jesus provided certain important concerns for reflection by those present during the novena in the Upper Room immediately after his ascension; the Priestly Prayer for himself (John 17:1-5), the intercessory prayer for his apostles (John 17:6-8, 9—19), and all those who would later follow him (John 17:20-26). Jesus' Priestly Prayer came from his Sacred Heart, a heart that beats with the message of unity and love. It is up to us to keep his message in our own hearts as we endeavor to life as true witnesses of Jesus. Nothing else we do could please him more.

How do you bear the costs and sufferings of being a disciple of Jesus?

What gifts of the Holy Spirit have you identified in your life that will contribute to unity among God's people?

How are you using these gifts to help you walk in the footsteps of Jesus?

Prayer,
Father, unite us in love and in fervent prayer to receive the gifts of the Holy Spirit which will strengthen us to spread the message of Jesus by our words and deeds. Amen.

PENTECOST SUNDAY

Acts 2:1-11; 1 Corinthians 12:3b-7, 12-13; John 20:19-23

THE POWER OF THE HOLY SPIRIT IN THE WORLD

The Feast of Pentecost commemorates the descent of the Holy Spirit on the apostles and other believers. It occurred ten days after Jesus' Ascension or fifty days or seven weeks after his resurrection on Easter Sunday, Jesus' victory over death. We understand traditionally that the event occurred in the Upper Room where Jesus celebrated the Passover (Luke 22:12-13). It was also in the Upper Room that Jesus had the Last Supper with his apostles when he instituted the Sacraments of the Holy Orders (Priesthood) and the Eucharist (Luke 22:14-20). It was at the same place where Matthias was chosen and consecrated as an apostle replacing Judas Iscariot (Act 1:15-26). Again, the believers, including women, regularly gathered in the Upper Room to pray (Acts 1:13-14).

Pentecost was originally a Jewish agricultural thanksgiving festival known as Shavuot, or the Feast of Weeks, when the people offered their first fruits of grain harvest to God (Deuteronomy 16:9-12). Since Hellenistic Jews observed Shavuot fifty days after the second day of Passover, they called it Pentecost (meaning fiftieth day). Spiritually, the day was later associated with the giving of the written Torah (Mosaic Law) to commemorate its promulgation on Mount Sinai (Leviticus 23 and Numbers 28). Jewish teachings stated Mount Sinai was the place for sharing the oral Torah. People dedicated the morning of the first day of Shavuot to reciting Exodus 19 and 20 to remember when the Law on Mount Sinai was given. Shavuot is considered the birthday of Judaism, and Pentecost the birthday of Christianity, as well as the fulfillment of Shavuot. The Feast was later also associated with the earlier covenants with Noah after the Flood. Pentecost, Unleavened Bread, and

Tabernacles were the three festivals which brought many "devout Jews from every nation under heaven" to Jerusalem, and vast crowds came into the city (Acts 2:8-11).

The disciples had gathered in prayer when suddenly a strong wind gushed into the entire house and into the Upper Room, followed by dancing tongues of fire that spread out and rested on each of them. Filled with great joy, gladness, eagerness, and with a look of ecstasy on their faces, they went out preaching "in other languages, as the Spirit enabled them to speak" (Acts 2:2-4). The Holy Spirit's anointing would go beyond the "gift of tongues" to reveal "the truth about God" (John 16:13), and the progression in his salvation plan. The Spirit would fill the disciples with power to witness boldly to Jesus "in Jerusalem, in all Judea and Samaria, and to the ends of the earth" (Acts 1:8). The Holy Spirit would lead them to understand the meaning of the Scriptures about Jesus, "beginning with the books of Moses and the writings of all the prophets" (Luke 24:27). The Holy Spirit would empower them to be fearless witnesses who braved martyrdom for Jesus Christ.

Jesus' promise to send the Holy Spirit (Acts 1:8) and the prophecy of the Prophet Joel came true (Joel 3:1-2). The apostles and others received the Holy Spirit and witnessed in languages spoken by pilgrims to the city. The people were overwhelmed by the "miracle of fire" and the "miracle of languages." The depth of knowledge the apostles showed regarding the Scriptures amazed them. When Peter blamed them for their connivance in Jesus' death, they asked the apostles about what to do (Acts 2:37). Peter urged them to repent, accept the Good News, and embrace baptism in Jesus' name to receive forgiveness and the Holy Spirit. About 3,000 believers blessed the fledgling movement. We refer to this historic moment as "the birthday of the Church" or the inauguration of a New Covenant or the New Testament. Also seen as the beginning of the role of the Church in "salvation history," it extended the message of Jesus through the power of the Holy Spirit to believers throughout the world (Matthew 28:18-20).

What is the Holy Spirit to the Church and Christians today? Pentecost is the feast of God's "grace-giving" which gives full meaning to the Easter Sunday story of Jesus Christ. It is a moment of renewal of faith in Jesus through the power of the Spirit and showing Jesus' presence in the world as he promised (Matthew 28:20). In the second reading, Paul admonishes Christians to appreciate their gifts, since various gifts mean different services given by the Spirit to benefit the community as one body.

Traditionally, we associated God's Holy Spirit with the Sacraments of Initiation—Baptism, Confirmation, and the Eucharist—the pouring of water, and the laying on of hands. The 3,000 converts to Christianity on Pentecost Sunday received the Holy Spirit during baptism (Acts 2:38), as well as the baptized at Ephesus when Paul laid his hands on them (Acts 19:5-6). At the Sacrament of Confirmation, we receive the Holy Spirit by the laying on of hands and anointing. However, today's Gospel reading shows the experience of the Holy Spirit is not always in dramatic ways with winds blowing and fires erupting. Instead, Jesus breathed on them and said the words, "Receive the Holy Spirit." He imparted the gift of the Holy Spirit, which empowered the apostles with the Sacrament of Reconciliation. A more peculiar manner was at the home of Cornelius, where the Holy Spirit manifested during Peter's preaching. He immediately directed to baptize the household in the name of Jesus (Acts 10:44-48). Indeed, the Holy Spirit is the principal force behind all the Sacraments and all the other gifts granted to us by the Father through Jesus Christ.

Pentecost confirms that the Holy Spirit is the Spirit of love, peace, and unity in the Trinity. Jesus prays that the Spirit of God would bring his followers together in that same love, peace, and unity. According to Luke, the crowd comprising Jews from every nation understood the Spirit of God's message at Pentecost in their respective languages.

In the story of Babel, the command of God made humanity speak different languages, splitting into diverse communities (Genesis 11:1-9). This condition is reversed at Pentecost by the miracle of God bringing humanity together to understand each other's language and foster unity that will ensure peace and love. The Word of God espousing that God created humanity for love, peace, and unity is now spoken everywhere and understood in all languages in every nation. The Spirit of God keeps the world protected from the Evil One (John 17:15) who maliciously peddles untruths and preaches the ethos of individualism that glorifies ill-gotten wealth, status, pride, selfishness, envy, racism, corruption, hatred, war, and exploitation of the planet. Today, the Holy Spirit is consecrating the New People of God with the mantle of unity, love, compassion, and generosity, urging them to work together to reject all vices and lies to achieve peace. All this makes Pentecost a celebration of faith, hope, and grace, revealing that God's Spirit impels us to work together.

Here is a story from a couple: "When we visited the Franciscan monastery in Washington DC, we heard a story about a monk who was the head gardener. One day, a tourist asked him what he would do differently if he knew that today would be his last day on earth. He thought a moment, and then said, 'I would do nothing different than what I am doing right now. I am living in God's will, so I would change nothing.'"

Would you do anything differently if asked the same question? If you could honestly say no because you are living God's will, then your answer would be the same as that wise monk's. If your answer would be that you would do something different, then you have never recognized God's will in what you do.

Pentecost unites Christians as one body, the family of God, filled with and guided by the seven gifts of the Holy Spirit: wisdom, understanding, counsel, fortitude or courage, knowledge, piety, and the fear of the Lord (Isaiah 11:2-3). When imbued with these divine gifts, the true Christian must respond, as if by instinct, to live by love, joy, peace, patience, kindness, goodness, faithfulness, humility, and self-control (Galatians 5:22-23). Indeed, this is the fruit of the gifts that can

206

contribute to unity and harmony in every community. Do you recognize which of the gifts the Holy Spirit has given you?

Do you accept that any wonderful talent you feel so strongly about may be a gift from the Holy Spirit? How are you able to make the gift produce fruits for the benefit of family, friends, co-workers, community, and the Church? Do you believe that a talent or gift has excellent results when we pray for the guidance of the Holy Spirit to control the negative inclinations and desires that can make us deviate from that purpose?

The Holy Spirit comes to confirm the gift God has planted in us and strengthens us to be committed to them.

Looking at your life, are you convinced that you are living in God's will and reacting nimbly when you become increasingly concerned about the plight of people faced with seemingly unsurmountable problems of poverty, displacement, and disease?

May the power of the Holy Spirit fill your hearts and kindle in you the fire of His love.

The Peace of the Lord be with you.

Prayer to the Holy Spirit:

> *Come, Holy Spirit, fill the hearts of your faithful*
> *and kindle in them the fire of your love.*
> *Send forth your Spirit and they shall be created*
> *and you shall renew the face of the earth.*

Let us pray

> *O God, who have taught the hearts of the faithful*
> *by the light of the Holy Spirit,*
> *grant that in the same Spirit we may be truly wise*
> *and ever rejoice in his consolation.*
> *Through Christ our Lord. Amen.*

THE SOLEMNITY OF THE MOST HOLY TRINITY
(Trinity Sunday)

Exodus 34:4b-6, 8-9; 2 Corinthians 13:11-13; John 3:16-18

THE MYSTERY OF THE NATURE OF GOD REVEALED

The Solemnity of the Most Holy Trinity, which falls on the Sunday after Pentecost, is a Christian Feast celebrated by the Roman Catholic, Anglican, Lutheran, and some Presbyterian and Methodist Churches. The uniqueness of this Feast relative to the other Feasts is that it does not celebrate any historic event, nor is it associated with any person. The Feast commemorates a basic mystery of Christian faith and doctrine to honor the Holy Trinity, the "One Eternal God," existing eternally as three distinct Persons—the Father, the Son, and the Holy Spirit.

The doctrine shows that after the two great historic events of Ascension and Pentecost the Father, the Son, and the Holy Spirit united again in heaven. We feel their presence in the world through the Holy Spirit, who empowers us to profess Jesus as Savior to the glory of God the Father. Since the doctrine of the Trinity is a mystery, it is important to delve into its historical antecedents, current views of the various religious bodies, and the significance of Christian living.

The Latin theologian Tertullian (220 A.D.) first used the words "Trinity," "Person," and "Substance" and explained the Father, the Son, and the Holy Spirit are "One in essence, not One in Person." Some Scripture scholars, however, trace its first usage to Theophilus of Antioch (170 A.D.), bishop of Antioch, the third largest city in the Roman empire after Rome and Alexandria in Egypt. According to Acts 11:26, it was in Antioch that believers in Jesus were first called Christians. Theophilus, used the Greek word *triad* to refer to the Father, Son, and Holy Spirit as "God, his Word, and his Wisdom."

In the fourth century, a priest called Arius taught that the Father and the Son were not one true God or co-eternal. This view, known as Arianism, became popular at the time but the First Ecumenical Council of Nicaea in 325 A.D, and the First Council of Constantinople (381) rejected it. The latter states: "This is the Faith of our baptism that teaches us to believe in the Name of the Father, of the Son and of the Holy Spirit. According to this Faith, there is one Godhead, Power, and Being of the Father, of the Son, and of the Holy Spirit."

They adopted the doctrine in the Nicene Creed as an ancient, expressed faith or symbol derived from Scripture and Tradition. It declared that "the Son is eternally begotten of the Father, while the Holy Spirit proceeds from the Father through the Son."

The Trinity is therefore an article of faith, a mystery which natural reason cannot prove, but is known by divine revelation in Jesus as recorded by the New Testament writers and Early Church Fathers. Such Scriptural texts led to the development of the Doctrine of the Trinity, which was inconsistent with the Jewish belief in God. The Annunciation, as recorded in the Gospel of Luke, shows that the Father sent the angel Gabriel to the Virgin Mary announcing the birth of his Son, to be named Jesus, by the power of the Holy Spirit (Luke 1:31-35). At Jesus' baptism, the Father spoke from heaven and the Spirit descended in the form of a dove (Mark 1:10-11). In "the Great Commission," Jesus instructed his disciples to go "to all peoples" and "baptize them in the name of the Father, the Son, and the Holy Spirit" (Matthew 28:16-20).

The New Testament reveals the Father as creating the world, the Son redeeming it, and the Holy Spirit filling it with the love of the Father and the Son. The Father sent the Son into the world (John 3:16), and the Father and the Son sent the Holy Spirit into the world (John 14:26). Therefore, the Holy Spirit must be distinct from the Father and the Son. Similarly, God the Father and God the Son are distinct (John 8:18) and One (John 10:30). Other verses reveal Jesus is God but is not God the Father (John 1:1, 18; 8:19). Other Trinitarian sayings are "The Grace of our Lord Jesus Christ, the love of God, and the fellowship of the Holy Spirit be with you all" (2 Corinthians 13:13); "God's Spirit guides us to confess that Jesus is Lord" (1 Corinthians 12:3); and, "God the Father chose us and we were made holy by his Spirit to obey Jesus Christ" (1 Peter 1:2).

Christians, particularly Catholics, invoke the name of the Trinity at the beginning of prayers on all occasions, including private prayers and end praising the Trinity. Making the Sign of the Cross alone in the Name of the Holy Trinity is a great prayer for a blessing from the Holy Trinity.

The idea of observing a feast to venerate the Father-Son-Holy Spirit or the Divine Triad began in the tenth century with Bishop Stephen of Belgium. Over the years, the Church's calendar incorporated the feast. It gained popularity in England at Saint Thomas Becket's consecration as Archbishop of Canterbury on the Feast of the Trinity in 1162 and the subsequent observance of the Feast in the Church of Canterbury. In 1334, the Feast gained universal recognition following the decree of Pope John XXII.

For Christians, the Trinity is a mystery that must not be a mathematical puzzle, or an academic principle solved by physicists, philosophers, and theologians. It was a logical trend in the divine realm which the mind "ultimately must know through worship, symbol, and faith." The Greek word for essence is *ousia* and the word for a person is *hypostasis*. However, "hypostasis" does not imply three different human persons, but it means "that which stands on its own," implying distinct or individual realities. One way of trying to understand and explain the Trinity looks at one's sense of vision using the eyes. The eyes are two distinct organs which act as one to produce a completed single image.

Some religious groups, such as the Jehovah's Witnesses and Apostolic Pentecostals, deny the Trinity by saying that Scripture is not explicit about it. They reject the Church's role to interpret Scripture and the assertion that Scripture reveals an interrelated dynamic Trinity at work in salvation history. The Apostles interpreted Scripture with reflection and with the gift of the Holy Spirit as promised by Jesus (Acts 15:22-32; Lk 24:45; Jn 14:16-17). Other groups such as the United Pentecostal Church believe the Father, Son, and Holy Spirit are all One God playing different roles in salvation history, a view known as *Modalism*. This view, propounded before Arianism, asserted that the same God created the world as Father, died on the Cross as Son, and strengthened the apostles as Holy Spirit, thus plainly assuming a historic moment that God was not alive when he died on the Cross.

In the Gospel, we see a significant teaching about the Holy Trinity and an emphasis on the reality of the Holy Spirit and his role in Salvation History.

If we live a sincere Christian life, the Holy Spirit will dwell in us and enable us to fully experience the Father and the Son in our innermost self. The remarkable result of this singular relationship will be Christian charity in genuine love.

The Trinity, which is a "community of relationships," teaches us we live for relationships. Paul's message in the second reading urges Christians to repent and "encourage one another, agree with one another, live in peace," and "greet one another with a holy kiss" as evidence that the Holy Trinity is dwelling in you.

The Peace of the Lord be with you all.

Prayer

O Holy Trinity, let your people acknowledge you and praise you every day as we pray:

> *Glory be to the Father, and to the Son, and to the Holy Spirit. As it was in the beginning, is now and ever shall be, world without end. Amen.*

The Season of Ordinary Time

SECOND SUNDAY OF THE YEAR

Isaiah 49:3. 5-6; 1 Corinthians 1:1-3; John 1:29-34

WE MUST DO BETTER

On a Saturday morning in Tucson, Arizona (USA), January 8, 2011, there was a mass shooting at the parking lot of a shopping center where the Congresswoman Gabrielle Giffords was interacting with her constituents. A shot hit her in the head, six people died, and about eighteen others were wounded. Since then, each year, Tucson celebrates January 8, one of its darkest days, to remember the incident, honor those who died and the survivors, and encourage the community to move forward for change.

The Gun Violence Archive, an organization that tracks gun violence cases in the U.S., defines mass shooting as an incident with at least four people shot, excluding the shooter. In the year 2022, the organization counted about 604 mass shootings and about 40,000 deaths and thousands of people wounded by November 22, 2022. The Walmart massacre (November 22, 2022) in Chesapeake, Virginia, claimed seven persons and other injuries three days after five people lost their lives with dozens injured in a mass shooting at an LGBTQ nightclub in Colorado. Mass shootings continue to occur regularly throughout the world killing thousands of people yearly and changing the lives of survivors. At the January 8, 2025 anniversary of the Tucson shooting, Gabrielle (Gabby) Giffords, now leading an organization working to end gun violence, commented about her life changing so quickly after she was shot, and how she was starting to learn and do things again in life like talking and walking.

Scott Kelly, the American astronaut, was the commander on the International Space Station (ISS, Expedition 26) when the shooting took place in Tucson. His sibling, Mark Kelly (astronaut and politician), was married to Gabrielle

Giffords. Peering down from his spacecraft, Scott Kelly measured the disturbing conflict between good and evil on earth. Scott remarked: "We have a unique vantage point here aboard the International Space Station. As I look out the window, I see a very beautiful planet that seems very inviting and peaceful. Unfortunately, it is not. These days, we are constantly reminded of the unspeakable acts of violence and the damage we can inflict upon one another, not just with our actions, but also with our irresponsible words." He added, "We're better than this. We must do better," (Associated Press, January 11, 2011).

Can we visualize the Lord Jesus looking at Planet Earth from the heavens and seeing a once beautifully created paradise convulsing because of humanity's sins of hatred, violence, prejudice, dishonesty, selfishness, and human untoward actions on earth leading to climate change?

Today's readings establish a link between the Feast of the Baptism of the Jesus when he accepted the rite of purification (Baptism) from John the Baptist. He became mindful of his identity as the Son of God and was filled with the Holy Spirit, symbolized by the presence of a dove (John 1:32). Likewise, he realized his mission as the "the Lamb of God who takes away the sin of the world" (John 1:29).

The first reading is a follow-up to last week's reading from the Book of Isaiah, describing the universal mission of the Suffering Servant to announce God's gratuitous love for his people and his readiness to execute God's plan to save the world from sin.

After his baptism, Jesus preached in towns, villages, and synagogues, and performed miracles (Mark 1:49). This amazed the people who remarked: "This man has authority to give orders to the evil spirits, and they obey him!" (Mark 1:21-28). Two miracles stand out: the healing of a leper (Mark 1:40-45) and the healing of a paralyzed man. During the time of Jesus, leprosy indicated sin that alienated the victim from social life, family, and friends into a state of loneliness, squalor, and disease. The physical condition of lepers was horrible, and all regarded them as the living dead. In the story, Jesus approached the leper, touched him, and showed him love and compassion, and cured his disease.

Humanity is smeared in the leprosy of hatred, violence, prejudice, dishonesty, and selfishness. Like the leper in the Gospel, we must humbly approach Jesus and beg for healing. Are you sincerely approaching Jesus to heal you of your personal leprosy of hate, pride, and prejudice? Do you find it difficult to show love and compassion to those pushed to the fringes of society because of birth, poverty, or place of origin?

The story of the paralytic is essentially about four good friends who helped a friend in need. The story does not show how far the four people walked or traveled with the seriously physically disabled man to reach Jesus. They faced the problem of entering the house blocked by an immense crowd. Unperturbed by the desperate situation, they devised a challenging plan using a ladder to climb to the rooftop while carrying the paralytic. They widened an opening and lowered their friend right at the feet of Jesus. Jesus might have looked up and smiled at the bewildered and yet courageous strangers with admiration because of their faith and tenacity of purpose. Their faith, love, compassion, empathy, and persistence for their suffering friend contributed to his eventual healing.

It is true that boundaries do not limit love. What friend or person do you know who needs love and compassion? Who do you want to bring to Jesus for healing? Is it your wife, husband, child, or co-worker troubled by a sad habit—a kind of sin—who you want to bring to Jesus for healing? Sometimes, Jesus wants to bring healing to others through us. Like the four friends who carried the paralytic, are you a good friend to persons in need, like older adults or those depressed, marginalized, and handicapped who lack the ability to function properly physically, mentally, or socially?

We ought to strengthen each other's sense of goodness. We can achieve this when we embrace forgiveness, are cloaked in love as taught by Jesus, and eschew violence, bitterness, grudges, and revenge. Such negative attitudes are detrimental to human progress, peace, hope, joy, and spiritual well-being.

The second reading is an example of Christian resolve. Saint Paul's reception in Athens was lukewarm (Acts 17:16-33) but it did not discourage him. He sailed further on to Corinth and successfully preached the gospel. The results of his preaching and missionary activities in Corinth were remarkable, especially when Sosthenes, the head of the Jewish synagogue in Corinth, became a Christian. However, the Jews of Corinth appealed to the new Roman Consul, Gallio, to persecute Paul. When the Gallio refused, the mob attacked the head of the synagogue, convinced that he had prevented Paul's persecution. They manhandled Sosthenes in the Consul's presence (Acts 18:12-17).

Sosthenes became Paul's friend in the Church and is believed by others to have been a co-author of the Letter to the Corinthians. Paul referred to Sosthenes as "my brother." We would have a perfect world if we saw ourselves as brothers and sisters in Christ Jesus, our Lord.

To echo Scott Kelly, humanity must strive to do better for itself and Planet Earth than it is doing.

From today forward, your mission must be to bring God's love to all peoples.

Think of the ways you can show compassion and generosity to your fellow human beings, family, friends, neighbors, especially the needy, sick, and elderly.

As you reflect on the love of Jesus for you, endeavor to bring the same love to someone.

Look for daily signs of how your efforts can change your life positively and the lives of those around you.

The Peace of the Lord be with you.

Prayer
Father, Your Son laid down his life to save us because of his love and expects we follow his footsteps. As my people deeply meditate on Jesus' great love, may they become his disciples of love, compassion, and generosity. Amen.

THIRD SUNDAY OF THE YEAR

Isaiah 8:23–9:3; 1 Corinthians 1:10-13. 17; Matthew 4:12-23

BROTHERS AND SISTERS IN GOD'S KINGDOM

A couple of years ago, on a humid afternoon, I was taking a walk through Prospect Park in Brooklyn, New York, and I passed by two women and their children. Apparently, the women were engaged in a kind of adult chatter in which their children also took an interest. One child, about seven years old, was incessantly asking his mother if the person who was the topic of their conversation was a Jew. "Mama, is he Jewish?" the boy asked several times.

From infancy, we seem to gain certain erroneous opinions and perceptions from home, peer groups, and schools; as we grow, such seemingly small foibles develop into sheer prejudice, hatred, mistrust, and a sense of superiority over those from different social, religious, or national backgrounds. We categorize our minds into extreme cases of suspicion regarding others who differ from us culturally, socially, or academically. With raised eyebrows, smirks on our faces, and arrogant shrugs of our shoulders, we frequently inquire about these "other" people: He's not American, is he? What's her background? Are they Chinese or Africans? Is the man a Northerner? Is the woman a Southerner? Is the person she wants to marry Ghanaian, Nigerian, French, British, German, or Spanish?

The story of Jonah is a case in point. Jonah grew up within a biased society, taught to believe that his tribe was superior to all others. He learned to dislike and mistrust the people of Nineveh and the foreign Assyrians. Besides, moral life in the city of Nineveh had totally worsened; most Ninevites obsessed over physical needs and cared less about nourishing their spiritual lives. Israelites, on the other hand, lived much differently. The Assyrian Empire looked down upon Israel as a vassal state, treated her people harshly, and deported them from their own country as a deterrent to Israel considering any rebellion.

As noted last week, humanity seems to head towards self-destruction with violence igniting and exploding all around the globe. Several countries fight or have fought in drawn out wars, driven by ethnic power struggles or influenced by distorted nationalistic sentiments. We have seen the devastating effects of this throughout the world: the Middle East, the Balkans, the Central African Republic, the Democratic Republic of Congo, Liberia, Sierra Leone, La Cote D'Ivoire, Sri Lanka, and recently in Ukraine, a war described by most people as ridiculous and totally unnecessary.

It becomes increasingly clear that prejudice, hatred, violence, and dishonesty poison our world today. Openly, we decline opportunities to learn about other ethnic groups and religions. We do not respect the way of life and beliefs of others; hence, we cannot live together in peace. The old concept of the village (whereby individuals in the community interacted as brothers and sisters and shared things in common) is no longer the case in our so-called global village now tainted with individualism, greediness, corruption, and disregard for others.

Today's readings again emphasize the deep-rooted belief in divine presence in the world saving it from destroying itself. The Gospels plainly present Jesus as the Light of the world (John 8:12) drawing all peoples living in spiritual darkness to himself. He is the Light rising like the first light of the day over a murky world. He is also the Light that fills the hearts of those who live in darkness with "abundant joy and great rejoicing."

After his baptism in the Jordan, Jesus went for a retreat in the desert mountains during which the devil tempted him (Luke 4:1-13). Then, beginning from Galilee and settling in Capernaum, he started his public ministry preaching the Word of God after hearing of John's arrest (Luke 4:18-20). He preached to remind us we are brothers and sisters created by

God, whose kingdom has been established for everyone. Therefore, if we allow our minds to be riddled with prejudice and hatred, we cannot appreciate this priceless gift from God.

In the narrative regarding Jonah, God healed his prejudiced mind. He went to Nineveh with a message of repentance and forgiveness. The people exhibited genuine repentance, which resulted in peace and harmony. The story of Jonah teaches about the ability to repent and to be forgiven by God. Jonah recognized and accepted God's infinite love towards other peoples.

The Gospel reading of today describes how Jesus chose some people for help in his glorious act of redemption. God's Plan of Salvation is about people who are also called to play the crucial role of inviting others into the new kingdom, and of helping them to know, love, and serve God. Hearing the Word of God inspires faith, and therefore, the Word ought to be preached throughout the entire world (Matthew 28:19-20).

Jesus called his first group of disciples who were fishermen, Peter, Andrew, James and John, to join in the new evangelization. They immediately detached themselves from many physical things, followed Jesus, and identified with his way of life. His presence at the shore was so powerful to provoke an immediate positive response in his call to discipleship. Can you allow the powerful personality and divine grace of Jesus to assist you in detaching yourself from a habit or weakness that is detrimental to you personally, or family and community?

When we cannot find our way in a busy city despite our sophisticated gadgets for directions, we are relieved when a police officer or some kind person courteously offers to lead us to our destination. In the same way, we are grateful when we cannot find an item we want to buy in a large shop and a sales associate escorts us to its location. An employee who merely points to the item is not a good one, behaving in a way that goes against their training.

221

We are also called to walk alongside people who are desperate and looking for meaning in life, leading them to know, love, and follow Jesus. Is your lifestyle leading your family, a friend, or a neighbor to Jesus? Are you boldly preaching about Jesus at your workplace or at a place of camaraderie?

Jesus knows our strengths and limitations, sometimes impulsive like Simon Peter, or explosive like James and John, or reckless and immature like Judas Iscariot. Jesus approached and called each person to follow him, transformed the person, and made him or her a blessing to others. Jesus comes to us at the door of our homes and hearts (Revelations 3:20) to offer us salvation. Our mission is to be altruistic and generous towards one another and to communicate in ways that bind people together, resolve issues, and heal differences.

The second reading shows Saint Paul's worry about factions, tensions, dissensions, and disputes in the Church at Corinth. Spirituality and moral life in the Church had weakened, giving way to apathy, nepotism, envy, suspicion, power struggles, selfishness, sycophancy, and slanderous criticism. Each group claimed to belong to an authority in the church, like Apollos, a learned and influential man, or Cephas (Peter), or Paul. Paul told them that Christ did not portion himself out to the apostles. He, therefore, urged them to preach as one group, baptized in the name of Jesus Christ, about the Messiah's crucifixion for salvation.

Are there divisions in our parishes and dioceses? Are you part of the defamatory criticisms not promoting progress, instead aligning with character assassination?

What is the level of your participation in the life of the church or local community?

As witnesses to the Word of God and God's new kingdom, let us endeavor to maintain the unity of the Christian communities and ensure that we all work for peace in the Church and in the world.

Words can hurt when used as put downs. How can you replace the words that put others down with words and terms that serve to lift others up instead?

How are you, your brother's keeper?

What are some ways you can help recreate and preserve peace in the community through your kind words, attitudes, and actions?

The Peace of the Lord be with you.

Prayer
Father, soften the hearts of all people to receive each other as brothers and sisters and melt their prejudices so they will live in genuine peace and lasting love. Amen.

FOURTH SUNDAY OF THE YEAR

Zephaniah 2:3; 3:12-13; 1 Corinthians 1:26-31; Matthew 5:1-12a

THE BE-ATTITUDES THAT BRING PEACE AND HAPPINESS

From time immemorial, there have been many theories purporting to give answers to the human quest for true happiness in the world. The ideas of the ancient Greek philosophers like Socrates, Plato, Aristotle (known as the triumvirate of ancient Greek philosophers), the Stoics, and many others, provoke feelings of déjà vu as they opine similar conclusions that true happiness is not derived from wealth, fame, status, power, good health, and excellent relationships. Such circumstances are not ends to themselves because they create the sense of inadequacy; hence, there is always the insatiable hunger to get more. The desire for more things creates anxiety or fear which erodes happiness. Thus, a school of thought associated with Epicurean ideas gaining currency currently suggests that overcoming anxiety or fear would be the only good thing to guide one to happiness.

Social Sciences studying human behavior in its social, cultural, and scientific aspects have joined in the search for how one can find happiness. The studies address many existential concerns, such as, "How does a person obtain happiness?" or "What are the ways to cultivate happiness?" or "What are the simple steps to finding happiness?"

Society has several people making it to the top in terms of wealth, status, and fame. However, many acknowledge that their situation has not brought ultimate contentment in their lives. They have sought the alternate way of viewing life through the lens of faith. They have discovered that life has a spiritual element as essential as air, food, drink, and love. They have found Jesus Christ to be the greatest model through whom they can achieve joy, peace, and happiness.

We are following the trails of Jesus as he tours Galilee spreading the Word of God and healing the sick. Many years before Jesus, the prophets, like Zephaniah in today's first reading, had preached about the Word of God and the need for the people to be meek and humble. Zephaniah, the seventh century prophet also prophesied before the Babylonian exile against moral decadence, arrogance, prejudice, and apathy to religion because of widespread wealth, prosperity, and well-established foreign relations between Israel and neighboring nations. The prophet forewarned the leaders of Israel who ignored the needy about imminent punishment, while the poor who relied on God would receive protection.

In the second reading, Saint Paul writes that God chooses the poor, lowly, and rejected, "those who count for nothing," over the arrogant. He urges the Christians to turn their lives into living sacrifices for God and for others.

This kind of disclosure manifests in Jesus' teaching, notably called the Sermon on the Mount (Matthew 5-7). He delivered the sermon soon after his Baptism in the Jordan River by John the Baptist. According to the Gospel of Matthew, Jesus had selected his first disciples before meeting the crowd following him, who looked for spiritual nourishment and happiness. Jesus' ascent to the mountain to deliver his sermon (hence, The Sermon on the Mount) is reminiscent of Moses' proclamation of the Law on Mount Sinai. This makes Jesus the New Moses proclaiming the Law from the mountain. Again, Matthew's emphasis that Jesus "opened his mouth" (as in some translations) to teach his disciples is a reference to the Old Testament times when God "touched" or "opened the mouths" of prophets to speak, signifying that the speakers were messengers of God (Jeremiah 1: 9; Isaiah 6:6-7). Saint Luke has a parallel version of the Sermon on the Mount known as the Sermon on the Plain because Jesus preached from a tableland (Luke 6:20-23).

In the Sermon on the Mount, Jesus presents the general ideals of discipleship. He teaches about true happiness, salt and light, the Law and Justice, anger, marriage, good relationships, general prayer (the Lord's Prayer), forgiveness, fasting, and many more. Jesus recommends a higher standard of conduct for his followers founded mainly on love, selflessness, and forgiveness.

Today's Gospel presents the Beatitudes which are part of the Sermon on the Mount. The Beatitudes are nine declarations or proverb-like sayings of Jesus, which mark the grand opening of his teachings. Each Beatitude promises a blessing, happiness or "divine favor" to those who affirm the qualities and virtues espoused by the Beatitudes. Although the reward of happiness seems to be set in the future, observing them will ensure current "divine joy and perfect happiness" to anyone who accepts them. For example, the one who is a peacemaker will be a peaceful and happy person who can also promote peace in the community.

The word blessedness comes from the Latin word *beatus* or *beatitudo* from which is derived the word Beatitude. Though stated in simple words, the Beatitudes have profound meanings acting as a "road map of life," or virtues ("Be-attitudes") that Christians ought to apply to their everyday lives. Such insightful virtues establish close relationship with God and one another to bring about peace and happiness.

"Blessed are the poor in spirit, for theirs is the kingdom of Heaven."

The phrase "poor in spirit" refers to a state of humility when one does not consider oneself better than the other. It is "a spiritual condition of poverty," a recognition of one's need for God, when one acknowledges he or she possesses nothing but relies on God's providence rather than on physical things. One makes a complete surrender to God. Such a person accepts humility as "a sign of godly strength and purpose, not weakness." In Christianity, the "poor in spirit" are those who humbly acknowledge their need for God and humbly surrender to him with absolute faith and trust. The term

"Islam" means "surrender (to God), in humility" exhorting believers to "bow in humility before God." Pride shames and destroys a person, but a lowly spirited or humbled person is fortunate and blessed (Proverbs 3:34; 1 Peter 5:5; James 4:6). The proud will be humbled, but the humble will be made great (Luke 14:11; 18:14). As the archetype of humility, Jesus succumbs to human cruelty and death and God raises him from the dead. Again, Jesus teaches we must conduct ourselves like children in our attitude towards many of the things in the world (Matthew 18:3-5).

"Blessed are they who mourn, for they shall be comforted."

The Beatitude refers to those who grieve or mourn over their sins and repent to receive comfort and forgiveness from God. Accepting to follow Jesus means total surrender of one's will which can cause grief because surrendering to God's will is the path to the Cross. In this Beatitude, Jesus reassures his followers of God's presence and protection in times of grief.

"Blessed are the meek, for they shall possess the earth."

The word "meek" comes from the Greek word *praus*. Typically, it pertains to a strong or wild animal, like a horse or an ox, disciplined to respond to its owner. In this context, a meek person is under the absolute control of God, "in thought, word, will, emotion, and action." The meek or humble person is, however, not physically or emotionally weak. Rather, while accepting God in their lives, they are resolute in faith and less affected by the vagaries of the secular world.

"Blessed are they who hunger and thirst for righteousness, for they shall be satisfied."

The words "hunger" and "thirst" are human drives that connote a deep need and strong passion for something. The

227

word "righteousness" implies a virtuous and morally upright lifestyle. Jesus is the epitome of righteousness, and in this Beatitude, those passionately longing for justice and honesty will receive copious blessings and contentment.

"Blessed are the merciful, for they shall obtain mercy."

Mercy and charity are expressed through love and compassion for the poor, the sick, and the needy by providing them help, kindness, and forgiveness (Matthew 6:14-15). A merciful person experiences an emotional attachment towards those who are hurting and will reach out to them. Jesus is our greatest model of Divine Mercy and entreats us to be compassionate, kind, and forgiving. Indeed, mercy and charity offered to the needy is actually offered to Jesus Christ (Matthew 25:40).

"Blessed are the pure of heart, for they shall see God."

Jesus criticized the double standards of the teachers of the Law. They presented themselves obsequiously in the synagogues and in public, while within their hearts, they harbored "violence and selfishness" (Matthew 23). Jesus teaches we wash our hearts clean of hypocrisy, prejudice, and selfishness. We need to desist from outward righteousness that can be pretenses from our genuine feelings. Thus, Jesus blesses those who have purged themselves from inside out, refraining from self-serving behavior, and providing help and support for the marginalized.

"Blessed are the peacemakers, for they shall be called sons of God."

A peacemaker possesses amicable disposition and believes God is the ultimate source of peace. A peaceful environment is necessary to enhance our lives. Therefore, we must seek reconciliation to restore peace and harmony (Romans

14:19). God regards the person who reconciles opposing parties as a true son or daughter of God.

"Blessed are they who suffer persecution for justice's sake for theirs is the kingdom of Heaven."

Living according to Jesus' message in a world that defines its own values can lead to persecution. This kind of suffering can be the consequence of one's belief and commitment to God and his Word.

"Blessed are you when they insult you and persecute you and utter every kind of evil against you falsely because of me. Rejoice and be glad, for your reward will be great in heaven."

This last Beatitude shifts to the second person to reflect the trials and persecutions of Christians at the time Matthew and ever since Christianity was born.

Let us frequently read the Beatitudes. How can you carry them in your heart?

Let us endeavor to live with hope and pray for the strength to incorporate the message of the Beatitudes into our everyday connections.

How can you become the positive change you want to see in yourself, family, and community as you live according to the Beatitudes?

The Peace of the Lord be with you.

Prayer
Father, let the Beatitudes of Your Son become first among the routine things we look up to in life. May the Beatitudes guide us to the happiness and joy that we seek in life. Amen.

FIFTH SUNDAY OF THE YEAR

Isaiah 58:7-10; 1 Corinthians 2:1-5; Matthew 5:13-16

BE SALT AND LIGHT OF THE WORLD

The first reading originates from a chapter in the Book of Isaiah (Third Isaiah) subtitled, "True Fasting." Fasting is abstinence from food or drink for an extended period. It is a worldwide phenomenon practiced as a religious or cultural act. In some religions, fasting is a spiritual exercise to establish a close relationship with a deity. In other traditions, the family fasts when mourning a dead member as a prayer for the deceased. In modern times, however, fasting or reducing food intake is a popular way of quickly achieving a good physical shape.

While in exile in Assyria (597-538 B.C.), the Jews were far away from the Temple in Jerusalem to worship and offer sacrifices. They observed fasting and kept the Sabbath as a way of worshiping Yahweh. This ancient practice of fasting continued after the return from captivity, particularly when they met a dilapidated Jerusalem and Temple, and they had to rebuild the city and the Temple. The socio-political life of the people continued to deteriorate; corrupt officials manned both the civil and religious courts, the tax structures were appalling, and disputes and conflicts were widespread. The people were, however, upset that God's favor was not reciprocating their pious practice of fasting to ease them from continued abject poverty and misery. They lamented that God had turned a deaf ear to their pleas and problems: "Look at our elaborate fasting," the people said, "and Yahweh does not favor us," they complained (Isaiah 58:3a). Apparently, they understood fasting as putting God under obligation to intervene and improve their dire social state. God was to blame for ignoring their extensive public display of religious zeal in fasting.

230

The sense of dejection was exacerbated by Isaiah's criticism that their fasting was mere outward form of worship. According to Isaiah, the people dishonored the spirit of fasting when it did not lead to inner conversion and a positive attitude towards others. While they fasted, they pursued their own interests by oppressing and exploiting the poor. Their understanding of faith, as well as the shape and form of worship, were dishonest, Isaiah told them.

As a prophet, Isaiah's mandate from God was to announce what God desired from his people as proper fasting. They must set the oppressed free and show sincere love, unbiased justice, and compassion towards one another. They had to share food with the hungry, cloak the poor, shelter the homeless, provide for the sick and the needy, and avoid nepotism. Their acts of love and mercy would induce and spark off God's light or Spirit that would subdue "the darkness and the gloom" surrounding them.

During the time of Jesus, the nature, eagerness, and intention for fasting had not changed. It was common, competitive, overtly staged, and self-righteous. Jesus' disciples were not seen fasting and this surprised the disciples of John the Baptist (Matthew 9:14). Jesus echoed the concerns of Isaiah and forthrightly rejected the excessive elaboration regarding fasting, such as showing oneself in public places when fasting (Matt 6:18). He condemned similar popular and big performances when praying or giving to charity (Matthew 6:1-8). In addition, he said the greatest in the Kingdom of Heaven were those who were humble, like children (Mathew 18:4): they would be heirs of the Kingdom (Matthew 19:14).

The world today is like a stage with a huge blend of characters performing acts and scenes that have lost every godly element. Religion, fasting, and praying have become nothing less than persuading God to provide our desires to be wealthy, famous, and powerful, and to be healed of our human disorders and muddles resulting mostly from our selfish interests. Love is no more divine. An act of love does not radiate from one's love of God and neighbor. Love and charity become relevant merely at the human level meant to be reciprocated. The absence of paybacks or profits renders the act of love unnecessary. An individual's needs take priority over those of others. Truth is no longer regarded as absolute, standard, or definite. Others redefine truth severally as it suits the individual's conscience.

Today's Gospel is a continuation of the Beatitudes, additional directives given by Jesus to his disciples. Jesus uses the metaphor of salt and light to describe the urgent mission of Christians to prevent the gloom around the globe, the violent human relationships, widespread hate, and hurtful revenge. We must be salt to a world that is oblivious to the joy in knowing God and serving him and neighbor. The essence of our humanness is to be salt, and we must not misplace or replace it. Salt also signifies purity and reminds us to let the virtues of goodness, integrity, and righteousness be our mark in all we do in life. Again, salt is used to preserve food, and that reminds us to preserve the gift of faith and our Christian moral principles and let others benefit from us.

On Holy Saturday, we acknowledge Christ as Light of the world glowing in the darkness surrounding it (John 1:5). We are also called to be the light that glows from a hilltop or a lighthouse, revealing God's presence on earth and in every human being, especially those who need love and care, by providing them clothing, attention, justice, and compassion.

The Prophet Isaiah in the first reading, and Jesus in the Beatitudes, show us how we can shine the light of Christ in us: the light of love, compassion, goodness, forgiveness, wisdom, perseverance, patience, humility, and respect. In the second reading, Paul shares the light of faith, "Jesus Christ, and him crucified," to the Christians in Corinth; he shows how the Holy Spirit enhances one's belief in God and reliance on his power and wisdom. The antiphon to the Psalmist's song "The just man is a light in darkness to the upright," shows the graciousness of beaming with the light of Christ if one is just and "conducts his affairs with justice" (Responsorial Psalm).

232

How can you become salt and light in your home, in the community, among friends, and in the world?

What are some random acts of kindness that you can perform daily to reflect the message and teachings of the Beatitudes?

Jesus Christ, "The Word of God is the source of life, and this life brought light to humanity" (John 1:4). As you hear the Word and receive the Eucharist, will you accept the challenge to be the light of Christ wherever you are?

The Peace of the Lord be with you.

Prayer
Father, let Your Light, Jesus Christ, shine through the hidden places of our hearts. Help us to be kind and considerate to one another and encourage each other to be faithful to Your Word. Amen.

SIXTH SUNDAY OF THE YEAR

Sirach 15:15-20; 1 Corinthians 2:6-10; Matthew 5:17-37
or Matthew 5:20-22a, 27-28, 33-34a, 37

BLESSED ARE THEY WHO FOLLOW THE LAW OF THE LORD

The Responsorial Psalm sets the theme for today's liturgy: "Blessed are they who follow the Law of the Lord." Its direct opposite is: "Cursed are they who do not follow the Law of the Lord." Both statements suggest that people have two choices in relating to God regarding their way of life on earth. They also teach us about God's respect for the freedom of human will. Since God is all good and perfect, we understand that the evil which comes from not obeying God's Law cannot come from God. We are, therefore, admonished to choose to follow the Law of God without reservation.

Every society, ethnic group, or community has a history (oral and written) rooted in its culture, traditions, beliefs, and customs. These values, principles, and social norms have symbolic meanings passed on from one generation to the next. The goal is to perfect the behavior of members towards the common good. The values instill in people the sense of purpose in life: integrity, individual and collective responsibilities, religion, self-sacrifice, a sense of belonging, and strong morals. When a society disregards its values and rules, there are serious and harmful consequences like immorality, decadence, hatred, conflict, crime, greed, clamor for power, corruption, and lack of peace and harmony.

The Torah, or the Law of Moses (the first five Books of the Hebrew Bible or Old Testament, also known as the Pentateuch in Christianity) was the most sacred text in Judaism. The Torah rooted itself in believing in the one true God and, through it, a person became connected to God. It originated from God's covenant with Israel, guiding its people's lives, beliefs, and rituals. It required the total allegiance of every Israelite to the covenant, which ensured their protection during the journey to the Promised Land. The Torah contained teachings and instructions believed to have been written by Moses through divine revelation.

While crossing the desert, the people of Israel encountered different ethnic groups who influenced them with their traditions and religions. Moses explained to them to follow God's Law so that God would bless and take care of them. God's Law, Moses told them, was not too difficult to follow, nor was it beyond their understanding (Deuteronomy 30:11-14). The people were, however, free to make their own choice "between blessing and a curse... between good and evil, between life and death." Moses counseled them to "choose life" and "Love the Lord your God, obey him and be faithful to him" (Deuteronomy 30:15-20).

It became apparent during the leadership of Joshua that many of the people had abandoned the precepts and commandments of Yahweh, which guided Israel as a nation. They worshiped foreign gods and accepted the traditions and ways of life of neighboring nations. Joshua summoned them to Shechem and confronted them about their wrongful behavior. He urged them to fear the Lord and serve him in sincerity and in truth (Joshua 24:14). But even if serving the Lord was undesirable to them, Joshua said, he and his household would serve and obey the Lord.

Earlier in the history of Israel, Jacob had urged people to rid themselves of foreign idols (Genesis 35:2). In later years, Solomon, Jeroboam, and the kings of Judah and the Northern Kingdom "built places of worship for false gods" (1 Kings 14:23). At the time of King Ahab, Prophet Elijah challenged priests of Baal and the people to decide between God and Baal (1 Kings 18:21). The Prophet Daniel and his colleagues would not kowtow to a golden statue presented as a god erected by King Nebuchadnezzar (Daniel 3:18). The prophets consistently reminded the people of Israel about the urgent need to abide by God's laws, warning about dangerous consequences if they disobeyed God.

Today's first reading from Sirach reminds us we have freedom of will in choosing our way of life. The author recommends we appreciate the value of wisdom which God gives to those who fear him. He also contends that failure to trust in God is denouncing God, the kind of sin that will lead one to a wrong path leading to disaster or death.

Ben Sira, a resident in Jerusalem about 200 B.C., wrote the Book of Sirach (or Ecclesiasticus) in the Hebrew language. Fifty years later, the book was translated into Greek by his unnamed grandson in Egypt who added a foreword. There was a clarion call to people in diaspora (Jews outside Palestine), particularly young women and men in Alexandria, Egypt, inclined or forced to adopt the Greek culture to learn the Jewish religion and custom. In the foreword, the author states that the legacy of wisdom, tradition, and moral instruction which Jewish people had received through "the Law of God, the Prophets, and later writers" was "a wealth of valuable teachings" they must not ignore.

As in the other books of Wisdom, the author notes, "the fear of the Lord is the beginning of wisdom," and "to fear the Lord is the flower of Wisdom that blossoms with peace and good health" (Sirach 1:14-18). Likewise, God withholds his grace and blessings from those who denounce him (Sirach 15:7-9) and denying God has consequences. Therefore, we ought to choose to stay close to God and serve the Lord alone.

In the Gospels, John the Baptist is seen as the last of the Old Testament prophets reminding people to follow God and his laws. He prepares them to receive the new Moses, Jesus Christ, who provides the authentic interpretation of God's Law.

According to the Gospel of Matthew, Jesus goes up to the mountain in the same way as Moses to receive the Law. Again, like Moses, Jesus comes a couple of steps down from the mountain to meet a large crowd, and with his disciples around him, gives them the Law. During his preaching (today's Gospel), Jesus declares he had not come to nullify the Law but fulfill it by providing its authentic meaning as God really intended it. Indeed, he asserts the Law is of primordial essence (some traditions believed that the Law even existed before creation), which would endure until the end of time, and that, those who live by God's Law and teach others to observe them would be called the "greatest in the kingdom of heaven."

While the Pharisees and the Scribes, the so-called role models, see themselves as righteous before the Law, Jesus perceives them, vis-à-vis the Law, as hypocrites due to their superficial knowledge of the Law and sanctimonious attitude. Therefore, Jesus advises his disciples and the people that their way of life must outshine the Pharisees who only give lip service to the Law.

Jesus offers a high standard explanation about the true meaning of the values and principles of God's Law. For example, Jesus upholds the sixth of the Ten Commandments, "You shall not murder" (Exodus 20:13), and its punishment of death (Numbers 35:31), but he expands its interpretation. Murder is a sin, and one should not take the life of another person. But Jesus explains further that murder as sin goes beyond the physical act of killing to plain evil thoughts, feelings, attitudes, gossips, hatred, and lying about another person; this is tantamount to character assassination. In the same vein, though the mind can commit immorality, marriage is indissoluble, and couples must be sincere with one another. Jesus offers a new teaching about love, mercy, compassion, forgiveness, and justice. It is when we recognize God and relate to him closely that we will know his love; it is when we know and experience God's love that we can show love to others; it is when we show mercy and compassion to others that God will be merciful to us; and it is when we forgive others that we will be forgiven.

Are we going to build bridges in a world beset with ethnic tensions, hatred, and prejudice, and see ourselves as sisters and brothers, or will we choose evil and actively ferment violence and racial tensions? Are we obsessed with power, wealth, self-esteem, greed, or pride? The purpose of the Law is to guard against such wrong choices that will lead us astray.

The message of Saint Paul (second reading) is for Christians to accept Jesus as the wisdom of God instead of accepting "the wisdom of this age." According to Paul, this is a doctrine of truth hidden in the lives of the Jewish Patriarchs but now revealed by the Holy Spirit in Jesus. Indeed, "in Jesus is revealed a new wisdom" (1 Cor 2:6-10). Jesus personifies the Law of God and a new way of life. The new Law is designed for the new "People of God," saved by the sacrifice of Jesus on the Cross, leading the world to God. As Scott-Hahn comments, Jesus' "Gospel reveals the deeper meaning and purpose of the Ten Commandments and the moral Law of the Old Testament. But His Gospel also transcends the Law. He demands a morality far greater than that accomplished by the most pious Jews, the scribes and Pharisees."

We gather around the altar of grace to listen to Jesus' teaching, and he will feed us with his spiritual food, the Eucharist.

Let us allow the Holy Spirit to help us understand the teachings of Jesus so we can stay close to God the Father and accept his Son Jesus Christ as our Lord and Savior.

The Peace of the Lord be with you.

Prayer
Father, help us to meditate on the Beatitudes daily. May the Holy Spirit enlighten and strengthen us to humbly abide by these profound teachings of Your Son. Amen.

SEVENTH SUNDAY OF THE YEAR

Leviticus 19:1-2; 17-18; 1 Corinthians 3:16-23; Matthew 5:38-48

"BUT I SAY TO YOU, LOVE YOUR ENEMIES..."

The Ancient Near East, now known as the Middle East, has often been described as the "cradle of civilization." Noted for its year-round mechanized agricultural systems and general education, particularly in astrology, mathematics, and writing systems, it was also well-known for its centralized governments and very elaborate law codes. Kingdoms and empires in the region enacted scores of law codes dated before 2000 B.C.

One such code was the famous Code of Hammurabi, enacted by the sixth Babylonian king, Hammurabi, about 1790 B.C. Other cultures and kingdoms within the relatively small geographical area adopted the Code of Hammurabi almost in its entirety. It was included in the Hittite Law, the Assyrian Law, and the Mosaic Law. An almost completely intact copy of the original Code of Hammurabi, comprising about 282 laws, has survived over the millennia and is preserved at the Louvre in Paris. The codes were nearly the equivalent of the constitutions or justice systems of modern democracies. It was difficult for a king or emperor to affect an arbitrary change upon them. Some codes contained the concept of "presumed innocence," that is, the accused person was innocent until proven guilty with overt evidence. Such laws survived in the Roman Empire at the time of Jesus.

In the Old Testament, this system of law captioned the Code of Hammurabi as "life for life, eye for eye, tooth for tooth, hand for hand, foot for foot, burn for burn, wound for wound, bruise for bruise" (Exodus 21:23-25) or as *lex talionis*, a Latin expression meaning "tit-for-tat" or "law of retaliation." For example, the Code of Hammurabi stated that, "If a man puts out the eye of an equal, his eye shall be put out. If a man knocks the teeth out of another man, his own teeth will be knocked out."

"An eye for an eye, a tooth for a tooth," as an expression today means that for someone treated wrongly, retaliation or compensation must be in kind. By this meaning, we may judge the *lex talionis* as unusually harsh, especially when the Mosaic Law believed such a law emanated from God.

This, however, was not what the *lex talionis* meant. It was not an encouragement to take revenge or retaliation, but to restrain a victim from exceeding a punishment beyond the severity or brutality of a crime. It was against excessive retaliation or vengeance and therefore did not recommend or encourage retaliation like a wrong or injury. Again, the basis of the "an eye for an eye and a tooth for a tooth" type of law was to guard against people taking the law into their own hands to punish minor offenses with severe punishments or uncontrolled vengeance. For example, if someone slapped a man or lost a tooth or eye in a fight, that did not mean the culprit should suffer capital punishment.

Furthermore, the law sought to "protect the weak and the poor against injustice at the hands of the rich and powerful." It promoted a concept of providing "proportionate punishment" or "equitable retaliation for an offended party" under the maxim "let the punishment fit the crime." Thus, the code "defined and restricted the extent of retaliation."

In Mosaic Law, retaliation or a proportionate punishment could come as monetary reimbursements or similar forms of compensation for minor offenses (Exodus 21). Again, sometimes the preference at the time was forgiveness for a wrongdoing (Leviticus 19:18). There is ample evidence in the Torah to conclude that the *lex talionis* was only a guiding principle in the Jewish culture and not to be carried out literally, although Leviticus writes about two incidents that resulted in stoning (Leviticus 24:10-16; Numbers 25:1-16).

In other religions or cultures, such as Islam, there was a literal interpretation of the law. Thus, in the Shariah Law (the Sacred Law of Islam), a minor offense of stealing or shoplifting could lead to a thief's hand being cut off in punishment. Indeed, the philosophy of law in the world today is basically akin to the *lex talionis*. We enact laws to ensure that punishments meted out either "in kind or in cash" are not disproportionate to the original wrongdoing.

Biblical scholars agree that Matthew's Gospel shows Jesus as the promised Messiah, teaching about the Law of God. The book has more Jewish traditions than the others. Again, Matthew presents Jesus as the new Abraham who creates a new people of God comprising all peoples of the world. The Church Father, Eusebius, in the fourth century, wrote that the Church had replaced Israel as God's people. Matthew ends his Gospel with the Great Commission or command of Jesus instructing his disciples to preach to all Nations and baptize all peoples of the world (Matthew 26:10-20). Jesus is also the new Moses and delivers his people from the slavery of sin giving them God's new Law. Herod's order to kill children parallels Pharaoh's directive to execute the children of Israel. Again, the Holy Family crossing the Red Sea from Egypt to Nazareth, the miracles of the loaves and fish depicting the manna in the desert, and the Sermon on the Mount are examples showing Jesus as the New Moses leading God's people.

In today's Gospel, Jesus continues his role as the new Moses teaching about the Law of God. He declared he had not come to abolish the Law but to fulfill it, which means to interpret it the proper way since the so-called scholars of the Law had misplaced the authentic meaning and spirit of the Law. Indeed, even the prophets had in their times decried civil and religious leaders for not following God's Law in the right sense, who instead interpreted the Law to support and effect injustice, corruption, mistreatment, and exploitation of the poor.

Jesus is the Great Teacher with authority to interpret God's Law. Moses received the Law from God by encountering the glory of God on the mountain. Similarly, Jesus sits on the Mount as one sitting on the seat of Moses to

241

teach the Law. He instructs his disciples to go beyond religious practices and make God's Law a way of life. After quoting Moses or the *lex talionis*, Jesus exerts his authority with the dictum, "But I say to you," and introduces the new Law. Jesus' new law is about the unconditional and radical response of love, forgiveness, understanding, reconciliation, and zero tolerance for retaliation. His disciples must show restraint and patience, forgiving their enemies who cause them harm by hurting their eyes or teeth, striking them to humiliate them in public, battling them in court for their belongings, and forcing them to work.

Though a major Christian challenge, Jesus' new Law is the way to holiness and perfection that today's readings advise everyone to achieve. The Book of Leviticus is about "the truth that God is Holy," meaning God is "completely and perfectly good," and therefore "worthy of total allegiance, exclusive worship, and loving obedience" (Commentary: Theology of Work). Thus, Moses urged the people of Israel to be holy because the Lord is holy. In Jesus' new Law, holiness or perfection is not merely following directives and rules to the letter as taught and meticulously observed by Pharisees and Scribes. It is rather about how one relates to another person and how both relate to the community and work together as brothers and sisters in God's kingdom.

"The Golden Rule" or "the Ethic of Reciprocity" specifying we ought to treat our neighbor as we would want our neighbor to treat us is basic to almost all religions, cultures, and philosophies. Rabbi Hillel, a contemporary of Jesus who was asked to sum up the Torah, said: "Do not do to your neighbor that which you would hate to have done to you. There you have the Torah. Everything else is commentary" (Talmud, Shabbat. 31a). Jesus places it positively: "Do for others what you want them to do for you: this is the meaning of the Law of Moses and the teachings of the prophets" (Matthew 7:12). Essentially, therefore, the Law is about loving God and your neighbor as yourself. In the Book of Leviticus, the concept of neighbor included the foreigner (Leviticus 19:33-34). Jesus stresses this as the universal meaning of neighbor to constitute every human being, especially one injured or in need of help.

Therefore, loving neighbor implies showing love to all peoples including those who do not like you, begrudge or gossip against you, and preach hatred, racism, and violence. Instead of applying the law of retaliation, one must go the extra mile and show kindness and love to all. Indeed, a non-aggressive response by Christians to ill treatment would not be a sign of human weakness. Rather, it would be a noble gesture of holiness desired to motivate their offenders to repent and accept all people as sisters and brothers. Besides, retaliation is reserved solely for God (Hebrews 10:30; Colossians 3:25) who is just and "will pay back trouble to those who trouble you" (2 Thessalonians 1:6).

What seems to be most challenging in our Christian life is what we read in the Gospel today: a call to self-sacrifice, like Christ dying on the cross, and a call to be perfect, like God. All this means turning the other cheek to someone who strikes you; giving away your best clothes; and perhaps the most radical, to love your enemy and pray for those who harm you; have hurt you; lie to you and cheat you; stab you in the back; consciously, deliberately, and purposefully spread vicious rumors to defame and destroy you; have judged you unfairly, disrespected, and betrayed you; and to those beside you, like the co-worker, whom you cannot trust. The list is tall! Jesus teaches us to love the people who wrong us, and this will make us holy. Let us reverse the list and think about the people we have offended, hated, and disrespected. This list is also unending.

It is said, "To be holy is to be like God." Is this an abstract concept in your life or do you really seek to live a life of holiness by your love of God and neighbor? Have you tried to assess how you love yourself, which then becomes a measuring stick of your love for your neighbor?

Remember the words of the prayer Jesus himself taught: "... forgive us our sins as we forgive those who sin against us

..." Have you forgiven someone from your heart? What are some ways you personally can show your forgiveness to those who dislike you, resent you, and gossip about you?

The Peace of the Lord be with you.

Prayer
Father, Your Son is always kind and merciful to us. Enlighten us to show the same attitude towards each other. Amen.

Note:
Following three Sundays are replaced by Feasts of Pentecost, The Most Holy Trinity, and The Most Holy Body and Blood of Christ.

ELEVENTH SUNDAY OF THE YEAR

Exodus 19:2-6a; Romans 5:6-11; Matthew 9:36-10:8

GOD'S PEOPLE NEED TEACHERS

Today's Gospel reading is preceded by a verse describing Jesus on a special mission, proclaiming "the Good News about the Kingdom" (Matthew 9:35). He is a charismatic leader, performing his task with divine authority. His appeal is extraordinary, affirmed by his miracles manifested by mere touching (Matthew 9:20-22). He travels to "towns and villages" preaching in synagogues and open places with sizable crowds pouring out to listen to him.

Sadly, Jesus sees a crowd "worried and helpless" about life's uncertainties, challenges, and lacking direction regarding life. He sees their lives visibly disoriented. They appear "like sheep without a shepherd." Turning to his disciples, Jesus says: "The harvest is large, but there are few workers to gather it in." Jesus contemplates expanding his outreach in his public ministry. He knows his time in the world would be short and the work would have to be continued by others. He prepares his disciples for the huge task ahead and to get them actively involved. He directs his followers to pray to the "Lord of the harvest" for more workers to preach about the loving mercy of God.

The second part of today's Gospel (beginning of Chapter 10) shows Jesus picking an inner circle of Twelve Apostles whom he sends to preach about God's Kingdom. Another time, he would send an additional seventy-two disciples to towns, villages, and crossroads on a similar mission. He instructs them about his way of life and how to respond to the world's challenges with love and humility even when maltreated by others (Luke 10:1-20).

The special directive in the Gospel to the apostles to go to "the lost sheep of the House of Israel" (Matthew 10:5-6) shows a peculiarity of Matthew at the time of writing. Many perceived the Messiah's mission was to restore the kingdom of David and announce freedom from all forms of foreign domination (Isaiah 61:1-4). Divine design, however, resonated in Jesus' Great Commission to his disciples to preach about the loving and merciful outreach of the Father to the entire world: "Go, then, to all peoples everywhere and make them my disciples" (Matthew 28:19). The kingdom of God would comprise large numbers of people spread throughout the world who would need more workers to evangelize and announce God's gratuitous love and compassionate affection.

The theme of today's liturgy is certainly about the call to discipleship, to be teachers of evangelization and to live the faith. Jesus turns to the crowd and explains to them the meaning of true discipleship for those who want to follow him. Discipleship calls for total surrender to him with a spirit of undivided heart (Luke 14:25-27).

Discipleship has its roots in mentorship, whereby a pupil or student understudied a master or teacher to adopt his way of life emanating from the master's philosophy or ideas about life. Usually, pupils learned by staying with the teachers to observe their social and spiritual lives. For example, Elisha was called to follow Elijah (1 King s19:19-21) and for several years, Elisha stayed with the prophet as his protégé until Elijah was lifted into heaven (2 Kings:11-12). Among the Greek philosophers and mathematicians (4th and 3rd centuries B.C.), Plato was the most famous pupil or disciple of Socrates, Aristotle was one of the brightest students of Plato, and Alexander the Great was a student of Aristotle. Sometimes, one had to leave family and friends like the first followers of Jesus—Simon Peter, Andrew, James, and John—who left their families and professions to live with Jesus (Matthew 4:18-22). Jesus taught that a leaning towards him would not be a matter of tolerating half-truths or showing allegiance to multiple desires.

The first lesson Jesus teaches his disciples, all of us included, is to be his eyes to see the hopelessness around us, suffering, poverty, hatred, violence, selfishness, increasing secularization, deception, cheating, and untimely deaths. and give emotional response to what we see around us. Our hearts must move with pity to these desperate situations of our times and respond accordingly.

The second lesson Jesus gives is that people "worried and helpless" are dear to God and he desires to save them. Although set during the Exodus period, the first reading looks back to Israel in slavery and hardship in Egypt. Moses told the people about how divine liberation, carried out with resolve and tender loving care, brought them to Mount Sinai, the Mountain of the Lord, in freedom. The image of an eagle illustrated the divine intervention: "I bore you up on eagle wings and brought you here to myself." God further declared that if they kept his covenant and obeyed his commandments, they would be his special possession, a kingdom of priests, and a holy nation. The Responsorial Psalm reiterates God's goodness and tenderness to his sheep, for which reason he ought to be praised and served.

The reading looks forward to a new covenant through Jesus, symbolized by divine love: "For God loved the world so much that he gave his only Son, so that everyone who believes in him may not die but have eternal life" (John 3:16). Just as God showed empathy to the people of Israel and delivered them, Jesus had compassion for the crowds. He chose twelve of his disciples to attend to them, heal their sicknesses, raise their dead, and spread the Good News of the new kingdom among them. He reminded them to give freely with love and generosity what the Holy Spirit gifted them. Similarly, Jesus is always present when we find ourselves in the wasteland of our life, when feeling lost and depressed.

The third lesson is that we should not lose sight of the importance of remaining faithful, hospitable, generous, and inclusive. For example, the challenges of today's Church should not destroy the vibrant faith received. It demands giving up one's old way of life and finding a new life, an authentic life in Jesus, who is the same yesterday, today, and tomorrow.

The fourth lesson is Jesus' message on love and peace. Indeed, it was the hub and summation of his ministry—peace with God, peace with others, and peace within each other. This sequence of experiences brings peace of mind and peace of heart and enables us to love. It ensures our own interests do not preoccupy us, but we are aware of our neighbors, recognizing them as children of God. Again, the knowledge of peace and the experience of it brings peace even among enemies, forgiving them, loving them, and making them feel loved.

Jesus gave instructions to the disciples to preach salvation to the entire world, lead the Christian way of life, and address societal dilemmas and dreadful spiritual conditions; today, he directs us, called to be disciples, to do the same.

The Peace of the Lord be with you.

Prayer
Father, let all people receive Jesus and his lessons with joy. May the Holy Spirit enlighten us as we endeavor to live by his teachings. Amen.

TWELFTH SUNDAY OF THE YEAR

Jeremiah 20:10-13; Romans 5:12-15; Matthew 10:26-33

FAITH AND DISCIPLESHIP

The readings of today acknowledge the challenges, particularly in the life of faith, for the Christian to persevere in following Jesus Christ. The readings from the Book of Jeremiah, Romans, and the Gospel give the assurance that amidst difficulties, challenges, and misfortunes we struggle with, victory will always come from God, who is close and cares for us. Faith in a loving and merciful God is paramount to living a life of hope. Jeremiah is a model articulating confidence that God will always be with the righteous despite physical and spiritual challenges. Saint Paul establishes that sin and its consequence (death) entered the world through Adam, but gratuitous grace and salvation have come to the world through the gracious gift of Jesus Christ. Through him, we receive a new life in baptism and God's gift of forgiveness. In the Gospel, Jesus Christ inspires us not to be afraid of the devil's machinations because only God has power over both body and soul. The Responsorial Psalm is a hymn of hope in God's presence in times of seemingly unsurmountable distress.

Judaism considers Jeremiah as one of the major prophets whose faithful secretary and disciple, Baruch, assisted him in documenting most of his prophecies. Though not mentioned in the Qur'an, Islam regards Jeremiah as a prophet in Islam. Scripture scholars highlight that Jeremiah preached about developing a close relationship with God. His primary mission was, therefore, to tell people to turn away from the worship of Baal and other foreign gods after widespread idolatrous practices during the reign of King Josiah. He urged the materialistic priestly class, false prophets of Baal, and corrupt civil leaders to be faithful to God or face his

249

wrath. The people did not change and soon saw the serious consequences of famine, the Babylonian invasion, the destruction of Jerusalem and the Temple, and the deportation in 586 B.C.

Called to the prophetic ministry around 626 B.C., Jeremiah faced fierce resistance, assault, and persecution from other people: the king and his powerful officials, prophets, priests, army officers, and his own townspeople. They indulged in character assassination to smear his reputation. They beat him, imprisoned him, sent death threats, and finally threw him into a borehole and left him to sink in the mud. The priest called Pashur, understood he would not be guilty of murder if the prophet died in this manner.

It is said Jeremiah spoke passionately about his desperation and unsettling situation and so Biblical scholars refer to him as "the Weeping Prophet." Despite the ill-treatment and opposition, he dared to confront his detractors and prophesied for forty years under five kings. He affirmed God's Word was a fire in his heart that his opposition could not suppress, and he could not resist speaking out. Jeremiah was in prison when Jerusalem was besieged and destroyed in 586 B.C. by Nebuchadnezzar, king of Babylon. Since he prophesied the Babylonians would conquer Jerusalem, he was considered a defector to the Babylonian camp (Jeremiah 37: 6-15). However, king Nebuchadnezzar released him and ordered that he be well-treated (Jeremiah 39:11-14).

Jeremiah was "the son of a Priest" (Jeremiah 1:1) whom scholars suggest was the High Priest who discovered the "Law of the Lord" in the Temple (2 Kings 22:4) after it had gone missing for many years. Therefore, it is possible the zest and zeal of his father regarding the "Law of the Lord" affected Jeremiah. It is also possible he was trained at a scribal school to enhance his mission as a dedicated and focused prophet. It seemed he lived an ascetic life by "not turning to the people, not marrying or fathering children, not going to weddings or funerals, not sitting in a house with feasting, and not sitting

250

in the company of merrymakers" (Jeremiah 16). He was disciplined, truthful, fearless, obedient to God's Word, and trusted God's protection (Jeremiah 1:7-8).

In today's Gospel, Jesus gives instructions to his twelve apostles, most likely referring to the prophet Jeremiah. Last week, Jesus urged them to pray for more people to gather the harvest (Matthew 9:38). He saw a crowd "worried and helpless, like sheep without a shepherd," and needing direction (Matthew 9:36). Then, he selected a core group and spoke with them about what they should do and how they should live the faith. He cautioned them about difficulties, challenges, and rejections they would face in their urgent mission. Indeed, like Jeremiah, they would "cry and weep" (John 16:20). However, Jesus gave the apostles words of consolation, assuring them of God's protection. Just as God told Jeremiah not to be afraid, and assured him protection, Jesus told his disciples to be firm and unafraid, and guaranteed their safety: "you are worth much more than many sparrows" and "even the hairs of your head have all been counted."

At this juncture, we reflect on how the readings relate to our call to maintain faith and trust in God with strong confidence and reliance on him. We are sometimes doubtful of our faith and fear losing the eagerness required of us. We fall away from our affection and connection to God, and our Christian beliefs and values become immaterial and subjective. We discard our hitherto strong obligations and pledges to be faithful to the Word of God. We furtively compromise truth and sincerity in our dealings with one another, resulting in dishonesty and betrayal.

Physical challenges sometimes negatively affect our faith. The entire world panicked when the COVID-19 pandemic did not show a hint of coming under control, let alone going away. Everyone feared how all were at risk with increasing numbers of infections and deaths.

We all share common dreads, about our health and how our medical labs turn out; what our employment status will be; worry about our children as they grow. We are concerned about military deployments and how they affect our dear ones. We are anxious about our marriage status and wonder why we cannot be better parents. We do not understand why we cannot change a habit always haunting us.

The Prophet Jeremiah, the disciples, and Paul must be great examples of how we can confidently show truthfulness, determination, and steadiness in our relationship with God. All this is possible when faith in God makes us fully aware of his presence in our lives and we rely fully on his protection when we face difficulties and challenges in life. Like Jeremiah, we need to experience God's presence in every step of our lives: to believe and sense the Spirit of Christ alight in us to console and give us confidence, hope, and trust in him. Can the measure of our faith be like the mustard seed, strong and tall? Can we feel with Jeremiah that "the Lord is at my side, a mighty hero?"

We are also called as disciples to preach that people turn to God. We have the onerous task of affecting others' lives with the Gospel message. We must proclaim Jesus and his salvation mission for the world to be transformed, and people's hearts to be filled with generosity, patience, and forgiveness. The Christian must confront a world of multifaceted social persuasions, many of which are extreme and at variance with the teachings of the Gospel. It is a world endorsing individualism that justifies selfishness, injustice, and untruth as a perfect means to an end. Christians must not be indifferent, but take the responsibility with boldness and courage like Jeremiah.

Jeremiah was disciplined, truthful, fearless, and obedient to God's word. The Church continues to guide us in our faith so that our lives will radiate discipline, faithfulness, and truthfulness. Which qualities do you focus on and nurture to take roots and thrive as proof of your love, close relationship, and reliance on Jesus? Like Jeremiah, you must face the test to preach Jesus through word and deed without fear. One need not be afraid of opposition when doing the right thing for the sake of Jesus. One needs to persevere in the faith while facing life's challenges.

Recently, we observed Mother's Day and prayed for all women for their gentle and loving care at home. We also observed Father's Day and prayed for all men for their support and protection. Invariably, the two commemorations bring parents together to bring about peace, love, security, and progress in the home. Both must practice Christian love, faithfulness, kindness, generosity, respect, and the fear of the Lord as values worthy of emulation by their children. Research proves that a peaceful and compassionate child mirrors peace and compassion experienced at home. A respectful and loving child reflects respect and tolerance at home. A smiling and cheerful child shows how her parents smile and laugh at home.

The Peace of the Lord be with you.

Prayer
Father, may Your Spirit sow in our hearts God's love and make us strong in faith to do what is right and not fear challenges around us. May all your people be encouraged to move on and trust in Your providential care and protection. Amen.

THIRTEENTH SUNDAY OF THE YEAR

2 Kings 4:8-11, 14-16a; Romans 6:3-4, 8-11; Matthew 10:37-42

CALLED TO TRUE DISCIPLESHIP

Elijah inducted Elisha into the prophetic ministry, where Elijah's cloak and staff became symbols of Elisha's spiritual powers. With these revered objects, Elisha performed miracles, healing the sick and helping the distraught. He trekked across the towns and villages surrounding the foot of mountains such as Carmel, going beyond Samaria, Bethel, and Jericho. Elisha regularly passed through the small city of Shunem and later became a routine visitor to the home of an elderly and childless couple. The woman, related to king David in a variety of ways, was a great and pious woman of significant wealth, who feared God and sin, and showed incredible generosity to others.

Apparently, Elisha's demeanor, while prophesying in the area, made the woman infer that the prophet was a holy person to be revered. She extended her generosity to accommodate Elisha. Though initially reluctant to accept the offer, Elisha soon became a regular visitor. She fixed an extra room in their home and furnished it with a bed, table, and lamb. Elisha rewarded her kindness with a promise of the birth of a son. When the boy died, Elisha raised him from death (2 Kings 4:18-37). This resonates in the Gospel reading of today where Jesus states: "Whoever receives a prophet because he is a prophet will receive a prophet's reward, and whoever receives a righteous man because he is a righteous man will receive a righteous man's reward."

In the first reading, we deduce an important message about the call to discipleship, which is a common theme in today's liturgy. The host welcomed and accepted the prophet Elisha because his affection revealed him as a man of God. In taking care of Elisha, who exuded God's presence, the woman knew she was serving God. The first step to discipleship is holiness:

"Be holy, for I, the Lord, your God, am holy" (Leviticus 19:2; 1 Peter 1:15-16). As both clergy and laypeople, our way of life, character, and attitude must be outward signs of inward holiness and grace. Other people's generosity or respect towards us may not be because of our priesthood, personality, or status, but deportment that gives a sense of God's spirit around us.

Another distinguishing trait about the woman was her eagerness for God's Word. Elisha's presence enhanced her faith when his promise that she would bear a child came to pass. The woman of Shunem teaches us that hospitality, generosity, and compassion must go beyond the circles of ethnicity and status to reach many people: strangers, foreigners, the poor, the needy, and the sick. When we attend Mass or any religious service, for example, and listen to God's Word, we must practice what we hear by showing profound kindness to all and teach our children to do the same.

In the second reading, Paul explains that baptism makes us disciples of Jesus Christ. It ushers us into a life of faith that calls for complete *metanoia,* or a dramatic change to a new way of life and a conversion into the spiritual awareness of the Spirit of Christ within us. The first time we received any of the Sacraments was a moment of great spiritual experience of God in our lives-—Baptism, Confirmation, First Holy Communion, Marriage, Priesthood, Penance, or Sacrament of the Sick. Soon, however, we lose the fervor and passion brought about by the Sacrament.

Paul is bringing us back to our baptismal faith as the mark of true discipleship, even in the hustle and bustle around us. Indeed, the Early Church built the baptismal fonts into the ground as a cross. The catechumens descended three steps in honor of the Father, the Son, and Holy Spirit, and finally stepped into the pool for the baptism. After the words of baptism by the priest, the catechumens plunged into the water to symbolize burial with Jesus in the tomb. It also signified death to sin with a new life in the love of God to live free from sin. The newly baptized rose and walked up to receive new clothes symbolizing resurrection with Jesus. The baptized enacted his or her death and resurrection in the baptismal ritual. It was a new spiritual experience and admittance into the Body of Christ, the Church.

Thus, for Paul, baptism shows discipleship as a compelling commitment to embracing sacrifice and suffering as part and parcel of witnessing to the faith. In today's Gospel, we are told families, worldly matters, and the toils of life could create conflicts within families and among friends. There are examples of conflicts, heated debates, and opposition that occur between converts to the Catholic Faith and their families.

The Gospel of today ends the "mission instructions" of Jesus to the apostles about true discipleship, suffering, and the rewards involved in committing themselves to him. First, Jesus is concerned about commitment from his disciples. They must love him, show commitment to his word, and accept suffering as crosses. If they persevere, they will have their reward.

The second part of Jesus' discourse concerns the attitude of others to his disciples and their reward if they are welcoming and friendly. By our baptism into the Body of Christ, we are both believers and disciples called to show generosity and compassion towards all other believers. The woman of Shunem received God's reward because she showed kindness and generosity of spirit. Being baptized into the Body of Christ makes us brothers and sisters with God as Father and called to lead a specific way of Christian life. Jesus, therefore, calls us to show love, generosity, and compassion to one another, and we will be rewarded for our hospitality. Like the woman of Shunem, showing hospitality to others is a sign of serving God himself. Let us cooperate with the Grace of Christ to show commitment to our call to discipleship.

The Peace of the Lord be with you.

Prayer
Father, bless us with Your Grace. Enable your people to love Your Son above all things. Let our love for him enhance our love for one another. Amen.

FOURTEENTH SUNDAY OF THE YEAR

Zechariah 9:9-10; Romans 8:9, 11-13; Matthew 11:25-30

LOVE MAKES OUR BURDENS LIGHT

The Prophet Zechariah prophesied between 520-518 B.C. in Jerusalem. This was after the Persian king, Cyrus the Great, conquered the Babylonians (539 B.C.) and issued the Edict of Cyrus (538 B.C.) to free the Jews exiled by the Babylonian king, **Nebuchadnezzar (586 B.C.)** into Babylon. The Jews could return to Jerusalem to rebuild the city and the Temple (Zechariah 2:6-8). After the death of King Cyrus (530 B.C.), Darius asserted power in the Persian empire. The new emperor established a cordial rapprochement with the empire's vassal states, including Israel, and endorsed the reconstruction effort. The Jews perceived the engagement as divinely guided and a favor from God.

Biblical scholars opine Zechariah was priest and prophet who started his ministry under the reign of Darius about sixteen years after the return of the first group of exiles. He prophesied about the restoration of Jerusalem, rebuilding of the Temple, future of Jerusalem, expected Messiah, and final judgment. Zechariah—the name meaning "God remembered"—underscored God's wish to accept his people again, purify them, and protect them from their enemies. Thus, he preached about repentance, avoidance of sin, faithfulness to God, and profound spirituality as a new way of life for God's people.

The Book of Zechariah is not chock-full of historical background as other Old Testament books, but mainly theological and pastoral. It is a discourse or guide underlining God's purpose for his people; rebuilding the Temple, promise of a future king, and plans for Israel in "the latter day." The Book of Zechariah is one often referenced in the Gospels and other Christian literature as fulfilled by Jesus Christ.

The first reading is a call to rejoice in the Messiah-king, the ideal Davidic king, destined to bring liberty and peace to Israel, and ultimately to all nations. In Christian theological parlance, the oracle prefigured Jesus' entry into Jerusalem amidst songs of joy from the crowd (Matthew 21:1-11). The donkey depicted the custom of royal humility in the ancient Near East and the kingdom he would build: a spiritual, peaceful, and welcoming kingdom established by God, not upon the ideals of the world. The future king would end wars and divisions and establish peace for the nations.

The Psalmist praises God, our king, for his kindness and mercy, aiding those struggling with many earthly yokes.

Throughout the Gospel of Matthew, there are references to prophecies showing Jesus as the Messiah. For example, Matthew narrates "the birth of Jesus the Messiah" (Matthew 1:18-25) and quotes the Prophet Isaiah, "A virgin is with child, and she will bear a son, and will call his name Immanuel" which means, *God is with us* (Isaiah 7:14).

Today's Gospel reading is another example showing how Jesus fulfills an Old Testament prophecy. The Old Testament frequently describes Moses' hindrances while leading the Israelites across the wilderness. Often, the people were distrustful of him and disobeyed God despite the miracles, which apparently had little meaningful influence on them. Matthew sees Jesus in a similar situation and considers him as the new Moses. Today's Gospel is preceded by Jesus reprimanding the people of the regions of Chorazin, Bethsaida, and Capernaum for their disbelief in attributing his miracles to the power of Satan.

In the first part of the Gospel, Jesus thanks God, praising him for making himself known to the disciples. Though not regarded as "learned" and "wise" as the unbelieving Scribes and Pharisees, the "little ones," that is, his disciples comprising ordinary people, tax collectors, and sinners, have accepted him and his message. The "little ones" share God's gift of faith: Jesus is God's Son, "all things have been handed over to me by my Father," and Jesus reveals the Father to

258

those committed to true discipleship, the little ones. For Matthew and his Christian community, following Jesus, the new Moses, was obeying the Torah. Jesus calls for a profound profession of faith in him, as well as obedience to his new Commandment of Love.

In the second part of the Gospel, Jesus explains that the Mosaic Law, as explained by him, was based on the Commandment of Love, and easy and light to observe, unlike the Mosaic Law taught by the Pharisees. The Pharisaic interpretation of the Law was stringent and burdensome, hence the common expression "bear the yoke." "My burden is light" refers to Jesus' Commandment of Love, which is the key to salvation and happiness. Jesus summarizes the Law as loving God and neighbor with humility of spirit and endurance, not arrogance, pride, selfishness, or scorn. Love is from God, a path to joy, peace, and security, when followed by a gentle and humble spirit. Thus, Jesus' compelling call: "Come to me, all you who labor and are burdened, and I will give you rest," because "my yoke is easy, and my burden light." The "yoke" exerted by Jesus' call to loving, meekness, humility, and obedience is not cumbersome but light and ensures peace.

In the second reading, Paul addresses first-century Christian converts in Rome, saying true Christian living is relishing an unadulterated relationship with God, a holy connection which is gifted by God's Spirit through the death of Jesus Christ. This is divine power conferred through baptism, which enlightens the Christian to develop spiritual discipline and reject the sinful spirit of human desires or flesh. When we have personal relationships with Jesus Christ, we learn spiritual discipline and move away from the enticements of the world. We are not indebted to the Devil to succumb to his inducements to legitimize hatred for others; zeal for power, influence, and status; cravings to lie and corrupt systems; desire to cause lawlessness; daring to be disrespectful, immoral, and irresponsible. If we do not focus on the Lord Jesus, the Devil will take over our lives. We would lose the rewards abundantly received when we are under the reign of the Spirit of Jesus Christ.

Paul termed the way of the Devil and the way of Jesus as the flesh versus the spirit, respectively, or the hard and dangerous yoke of the Pharisees and the light and warming yoke of Jesus Christ. When attracted by greediness for material things, power, influence, and self-gratification, the consequences thereafter can be detrimental. When engulfed in the love of Jesus, our hearts melt within his. We become "other Christs," and radiate his virtues of love, which among others include knowledge of God, the spirit of generosity, humility, meekness, holiness, and compassion. Harvested from nurturing such virtues are the fruits of the Holy Spirit: love, joy, peace, patience, kindness, goodness, faithfulness, humility, and self-control (Galatians 5:22-23).

A parishioner who recently attended her family reunion wrote me an emailing stating, "I am home now from the family reunion! I cannot tell you how little time I had to myself, as my sisters and I prayed daily and went to Mass. Just busy, talking, and laughing; cooking, talking, and laughing; knitting, talking, and laughing, and more talking and more laughing. I absolutely love my family and had such a great time with them. I am so blessed that God gave them to me!" My reply was, "Aren't you lucky to have wonderful and generous sisters you can visit together and spend time reminiscing your past and looking into the future together? You know, few people today will say such generous comments about their siblings, always problems! What are brothers, sisters, and friends for?"

The burden of this parishioner became light, and her yoke was easy when she went to her siblings with a good and loving heart and received great affection with an open heart. She prays and thanks God for the happiness and blessings for the gift of her siblings. She would endure all the pain to sustain the joy and blessings that her siblings brought into her life. She wrote back: "From now on, in all my interactions with others, no matter my mood, I will approach them in that way. As for being yoked with Jesus Christ, it is only then that I can look at the world through his eyes since we are walking side by side. Pray that I always stay yoked to Him!" The yoke for obeying Jesus' commandment of love may not always be easy as we know, but it carries a noticeably lighter burden.

What are some mistakes you have made that found you swerving off the path Jesus wants you to take?

Have your alternative paths in life led to meeting hardships?

Are you struggling to be humble to family, co-workers, and the people you meet?

This week, take time to use the power of prayer to help you become more intimate with Jesus Christ and learn from his meekness and humility.

Lean on Jesus to help carry your worries and burdens so that you may trust that you need him.

If you do not focus on the Lord Jesus, the Devil will take over your life.

The Peace of the Lord be with you.

Prayer
Father, fill the hearts of your people with fervent desire to be close to Your Son Jesus Christ through the power of the Holy Spirit. Amen.

FIFTEENTH SUNDAY OF THE YEAR

Isaiah 55:10-11; Romans 8:18-23; Matthew 13:1-23

CULTIVATING THE WORD OF GOD

At certain times of the year, farmers in developing countries, where crop cultivation is not all- year-round, use traditional farming tools and methods to prepare pieces of land in anticipation of the rainy season. Part of the groundwork ensures plowing the soil with manure and cutting trees to bring in ample sunlight. When the weather forecast for the rains is precise and there is adequate sunlight and proper pesticide, yields could hopefully be bountiful. Crops harvested enable farmers to support their families for the greater part of the year. What is most essential in this system of farming is hard work in preparing the land and diligently attending to growing crops.

In the spiritual context of today's gospel, we are called upon to cultivate and nurture God's Word, his seed of love (1Corinthians 13). This will ensure that we harvest immeasurable righteousness whose fruits include wisdom, knowledge, faith, healing, preaching, and speaking in tongues (1Corinthians 12:8-10), as well as charity, compassion, and forgiveness that benefit God's people (1Corinthians 12:7).

The Parable of the Sower is one of the well-known parables of Jesus. The story is about a farmer who set out with a sack of seeds to sow on the farm. On his way, some seeds accidentally dropped on the footpath. Many people using the footpath crushed or pressed the seeds deep into the ground and birds pecked on some. As the farmer walked across a rocky landscape, seeds dropped on the rock and into the cracks between the rocks. In the thin soil on the rock and between the cracks, the seeds sprouted, but soon became parched and sapless. The plants died from lack of water and suitable soil. Some seeds fell into a bush of thorns, but the thorny bush choked them as they germinated. The farmer finally reached his farm, a well-manured and gated field where the seeds, carefully planted and well-nurtured, yielded a bumper harvest.

In the Parable of the Sower, Jesus teaches about the transforming nature of God's Word. It should bear fruit, and one must work hard, especially while facing anguish and difficulties. The Word of God flourishes or perishes depending on the disposition of the heart it reaches. Just as a seed cannot thrive on a hard-trodden footpath or soil-less rocky surface, the Word of God cannot grow in a hardened and unbelieving heart. Similarly, a heart with superficial or shallow faith cannot sustain the Word of God nor commit itself to the tenets of God's Word. However, God will effectively nurture a spiritual and submissive heart just as his rain and snow from the heavens water the field to "make it fertile and fruitful." Faith in the Word of God, even like a mustard seed, flourishes, and bears lots of fruits according to God's will. Thus, the subservient heart, well-prepared to receive God's Word, must not become disheartened when the challenges of life seem overwhelming.

In the parable, Jesus talks about four kinds of soils. The seed to be sown is the Word, God's message of Love. The Sower is Jesus, represented by all called to discipleship or ministerial priesthood through their preaching and administering of the Holy Sacraments.

The first soil is the path trod on by humans and animals. Feet trample and crush down the seeds, or birds and rodents scoop them up or eat them. Obviously, this is not an intentionally well-prepared strip of land. The seeds destroyed or eaten by animals are the equivalent of people lacking a real understanding of the Word of God, and who speedily snub and disregard it at the least incitement from the evil one.

The second soil is on a rocky surface lacking proper soil structure to sustain plant roots and the sprouting seeds experience premature death. This type of soil represents people without willpower and steadfastness. They easily abandon the faith in the wake of apparently stringent demands of the Word of God.

The third type of soil has thorns and prickly shrubs as the main vegetation. In this scenario, germinating good seeds struggle to survive. This category of people discards God's Word because of life's debilitating anxieties and a penchant for worldly interests and joys.

The fourth soil is meticulously plowed with seeds carefully spaced and farm weeds destroyed. As a result, plants thrive well and produce an abundance of fruits. These are the men and women of faith who receive the Word joyfully, cultivate, nurture, and allow it to affect their lives. They exude God's Spirit within them and share their lives with the fruits of the seed of love, wisdom, generosity, compassion, forgiveness, faith, respect, and acceptance. God's love prevails in their lives.

A phrase in the Akan Ethnic group in Ghana says, "no one shows a child where to find God," a notion also echoed by the Prophet Jeremiah (Jeremiah 31:33-34). God's seed of love is already planted or written in each heart. It is incumbent, therefore, on all to allow the seed of love to grow. This endeavor will lift up a world known to be ungodly, purposeless, and heading towards self-destruction.

Isaiah's analogy in the first reading was a consolation message to the Israelites in exile in Babylon. God provides rain and snow for watering the soil so that seeds will receive nourishment and grow to bear fruit for use by humans and animals. With this analogy, Isaiah assured the people that God's Word to bring back the exiles to Jerusalem would be fulfilled.

The Church applies the same analogy to Christians as they respond to God's Word. If our hearts are adequately prepared and ready, God will sow his Word and provide us with the rain to grow the Word, bearing beautiful fruits. The Holy Spirit who gives life (Galatians 4:25) is associated with the rain, snow, dew, and air in the first reading. The Spirit gives his seven-fold gifts of wisdom, understanding, counsel, fortitude, knowledge, holiness, and fear of the Lord. We receive these gifts which enable us to bear the fruit of the Spirit: love, joy, peace, patience, kindness, goodness, faithfulness, gentleness, and self-control (Galatians 5:22). Preceding his discourse about the fruit of the Spirit, Paul talks about certain human behaviors and attitudes that are bad fruit, such as indecent actions, idol worshiping, jealousy, hatred, anger, fighting, and ambition (Galatians 5:19-21).

Ultimately, God's Word is Jesus Christ, the "source of life" who has brought "light to humanity" (John 1:1-5). His divine calling was to come into the world as Seed (Word) and Sower. As Saint Paul intimates in the second reading, the whole of creation was meaningless and groaned without the presence of Jesus Christ. Indeed, today, there is still "inward groaning" among people looking for meaning in life. They desire to experience the Word, signifying life, love, and peace. Still, there are others allowing the vicissitudes of life and love for wealth to choke the natural yearning for God's Word.

There is a regular advert in the media where a self-confessed atheist advocating for separation of church and state in the United States of America says, "I am not afraid to burn in hell." Here is an example of the Word of God touching a hardened and impervious heart but quickly passing like a water run-off. The heart will not endorse finding the Word to be nurtured, nor allow the Word to function for its created purpose. Another example is the dilemma of parents whose children come home from college with alternate ideas and values completely at variance with those taught from their childhood. Away from the routine at home, the students are embarking on a journey of self-discovery, emotionally and mentally. They are seriously affected by social media and the inexorable detraction of religion and traditional standards among peers. Amid self-doubt and uncertainty, faith is wavering among many of them who now think God is irrelevant, the Word of God unattractive and powerless, and God not even existing. Social media, for example, is advertised as a powerful novelty, a panacea, or the goddess of universal remedy. These young men and women ought to realize that hard work by the farmer in the Gospel, who plowed and fertilized his farm to allow God's rain to nourish it, manifests in every aspect of life: business, career, marriage, family relationships, health, and religion.

Whenever you think of farmers cultivating their lands and working to grow their crops, think of how the Lord wants to cultivate and grow his Word in your heart and in the hearts of all people throughout the world.

How would you describe the soil of your heart? Would it be like the heavily compacted soil one might find on a footpath? Would it be like the scant or poor soil one would find between the cracks among rocks? Would it be like the soil found under thorny bushes?

What can you do to turn the soil of your heart into a well-nourished one, ever ready to yield a bumper harvest for the benefit of the People of God?

Saint Paul enjoins us in the second reading to continue to bear fruit, even if we must go through pain and suffering as the Lord Jesus endured.

The Peace of the Lord be with you.

Prayer
Father, kindly prepare the hearts and minds of your people to eagerly receive Your Word, Jesus Christ, and bear fruit to benefit and change our world. Amen.

SIXTEENTH SUNDAY OF THE YEAR

Wisdom 12:13, 16-19; Romans 8:26-27; Matthew 13:24-43

THE PATIENCE OF GOD FOR US TO CHANGE

The Parable of the Sower (last week's Gospel) with today's trilogy of parables is laden with profound meanings and symbolisms. Indeed, the stories represent an important stage in God's Salvation History. In the Book of Genesis, God's Word (Spirit) was sowed in the soil fashioned by God that gave birth to Adam (Genesis 2:7), who together with the partner, Eve, was told to "increase and multiply" (Genesis 1:28) to build the kingdom of God. Satan sowed the seed of evil into them and sin entered the world: "Sin came into the world through one man, and his sin brought death with it. As a result, death has spread to the whole human race because everyone has sinned" (Romans 5:12). Alyssa Roat (September 2022) puts it succinctly, "The cycle of sin and decay were etched into the DNA of mankind." God started a salvation plan through the Patriarchs and oracles to the prophets, and yet, sin was not overcome. From time immemorial, the Word of God had been "despised and rejected" (Isaiah 53:3). The people broke their covenants with God, tore apart God's altars, and denounced the prophets of God and killed them (1 Kings 19:10).

After centuries, God sowed a seed through Mary (Luke 1:31), "For God loved the world so much that he gave his only begotten Son" (John 3:16). He is Immanuel, "God with us" (Isaiah 14:7), "a shoot from the stump of David's family (Isaiah 11:1), raised to bring freedom to his people (Luke 4:18-19). By one man's disobedience, humanity became sin. In the same way, by one man's obedience, "the mass of people will all be put right with God" (Romans 5:19).

We may therefore see the Parable of the Sower as the work of God through Jesus to establish the new kingdom of God. Jesus battled with the Evil One who tried in various ways to tempt him (Luke 4:13). His Word was trampled upon on pathways, rocky surfaces, and choked by thorns and prickles (Matthew 11:20-24). In the Parable of the Tenants in the Vineyard (Matthew 21:33-44), the vinedressers, symbolized by the Pharisees, Scribes, and Religious Elite, killed the son and heir to the vineyard, a story that clearly anticipates the suffering and death of Jesus. In his burial, they sowed the body of Jesus as seed in the earth, without knowing it was good soil, and sprouted in his resurrection to sanctify all those raised up with him through baptism.

On this new earth, which is the new kingdom of God, the baptized are planted on a well-fertilized soil expected to grow, thrive, and become productive. This is because the Sower in the Parable of the Sower will provide abundant grace through the Holy Spirit which, like the rain, will accomplish its purpose on earth (Isaiah 55:10-11). Like the mustard seed, the Word must grow into a huge shrub, yielding thirty, sixty, or one hundred-fold to provide sustenance and comfort to us and others. We ensure that the fruits we share, including our actions and words, become good seeds as well to be sowed in others. Thus, the role of God as Sower and the task to prepare hearts and minds for the seed are entrusted to the Church and all who believe the Word of God personified in Jesus Christ. In the parable, we realize that spiritual and physical fruits will be contingent on how we accept and respond to the Word of God.

Jesus now focuses on the kingdom of God where the wheat is sprouting and there is hope for healthy growth and a bumper harvest. The kingdom will expand and grow to include all nations, peoples, and cultures. Jesus has called people to true discipleship to preach about the love of God and neighbor. The faithful will be kind, merciful, and charitable to one another. However, Jesus recognizes the harmful influence of the Evil One to sabotage the kingdom (the Church) both from outside and within, and assures his disciples, "But be brave! I have defeated the world" (John 15:33).

In the Wheat and the Weed parable, God, the owner of the farm, sends the Sower, the "Son of Man," who supervises a well-fertilized field. He and his disciples sow wheat seeds hoping that they will sprout into healthy growing crops and yield a plentiful harvest. However, there is another Sower, "an enemy," described variously as "diabolos," the Devil, the Evil One, Satan, the Deceiver, and the Betrayer as the one who tempted our first parents and Jesus before his mission (Matthew 4:1-11). At night, he leads his cohort out to sow the seeds of invasive weeds on the same well-tended land, potentially able to grow into healthy destructive plants. This occurred after the field workers had finished their work on the farm and closed for the day. Indeed, the darkness reveals the Devil's cunning nature when he divulges his devious acts. It amazed everyone at the presence of weeds sprouting alongside wheat.

In Palestine, an annual weed typically known as darnel or tares with deleterious properties is similar in appearance to wheat as it sprouts to grow up to about one meter tall. It is recognizable when it flowers or at harvest time, before which farmers would not even try to separate wheat from darnel. Again, by this time, its roots would entangle the wheat roots, making it difficult to separate it without damaging the wheat. The farmer considers it a serious enemy in the East. Concerned that he might lose a lot of wheat stalks should the weeds be uprooted, the owner in the parable instructs the workers to allow both plants to grow side by side until harvest time when the wheat could be carefully picked, and the weeds destroyed. When not separated from wheat, bread made from flour from a mixture of wheat and darnel often causes dizziness, nausea, paralysis, and, in extreme cases, death. There is a story from Northern France alleging that in the past ejected and disgruntled tenants would sometimes covertly plant darnel on the farm to punish their landlords. The parable would, therefore, have been well understood by Jesus' audience.

The three parables are about the Kingdom of God and dwell on our conduct and how we prepare to attain eternal life. The first parable addresses the old-age mystery of the presence of evil and how the Devil could sway the disciples from the good. It reminds us of the two predispositions within humanity and in ourselves as individuals, namely the good and the bad. The human mind is the battlefield for evil and good (the flesh and the spiritual). The evil is perpetually gaining the upper hand because of the human inclination to succumb to sin (second reading). Christians must not be complacent lest they live their lives embracing evil ways. They must persevere with the help of the Sacraments, especially the Sacraments of the Eucharist and Reconciliation, which affects God's grace that bolsters and sustains God's love for us.

Jesus warns his disciples about the malevolent children of the Devil working in the dark to confuse the true children of the kingdom. All should be consistently upright, prayerful, and watchful so that the Devil would not lure them into sin. They should be wary of the children of the night who would flatter and woo them to their side, sometimes pretending to be faithful members in the church. Their machinations bring hardships, sorrows, struggles to discredit the power of God. Each day we are shocked and horrified about gruesome murders, swindling, abuse, unhealthy relationships, and the apparent successes and triumphs of the bad.

In the parable, God would allow the co-existence of good and Evil (believers and unbelievers) in the same way as the owner of the farm allowed the wheat and weeds to grow together. We wonder why God will not punish those who take advantage of innocent people and use position and power to pilfer the fortunes of society. During harvest, however, the weeds would be separated and burned, and the wheat gathered to safety. Similarly, we will reap what we sow: those of evil disposition will be punished for the evil they perpetrated. Those who remained faithful despite the temptations and lures of the world will be handsomely rewarded. Jesus is admonishing his followers to be patient and endure challenges as loyal disciples, expecting that God's forbearance and promise of justice will prevail. Since we cannot accurately differentiate between the true and the false, God will do the separation during harvest time (judgment day).

All this should serve as a reminder that we have to work hard towards our goal, which is heaven. We hope that in the end, the Angels will pick us and preserve us in God's Kingdom. It will not be the Devil but God, who will sit on the Judgment Seat directing his angels to do the harvesting. We must decide if we want to be wheat or weed, children of God, or protégées of Diabolus.

Another significant message from the parable is about the divine **patience and forbearance** which characterizes God's nature as he guides creation (first reading). Although the fundamental nature of the weeds in the parable could not be altered, the "weeds" among us or within us, as individuals, can change. Our mistakes can change into wheat and sinners can change to become saints. This underlines what the prophets had taught that the Messiah would come and save sinners, and Jesus reiterates he had come to save sinners. As Jesus did not condemn, we must not hasten to judge others but hope with our prayers, patience, and encouragement that people can change. It also reinforces the expectation that Christians must be instruments of change in themselves, families, communities, and the entire world. This will help uproot and destroy evil tendencies and allow accepting each other as brothers and sisters.

The second parable is a clarion call to Christians to see themselves as mustard seeds that must grow in God's love and invite others to benefit from this remarkable experience. The Christian must be like the yeast that makes the dough expand so that the bread can benefit everyone. Each of us has the potential of bearing good fruit and influencing other hearts to return to God. We rejoice in the assurance given by Saint Paul in the second reading that the Holy Spirit is always

271

present to assist us. Let us be humble in recognizing the weeds in our lives and turn our bad stories into good ones. God is merciful and patient. But we cannot let him wait interminably.

How would you describe the "weeds" in your life?

How do you help to keep these "destructive weeds" from taking root and spreading in your spiritual garden?

How do you grow the gifts God has given you to help your spouse, children, family, friends, co-workers, the Church, and all others who may have fallen by the wayside?

The Peace of the Lord be with you.

Prayer
Father, Let Your Holy Spirit continue to guide everyone who finds themselves struggling each day to survive within an environment strongly influenced by the Evil One. Amen.

SEVENTEENTH SUNDAY OF THE YEAR

1 Kings 3:5.7-12; Romans 8:28-30; Matthew 13:44-52

SELLING EVERYTHING TO POSSESS THE KINGDOM

Chapter Thirteen of Matthew's Gospel is referred to as the "Parable Chapter," and today, Matthew presents us with the last three parables: the Parable of the Hidden Treasure, the Parable of the Pearl of Great Price, and the Parable of the Dragnet. The parables, which are short morsels together with the earlier ones in the chapter, are about the Kingdom of God and have received much consideration, profound reflection, and interpretations over the years.

The first parable in today's Gospel is about a hidden treasure a man discovers on a piece of land. Although the price of the land is exorbitant, he sells his property and works assiduously to gain the land to get access to the land's ultimate riches. The parable suggests a scenario where the original owner of the land might have buried the treasure and died with the present owner not knowing about the valuable treasure. A hired laborer or daring investor accidentally stumbles upon the jackpot and works hard for capital to purchase the land and legally extract the hidden treasure.

The second parable is like someone who goes to an antique shop and finds an artifact of historic importance or huge monetary value that he spent years researching. He quickly mobilizes resources to purchase it and celebrates with joy. The first and second parables are about the value and preciousness of the kingdom of God, a treasure or pearl of utmost value which must be the ultimate desire of all, for which reason we should do everything possible to gain it. It is in the kingdom that we find meaning in life and the relevance of God in the world.

The third parable is a sequel to the earlier two showing the rewards for those who work hard to gain treasures and put them to good use. It is like the ending of the Parable of the Sower in the Gospel of last week showing how, at harvest time, God's angels would save the wheat and burn the weeds. In this third parable, the kingdom of heaven compares to fishermen who cast a wide net and catch different fish and other materials like weeds. At the shore, the fishermen sort out the fish to preserve edible ones and throw the bad back into the sea before discarding the other useless materials. The parable portrays the Church as God's wide net, the sea as the world, the good and bad people, and everything evil as the kinds of fish to be sorted out on judgment day.

There is a plethora of evidence in the Old and New Testaments, as well as other religions, to suggest that God takes initiative to redeem his creatures who cannot redeem themselves. Relying on Paul (Romans 5:1; Galatians 3:24), Martin Luther emphasized that justification or salvation comes by faith in Jesus Christ. We do not earn it through our own works but through the redeeming work or righteousness of Jesus Christ (Ephesians 2:8; Titus 3:5). We cannot work to save ourselves. Thanks to the mercy of God, there seems to be a growing consensus about this truth in Scripture raised over 500 years ago by Martin Luther. Fr. Raniero Cantalamessa, preaching at a Good Friday sermon in 2016 to the Papal household including Pope Francis, said that Saint Augustine had already clearly explained the righteousness of God centuries ago. Fr. Cantalamessa continued that, ".... Luther deserves the credit for bringing this truth back when its meaning had been lost over the centuries, at least in the Christian preaching, and it is this above all for which Christianity is indebted to the Reformation..."

In his book *Evangelii Gaudium*, Pope Francis writes, "The salvation which God offers us is the work of his mercy. No human efforts, however good they may be, can enable us to merit so great a gift. God, by his sheer grace, draws us to himself and makes us one with him." The Pope gives "a theological emphasis on the mercy mentioned in Paul's writings and a key to a true comprehension of the doctrine of justification." All this lends credence to the interpretation that the parables being considered point to the kingdom as the treasure or pearl. St. Thomas Aquinas (died 1274) likened the hidden treasure to the Gospel, which he said cost nothing and is free for all. However, he adds, one must give up the world to buy the heavenly riches.

The parables about The Hidden Treasure and The Pearl of Great Price are not about actual precious stones or oil underground that have the value of millions of dollars, though people may pine for such. There is something alluring about the possibility of possessing riches and assets in the world. Many people get caught up in strange and wild adventures to possess material wealth.

Indeed, the traditional interpretation over the centuries regarding the parables portrays the kingdom of God as the precious treasure or pearl that we must work hard to possess, even at the cost of life. It is a great joy to find the kingdom of God as the ultimate meaning of life, but it also calls for hard work and sacrifice to attain and preserve it. As John Calvin commented, we need to opt for the kingdom of God and deny ourselves the lures of the world that could stop us from discovering and receiving the precious kingdom. The kingdom of heaven becomes the utmost good, which should inspire the seeker to do everything possible to possess it in the end.

Early Church Fathers, like second century Father Irenaeus, wrote that the Hidden Treasure refers to Jesus. The Church Father Origen described Jesus as the "autobasileia" (the kingdom itself). The word *auto* means "self," and *basileia* means "kingdom." Jesus is the Kingdom of God. Pope Benedict XVI restates this in his book, *Jesus of Nazareth*, and writes, "Jesus is the Kingdom." The Pope continues, "the king said it is not a thing; it is not a geographical dominion like worldly kingdoms. It is a person; it is He," Jesus Christ. If the kingdom is Jesus, then Jesus is what the kingdom is made of. Jesus is the "Good News." He is the Way, and the Truth, and the Life (John 14:6). He is Charity, Justice, and Salvation. Christians must, therefore, "turn away from sin" (Mark 1:15) and pursue and cherish the treasure and pearl personified in Jesus. If Jesus is the kingdom, then the kingdom of God can be within us (Luke 17:20-21) when we associate with Jesus. Thus, if we look for Jesus as our precious treasure, the primary goal in life, we shall reflect the extraordinary values of the kingdom anywhere: from home, our place of work, our community, and our church.

By our acquisitive disposition, distractions confront our lives daily that could lead us away from the kingdom of God. We must stem the tides that may carry us away from the kingdom, such as wealth, power, self-gratification, and the spate of spurious freedoms and "isms" that engulf the world today. We need to embrace the virtues that have the profound potential of bringing the kingdom into our hearts (Jeremiah 31:33). Then, completely wrapped in God's love, we would exude perfect joy and happiness.

These virtues are the spiritual gifts of faith, hope, and charity, as well as wisdom, understanding, and the fear of the Lord that guide our lives to serve God and the interests of God's people. The grace of God we seek to discover, "the knowledge about the secrets of the Kingdom of God" (Matthew 13:11), showers on the elect in the kingdom of God (Mark 1:15). These are the graces to profess faith and hope; judge with justice; empathize with the poor, the sick, and the lonely; and the grace to love all God's people. Anyone who possesses these spiritual gifts of the kingdom and practices them will be given more; faith, hope, and love will increase (Matthew 13:12). Thus, in this saying, Jesus is referring to spiritual goods rather than material ones.

The first reading is about Solomon as a young king, privileged to make a wish before the Lord. In his early days, he saw a priceless treasure in God and asked for wisdom, "an understanding heart to judge your people and to distinguish right from wrong." Scriptures had taught Solomon that wisdom represented all the spiritual values and benefits of the heavenly dominion. The Lord granted Solomon's request immediately, with additional promises of wealth and a long life. The young king was subsequently lauded everywhere for his "wise and discerning heart," as well as his abundant material assets. Towards the end of his life, however, he did not pursue wisdom in God.

Saint Paul had a glimpse of the kingship and glory of Jesus in a vision (Act 9:3-6). Jesus was the treasure he would value for the rest of his life and into which he would delve more deeply. He passionately preached about it and was prepared to die for it. Paul abandoned an apparently prestigious Rabbinic career since, for him, Jesus was his new paramount treasure. In all this, he hoped to enjoy the fullness of the glory he had witnessed (Romans 8:18; Eucharistic Prayer III).

The Parable of the Dragnet reiterates the theme of the Judgment Day. Those who have sold everything for the priceless kingdom and lived their lives by endeavoring to practice its virtues, like Saint Paul, would be redeemed at the end of time, marked with the sign of salvation.

We see in the first reading that Solomon did not ask for wealth or power from God, but wisdom and an understanding heart. The first verse of the Responsorial Psalm reads: "The law of your mouth is to me more precious than thousands of gold and silver pieces." What matters most to you in this life? What do you ask of God? How are you making a difference in God's kingdom here on earth?

We must not lose sight of our precious treasure, who is Jesus, by chasing false treasures like money, social status, and other worldly pleasures. Let us always keep in mind that heaven is within the reach of all of us. Let us always remember that the kingdom of God is a challenging choice and requires resolve and perseverance.

The Peace of the Lord be with you.

Prayer
Father, may we see the Kingdom as a hidden treasure and a pearl of great price. Let Your Spirit help us to seek its values and live by them. Amen.

277

EIGHTEENTH SUNDAY OF THE YEAR

Isaiah 55:1-3; Romans 8:35. 37-39; Matthew 14:13-21

GOD'S SPIRITUAL FOOD

Saint Matthew gives a prelude (verses 13-14) to the story of the Multiplication of Five Loaves and Two Fish in today's Gospel which many homilists would disregard. These verses summarize what Jesus did shortly after the death of John the Baptist. The Gospel begins with the disconcerting news about the gruesome murder of John the Baptist ordered by King Herod. Straightaway, Jesus takes a boat to a lonely place to pray. He returns from a short but intense retreat and meets a large crowd direly in need of spiritual direction. He feels sympathy for the people, preaches the Word of God to them, and attends to their physical needs by healing the sick and providing food.

The Gospel reading is an incredibly chilling story narrated by Matthew and Mark. King Herod Antipas ruled Galilee annexed to the Roman Empire. He divorced his first wife to marry Herodias, his brother's wife, while his brother was still living. Herodias hated John the Baptist for publicly condemning their marriage as unlawful. She used her daughter, named by some traditional sources as Salome, to get John the Baptist beheaded. She told her daughter to demand John's head on a tray after an exciting dance at Herod's state dinner. Herod, obviously in a drunken stupor, had sworn to offer the girl anything she requested. In the same state of murky mind and in a show of sheer bravado before the guests, Herod would not take back his oath and ordered the execution of John the Baptist.

The Jewish historian, Josephus, attests to the imprisonment and murder of John the Baptist by Herod, but attributes this to John's significant influence over the people and Herod's paranoia that they would start an uprising if he killed John. And according to Mark's version of the story, Herod admired John the Baptist for his integrity and honesty and wished to listen to him (Mark 6:20). Herod carried his guilty conscience for some time and when he heard about Jesus, he was upset that John had resurrected (Mark 6:16).

How do we treat those who criticize us or express opinions different from ours?

Do we manipulate others for our personal interests, especially the vulnerable like children, the poor, and the uneducated, and shatter their dreams?

Do we use our status, power, and wealth to benefit ourselves irrespective of how we hurt others?

Do we make promises we cannot rescind because of pride and pleasure?

Do we feel jealous of people who appear more successful or have more revered integrity than us?

Without a doubt, Jesus had gone to "a lonely place" to mourn the death of John the Baptist. He had gone to pray and meditate before embarking on a mission without John the Baptist on the scene. Understandably, the possibility of experiencing a similar fate overwhelmed him with sadness and apprehension. This might have been one of Jesus' most challenging moments. Yet, like his overwhelming temptation in the wilderness (Matthew 4:1) and the somber experience in the Garden of Gethsemane (Matthew 26:38), he emerged from a private contemplative prayer session fully strengthened. He had renewed vigor to preach, the power to heal, and humility to do God's will. He expressed compassionate care to the people who were thirsty, poor, hungry, and without hope or spiritual direction in life.

Time and again, Jesus secluded himself from the fatigue of traveling, evangelizing, and healing for prayer and meditation (Mark 6:31-32). He prayed all night before selecting his apostles (Luke 6:12-13); prayed for his disciples and future followers for their sanctification and safety from the influence of the Devil (John 17:9-11); prayed, thanking God (Matthew 11:25); and prayed for glorification from the Father (John 17:1). Sometimes, it was a prayer of supplication to be relieved from suffering and death (Luke 22:42), a prayer for total submission to God's will (Matthew 26:42), and a prayer imploring God to strengthen him (Luke 22:43).

Prayer is a human phenomenon, an act of acknowledging and connecting with the divine or Supreme Being with profound significance in the life of humankind. The act of prayer is foundational in various religions, which define a person's socio-economic ethos and spiritual growth.

The Catechism of the Catholic Church defines prayer as "a vital and personal relationship with the living and true God" (CCC, no.2558). For Christians, prayer is engaging in a profound personal relationship or union with God, and Jesus is our object of prayer acknowledged as God, the second person of the Trinity.

The Syrian theologian, Saint John of Damascus (c. 675-749 A.D.) defined prayer as "the raising of one's mind and heart to God or the requesting of good things from God." By accepting Jesus as Lord and Savior who cares for our daily needs, we usually earnestly ask for temporal and spiritual gifts or graces. This is called adoration prayer, an act of worship where we clearly acknowledge God as creator and praise him for his gratuitous love. St. John of Damascus also defended the veneration of the cross and other icons as forms of prayer.

In the Catholic Church, we pray through the intercession of saints for divine help, especially to the Virgin Mary, the quintessence of faith. We pray to show gratefulness to God for his abundant blessings bestowed upon us and forgiving our sins, which have broken our relationship with Him. The "Our Father Prayer" is the model of prayer encapsulating all forms of prayer. Finally, prayer leads us to grow in faith and dependence upon God, fortified in living the example of Jesus.

Prayer is one of the Five Pillars in Islam, making it a very important aspect of the religion. Officially, Muslims pray five times a day, referred to as Salah, to ensure constant union with Allah and to show one's resolve to do His will. In the magazine, Australia Unwrapped 2025, Teboho Ibrahim writes in the article "The Significance of Prayer in Different Religions" that, "Prayer not only deepens their faith (Muslims) but also fosters a sense of belonging to the global Muslim community."

In Judaism, synagogue and daily prayers, such as the Shema and Amidah, "are recited, fostering a sense of unity and shared purpose" (Ibrahim, 2025). Regarding Hinduism and prayer, Ibrahim (2025) writes, "Hindus believe that prayer cultivates spiritual awareness, promotes inner harmony, and facilitates a deeper understanding of one's true self."

In African Traditional Religion and other typical cultural religions, the people recite prayers and perform rituals to appease the Supreme Being and tutelary deities in thanks for the blessings of life, health, food, rain, and other gifts. The beliefs and practices are diverse and rooted in traditions and customs passed on in posterity in oral form. The religion reveres the concepts of nature, ancestors, and the sense of oneness and strong allegiance to the ethnic group.

Ibrahim (2025) succinctly concludes that humanity ought to "recognize the profound importance of prayer in fostering spiritual growth, connecting with the divine, and embracing our shared humanity."

As Christians, we must learn to go into private prayer with our Lord Jesus Christ to be blessed and strengthened for the mission of spreading the faith and the kingdom of God (Matthew 28:19-20), and the grace to live by his Commandment of Love by loving God and loving neighbor.

Do you have your own place to pray, a place that is separate, a place that allows you to pray free from the distractions of the day?

The Feeding of the Five Thousand People is one of the miracles narrated in the four Canonical Gospels. Like the Resurrection of Jesus, it buttresses the importance the Early Church accorded it in understanding Jesus as the Messiah and the church's mission to spread the "Good News" to all corners of the world (Matthew 28:17-29).

John the Baptist's death was certainly a sad presage of Jesus' fate amid rumors about the imminent moment to face his own death. After the connection with God in a quiet place emboldened him, Jesus performed one of his most revealing miracles. Jesus gave the multitude a first-hand glimpse of God's kingdom to fulfill the prophecy of Isaiah about God's invitation to all peoples to a banquet (first reading). The fulfillment of Isaiah's prophecy by Jesus was a sign of the Eucharist in the Church. This time, however, the meal would comprise his own body and blood (Matthew 26:26-29). This will also be the greatest sign of God's love to his people (John

3:16), through Jesus Christ, never to be obliterated by any power "neither the present nor the future" (second reading).

Indeed, the Early Church well understood the notion of the Eucharist. The image of food, as understood by the Prophet Isaiah, the Early Church, and the four Gospel writers symbolized spiritual food. In Jesus' Prayer of Consecration at his Last Supper, he took bread, blessed it, and gave it to the disciples to eat. A similar action happens at the Eucharistic celebration when the priest, representing Jesus, takes bread and wine and consecrates them to become the Body and Blood of Jesus Christ. The Ministers of the Eucharist move to the altar, receive the body and the blood of Christ, and distribute them to "feed" all present. The Body of Christ and his Precious Blood feed and nourish all believers. The Eucharist binds us together as "the People of God," expressing the same faith.

God's invitation to the Eucharist is open to the "People of God." How have you availed yourself to adequately receive God's free spiritual food?

What would you say threatens your intimate relationship with Jesus?

Are you prepared to give what you have, like the boy in today's Gospel, to the Lord to bless and multiply to benefit the poor and the needy?

The Peace of the Lord be with you.

Prayer
Father, we are gathered at your table to share in Your divine life through receiving the Body and Blood of Jesus, Your Son. Through this gift, renew us to live like Jesus, loving you and one another. Amen.

283

NINETEENTH SUNDAY OF THE YEAR

1 Kings 19:9a, 11-13a; Romans 9:1-5; Matthew 14:22-23

JESUS CHRIST, THE WISDOM OF THE WORLD

In many traditional cultures and societies, elders are the personification and repositories of wisdom, custodians of tribal ethos, and expressions of family identity, language, and religion. They apply valued experiences and long developed codes of conduct in discerning what is socially appropriate or otherwise in separating cultural facts from fictions. Many believe these values and moral principles are of divine origin handed down over the years through the ancestors as spiritually present among the tribes. The social norms are close knit to religion and systems of rituals in daily life designed to ensure peace, harmony, and progress in the society and in the individual.

Such is the case among the "Inuit" (indigenous inhabitants of the Arctic Regions) and in most African traditions, as well as in other traditional societies, holding the belief that one must live in harmony with the divine who is the source of life and manifests itself also in nature. Elders must pass on the tribal wealth of wisdom and knowledge to younger generations. They must teach them the meaning and value of human life, reverence, and obedience towards older adults as gauges of wisdom distinguished from intellectual pursuits of knowledge or academia. Saint Thomas Aquinas spoke of wisdom as the "father" of all virtues. The Philosopher, Nicholas Maxwell (born 1937), has intimated that wisdom, defined as the "capacity to realize what is of value in life, for oneself and others," differs from just gaining knowledge officially taught in academia.

The nation of Israel was one such ethnic group that systematically chronicled the pursuit of wisdom as preserved in the Old Testament. Proverbs 9:10 said, "The fear of the

Lord is the beginning of wisdom, and knowledge of the Holy One is understanding." It begins with knowing God, who is Wisdom, and we gain wisdom by humbly accepting his Word and living by it (Psalm 111:10). Thus, anyone who diverged from God's Word lost the wisdom and understanding needed to lead a meaningful life. The young King Solomon perceived a valuable treasure in wisdom. He asked for wisdom from God to enable him to rule the people justly, making him a successful leader, at least initially (1Kings 3:5, 7-11).

Today's first reading takes us back to a divided Israel after Solomon's death (922 B. C.). Under the influence of the fearful Queen Jezebel, the foreign wife of King Ahab, the Northern Kingdom began Baal worship. Most of the people lost the unique experience of God that had shaped and directed the existence of the ethnic group for generations. The Prophet Elijah strongly denounced the false wind of change and fought to preserve the true faith. He led a fierce contest with over four hundred priests of Baal on Mount Carmel. Vindicated by his faith, Elijah proved once again that it was in the purview of wisdom to listen and serve the true God (1Kings 18:16-40). After besting the prophets of Baal, Elijah went on a pilgrimage to avoid the vengeful Jezebel, following the footsteps of Moses to seek God's guidance and wisdom (Exodus 19:1-23). The gift of wisdom revealed to him that God did not always manifest himself in dramatic events such as huge fires, storms, and earthquakes, but sometimes, his presence appeared in tiny whispering sounds. Elijah became the "tiny whispering sound" of God, alluding to a simple life in a kind and charitable manner. Indeed, God continues to reveal himself in less dramatic events which surround us and urges us to accept our mission to be humble, kind, charitable, and respectful even when we experience difficulties and face the unknown, as well as the things we cannot control.

In today's second reading, Saint Paul expresses sorrowful sentiment for the people beloved and chosen by God to spread his love throughout the world. He grieves about his own people concerning their lack of wisdom to recognize in Jesus Christ, the personification of God, and the quintessence of God's wisdom. In the preceding chapters of his "Letter to the Romans," Paul appeals to the Jews to accept Jesus as fulfilling God's salvation promised to their ancestors. Paul pledges to give away everything, even his life, if that would bring his fellow Jews to Jesus, the Messiah.

In today's Gospel reading, Matthew narrates other dramatic and awesome miracles after Jesus' feeding of thousands of people. He had sent the apostles to cross the sea to the other side while we went by himself to the mountain to pray. A violent storm confronts the disciples while crossing the lake. They express fear. They see Jesus is walking on the water. He calms the fierce storm. The apostles witness Peter's euphoric attempt to walk on the sea. They hear the echo of his astonishing statement during a fearful and near-death experience, "Lord, save me!" Peter expresses the fear of the rest of the apostles caught up in the turbulent waters.

Fear is like an epidemic, rampant in our lives, infecting us in sickness and endangering peace and security when facing challenges such as the struggles of marriage, grappling with unemployment, when faced with the politics at work or within business, and frustration among others, leaving many in silent despair. But when struggling with difficulties and the storms of life, a time comes when we believe we cannot conquer our fears and heal our troubled lives ourselves, except by the grace of God. It is when we hear the echo of Jesus' gentle and comforting words subduing the turmoil surrounding us and beckoning us, "Do not be afraid."

Let us not disregard the sound of Jesus' words even when they come to us in tiny whispering sound. Our faith and hope in the power of Jesus Christ must give us strength when faced with stressful moments in life. God's assurance to the Prophet Isaiah is most riveting: "Do not fear, for I am with you" (Isaiah 41:10).

Another statement in the Gospel scene is from the people in the boat who acknowledged the divinity of Jesus: "Truly, you are the Son of God." They put their faith in Jesus to save them. They were colleague fishermen and knew many skilled seafarers and fishers had lost their lives in similar storms on the Sea of Galilee. They were afraid of drowning in the boat. Mark describes the storm as "a furious squall" accompanied by broken waves that threatened the boat of the disciples (Mark 4:37). Luke said the storm brought about heavy winds and raging waves (Luke 8), and Matthew in today's Gospel mentions "a furious storm without warning."

The power of this storm is significant because of the design of the Sea of Galilee. It is about 680 feet below sea level and surrounded by high hills about 2000 feet, particularly to the East. The contrast between temperatures of cool dry winds from the hills and the near semi-tropical warm and moist air rising from the sea could usually result to storms on the Sea of Galilee which can be detrimental to smaller boasts like what the disciples might have been using. A worse danger could result in the shallow Sea of Galilee (about 200 feet at its deepest point) when "a shallow lake is 'whipped up' by wind more rapidly than deep water, where energy is more readily absorbed" (Donald B. DeYoung, 2003). In the time of Jesus, the Sea of Galilee, which looks exceedingly quiet today, was the center of commercial activities, with fishing as the primary activity, and boats, cities and villages along its shores. They described the Sea of Galilee as the "Cradle of the Gospel" or the "Center of Jesus' public ministry, where Jesus called his first disciples. He called them to be "fishers of men" referencing the large quantities of fish that teamed up the shores of the Sea, attracting migrations to the area.

The profession of faith by Peter and the people in the boat was not because of their intellectual ability to discern the divine, but the gift of God's wisdom they knew from their upbringing. After the resurrection of Jesus, such manifestations of faith would become the hinges anchoring the faith of the Early Church: Jesus as Lord and Savior, the

Messiah that the Law and Prophets foretold as "Emmanuel," God with us.

There is an increasing spread of disbelief in God today, diminishing the faith of families, as science and other intellectual pursuits attempt to explain everything beyond our bodily senses. Many people shun the experiences and wisdom of parents, grandparents, and ancestors to answer questions about life. This is a social pattern geared towards a world of economics and trade aided by science, manipulated by the influence of money and material wealth, power and politics. There are many people wearing their academic gowns and laboratory instruments and scissors to analyze the first and the Gospel readings of today to conclude that the events are mere faith stories. As we reflect on today's readings, we must trust God and pray with the fervent hope that he will grant us wisdom to know Jesus Christ, listen to his Word, and follow in his footsteps.

In an article, "Unshakeable Faith for Life" (February 4, 2019), Kathy Howard sums up the characteristics of wisdom from James 3:13-18 and how one would be amazed to discover Jesus in one's quiet surroundings, actions, thoughts, and in those around us. She writes James exhorts us to be humble because "wise people do not constantly brag, boast, or display a prideful attitude"; to have good deeds as "wise people live an upright and moral life"; to be gentle as "wise people treat others with care and respect"; to be considerate as "wise people put the needs of others ahead of themselves whenever possible"; to be peace-loving as "wise people do not foster division... the wise work to end strife and turmoil"; to be merciful as "wise people demonstrate compassion, forgiveness, and kindness to others"; to be sincere as "wise people are genuine, real, and honest; not deceitful, hypocritical, or false"; and to be impartial as "wise people are fair and just. They do not show partiality toward others for their own benefit." The author ends by challenging herself and us all to let our lives show godly wisdom.

Are you humble, charitable, gentle, considerate, peace-loving, merciful, sincere, and impartial when it comes to your relationships with family, friends, co-workers, and neighbors?

The Peace of the Lord be with you.

Prayer
Father, Your Son embodies Your wisdom which he offers as his greatest gift to ensure unity of mind and heart among those who accept him. Grant all people the grace to know Jesus Christ, listen to his Word, and follow in his footsteps. Amen.

TWENTIETH SUNDAY OF THE YEAR

Isaiah 56:1. 6-7; Romans 11: 13-15. 29-32; Matthew 15:21-28

JESUS, THE MESSIAH FOR ALL

After calming the ferocious storm on the Sea of Galilee that threatened the people in the boat (last Sunday's Gospel), Jesus crossed the sea to the Gennesaret Region, where he healed many sick people (Matthew 14:34-36). The Pharisees and scribes often sparred with him regarding his objective opinions on some aspects of the Law, traditions, and purity procedures. With respect to eating with unwashed hands, for example, Jesus told them what one speaks out would defame a person rather than what one eats (Matthew 15:1-20). The Pharisees and scribes were harsh, aggressive, and unfriendly towards Jesus, and looked for means to vilify him and arraign him before the Sanhedrin. Realizing that his opponents unduly interrupted his private moments, he trekked through the territory of Tyre and Sidon, a non-Jewish region where he planned to take some rest or a brief spiritual retreat.

The parallel story in the Gospel of Mark shows Jesus in a Syrian village apparently to withdraw from the people, but "he could not stay hidden" as the people heard about him in the area. One of those who pressed to see him to cure her daughter was a woman, "a Gentile, born in the region of Phoenicia in Syria" (Mark 7:24-30).

Matthew's adaptation of the story from the Gospel of Mark was to accomplish a certain theological objective. The woman's background as a "Canaanite woman" (Gentile) and the intriguing dialogue with Jesus were exceptionally significant to Matthew. His Gospel initially presents Jesus as the new Moses for the salvation of Israel, who had not come to destroy the Law and the Prophets but to fulfill them. Jesus' genealogy traces back to Abraham and Jesus testifies to being sent purposefully to "the lost sheep of Israel" and therefore, it was not a good idea to "offer children's bread to dogs." Thus, the woman coming from the region of Tyre (present-day Lebanon), the home of Queen Jezebel (1 Kings 16:31-32), is an outsider, a Gentile.

However, the woman shows her knowledge that God's grace reaches everybody. She declares her profound faith and dogged persistence despite Jesus' apparent cynical remark and rebuff from the disciples who urge Jesus to send her away. Indeed, deducing from Jesus' own analogy to what defiles a person, she sends the message that what is more valuable is her profession of faith (what comes out), and not her race, gender, or status (seen as the food that goes into a person) (Matthew 15:10-11). The woman continues to express the truth that God's kingdom is established for the Jews and all nations. This is a touching experience for Jesus, who applauds her wisdom, faith, and courage, and immediately extends God's compassion and love towards her. Indeed, Jesus reaches out to anyone who professes faith in him.

The story ends with the healing of the woman's daughter because of her strong faith. Her initial statement, "Son of David," shows how a Gentile identified with the Jewish Messianic expectation and recognized Jesus as Messiah. She represents the foreign world outside of Israel, which is a turning point in Matthew's Gospel. God is "Lord of the Universe," and Israel was a channel through which God's salvation plan would reach all nations (Genesis 12:1-3). The story suggests that at the time of writing, Matthew had seen non-Jews as part of the Early Christian Community. In addition, Matthew writes about the "Great Commission" of Jesus at the end of his Gospel, urged the disciples to preach the "Good News" throughout the world (Matthew 28:19). Thus, through baptism, all peoples would incorporate into the New People of God, the Body of Christ. Matthew's theology about universal salvation is brilliantly accomplished.

The three readings of today provide an insightful genre to the universal mission designed by God for the world. God's mantle is extensive and wider than our imagining, covering and protecting the universe. The Prophet Isaiah (first reading) had revealed God's prophecy: "My house shall be called a house of prayer for all peoples" who profess faith in him, keep justice, and do what is righteous as a positive response to following God's precepts and commandments.

The mission of Paul was to make the Good News known throughout the entire Gentile world. The Jews had failed to recognize Jesus as the "Son of David" because of their jealously guarded borders. Their rejection of Jesus was the reason for Paul's expression of grief (last week's second reading). In today's second reading, Paul stresses he had not renounced his people. However, he hoped that his experience of Jesus Christ would spread to his fellow Jews. God's salvation plan would come to completion when the Jews and Gentiles, who expressed faith in the Lord Jesus, received the Gospel. According to Paul, this had been the grand purpose of God when he set his salvation plan in progress.

The woman in the Gospel reading acknowledges the Messiah out of her knowledge about the Scriptures, wisdom, and strength of faith. We ought to emulate her by seeking to discover Jesus through the Scriptures and the Church Fathers who were close to the Apostles and their traditions. We must listen to contemporary homilies, meditate on them, experience the presence of Jesus daily in the Sacraments, and allow him to influence our lives.

The woman teaches us perseverance in prayer when answers to our prayers do not seem imminent and those who do not share the faith ridicule us. Sometimes, too, discouragement leads us to give up Church or religion and stop inviting Jesus into our lives. Jesus says we should not lose heart but pray continuously (Luke 18:1). The woman in the Gospel story today encountered opposition at each point of her journey to get healing for her daughter: even shouting at the top of her voice, Jesus seemed to ignore her; her presence and persistence to get close to Jesus irritated the disciples, and they asked Jesus to get rid of her; and she faced the embarrassment from Jesus' apparent cold and unfriendly analogy about dogs during their tête-à-tête.

The life of Jesus is replete with instances when he withdrew from the disciples to pray. His prayer life enamored them, and they asked him to teach them how to pray (Luke 11:1). Jesus prayed because the Devil was always after him (Luke 4:13). He prayed when, like many of us, he felt fate had to decide the course of his life, as in the Garden of Gethsemane (Matthew 26:39). He prayed when matters looked terrible and he seemed to feel no meaning in his life again while dying on the cross, as he "cried out" before he died, "Eli, Eli, lema sabachthani" ("My Lord, my Lord, why have you abandoned me?").

Again, the woman teaches us humility both in our social and spiritual life for, "Happy are the humble; they will receive what God has promised" (Matthew 5:5). The woman's sense of hope, which strengthened her faith, is a lesson for all of us. Hope gives us a deep sense of the presence and connection with the divine in our lives and helps us to grow in the Lord despite our desperate situation. Hope gives us strength when our intercessory prayers seem shelved somewhere by God. Again, hope gives meaning to life and animates our connection to God, who is the source of comfort and the inner peace we all seek. We may lose hope in early adult life, but experts opine that many people in later life usually return to the spirituality and traditions that nurtured them as they grew up. They realize that closeness to God, love of fellow human beings, compassion, generosity, and peaceful togetherness define life, which is God's gift.

Therefore, under the universal umbrella of God's salvation, love, and protection, we must accept each other as children of God created to live together in love. The spirit of hope addressed to refugees coming back from exile in Babylon is inculcated in us (First reading). We must answer the call to observe what is right, do what is just, and construct bridges of love peacefully connected to communities, churches, families, and countries in our world environment which are infested by barriers, hostility, strife, jealousy, and discrimination. We must be patient with others who, by sheer desperation in life, cry out daily for help and shower upon them love, acceptance, and compassion that will make them live with hope.

The essence of Christianity goes beyond doctrine, church laws, hierarchical structures, and even spirituality. It is ultimately about accepting others as children of God and relating with one another to be loving, compassionate, supportive, trustworthy, merciful, thoughtful, and kind.

The Peace of the Lord be with you.

Prayer
Father, we thank you for the gift of faith, making us realize we all have one Father in Heaven. May Your Holy Spirit unite the whole world to stay together in love, O Lord. Amen.

TWENTY-FIRST SUNDAY OF THE YEAR

Isaiah 22:19-23; Romans 11:33-36; Matthew 16:13-20

JESUS, SON OF THE LIVING GOD: PETER, HIS ROCK

The first part of today's Gospel reading is recorded in the Synoptic Gospels comprising Matthew, Mark, and Luke. The second part, which is about the confession of Peter, is exclusive to Matthew. According to the Gospel, Jesus traveled through the region of Caesarea Philippi with his disciples, apparently visiting villages and towns on his way to Jerusalem. A detailed historical and geographical background regarding Caesarea Philippi and the religious importance of the region and its significance to the ministry of Jesus Christ will be appropriate. Caesarea Philippi differed from Caesarea Maritima, one of the most economically thriving cities along the Mediterranean Coast.

In ancient times, Caesarea Philippi was particularly known for its pagan worship with many temples such as the Temples dedicated to Zeus, Hades, and Augustus. The city had different names depending on who ruled the territory. It was originally called Panias (usually spelled Paneas) after the Greek god Pan, the god of nature representing fields, forests, mountains, flocks, and shepherds. In 2 B.C., the city was renamed Caesarea Philippi by Philip II in honor of Caesar Augustus and himself. Later, Herod Agrippa II, the grandson of Herod the Great, named it Neroneas after Emperor Nero. After Nero's death, the city regained its original name, Paneas. The modern name of Paneas is Banias (as the Arabic alphabets do not include the letter "P").

Paneas (Caesarea Philippi) was about twenty-five miles north of the Sea of Galilee at the foot of Mount Hermon. The city was noted for its springs that fed the Jordan River, making the surrounding districts fertile. The city blossomed into an area of agricultural and economic activity where many people moved their families. It grew into the crossroad of political and religious struggles. Vespasian, a Roman General during the Jewish-Roman War (66-70 A.D.), encamped near the city. After the destruction of Jerusalem, the Romans used gladiators to punish and kill hundreds of Jewish prisoners in amphitheaters, much to the amusement of spectators in the city.

Sozomen, a Christian Church historian who died about A.D. 450, wrote that it was in Paneas that Jesus miraculously cured the woman with bleeding difficulties (Matthew 9:20). He added that, after the cure, the woman had a statue of Jesus placed in the city. Later, the Roman Emperor, Julian the Apostate, had it replaced with his own statue, which shortly thereafter was destroyed by a miraculous fire from heaven.

It is likely Jesus often visited the district of Caesarea Philippi for several reasons. For one, the aesthetic landscape from the relatively attractive, luxuriant vegetation far exceeded the typical desert environment of Galilee. It was also the non-Jewish district closest to Galilee, Nazareth, and Capernaum, which served as a haven for Jesus to flee from the hostile Jewish leadership. In Caesarea Philippi, Jesus might have had uninterrupted periods of time for meditative prayer and retreats away from the people who continually thronged around him in Jewish towns.

Some Biblical scholars opine that the incredibly significant Transfiguration occurred on Mount Hermon, which was considered a Holy Mountain at the time (2 Peter 1:18). It was about fourteen miles from Caesarea Philippi and the highest peak in the vicinity. It was therefore appropriate that in the peaceful backdrop of the region, Jesus had ample time to teach profound and confidential religious concepts to his disciples without interruption. That Jesus would bring his apostles to Caesarea Philippi, the center of many pagan beliefs and temples, to confront them with the notion of the Messiah, was remarkable. It was amid all the pagan religions, local gods, and fertility cults that Jesus inaugurated his Church after being acclaimed Messiah and "Master" over Satan and the gathering of gods (see homily on the Transfiguration of the Lord).

Responding to Jesus' question concerning people's views about him, the disciples said they perceived him as John the Baptist, who had re-appeared after his murder by Herod Antipas. According to the Church Father Origen (185-254 A. D.), Jesus and John the Baptist were cousins and bore a physical resemblance. The disciples also said the people regarded Jesus as the Prophet Elijah whom Scriptures had predicted would return before the coming of the Messianic age. Some people, the apostles said, saw him as either Jeremiah or one of the other great prophets. Jesus' best litmus test for his own followers was the question, "Who do you say I am?" Peter quickly and ardently responded, professing Jesus as the "Messiah" and "the Son of the Living God." Thereafter, Peter was called "Blessed," decorated with the title "Rock of the Church" and allegorically given the "keys of the kingdom of heaven" and earth.

After the confession of Peter and his installation, so to speak, as leader of the apostles, Jesus talked about his journey to his crucifixion, death, and resurrection. A couple of days after this, the Transfiguration revealed Jesus' identity again as the beloved Son of God. Peter's profession of faith, his mandate as custodian of the kingdom, and the Transfiguration scene were some of the climactic moments in the life of Jesus. They were moments of great insights for the disciples who, like the people, had not been sure about the identity of Jesus.

Today's revelation of Jesus' personality and the Transfiguration scene following later were of crucial concern to the Early Church when leadership and church structures had to be underscored by divine or scriptural authority. The second reading seems to be an affecting observation by Saint Paul on these significant events about Jesus Christ and the Church. They were overwhelming encounters for which he praises "the depth of the riches and wisdom and knowledge of

God," and ponders over God's "unsearchable judgments" and "inscrutable ways." The first reading was another remarkable revelation about the identity of Jesus Christ for the Early Church.

Scholars often date the reign of King Hezekiah from 715 to about 686 B.C. which was marked by frequent conflicts with the Assyrian empire. Jewish history presents him as "a man of extraordinary qualities and piety," who reversed the ungodly policies of his father, Ahaz; destroyed many idol temples; and restored the Temple worship in Jerusalem (Jacob Isaacs, 1946). Hezekiah, encouraged by the Prophet Isaiah, showed great faith and confidence in God. However, some of the king's advisers, especially the Chancellor Shebna, used their positions to serve their own selfish interests, leaving a weakened nation at the mercy of the Assyrians.

In the first reading, Isaiah announces Shebna's looming demotion from "Master of the Palace" or "Steward of the Palace," to the common position of a Scribe for arrogance and selfishness. He would be replaced by Hilkiah's son, Eliakim, who would be a true father to all the people and serve the Royal house with enormous authority. The symbols of his new office would mark his rise to fame as holding the "keys of the House of David."

The first reading evidently speaks about God's wrath with proud, selfish, and inconsiderate leaders who abuse their positions and unashamedly ignore their responsibilities, especially to the poor and needy (Isaiah 13:11). Even though we all struggle with the sin of pride and greed in life, we need to see the invaluable prize of generosity by humbling ourselves before God and others (James 4:6).

However, it is believed the reading foreshadows the role of Jesus in God's salvation plan. Because of his obedience and sacrifice, Jesus holds the "key of David," the symbol of his power in the kingdom of God, where he has absolute authority. He is accorded the power to open its gates for the righteous and refuse entry to others. Jesus is the key to life. He is "the Way, the Truth, and the Life; no one goes to the

Father except by me" (John 16:6). He is the Way that leads to eternal life, the Truth showing true knowledge about God because he is God, and the author and giver of life (John 6:68-69). Jesus is strong and stable like the nail, peg, or spike on a wall on which heirs of his kingdom will hang for safety and glory. Jesus is the ultimate Rock "rejected by the builders" but became the cornerstone of the new Temple of God.

Peter became empowered to be the visible leader of the Church, a role he diligently performed as evident in the Acts of the Apostles. Jesus handed the baton of leadership to Peter, which would also be passed on to the Church. The authority to enact laws (deepen doctrine and liturgy) to govern the Church at all seasons and in each millennium would be a continuum because "not even death will ever be able to overcome" Christ's Church (John 20:23).

There is a parallel in the passing of the keys to Peter in the first reading. But, whereas Eliakim's authority could "break and fall off," as it did with Shebna, Peter's authority "reaches beyond death and extends to his successors." Again, whereas Eliakim's office was consequential through human institution, Peter's office is the creation of Jesus, the Messiah and Son of God, whose command requires respect and obedience to and in harmony with the "Chair" or "Office" of Peter. The other Apostles symbolized the pillars supporting the new Temple in which all people of the world would worship (last week's reflection). The place to find our relationship with Jesus and build the unity with all those professing the same faith is in the Church founded on Petros (a piece of rock or a stone that is easily movable and insecure) now transformed as Petra (a huge projected and solid landmass) in Christ Jesus and guarded by the Holy Spirit as promised by Jesus.

Can you visualize Jesus asking you, "But who do you say that I am?" What would you have said? Hopefully, you will quickly profess him as Lord and Savior, and rightly so. The next question may be more challenging: "Do you walk the talk?" Do you merely profess Jesus as your "Lord and Savior" without living that faith in love, compassion, and charity? Is Jesus your Way and do you walk in his footsteps and listen to him, not veering out of his sight into worldly corruptions and temporal desires? How do you sincerely and boldly introduce Jesus to others with zest and zeal, like Peter and Paul in the readings of today? Are you truthful to Jesus, to yourself, work, and relationships with family, friendship, and in marriage?

Is Jesus the way of life for you, defining the essence of your life to love God and neighbor by helping, forgiving, and accepting others irrespective of societal prejudices and injustices? Are you close to Jesus in your prayer life, accepting that he is your pillar and your support both in good and bad times?

Are you part of the Church's mission to spread the Good News despite opposition from a world systematically working to destroy Jesus' Church? Are you prepared to influence the world, win hearts for Jesus, and change the world and your environment into peaceful places?

The Peace of the Lord be with you.

Prayer
Father, we are overwhelmed by your Plan of Salvation. Let us, and the entire world, profess Jesus as Your Son and Messiah. Amen.

TWENTY-SECOND SUNDAY OF THE YEAR

Jeremiah 20:7-9; Romans 12:1-2; Matthew 16:21-27

DENYING SELF FOR JESUS' MISSION

Today's Gospel reading continues with Jesus and his disciples in the territory of Caesarea Philippi, away from the frequent interruptions of the crowds in Galilee. More significantly, they are away from the habitual harassment, relentless aggressive opposition, and resentment towards Jesus. In Galilee, the Jewish religious leaders and "teachers of the law" (Pharisees and Scribes) blatantly exhibit arrogance, with the sinister objective of having him killed. This is exactly what Jesus predicts at the beginning of today's Gospel: He would be manhandled, and he would suffer; he would be killed and then resurrect from death. At this point in his ministry, he is dialoguing with his disciples and teaching them about himself, particularly after Peter's exclusive confession: "You are the Messiah, Son of the Living God."

The springs and lush vegetation of Caesarea Philippi, as we have learned in previous homilies, led to the construction of sanatoriums, which were popular. The city was also the center for the worship of many deities, local gods, fertility rituals, different philosophies and ideologies, and pagan thought-systems in the region. Some kings of Israel encouraged deity worship and Baal worship, which dates to the third century, with King Jeroboam building a temple in the city of Dan nearby. The ancient Greeks worshiped their fertility god Pan, the god of nature, caves, and grottos, associated with fertility cults. They named the city Panias to honor Pan. There was a Greek temple in honor of Zeus, the king of the gods and the god of the sky, thunder, law, order, and justice. The Romans continued the practice and built temples to worship their own gods and dead emperors considered as gods. The people carved niches in the cliffs, placed their individual or family gods in the rocks, and came there to worship periodically. The major attraction was a cave at Caesarea Philippi where the entrance, with its spring waters, depicted a gate to the underworld. They considered this as the abode of fertility gods who came into the world at springtime and went back in the winter to live there. It is profoundly amazing that Jesus would bring his devout Jewish group to a place of immoral pagan worship comparable to a modern-day red-light district, aptly called the Gate of Hell or the Gate of Hades.

It was at Caesarea Philippi, the center of pagan worship and the gate to the evil world that Jesus stopped to ask his disciples, "Who do you say that I am?" Peter spoke immediately, "You are the Messiah, Son of the Living God." Obviously, Peter was expressing the faith of the disciples revealed by God. The faith would lead to the inauguration of the Church of Christ to overcome evil. The disciples were to attack evil head-on because the Gates of Hades could not overcome it (Matthew 16:13-20). During this period, they built gates not as fences but for defense to keep away the enemy. Thus, the Church of Jesus would break the defenses of Satan and take his kingdom by storm. According to Christian tradition, Jesus stormed the underworld after his resurrection and freed those in the shackles of the Prince of Evil (The Apostles Creed). However, Jesus knew his disciples had not understood the spiritual character of his mission. Indeed, they had not understood the real meaning of the concept of the Messiah which Peter had proclaimed.

During many of his private prayers and meditations, Jesus had related the Messiah to the "Suffering Servant" of Isaiah 53 and had indirectly referenced Daniel 7 verse 13. Jesus announced to his disciples that the people would reject the true Messiah, who would endure excruciating suffering and experience violent death. The expected Messiah would not suffer because of his own shortcomings. Indeed, his humble countenance would not even lead to any attempt at evasion, either by trying to escape or by fighting back (Matthew 26:51-56). Fulfillment of his Messianic mission would depend

302

upon his martyrdom (Matthew 20:28). The Messiah was destined to exchange his death for the lives of sinful people, a new life symbolized by his resurrection. He became sin to save sinful humankind. The sequence emphasizes: He "must go to Jerusalem ... suffer ... and rise on the third day," all as prophesied by Scripture (Luke 24:25-27; Mark 9:12).

Another significant dimension least expected by the disciples was Jesus' revelation that those who acknowledge him as Messiah and associate with him would have to follow in his footsteps and embrace pain and suffering. While Jesus is teaching the disciples about the secrets regarding the Messiah, Peter bursts out with a strong rebuff to the concept of a suffering Messiah. Again, Peter is speaking the mind of the disciples. His spontaneous reaction is a manifestation of his human nature when he replies he will thwart any opposition against Jesus. He would fight any potential difficulty in the way of Jesus from accomplishing the spiritual tasks expected of the true Messiah. Peter, like the others, could not fathom the Messiah's divine powers being restrained and subjected to humiliation, suffering, and death as perpetrated by the Jewish leadership. This would be undignified and degrading for "the Christ, the Son of the Living God." God would not permit it!

Although the Prophet Isaiah preached about the "Suffering Servant," the people of Israel could not relate it to the Messiah. The Messiah in Judaism was the "Anointed One." He would be a descendant of King David to restore the kingdom of David. He would subdue all foreign occupations in Israel. By extension, this powerful king would bring about world peace. He would wield absolute secular power (Daniel 7:14) and free Israel from foreign domination. Thus, the Jews at the time of Jesus could not accept a Messiah who would suffer at the hands of mere mortals. As Messiah, he would save the world from sin and give it back to God. This spiritual task would be extremely difficult since it would meet opposition and suffering.

A case in point was the difficult vocation embraced by the prophet Jeremiah (first reading) in which he experienced great frustration. He proclaimed God's Word so that the people would turn away from idolatry and infidelity and walk towards God. Yet, the people regarded Jeremiah as a traitor. They mocked and derided him. Even his closest friends denounced and conspired against him (Jeremiah 20:10-13). At one point in his life, he regretted being born (Jeremiah 20:14). Other times, he did not have kind words for those who disparaged him and refused to listen to him (Jeremiah 20: 12).

Jeremiah had prayed to God to let him die, but he could also not resist God's Word burning like fire within him to preach, even if it would hurt and make him the subject of ridicule and scorn. Jeremiah's story ended with praise to God and fervent hope in him. He was steadfast in his belief that God would triumph over his enemies (Jeremiah 20:13). In the same way, Jesus' suffering and death would be crowned by his resurrection from the dead. Jesus reminds us of Jeremiah's humble submission to the power and will of God. Jesus, the Messiah, would accept all suffering because of his inherent love for all people, even those who wished to destroy him. Similarly, the Psalmist has a soul thirsting for God "like the earth, parched, lifeless, and without water." He has seen the power, glory, and kindness of God, and his soul will always acknowledge God, whose arm will always support him.

Denying self or losing one's life—that is, taking up the Cross of Christ or living the often-recognized difficult tenets of Christianity—becomes the central focus of Christian discipleship. The sacrifice of going a further mile, even with the enemy to win him or her back as a friend, sister, or brother, is worth more than all the wealth of the world. God inspires this sacred journey and guarded by his Spirit's blazing fire of love within us Jesus calls us to love and to "die" for one another.

The readings are also referring to us as believers in Jesus Christ who follow him and desire to attain his level of holiness, selflessness, love, and compassion. The readings teach us that

God created us with a seed programed to bear the fruits of love. We radiate that natural propensity for these fruitful values to blossom for the benefit of the people around us and for the whole world. In a world filled with hate, racism, prejudice, and fighting, we ought to yield to the natural burning desire to do God's will like Jeremiah and Jesus in today's readings. In the second reading, Paul tells us we can achieve God's will for us when we align ourselves with Jesus Christ to learn how to make sacrifices, even when the world mocks our choices, making us suffer for our commitment.

How are you committed to the Word of God? Do you live by accepting and reading it, obeying it, and following it? Science and the secular world will laugh in derision of your faith, but we should not be ashamed of your belief and mission to spread the Word of God (Luke 9:26). You must not hide or suppress the fire of the Spirit burning within you and urging you to give testimony of the joy of being associated with Jesus Christ (1 Peter 3:15) and following him (John 8:31-32).

Are you living Jesus' Commandment of loving God and neighbor by denying yourself for the wellbeing of your neighbor?

Each day, how can you thank God for the graces and blessings he has bestowed on you and your loved ones, and how can you pass along that appreciation in whatever way you can to those in need of your love?

What can you do to go that extra mile for the People of God who are in need?

In the battle against Satan, how determined are you to fight back?

The Peace of the Lord be with you.

Prayer
Father, following Your Son is a sacred and worthy journey defining our purpose on earth. Guarded by Your Spirit within us, let all peoples follow the footpath of Jesus, loving and sacrificing for one another. Amen.

TWENTY-THIRD SUNDAY OF THE YEAR

Ezekiel 33:7-9; Romans 13:8-10; Matthew 18:15-20

LOVING NEIGHBOR AS SELF, A CO-CREATOR OF GOD

The New York Times featured a photograph of a gravely emaciated child—down to skin and bone—in the Banadir Hospital in Mogadishu, Somalia (August 2, 2011). At first sight, it looked like a skillful painter's depiction of a child of poverty: suffering, despairing, and dying. The child's condition, portrayed in the detailed pictorial presentation, looked shocking and too unnatural to be an accurate rendition of human existence. But the critically impoverished child was one of over 500,000 children deprived of food, in a den of starvation, and on the brink of death.

The inside page of the same newspaper showed another photograph that could be termed "The African Mother of Sorrows!" It was a woman, lean to the bone from starvation, outstretching a hand to touch her motionless, emaciated, and skeletal child who was on the verge of death. The photograph, also resembling an impressionist's work of art, depicted the gravity and stench of human suffering.

A third picture showed a visibly horrified, distressed, and helpless man "gently carrying a small package in his arms wrapped in blue cloth," looking "almost like a swaddled newborn," but it was not the case. The cloth carried "the body of his 3-year-old daughter, Kadija, who had just succumbed to measles."

The famine in Somalia's Shaba territory that year was one of the most horrific, affecting several people in their death throes. The situation was worsened by insurgents mired in political struggles in the region. All this had exacerbated a difficult situation, blocking thousands of starving women,

men, children, and domestic animals from leaving the area or getting critical access to aid. The newspaper article further reported that emaciated parents holding malnourished babies with chests exposing visible ribs and hands hanging weakly— were crowding the hospitals for medical care, food, and water.

The world community, churches, charity donors, and individuals have always shown concern in Somalia and other areas with similar conditions and responded to the urgent need to assist the needy and dying. The U.S. Conference of Catholic Bishops appealed to their priests and the lay faithful to contribute to a special solidarity fund established to provide food, water, and sanitation supplies to the people "facing an uncertain future." The bishops asked for blessings of the faithful in their singular effort to "reach out to help our brothers and sisters in East Africa." They echoed Pope Benedict's clarion call at the time to the Catholic community and the entire world to assist the people of East Africa.

The common theme underlying today's liturgy is that God is present among his people and concerned that his children will live in harmony and peace as brothers and sisters, correcting and forgiving each other, and caring for one another especially the poor, sick, needy, neglected, and underprivileged throughout the world. Jesus said in today's Gospel, "Where two or three are gathered together in my name, I am in the midst of them." We often quote the verse when we gather to pray, reminding ourselves of Jesus' presence, but Jesus goes beyond the context of community prayer. Jesus is Emmanuel, "God is with us." Jesus shares his spirit with us, both as individuals and as a community. This is our faith. We can therefore pray as individuals or with the community for God's forgiveness, aid, and favors.

We also pray that God would take temptation from us, establish justice and peace on earth, and receive our praise for his glory and goodness in our lives. The verse is about God's close connection with the community or the church in handling disputes and other human concerns. Jesus gives some guidelines to follow; talk to the offender, get two or

307

three others to intervene, consult with the church community, and if none of the protocols work, let the person be on his or her own. The disciples would have been familiar with having two or three witnesses in a dispute (Deuteronomy 19:15). Jesus involves the church in disputes, and he promises a divine presence throughout the process of solving issues. The Church must do everything possible to bring back a lost sheep (Matthew 18:12-14), and, if possible, pronounce justice. Because Jesus is spiritually present in the church, the decisions of the church would be binding both on earth and in heaven. But the church or the individual must forgive and reconcile with the offender like the master who was merciful to his debtor (Matthew 18:22-35).

Again, Peter speaks the mind of the rest, asking Jesus if one must forgive an offender seven times, a recommendation well known in the Jewish culture. Jesus replies, "No, not seven times, but seventy times seven," and told them the story of the forgiving Master. Jesus means we must love and forgive as many times as we are offended, as the Book of Lamentations says God's mercy and faithful forgiveness comes to us abundantly fresh like the morning and as sure as sunrise (Lamentations 3:22-23). Jesus ends the parable by saying that because of God's copious mercy to us, we too must forgive from our hearts (Matthew 18:35).

All religions hold the belief that human values, concerns, and abilities originate from God and, therefore, are intrinsic to the human being (Jeremiah 31:33). His commandments express these ideals as revealed in the Holy Scriptures. God's supernatural presence and influence is at the core of human life and must affect our interconnectedness and decision-making. As Christians, we are called to live in a close relationship with Jesus, the Son of God, in a bond which should be so intimate as to grow into his life. The core of Jesus' life was love, and he gave his life away to save us. In the same way, those who are in union with Jesus must live in that very self-giving love that animated his life. Christians must readily show love and give their lives to their brothers

308

and sisters (1 John 3:16). We express love in concrete ways and not merely in good intentions and kind thoughts. We are tested in proving our claim to love God by how concrete we are in charity to our fellow human beings (1 John 3:18).

Saint Paul says in the second reading that our singular obligation to other people is to love them and work for their good. We do not restrict the responsibility and commitment to love to those who share our beliefs. It extends beyond ethnicity and political boundaries. It is our duty, Saint Paul says, to advise and correct those who think otherwise to repent and grow the love of God and neighbor. Our love must reach victims of disasters everywhere in the world, whether they be tsunamis, earthquakes, violent winds and floods, blazing fires, or wars, poverty, and famine.

Dr. Bruce Charash, a great friend with a Jewish background, believes that there will be total peace and stability in the entire world if we would love God, listen to the message of Jesus Christ, and serve God by living in peace with one another and taking care of the rest of God's creation. We are to intensify the concept of the Christian obligation of love, widen its range of operation, and spread it throughout the world by engaging in acts of love and caring for all people, especially the unloved, the sick, older adults, the marginalized, and starving children. This would be our way of assisting God in establishing his kingdom on Earth, comprising the suffering in Somalia, the underprivileged in the forests of Brazil, and the dying in Afghanistan and South Sudan.

Created in the image and divine likeness of God (Genesis 1:26), and sharing in his spiritual life, the *ruah* of God (2:7), humankind becomes *stewards* and *co-creators* with God to ensure that the perfect physicality of creation will maintain and sustain against the backdrop of evil and its forces working against God's purpose. Thus, "humans are meant to join God in further creating reality" (Patrick Engler, 2023), "and thus possessed of a special dignity which enables them, by the work of their hands, to reflect God's own *creative activity*" (Saint Pope John Paul II, *Laborem Exercens, 4*). Engler, (2023), again quotes human beings "are meant to be 'co-workers' with God, using their knowledge and skill to shape a cosmos in which the divine plane constantly moves towards fulfillment" (Gaudium et Spes, 34). Indeed, Jesus Christ reveals our divine likeness and makes a graced humanity possible as stewards and co-creators.

How can you show love, care, and concern to those you may not know, to those you may not realize are your brothers and sisters, and to any or all of God's children?

During the week, think of what you, as God's steward and co-creator, can do. What concrete steps you can take to make someone's burden or worry just a little lighter?

Think about how you can become God's co-creator to the lonely and distressed in a narcissistic, out of kilter, corrupt, and broken world of hate, division, prejudice, and fighting.

The Peace of the Lord be with you.

Prayer
Father, Your Son teaches that Christians must cheerfully show love and give their lives to their brothers and sisters. Help each of us to show love and support to all, especially those are suffering or in need. Amen.

TWENTY-FOURTH SUNDAY OF THE YEAR

Sirach 27:30-28:7; Romans 14:7-9; Matthew 18:21-35

FORGIVENESS, THE WAY TO RECONCILIATION

For a couple of weeks, we see Jesus based in Caesarea Philippi, where he does remarkable things in this center of idol worship in the area. He launches his Church in Caesarea Philippi after acknowledging Peter's "Declaration of Faith," when the disciple declared, "You are the Messiah, the Son of the Living God." Jesus distinguishes Peter as the "Rock," the bedrock foundation upon which the Church would be built (Matthew 16:13-19). Through Peter, the bequeathed of the keys to the kingdom of God, the Church will have power over Satan and his kingdom. Jesus reveals to them the real meaning of the mission of the Messiah: fated to suffer in Jerusalem at the hands of the elders and religious leaders. He further tells his disciples that the suffering will lead to his death, but after three days, there would be a victory in his resurrection. This is not good news for the disciples, and Peter calls Jesus aside to remind him about the common revered knowledge concerning the Messiah. That common notion is a huge hindrance in the way of the Messiah, Jesus tells them.

While moving with his disciples towards Jerusalem, Jesus teaches them about how the church should be organized. He deals with the matter regarding those aspiring to be great with top positions in the church. Such people ought to be the humble, welcoming, and compassionate (Matthew 18:1-9). The life of the church must not be scandalous to cause others to sin and Christians must reject anything that could entice them to sin (vv. 6-9). The members of the church are bound by the divine founder. They must always seek those who go astray and bring them back to the sheepfold like the good shepherd in the Parable of the Lost Sheep (vv. 10-14). Jesus underscores the need for the church to be forgiving and its members to forgive one another, practice fraternal correction and charity, and settle disputes (vv. 15-17). Indeed, when the church meets to discuss the good of the church, Jesus' spiritual presence would forever be assured and the church's decisions endorsed in heaven (vv. 18-20). Jesus prescribes certain guidelines to settle disputes with the purpose of bringing people together (vv. 15-17). All this would prevent individuals from taking advantage of their positions in the church to forge their own interests.

Peter, as "spokesperson for the others," selects forgiveness and asked the frequency of forgiving one another. At what point do we cease to tolerate those who take advantage of our silence to slight, hurt, or disgrace us all the time? He suggests to Jesus they could expand the Jewish custom of forgiving an offender three times to seven times as a perfect practice for the church. Jesus responds they should forgive "seventy times seven," implying that one should not count the many times one forgives an offender. Forgiveness is limitless and must come from one's heart where God dwells.

Jesus illustrates his instruction on forgiveness with the parable of "The Unmerciful Servant" followed by a strong warning that God will forgive no one who does not forgive an offender from the heart. In our daily prayers, we ask to "forgive us our trespasses, as we forgive those who trespass against us." The one who loves a good person must also show love, mercy, and forgiveness to an enemy. Such a person would be on the path to perfection (Matthew 5:48). We know that in life, it is a significant act of humility to stand before another person or a Council of Elders to ask for forgiveness or apologize for a fault. It is also a noble act of courage, charity, and dignity to forgive an offender and let go of anger, bitterness, revenge, and prejudice.

The readings chosen by the Church for today's liturgy stress the need for forgiveness and reconciliation in the world, church, communities, and families. The first reading

312

commonly known as "the Book of Sirach" has many other names: "The Wisdom of Ben Sira," "The Wisdom of Jesus Son of Sirach," "Sirach," and "Ecclesiasticus" (different from another Old Testament Book called Ecclesiastes).

Protestants refer to the "Book of Sirach" as one of the apocryphal (unauthentic) books because it was not part of the Hebrew Biblical Canonical Books. In the Roman Catholic and Eastern Orthodox traditions, however, the Greek translation of the Hebrew Old Testament (Septuagint) included books not found in the Hebrew version. These books are called "deuterocanonical" (the second canon). They are accepted as canonical (inspired by God) and part of the Christian Old Testament. This is partly because both the Greek and Latin Church Fathers accepted the books as canonical. For example, the Greek Fathers referred to "The Book of Sirach" as the "All-Virtuous Wisdom." The Latin Fathers, starting with Cyprian, called it "Ecclesiasticus" since they regularly read it in the church (ecclesia) and referred to it as the "church book" (Liber Ecclesiasticus).

In the author's mind in "The Book of Sirach," Wisdom is synonymous with the fear of God. Wisdom is also personified as the "Mind of God" that partnered in the world's creation. John the Evangelist continues the personification of Wisdom in the New Testament by developing the notion of the "Logos," the "Word" of God, Jesus Christ, who was with God in the beginning of time and became flesh to live among humanity (John 1:1-14). It increasingly becomes clear why Early Church Fathers referred to the Book of Sirach as the "church book" and accepted it as one of the inspired books of the Old Testament and therefore considered canonical.

Like the book of "Proverbs," the Book of Sirach is a collection of moral teachings. However, unlike Proverbs, only one person wrote the Book of Sirach—one of the great minds of Jewish philosophy and theology. He had made an in-depth study of the Jewish Mosaic Law and religion and wanted to share his knowledge of God with others. The book contains profound advice for parents and children, advice for forging and maintaining good relationships, and instructions regarding one's duty to oneself, to society, and to God. It also deals with certain phenomena in the world which seem beyond human understanding, such as the meaning of life, existence, the nature of God who created life, the nature of truth, and the reality of death and what follows thereafter. The author ponders the fundamental issues concerning wealth and poverty. In addition, the book is very much concerned about "fraternal sympathy" towards the poor and the oppressed.

In the verses of today's first reading, the author of the Book of Sirach, who lived about two hundred years before the birth of Jesus, shares his thoughts about the notion of forgiveness. He talks about the dangers of anger and resentment and urges us to forgive one another and not hang on to pride and self-righteousness. It is when we dispense mercy that God will shower his mercies upon us. God abhors anyone taking revenge on an offender. Indeed, revenge is reserved for God alone.

The author urges us to reflect on our mortal lives and the stark reality that each life will end. The inexplicable truths about life, its brevity, and uncertainty must ignite in us a sense of awe and wonder that must lead us to accept the divine whose commandments ought to be obeyed. Finally, the writer advises everyone to follow God's Commandments and show love to our neighbors, eschew hate, and overlook faults.

In today's second reading, Saint Paul compliments the belief that God created the world. He places creation or existence under the purview of God. Since we do not live by our own volition, it is logical that "if we live, it is for the Lord that we live, and if we die, it is for the Lord that we die." Like Saint John the evangelist's concept of the "Logos," Saint Paul refers to Jesus Christ as God Incarnate. By our baptism, we are incorporated into the universal "mystical body" of Christ. This means that as Christians, our entire lives find meaning in the life of Jesus, a life summarized or symbolized by love. We must, therefore, deepen our faith in Jesus, grow closer to him, and be faithful to our Creator (Galatians 2:20). This will enable us to face life's challenges while living together and forging close relationships.

Again, the readings of today explicitly vocalize the challenge to all peoples, particularly Christians, to accept everybody, irrespective of their cultural, social, and religious background. We must correct those observed to be recalcitrant, recognizing their weaknesses and frailties, and not ostracize them. We owe it as a moral and spiritual duty to be interested in the welfare of the poor and needy and show generosity to them. We ought to show love to one another and express it by embracing each other, forgiving those who hurt us, and ask for forgiveness from those we hurt.

We know that to "forgive and forget" is a lot easier said than done. Indeed, the mind is such that it might not forget a hurtful encounter. Each day is the anniversary of a wrong done to humanity: a mass shooting, execution and annihilation of an ethnic group, a senseless war, a horrible experience of racial slurs and killings, religious intolerance, family feuds, betrayals by friends, prejudices, jealousies, and sheer hatred. However, each moment we remember a wrong would be the time to forgive again and pray for the perpetrators of our injuries. Forgiveness gives us power to overcome Satan's tactics to create enmity and pain between us and our loved ones.

When is it more difficult for you to forgive a family member or co-worker who has "trespassed against you?" Do you pray for God's help at such times so that you harbor no ill will against them?

Nelson Mandela of South Africa is remembered as one of the most forgiving persons the world has seen. Before his arrest and during his 27 years in prison, mostly in the brutal Robben Island Prison, he was resentful and angry against the apartheid regime. But Mandela spoke of forgiveness and reconciliation, not revenge after his release from prison. He became a global advocate for peace and social justice and died in December 2013 at 95 years old.

Can you also forgive as a call from God all those who have wronged you, show them mercy and compassion, and then move on, always walking in the footsteps of Jesus?

The Peace of the Lord be with you.

Prayer
Father, we look for grace and strength from You to forgive one another as we also seek forgiveness from You. Amen.

TWENTY-FIFTH SUNDAY OF THE YEAR

Isaiah 55:6-9; Philippians 1:20c-24, 27a: Matthew 20:1-16

EMULATION OF GOD'S GENEROSITY

While traveling on a Rwanda Airplane a couple of years ago en route to Nairobi, Kenya, via Kigali, Rwanda, I came across a fascinating story written by Sam Kwizera, in one of the airlines' publications called INZOZI. It dates to about 400 years ago (1609-1642) when Mwami (King) Mibambwe Sekarongoro Gisanura ruled the Kingdom of Rwanda. He is remembered as a man of graceful disposition; a fair, and just ruler, who showed avid concern for the poor and needy in his kingdom.

In the story, there was a man caught stealing from the king. Once convicted of his crime, the king directed his two top chiefs to plan an appropriate punishment. The chiefs saw an opportunity to show they were hard on crime and innovative to suggest the toughest penalties. They believed their severe recommendations would ingratiate them with the king and gain prominent positions and honors in the royal court. Both proposed horrific forms of torture. The king asked the chiefs to demonstrate their ideas, so that he could better understand what they proposed. They eagerly went to work. One week later, the king arrived with his entourage to the scene of the punishment and inquired if everything was ready.

The chiefs nodded in agreement and with great pride, for they expected praise and some yet-to-be determined reward. They looked forward to watching with joy and satisfaction of their designed punishment meted out to the thief.

However, the king saw their apparent ingenuity as the work of depraved, evil, and merciless minds who had hearts of stone. He did not praise and reward them, but made them suffer the punishment they intended for the thief. He summoned the royal guards to whom he had already explained his intentions and told them to arrest the chiefs and "subject them to their own punishment! ...there is no place in my kingdom for men capable of such cruelty." The king echoed the words of the Scriptures and added, "the measure you use for others is the one that God will use for you" (Luke 6:38). Again, "God will judge you in the same way as you judge others, and he will apply to you the same rules you apply to others" (Matthew 7:2).

The rock at Ruhango on the Muhang-Huye Road, where the chiefs were cast to their fate and the people cheered their wise and compassionate ruler, continues to draw tourists every year.

Today's Gospel reminds us how we can show compassion to outcasts, from those we perceive to be unjust to those convicted of crimes. Jesus is nearing Jerusalem from Caesarea Philippi and continues to tell his disciples about his vision of the life of his Church founded on Peter, the Rock, and their role in it. He announces the incredibly irrefutable truths about the kingdom in parables and continues to give guidelines for managing the Church.

Only found in the Gospel of Matthew, the Gospel is a response to Peter's question about rewards for those who toil and sweat to build God's kingdom. Like the parable of the Prodigal Son and the Good Samaritan, this parable is a shock to the disciples because its context seems to be outside the normal social life. The workers in the parable are daily job seekers who rely on daily wages to feed their families. By law, it is incumbent on estate or farm owners to pay their workers by sunset (Deuteronomy 24:14-15). The hours of work specified in the parable range from six in the morning to six in the evening in the scorching summer sun of Palestine. Working in the vineyard is so exhausting that more workers are sometimes hired during the day to complete a task. The owner in the parable hires five groups of workers at various intervals, with the last batch going to the farm at five o'clock just one hour before pay time.

Here comes the shocking part: the owner gives the same pay to each group! The earlier group's expectation to receive more pay because they worked more hours is unfulfilled. They are indignant and protest strongly about the alleged injustice, although they would have kept quiet had they worked the whole day without knowing about the others being hired for just an hour.

Similarly, there was resentment in the Early Church among the first-century Jews against the Gentile late-comers to the faith. They considered the Gentiles the late hired workers. The Jews held the idea that they were God's chosen people. They were the first workers in the parable who, over the millennia from the time of Abraham, had enjoyed a special favor with God. But when Jesus announced the imminent coming of the new kingdom and the long-awaited Messiah rewarding people, he threw away the notion of special Jewish privilege, and invited Gentiles into the kingdom for the same reward. We are all God's children and heirs of God's promise to Abraham (Genesis 22:18), and there are no equity issues in the kingdom of God. Jesus begins the parable and ends it with, "But many who are first now will be last, and many who are last now will be first."

Traditionally, today's parable is used to address how God allows outcasts—that is, tax collectors and sinners, distanced from God's Salvation Plan in the life of Israel—to receive full recognition in the kingdom of God. We often refer to the call of Matthew, Zacchaeus, Paul, the criminal crucified with Jesus, and many proclaimed saints who had dreadful earlier lives. Hence, the Church has always readily accepted known notorious and wicked people, even those who convert on their sick beds and compelled her ministers and lay faithful to give them access to the Sacraments.

However, when viewing the first reading and the parable together, we also see another meaning to the parable from a traditional interpretation. The owner is fulfilling his part of an agreement with each group. The fortunes of the disgruntled first batch of workers could not change since they received the officially accepted daily wage. In fact, the owner also realizes that despite the number of hours the workers spend on the farm, each would need a full day's wage to feed his family. This is an incredible act of mercy and generosity, and the other workers should applaud and appreciate the owner's kindness.

319

In the parable, therefore, God is honoring his promise to Abraham's children spread beyond the borders of Israel to all nations. Thus, the Prophet Isaiah sends a welcoming message about God's generosity, of which all peoples are beneficiaries. At the eleventh-hour, Jesus fights for this dispensation on the Cross and his resurrection celebrates his victory. God's love shows that while we were sinners, Christ died for us (Romans 5:8). All of us, standing in need of God's grace, are saved by the gratuitous love of Jesus Christ, and not by our worthiness (Arland J. Hultgren, 2020). The disciples must therefore make this dispensation and Good News their ardent clarion call to all peoples (Acts 2:38) while traveling to the corners of the world (Matthew 28:19-20).

The parable goes beyond what Labor Unions may see as unjust regarding the posture of the farm owner. Isaiah provides us with a remarkable explanation and comparison in the first reading: "As high as the heavens are above the earth, so high are my ways and thoughts above yours." When we apply our human thought to appreciate God, we may fail in our analysis of him. Here, we see God's never-ending generosity and must focus on how we should emulate him and focus our love and generosity towards the poor and the needy and show them clemency, compassion, and empathy. Diseases, food shortages, and dreadful human conditions have rendered many people outcasts. Thousands of people, particularly in developing countries, struggle each day in abject poverty in refugee camps as victims of senseless and ruthless civil wars, ethnic cleansing, political persecution, and economic mismanagement. Our young men and women are exposed to readily available drugs that destroy their sense of judgment and usually make them a danger to themselves and society. We besmirch, abandon, and relegate such people into a world of isolation, pain, and loneliness, when they are better served by our sympathy and generosity.

In the Gospel, we meet manual workers willing to work hard to make ends meet, but wait for hours on end looking for work. Today, these include the well-qualified but unemployed, those laid off, or those at home on furlough. In many cities, they become marginalized and homeless. The unemployed and those struggling for simple things in life need our compassion and help.

An economist, Dr. David Stuckler, in an interview in "Oxford Today" (October 7, 2013) has suggested that "we should treat unemployment like the pandemic it is—a leading cause of suicide, alcoholism and heart attacks." In countries such as Sweden and Finland where politicians have better managed the social consequences of unemployment, suicides and depression have been reduced.

The introductory story becomes significant and a great lesson. The king, Gisanura, would not punish the thief by executing any of the means suggested by his wicked chiefs. He was kind and generous to the offender and probably thought about ways and means to rehabilitate him. But, as he rightly said, he would not tolerate chiefs who would seek vengeance and punishment instead of seeking to alter wickedness with mercy. The members of the "Family of God" must not behave like the two chiefs in our story. Yet, from the dissonance of the world, we hear of cruel acts of violence, including massacres, arsons, and kidnappings (both planned and executed) typically against innocent men, women, and children. We need to show sympathy to the perpetrators of such heinous crimes and pray that God touches their hearts to change them to serve the society in positive ways.

In the Kingdom of God, God rules with a kind and generous heart. However, Isaiah provides an important caveat in the first reading. God's mercy and forgiveness are beyond measure, but they come to us thorough repentance. Isaiah advises: "Seek the Lord while he may be found." He added that the villain and the wicked must change their way of life to deserve God's mercy.

How do you show the world and the surrounding people that you recognize your blessings, for which you should also show love, mercy, and generosity?

How is your life changed to be an example to others doing exactly what Jesus would have you do?

How do you think Jesus would have us react to people who have hurt us?

Someone shared her experience after reading last week's reflection. She stated, "Being human, I have at times found it hard to forgive, much less forget. But one time I was driving to Mass when I was really upset with someone and unable to forgive. I heard the voice of God ask me that if this were my last moment on earth, would I risk the loss of eternal life with God just because of some offense I might have suffered? I decided then and there that nothing and no one person was worth my losing the opportunity to be with God forever! And that was the end of my grudge! Of course, this happened after several months of bearing that grudge!"

"And something else that I say to myself that has helped me to be more accepting of others is to look at that person in the car next to me blaring his radio too loudly or the woman in Walmart who jumped in line is to say to myself, "Christ died for that person." Believe me, that has helped me in so many situations!"

May this experience change all of us.

Another person writes thus about this experience: "I find her story relevant because I think we all feel grudges in our heart and may think negative thoughts toward that person, the way the chiefs did (if not to the level of violence). Her story is a reminder to let go of that pain and negativity and replace it with patience and kindness."

The Peace of the Lord be with you.

Prayer
Father, Your Son teaches peace, love, and forgiveness. Teach us the ways to show love, sympathy, and compassion to those who offend us. Amen.

TWENTY-SIXTH SUNDAY OF THE YEAR

Ezekiel 18:25-28; Philippians 2:1-11; Matthew 21:28-32

TIME TO THINK RIGHT

A couple of years ago, my godson Gary visited me in Kumasi, Ghana, at Opoku Ware School, where I was a teacher. He was smiling and in high spirits, saying he had some exciting messages to share with me. He had just received his Advanced Level results, qualifying him to attend university. His grades were outstanding, and the three major universities in Ghana had offered him admission. I was not surprised because he was an intelligent and hardworking young man. I congratulated him and said I was very proud of him.

He thanked me profusely for my moral and physical support. He had once had problems with the school authorities, which could have affected his studies and, subsequently, his grades. In addition, he had not been born with a silver spoon in his mouth. In the primary school, he often had to sell newspapers or shine shoes in the streets of Kumasi to help finance his education. Both of us agreed we had to thank the Almighty God for his excellent achievement.

Again, he said he was happy to inform me that after many attempts, he and some of his friends had finally obtained entry visas to travel to the West Indies. Being the firstborn, Gary intended to make money elsewhere to support his family, especially his younger siblings. He and his friends had already purchased tickets and were ready to leave in just a few days. I rapped his shoulders gently and told him to sit. "Son," I told him, "think seriously about your decision to discontinue your education. You have performed well in your examinations. I think you should go to the university in Ghana with your excellent grades. I believe your grades are the foundation of greater things to come and I will do all I can to support you." This was a startling and unexpected message to him. Gary, struggling under the weight of my verbal pep-talk, continued to avert his eyes from me. I left him to think more about my advice. He sat quietly for about one hour, discombobulated, and sighing in between his thoughts. He was painfully weighing all the options and racking his brain about what to do, whether to go to school in Ghana or travel abroad with his friends.

Gary stayed in Ghana and worked hard at the University of Ghana Legon. While at the university, he had the opportunity to travel to the United Kingdom and other European countries, as well as to the United States and Canada. Soon after graduation, he established a travel and tour agency which I have used many times. Indeed, he built a house for his parents and established a mechanic shop for his biological father. He assisted his siblings through High School to the university, two of them furthering their education in London. Following this success, Gary discussed with me the idea of enrolling at the Law School. "What a wonderful idea," I said encouragingly.

Today, Gary is a lawyer. I am proud of him and delighted with his achievements at the Bar and in public life. He showed me, his godfather, due respect. He would not frustrate me and agreed to accept my advice. Admitting on the one hand, he had his own wonderful ideas and dreams for a bright future in wanting to travel, but on the other, he saw I desired the best for him. He believed I loved him. He trusted that somehow, by intuition and experience, I saw a brighter future for him at home. He listened.

The background to the Gospel reading of today is the concern from the traditional elders and the teachers of the Law regarding Jesus' acclaimed power to preach about God, work miracles, and, especially, interpret the Law. Jesus had confronted them about their silence when he challenged them to evaluate the mission of John the Baptist, who likewise had condemned them for their complacency and erroneous interpretations of the Law. John the Baptist advised them to repent of their self-righteousness and the pretense that they followed God's will.

Jesus argued using the analogy of the "The Parable of the two Sons." The first son had initially blatantly repudiated the father's request. This was tantamount to showing his father gross disrespect and defiance. Upon second thought, however, he complied with the father's will, notwithstanding his prior display of insolence. The second son, who had previously given an affirmative response as a deferential boy enthusiastic about undertaking the father's mission, refused to do it in the end.

The elders and teachers acknowledged before Jesus that the first boy who had said no to the father but had later carried out the task was the one who had done the father's will. The second boy, who presented himself as the more obliging and obsequious in the father's house, showed his true character as just a pretender.

Jesus uses their answer to condemn the religious leaders and the teachers of the Law. The basic message of John the Baptist (Matthew 3:7-9) echoed that of Ezekiel in the first reading. Jesus was preaching the same message. If the unrighteous one thinks seriously about his unrighteous ways and repents, he will not be punished for his unrighteousness. However, if the self-acclaimed righteous one remains unrepentant, he will die in his impenitent unrighteousness.

The tax collectors and sinners were acting like the first boy in the parable who move closer to Jesus and John the Baptist to think seriously about repentance. Indeed, those who have time for sinners are godly. Their principal aim is to make sinners repent and live in the Lord with joy and happiness. Thus, the people searched out John the Baptist in the desert to listen to the Good News. They had heard the kingdom of God was soon to appear. They had put the past behind them and were showing the fruit of repentance in sharing their lives with others (Luke 3:10-14).

On the other hand, the leaders were recalcitrant, refusing to change and obey the prophets (John the Baptist and Jesus included). They were paying lip-service to God. God would not condone their complacency; they would be rejected. However, the outcasts and the morally corrupt who would reject their past sinful lives and repent of their sins would be received into God's kingdom. Jesus, therefore, had an answer to the doubt and hostility of the leaders about his authority. They would be better off if they listened to him.

How better off too would be those of my godson Gary's generation, as well as the present generation of young students, if they would seriously consider the well-intentioned advice from their parents who want to guide them to prosperity? How abundant would their blessings be if they should listen to Jesus and follow in his footsteps?

What do I do, what can I do, and what should I do? How many times in your life have you asked yourself these same questions?

"Hindsight is 20/20," it is said. Looking far back, can you see how the early decisions you made have played out in your life?

Although it might be too late to undo the consequences of past decisions, it is never too late to pray to Jesus for his help and guidance when facing the decisions you will have to make in the future.

Follow in the footsteps of Jesus by making decisions that will keep you on the path you know he wants you to take.

The Peace of the Lord be with you.

Prayer
Father, we thank you for the gift of the young women and men you give to our society. Let the Holy Spirit help them to be patient in life and obedient to Your Son's Word, that brings joy and happiness. Amen.

TWENTY-SEVENTH SUNDAY OF THE YEAR

Isaiah 5:1-7; Philippians 4:6-9; Matthew 21:33-43

GOD'S SONG ABOUT THE NEW PEOPLE IN HIS VINEYARD

The Prophet Isaiah begins today's readings saying he will chant about the life of his friend and his vineyard; this homily will likewise be a song about a famous musician, a friend of the world, from some years ago.

The sad overture begins in July 2011, when the world was stunned and thrust into a state of profound grief about the sudden passing of Amy Winehouse, a 27-year-old British singer. Her untimely death resonated into a sad and distressing song that was echoed by the media throughout the world, including The Tablet (July 30, 2011) of the Catholic Diocese of Brooklyn, USA. The younger generation had seen her as a much-loved idol in the music industry for her remarkably "deeply moving and powerful contralto vocals," as observed by Father Frank Mann in an article in The Tablet. Father Mann acknowledged her as "the first British female to win five Grammy Awards in one shot for her riveting, soul-stirring album entitled *Back to Black*." He quoted a British columnist, Russell Brand, who described her voice as "... a wondrous resonance ... an awe that envelops when witnessing a genius," and again, as a voice that "seemed not to come from her but from somewhere beyond... from the font of all greatness. Hers was a voice that was filled with such power and pain that it was at once entirely human yet laced with the divine." I could not have agreed more with the attributes apportioned to Amy Winehouse after I had searched online to listen to *Back to Black* and many other songs.

Let me begin with the first stanza of Amy Winehouse's life-song. Her parents had a beautiful girl growing up in a palatial, peaceful, healthy, and flourishing home, likened to a vineyard (first reading), with well-prepared soils for roses and lilies blooming all seasons, beguiling numerous butterflies and hummingbirds. Amy was intelligent, ambitious, and exuded high expectations. She lived up to them. At age ten, she founded a short-lived rap group. Her own successful songs soon reached a crescendo. Everyone sang them and praised her high angelic contralto voice, streaming across the horizon to enthrall the entire world. She was singing them one by one: *Frank, Back to Black, Stronger Than Me,* and *Rehab,* receiving several accolades and awards for each.

Soon, however, the power of her performance withered away: not in her voice at first, but in her physical, spiritual, and emotional weakening. Her many admirers watched her swift, shattering descent and worsening performance in her concerts. The family members lamented their "daughter's openly courting of disaster," Father Mann wrote, and added it was "like a car crash." It was like watching "this person throwing all their gifts away," her mother bemoaned.

Everyone watched helplessly as her life-song became dissonant at the end, the chords misaligned as her life took a chaotic course. Her drug addictions ravaged her body and disintegrated her soul. Sadly, the final curtain lowered on the life of Amy Winehouse at the prime age of twenty-seven! Society had failed to protect one of its vulnerable children in its vineyard.

Do we create good vineyards for our children? Do we build opportunities for them? Do we build faith around them? Do we teach them Christian values and give them the right training and education? How can you express your love and concern for one of God's children who appears on the "crash and burn" path, like the pop-singer Amy Winehouse?

When so many marital couples who do not focus on the will of God, and day by day, drift away from God, they often affect their children when their relationships end in despair. Their lives should not end so hastily and disastrously.

With the spectacular analogy of a wine grower doing everything possible to produce the best of wines in the first reading, Isaiah serenades to show God's singular tender loving care and concern for his beloved. By careful planning and hard labor, Isaiah's friend prepares a large farm and creates an enabling environment for the finest planted vines to thrive and produce heavy and succulent fruits. Anticipating a good harvest, he prepares for the processing of the grapes by building a large wine vat. He constructs a watchtower so that enemies will not sneak into the farm to tamper with his top-quality winery. Despite his efforts, the farmer is distraught by the vineyard's yield of wild and rotten grapes, not at all useful returns for the vintner.

In Isaiah's story, God is the owner of the vineyard which represents the nation of Israel. The people are God's cherished plants, expected to bear good grapes for the best wine. But Isaiah's love-song about God's marvelous benevolence towards Israel changes into a song of lament. The expected outcome of God's love and protection turns sour and unpleasant. The people return God's affection and blessings with utter ingratitude and complacency as they avoid God in their day-to-day way of life.

Each life from cradle to grave is God's love-song about living in the vineyard. The vineyard is God's kingdom, which is everybody's home to live with the Lord. God creates the world as a paradise with the rhythm of the seasons to provide rain and sunshine to fertilize the soils and to produce vines heavy with fruit. God endows human life with wisdom and intelligence to co-exist in peace and harmony, "to know him, love him, and serve him," and extend the same courtesy to all life.

But we have failed to be good stewards to one another, to our children especially; even Mother Earth's previously soothing and peaceful songs have turned into dirges. Humanity does not have as much faith in God and continuously compromises God's justice and respect for human life. In the socio-political and religious milieus, leaders have abandoned the people assigned to them to govern with dignity and accountability. Many people remain in abject poverty, experiencing injustice and discrimination, feeling depressed or down, and lacking basic human needs while always singing sad choruses. We expose young people to deceiving information from self-seeking individuals and social media that lure them into other manners of life-styles detrimental to their physical and mental health. They are living through a higher rate of unhappiness and mental illness because of drug and alcohol prevalence. They feel a lot of pressure both at home and in school, and do not know how to live a stable life when affected by financial issues.

God is pruning and nurturing a new vineyard—a new covenant—through his Son (Hebrews 1:1). He is starting a new love-partnership with each life, more intense than before. All this shows God's love, generosity, and patience reflected in the parable in the Gospel of today. Therefore, God expects more from us, whom he has adopted and invited into his kingdom. We are the plants in the vineyard, and we have to protect each other from the man-made diseases that can plague our health: drugs, alcohol, and abuses of money and power, caused by instant fame and increased pressure to live life to its fullest in purely material terms.

God wants a full life to be found in caring for one another and for home (the vineyard), but society pushes people into caring only for themselves, to get rich quick, to do drugs and alcohol to take the edge off, to engage in risky behavior because there is only one life to live; don't miss out! Our children need to understand that a life lived to the fullest is possible in God's love and graces, which nurture and support our bodies, minds and souls, but not through addictive substances that hurt our bodies and our relationships. This is the hope that our young men and women must learn about and live.

Amy Winehouse had so many gifts from God, and yet, she did not know or feel the love God had for her. Her part of God's vineyard had everything it needed, but the vats still arrived to turn the fruits into personal profit. Again, those close to her took their eyes off God's tender loving care for their daughter and focused on the periphery, fame, fortune, vats, and turrets, thus allowing the withering of both Amy and the grapes.

Our covenant with God is a new love-song reminiscent of Paul's imitation of the life of Jesus Christ. Paul tells us to be determined in our love for Jesus to remain truthful, honorable, just, pure, lovely, and gracious (second reading), so that we can bear good fruits and sing comforting songs about our lives in Christ Jesus. As individuals and societies, we need to recognize our faults and seek God's forgiveness and grace to become responsible and productive stewards.

How do we apply the two parables of today to our own lives as new tenants in God's kingdom? In the new dispensation from Jesus for all, we are a new creation with the conscience, wisdom, and the blessings of God that should have protected young people like Amy Winehouse whose life-song we end with *Sileo in perficio pacis (Rest in perfect peace).*

The Peace of the Lord be with you.

Prayer
Father, many of our young women and men are struggling to find meaning in life. Let Your Spirit be a light to guide them in recognizing Your Son Jesus who is Life, so that they do not take the path to "crash and burn." Amen.

TWENTY-EIGHTH SUNDAY OF THE YEAR

Isaiah 25:6-10a; Philippians 4:12-14. 19-20; Matthew 22:1-14

GOD'S INSTRUMENTS ON EARTH

We are in the season of awarding Nobel Prizes. The Nobel Prizes are renowned yearly international awards conferred on individuals and groups who have excelled in cultural and scientific endeavors marked by intellectual and creative achievements. Alfred Nobel (1833-1896), a Swedish chemist, engineer, inventor, and philanthropist, established the award in 1895. His wealth acquired mostly from his recorded 355 inventions, of which dynamite was the most famous. What may be less well known is that while living in Paris, he had problems with the French over patent or exclusive rights regarding the production and sale of ballistite, another type of explosive material of his creation. France banned him from engaging in any further research and manufacturing explosives in France. He moved to Italy, successfully licensed the rights to the Italian government, and established a factory in the Italian town of Avigliana, Turin.

Mistaking his brother's death for his, a French newspaper published his obituary, entitled "The Merchant of Death is Dead." The epitaph read, "Dr. Alfred Nobel, who became rich by finding ways to kill more people faster than ever before, died yesterday." This was an obviously denigrating comment which disturbed him regarding his perceived legacy since he had never married nor had children. This motivated him to institute the Nobel Prizes for several awards in cultural and academic pursuits that would give the "greatest benefit to mankind." The funds were worth $472 million in 2012. The awards were initially in physics, chemistry, peace, physiology or medicine, and literature. The Nobel Foundation was subsequently established to manage his assets and organize the awarding of the prizes. Over the years, the foundation added other prizes, including one for economic sciences established by Sweden's Central Bank in 1968 in Nobel's memory.

Today, the coveted Nobel award is one of the most prestigious recognitions and awards in the world. Each Nobel laureate receives a gold medal, a diploma with a citation, and money. It is ironic that the once described "merchant of death" donated his fortunes to motivate others for finding antidotes against inflammatory diseases and promoting human understanding by saving lives and bringing about peace in the world.

Nelson Mandela, South Africa's first black president, received the award in 1993 for his belief in human rights for every person. Wangari Maathai (1940-2011), a Kenyan political activist and the first African woman to be awarded, received the Nobel Peace Prize in 2004 for her green belt movement, which led to a record planting of 50 million trees to combat climate change.

Awarding the 2020 prize in chemistry to Emmanuelle Charpentier (France) and Jennifer Doudna (USA), the Nobel Committee described their scientific innovation as "contributing to new cancer therapies to make the dream of curing inherited diseases come true" (Nell Greenfieldboyce and Mark Katkov, 2020). The authors write further that "Already, doctors have used the technology to experimentally treat sickle cell disease, with promising results."

Among the 2020 Nobel laureates was the World Food Program (WFP) which is the United Nations food-assistance initiative. The WFP won the award for its efforts to combat global hunger "and prevent it from being used as a weapon of war and conflict." The Norwegian Nobel Committee attests that "the world faces a hunger crisis of inconceivable proportions. The coronavirus pandemic has contributed to a strong upsurge in the number of victims of hunger." In 2019, WFP assisted about 100 million hunger victims in 88 countries (WFP, 2019 Report).

Additional motivating awards in 2023 included Narges Mohammadi "for her fight against the oppression of women in Iran and her fight to promote human rights and freedom for all" and Claudia Goldin "for having advanced our understanding of women's labor market outcomes."

Overall, the Alfred Nobel Prize has been awarded 621 times to 1,000 individuals and organizations from 1901 to 2023. As some have received it more than once, 965 people and 27 organizations have received it to date. This is an amazing testament to a universal value of life, inspired by people who want to change the world for the better.

Today's first reading presents the Prophet Isaiah's impressive image of a new age that would soon become a reality, a splendid vision portraying a grand banquet. It would be a gathering comprising all peoples of the world on God's Holy Mountain. It would be symbolic of a "global village" which all must joyfully be part of. It would be the start of an eternal coming together because "death and tears would have been conquered" (Isaiah 25). While experiencing God's presence forever, people's lives would be marked by extraordinary happiness with scrumptious meals and highly rated wines.

The prophet, however, deeply laments that people's pride, disloyalty to God, and strong desire for worldly things have combined to impede the intention of God to organize the glorious and luscious feast. The parable of the Wedding Feast is concerned about the responses and responsibilities of invitees. Many guests do not attend the feast for varied reasons. Some have blatantly ignored the invitation to be under God's reign and authority. They include atheists who have made the determination to obliterate the image of God from the face of the earth. They doubt God's existence and therefore flout his commandments and instructions. Others deliberately create mayhem, perpetuate terrorist attacks, and foment political and ethnic instability to destroy God's plans for peace.

The second part of the parable of today's Gospel, The Missing Wedding Garment, is about someone who appears at the wedding without the prescribed costume. This parable symbolizes Christian responsibility or the internal turning of one's heart to God. The "stranger" in the parable is punished for refusing to undergo spiritual formation to be incorporated into the Body of Christ. As Christians, we must accept Jesus Christ as Savior and Lord and reflect on our worthiness before honoring Jesus' invitation. Our outward actions must grow out of faith from within. We are not to take God's generous calling as an easy entry into the banquet hall, but to wear the proper garment embroidered with the right Christian codes that exude holiness and humility and show concern and gratitude towards other people.

The second reading introduces another Christian notion or garment of mutual relationship and of sharing of wealth, intelligence, and wisdom, as well as challenges. Saint Paul acknowledges with utmost gratitude the generosity he received from the community (Philippians 4:10-20) although desiring to be self-sufficient through his own hard work (1 Thessalonians 2:5-9). Paul continues to urge his audience, and all of us today, to acknowledge the power of Christ in our daily lives, exemplified by a life of charity, generosity, and compassion.

Although Isaiah's story of God's banquet and the parables in the Gospel are about the future, they also indicate a present reality of God's people coming together as brothers and sisters to ensure peace and harmony on earth (second reading). Likewise, Nobel laureates "expand our knowledge, improve our planet, and enrich our lives" (Dr. Matthew Sayers, 2016). By their selflessness, creativity, persistence, dedication, and readiness to work together, they "remind us that humans, with all of our obvious flaws, can still contribute substantially to advancing our collective progress.

There is an obvious connection made between the Nobel laureates and those who go to Mass to receive the Eucharist. The awardees do not make change simply to receive the award; their work is their passion to make change for the betterment of humanity, regardless of whether or not they receive an award for it. The same can be said for those who receive the Eucharist. We do not attend church and receive the Body and Blood simply because we want entrance into heaven. We go because we are passionate about being God's children, about embracing his word and each other, and in the hopes of receiving his graces in good times and bad. We pray collectively for the betterment of others; we provide donations to assist those in need, and we do so without the expectation of a reward.

But every act counts in the end, and even if we are not known worldwide for those we have helped, God knows, and we will attend his grand banquet in heaven to celebrate the lives we changed through his teachings and guidance. We wear our Eucharistic garment because we are humbled to be in God's presence, and to remind us we must assist each other in times of need. We do not expect any rewards for our actions, but trusting in the hope unified in Christ, we elevate each other and can celebrate together in heaven with those freed from pain and suffering.

Indeed, you may not stand out to the level of Nobel laureates working towards global solutions in promoting peace or contributing to eradicate diseases, poverty, corruption, and relentless evil. Yet, in "little ways" at home, work, school, and in the community, we have the capability of becoming instruments that can influence people to find peace, joy, and love on earth.

We must accept God's invitation and join him in mind, heart, and will, as well as put on the perfect Christian garment the Church bequeaths to us when we receive the Sacraments. The Eucharistic banquet, known as the Holy Eucharist, is the finest way to visualize the heavenly banquet. It is a gathering of all peoples in Christ, like a mosaic of colorful pieces when dressed in various ethnic costumes, seated around the Altar of Grace to be fed with the One Bread of Life.

How would you recognize and acknowledge the power of Jesus in the Eucharist?

Do you see that Jesus can help you to forgive others, reform and grace your day-to-day life, and allow your behavior to influence those in need to bring them peace, joy, and love?

You are God's instrument on earth, a Nobel laureate!

The Peace of the Lord be with you.

Prayer
Father, we thank you for touching the hearts of women and men to be instruments of your peace, joy, and love on earth. Let your Spirit guide more people to put on the perfect Christian garments. Amen.

TWENTY-NINTH SUNDAY OF THE YEAR

Isaiah 45:1, 4-6; 1 Thessalonians 1:1-5b; Matthew 22:15-21

USING ALL TO ACHIEVE GOD'S WILL

Traditionally, new lawyers are called to the Bar in Ghana during this time of the year. I had the honor of attending one of the graduation ceremonies. From a distance, the scene bore a resemblance to a large fertile ground of mushrooms, sprouting gracefully and glistening with the morning dewdrops waiting for chefs to come selecting. However, as one got nearer, the mirage of a meadow of mushrooms immediately transformed into a euphoric sight, screening nearly two hundred young women and men wearing the lawyer's wig. Smart in their dress suits, each candidate proudly wore the traditional wing collar, pin, bib, and gown. These were excited Law School candidates deemed qualified to be called to the Ghana Bar, with the women outnumbering the men for the first time in many years. The overall best performance award went to a lady. In addition, women won most of the awards for outstanding achievement in the various sectors of the Law course program.

The graduates had worked for four years pursuing their university degree and then another grueling three years in the Law School where competition for admission had always been intense. The last hurdle was the tough bar examination. And then graduation day! One by one, the candidates were called to approach the stage to receive their coveted law certificates. In this batch of new lawyers called to the Bar on October 1, 2011, at the Great Hall of the University of Legon, Accra, was my god-son Gary who had invited me to his graduation.

Every aspect of human life is directly influenced by society's legal systems behind which are lawyers who craft the laws of their sovereign countries. We therefore expect them to be experts who serve in varied legal jurisdictions as Attorney, Counsel, or Solicitor. The Judiciary Arm of Government applies the laws of the land to ensure good neighborliness, delivery of justice, peaceful co-existence, and political as well as social stability in the society. As we link laws to society in all its facets, we hold the practitioners of the law in high esteem as dependable members of the society who are duty-bound to subject themselves to a strict code of ethics.

The Chief Justice at the graduation, Georgina Wood, supervised the induction of the new lawyers into the Ghana Bar. She minced no words in drumming home to the newcomers that they should be women and men of integrity and sincerity who must always show a genuine passion for justice. As catalysts for peace and harmony in the society, they should "undertake their professional pursuits with civility and without acrimony." The Chief Justice intimated that a lawyer must not be distinguished by the garb, "the famous wig and gown alone; but, outstandingly, by his or her language and etiquette," differentiating him or her as a person of good moral fiber and of "noble character."

Our readings for today confirm the firm belief that God is the Lord of the Universe from its beginning. God permeates creation towards a purposeful end by his profound divine interest, sovereignty, and intervention in human life and its social institutions.

The first reading is a clear example of God's engagement, power, and control at another crucial period in the history of Israel. When Cyrus the Great of the Persian Empire defeated the Babylonian power (c.537 B.C.) and extended his rule into the territory of Israel, the Prophet Isaiah quickly reminded the people that Cyrus' mission was a divine plan. The new regime allowed the Jewish exiles' return to their original homeland to rebuild the Temple and Jerusalem. Indeed, Cyrus, a pagan king unaware of God's hand in his victories, was accorded the accolade "anointed," a Messianic title reserved for kings and religious leaders of Israel. It meant Israel recognized that God's power was universal, affecting those who did not even worship him. Again, it shows that God is also the intellect behind scientific discoveries that will lead the universe to a purposeful end. The reading reveals how God's salvation reaches all the earth and that he has given each person knowledge and responsibility to promote unity and peace.

Paul's letter to the Thessalonians is his earliest written document (c.51 A.D.). Today's reading commends the faithful for their "work of faith and labor of love and steadfastness in the hope of our Lord Jesus Christ" even through hardship. The triad or harmony of faith, hope, and love is stressed by Paul and his companions who praise God for letting the Christians know he loved them and chose them to live a new way of life directed by Jesus Christ with God's power through the Holy Spirit.

The nearly two hundred young women and men at the graduation in Ghana, and elsewhere throughout the world, need to know that God is keenly interested in their lives and that the lawyer's wig symbolizes the knowledge and wisdom conferred on them by God. The costume is a reminder that they are robed by God and called to represent him to effect peace and justice. They must put aside their personal interests and passions to demonstrate discipline, tolerance, and respect for the values in the society.

Similarly, God is actively behind all kinds of uniforms and dress-codes: soldiers and police officers, firefighters, medical personnel, and ministers of God's Word. There are also symbols, such as badges, stoles, hats, and scarves, that identify individuals and their jobs. There are certain positions ascribed by society to individuals, such as heads of states, ministers of states, politicians, chiefs and queens, parents, teachers, managers, household helpers, and community leaders. Each of these roles, positions, and talents are responsibilities and duties conferred by God to serve the society wherever we find ourselves.

Nothing in the universe is therefore contradictory. God's power or influence is always evident. Political institutions are part of a divine plan to bring about order and peace (Romans 13:1-7). The citizenry must respect and co-operate with civil authorities, assist with their assessments, and pray for leaders to be obedient to God in carrying out their roles assigned by God. Therefore, society must not see duty to God and nation as conflict, but complementary. God is working in the secular and

340

religious realms to establish his kingdom. But governments, certain clubs, and fraternities, who do not perceive God's hand in their work, tend to be oppressive and serve their own interests instead of the public good.

God's ways of bringing consistency, unity, and perfection to creation also include the wisdom of apportioning various ethnic or religious groups to specific areas. We are all different across the different ethnicities and religious affiliations, but we are all the same, woven together as a tapestry that is as beautiful in its diversity as in how complimentary we are to each other. Societies do not need to be completely uniform to still operate by God's intention, and that is why there are so many cultures that still operate in God's loving and peaceful ways. We can learn how to be better humans by understanding and recognizing the different rules and laws in each land, and perhaps adopting those laws that better serve humanity. We all have room to grow, and God encourages us to do so by bridging the gap with other societies. All these differences in human life and the unfortunate disturbances within, incomprehensible and disconcerting as they may seem, are unwittingly keeping to the plan of God towards a purposeful end.

In the Gospel, disciples from the Pharisees and Herodians, who regularly were at odds with each other, went to set-up Jesus into the mesh of the Roman authority. The Herodians were a kind of public, non-religious party different from the Pharisees and the Sadducees. They allied with Herod the Great and wished to promote the Herodian dynasty to the throne in Judea. It is opined that they saw Herod as Messiah. They agreed with the Roman authority and against Jesus' teaching that were against their interests.

The Pharisees belonged to an ancient Jewish sect who were meticulous in following their oral traditions and the written Law of Moses. They expected a Messiah to restore the Davidic kingdom and did not accept Jesus as the Messiah. Both groups reviled Jesus and wanted him killed. Still, they described Jesus as a truthful, excellent teacher, one who would not deviate from God's principles, was independent in thinking, respected people's opinions, and was bold enough to confront authorities unfazed by the prospect of arrest. They knew this was flattery and their trap question revealed their trickery, insincerity, and malice: To pay taxes or not to pay taxes? A "no" answer and the Herodians would accuse Jesus of treason before the Romans, and a "yes" answer would be tantamount to disloyalty as a Jew before the people. Besides, the image on the coin called a denarius was the emperor with the inscription Divine. A "yes" answer would have violated the first commandment. Jesus' response, "Give to Caesar what belongs to Caesar, and to God what belongs to God," stunned them and they left.

Society has an influence on everything we do in our lives, based on laws of the land that are enforced by those in authority. God also has influence on everything that happens in society, by touching the hearts and minds of those in authority, who make those decisions that affect the citizens. Those not aligned with God lead from a position of selfishness and drive the minds and behaviors of their people to live lawlessly. These are the people who try to entrap us to ignore God's teachings, based on the belief that we should care only for ourselves regardless of how our choices affect those around us. Each of us is in a battle every day to stand up for what is right. When we trust in Jesus and the Holy Spirit to continue working through us, we, too, can answer tricky questions and avoid being condemned. It is only Jesus' truth that can save us from falling victim to temptations of selfish abuse of power and position.

You ought to be aware of other people who will trap you in doing things that are not of God: to indulge in corrupt practices, draw you into prolonged conflict, to not show compassion to the poor, refugee, migrant, and to not be forgiving.

Do you remember every day that God has stamped his image on you and on everyone (Genesis 1:27) and that we must give ourselves to him because we belong to him?

Is your uniform or "badge" one of the good deeds that others will recognize? How do you show you wear the "stole" of a believer in Jesus and his teachings?

Have you experienced a conflict with God's active engagement in your life and his active engagement in the lives of those you meet every day? If so, how do you overcome this to avoid the entrapment that opposes God?

Can people recognize your truthfulness, sincerity, compassion, and charity at home, in the church, and in the neighborhood?

Traditionally, today is also celebrated as World Mission Sunday, instituted in 1926 by Pope Pius XI. It aims at fostering Christian evangelization throughout the world, emphasizing unity among God's people, and the unique role of each person in promoting the mission or the life of Jesus Christ. In his World Mission Day message (2019), Pope Francis wrote, "This missionary mandate touches us personally: I am a mission, always; you are a mission, always; every baptized man and woman is a mission." Indeed, in every situation, all of us—the newly inducted lawyers mentioned earlier, professionals, politicians, parents, clergy, young women and men, and members of the community—have a mission to bring our Lord Jesus Christ to one another. In his World Mission Day message (2020), Pope Francis wrote, "Jesus Christ desires that all people know him and his love, and every Catholic has the mission of sharing this love with the world."

The Peace of the Lord be with you.

Prayer
Father, we pray fervently that the power-filled faith within each of us will be more readily acknowledged and nurtured to bring the values of Your Son, Jesus Christ, to all corners of the world. Amen.

THIRTIETH SUNDAY OF THE YEAR

Exodus 22:20-26; 1 Thessalonians 1:5c-10; Matthew 22:34-40

THE TWO GREATEST COMMANDMENTS

Jesus began his ministry along the shores of the Sea of Galilee, preaching the Word of God and curing the sick. News about him spread throughout the province of Galilee (Mark 1:28); he amazed people with his teaching, eloquence, and ability to heal (Mark 1:27). About three years into his ministry, he repeatedly spoke about his impending suffering and death in Jerusalem, and resurrection after three days (Matthew 20:17-19). The Triumphant Entry into Jerusalem was his last visit to Jerusalem, where the people acclaimed him as the prophet from Nazareth (Matthew 21:11). But he incurred the wrath of the traditional authorities and teachers of the Law after healing the sick and particularly after driving out from the Temple "all those who were buying and selling," (Matthew 21:12-15).

The Pharisees and Sadducees, and sometimes the Herodians, turned increasingly ferocious towards Jesus and attacked him with tricky questions about issues of the Roman authority as in last Sunday's Gospel reading (Matthew 22:15-22), and about belief regarding the resurrection of the dead (Matthew 22:23-33). They calculated their questions to accuse and condemn him and dissuade his disciples from following him. In today's Gospel, a scholar of the law tests Jesus' knowledge about "the greatest commandment in the Law."

We learn from the Bible that God gave Moses the Ten Commandments (Exodus 20). Over the centuries, the leaders of Israel added more laws to expand the Ten Commandments. Traditionally, the number of commandments given was 613, although there is no Bible verse to show the exact number nor a common consensus in Jewish literature or Christian tradition. Thus, with a lot of laws during the time of Jesus, the scholar of law asked Jesus about the greatest commandment.

Most of the Christian New Testament versions translate Jesus' answer similarly as, "You shall love the Lord your God with all your heart, and with all your soul, and with all your mind. This is the greatest and first commandment." Then, without waiting for a follow-up question about the second greatest commandment, Jesus told him, "You shall love your neighbor as yourself." This is very important and complements the first. Indeed, Jesus concludes, "The whole law and the prophets depend on these two commandments," with other translations stating, "There is no other commandment greater than these."

A close look at Jesus' summary of the commandments reveals how he was accurate, saying, "all the Law and the prophets depend on these two commandments." Simply put, Jesus was saying, Love God. Love neighbor. The first three of the Ten Commandments are contained in this statement: "Love the Lord your God with all your heart and with all your soul and with all your mind." Then, the seven commandments that follow talk about "Love your neighbor as yourself." The two commandments sum up the Law and the teachings of the prophets. Jesus' summary is not only from the Ten Commandments but from all the 613 laws and the teachings of the prophets. We must love God like he is all we have and with everything we have in heart, soul, strength, and mind, and then do the same with our neighbor, to love him or her as we love ourselves.

Though explicitly enshrined in the Jewish Laws as a directive from God, the two great commandments, "Love God and love your neighbor as yourself," are sacrosanct in all human societies. God engraved them, so to speak, in the hearts of all peoples (Jeremiah 31:33-35). They are core to the Christian religion and perceived as a form of the "Golden Rule" which reiterates a central ethical rule known many centuries ago. Jesus gives it in the Sermon on the Mount: "In everything, do to others what you would have them do to you" (Matthew 7:12).

The Gospel reading of today is not only meant for a discussion of the clash between Jesus and the Jewish authorities over a very controversial issue. It is primarily about the two most essential moral standards that the Church is setting before all peoples of the world today as a command from God for all times and for all seasons: love of God and love of neighbor, as the greatest commandments.

Our first duty is to love God. However, love of neighbor is the grand litmus test for love of God. This was explicit in the covenant law code, as shown in Deuteronomy 6:5-9 and Leviticus 19:18. The true Israelite could not say he loved God when he turned away widows, orphans, and strangers, and lent money to the poor at a high interest or kept a poor man's things as collateral for a loan (first reading). The legacy of Christianity is Jesus' teaching on love of God and love of neighbor (Luke 10:25-37) as the principle behind the Law and the prophets. The teaching became the pillar of Christianity in the first century B.C. within the Early Church: "If anyone says, 'I love God,' and hates his brother, he is a liar" (1 John 4:20). The question was a big test for Jesus because in the Jewish society at the time of Jesus, one's neighbor was only a fellow Jew.

In Luke's Gospel, we read about the Parable of the Good Samaritan (Luke 10:25-37), when a teacher of the Law asked Jesus, "What must I do to inherit eternal life?" When Jesus asked what the Scriptures said, the man stated what Jesus had said about the two greatest commandments: "Love the Lord your God with all your heart, with all your soul, with all your strength, and with all your mind"; and "Love your neighbor as yourself." It is most likely that the teachers of the Law agreed on the first commandment but had problems with the second commandment. Hence, they had a follow-up question for Jesus: "And who is my neighbor?" warranting Jesus' narration of the Parable of the Good Samaritan.

Apparently, a Jewish traveler had been stripped of clothing by brigands, beaten, wounded, robbed, and left on the roadside to die. After a Jewish man of God and a Levite, one who served in the Temple, had failed to assist the dying man, a Samaritan who by institutionalized custom were enemies with Jews, stopped and took care of the wounded man. The neighbor in the story is the Samaritan, who showed compassion and assisted his fellow human being. The expression Good Samaritan means a person who assists a stranger in need.

Ryan and Wilhelm (Living the Word, 2022) have noted that the word "You" in the first reading and other words in the Book of Exodus were used in the plural sense "to address Jews of every generation." For example, "You were once aliens yourselves," made "later audiences' sharers in their ancestors' tribulations," which should induce compassion when they saw the hardships of others, especially aliens. God was close to the Israelites in their misery in Egypt and he would always be on the side of the poor, oppressed, and underprivileged.

Jesus lived and observed the two great commandments. Some scripture scholars suggest the Parable of the Good Samaritan "as exemplifying the ethics of Jesus" (Sanders, 1995). Jesus gave the gift of the Holy Spirit to transform the hearts and minds of people to show concern and affection for each other.

Sadly, however, we have not been true to practicing the law of love for neighbor. We do not show forgiveness, compassion, magnanimity, and tolerance towards neighbor. In our day-to-day interactions, we seem to define our own values. Conscience has become a personal matter, and we make our own choices about how to live and who to love. There is an increase in violence and injury to neighbor. Around us, we see abject poverty, homelessness, wars, and insecurity because of injustices, greed, and the struggle for power.

Some scholars emphasize envy and malice as the main reasons behind the attacks against Jesus. They opine that the Pharisees and the Scribes were envious of his talents

(Matthew 22:16). We need to be charitable and not harbor malice when we see our neighbor is more talented. Unfortunately, we see such envious and malicious tendencies in many areas of life.

The purpose of today's liturgy is also to remind us of the two most important commandments. Love of God means the wholehearted love of our neighbor because God resides in the neighbor. Love of neighbor is, therefore, love of God as an active and practical love. Love is the thread that knits creation together. Such saintly existence gives new hope and meaning to God's people despite life's afflictions (second reading).

Indeed, challenges of our day leave many people feeling like more and more societies are turning away from God. This development upsets many Christians and peoples of other religions. The situation is compounded by people's need to divide and conquer, to more strongly validate their own needs and lessen the needs of others. Unfortunately, this goes against what God wants us to do. Those who may have turned away from God need our love and kindness to re-enforce why God matters to all, and why we are all God's people. Our kindness to another should not be based on that individual's own beliefs, but on ours.

Furthermore, another purpose for today's readings is to remind us we can show God how much we love him by showing our neighbor we care no matter what their background, what their beliefs, what their mistakes in the past or their challenges in the future. To do this, God wants us to let go of our own judgments about others, and to remember everyone comes from God, so treat everyone as a son and daughter of God. We are all family, and we should love and support our family, no matter how much they may frustrate or annoy us with their own personal choices.

God gave us free will. Let us use it to show him we freely choose to love one another as strongly as we love God, and he loves us.

Can you develop the habit of reflecting on your day's actions and behaviors with love as the starting point?

If you have any opportunity, how would you demonstrate your love for the neighbor?

The Peace of the Lord be with you.

Prayer
Father, Your Son has taught all who believe in him that loving neighbor is proof of their love for You. Let Your Holy Spirit inspire each of us to always love our neighbors. Amen.

THIRTY-FIRST SUNDAY OF THE YEAR

Malachi 1:14b-2:2b, 8-10; 1 Thessalonians 2:7-9. 13; Matthew 23:1-1

UNDER TWO VANS, LEFT TO DIE

On October 13, 2011, in the city of Foshan, Guangdong in Southern China, two vans ran over a two-year-old Chinese girl, nicknamed "Little Yueyue," leaving her on a narrow road to die. When *SkyNews* (England) first transmitted the story, it appeared to be a bizarre video game, more so because my television was in the mute mode. Recorded by a surveillance camera, news stations repeatedly showed the incident in forensic detail. The video went viral, horrifying the world with the two drivers' sheer callousness, wickedness, indifference, and the outlandish behavior of the people at the scene.

In the afternoon of that fateful day, Little Yueyue became distracted and veered off from her parents' shop where she was playing. The vendors ignored her while they were dealing with financial matters in the shops and streets. The toddler was soon meandering around in the middle of a narrow, busy wholesale market street.

The film footage starts with a minibus approaching the girl but refusing to swerve out of her way. The van strikes the little girl who falls under the front wheel. The driver slows down but does not stop. The vehicle speeds off, running over her again with the back tire. Several passers-by walk away and some cycle past the tiny victim, although they have just witnessed a poignant, horrible accident. They stare at the mutilated and bleeding body of the helpless child and then turn their heads. Several minutes pass and a second vehicle approaches the scene. It hits the injured, bleeding, and unconscious baby girl and the driver speeds off!

According to the reporting, eighteen people walked past the girl and none of them stopped to assist her. Shopkeepers were too occupied with business as usual in and around their shops, with buyers more concerned about monetary transactions than what had just transpired in the street. A little child in severe agony and bleeding to death was of no concern to them. After much precious time had elapsed, an older woman—a rubbish scavenger—set her trash bag down. She approached the child and carried her bloodied, mangled body off the street and gave her to the woman identified as the child's mother. After one week in the hospital, Little Yueyue died from severe injuries to her brain and internal organs.

The recorded incident went viral and people throughout the world rapidly and furiously condemned the incident with one posting on the internet: "It takes a cold, dead soul to be able to do that," certainly referring to the drivers of the vans and all the people who witnessed Little Yueyue murdered in cold blood.

If the people around had immediately intervened after the first van had struck Little Yueyue, she might have survived. Although the drivers were arrested, it was unclear what their charges would be in a Communist China where God does not exist in official belief; where no one would say that Little Yueyue had a gift of life from God or had the right to live her life to the fullest, that she possessed a nature of God (her soul), or that she was a vulnerable child of God to be loved, treasured, and protected.

We are told that the incident ignited an ongoing, passionate conversation and debate. The country unanimously condemned the incident, demanding urgent and profound soul-searching about public moral principles and ethical reasoning. An outside opinion comment read: "I hope that this little angel who was discarded by society can act as a wake-up call to the nation about the importance of moral education." Another article reported a Communist party chief told provincial officials they needed to "take active and effective steps to raise the moral standards of the entire society," and that "we should look into the ugliness in ourselves with a dagger of conscience and bite the soul-searching bullet." The journalist of the article concluded her story with an undeniably worrying question:

"Have you seen the same sort of disconnect in America? Is Little Yueyue's death an isolated incident, or is this apathy rampant around the globe?"

A so-called "New World Order" seems to have engulfed the world today, an economic paradigm that has swiftly become a philosophy of life, an agenda for the populace designed and determined to transform society on a solely economic front to fight against religion. It asserts economic growth to be the goal of society. In this respect, the individual is the ultimate reality and free market forces operating within a strict but competitive milieu will enable one to achieve success in this world. The agenda does not recognize any Grand Designer, God-centered morals, or God-directed conscience. People are generous to another, not because an ultimate Grand Designer or God demands one to love the underprivileged, but because they expect a reward in return. If the other party cannot repay that generosity, loving action becomes unnecessary.

The new concept further purports that poverty is a choice for the poor who must "wake up" to work hard. People reject outright external moral values in this dispensation. Individual opinions, whether good or bad, take precedence and are protected as a person's individual right. With this way of life gaining currency over the length and breadth of the globe, Little Yueyue's gruesome death might not remain an isolated one. Indeed, Little Yueyue's situation is "what happens when people become mere instruments of productivity for the sake of economic prosperity." But China is not the only country tainted in shame with the blood of innocents. There is rampant apathy around the globe, and many of us often "look the other way."

The Communist Chief's suggestion of using moral education to awaken people's social conscience is hollow without the recognition of God as its true originator. Moral and ethical education must start with a belief in the divine, in the sanctity of human life, in the equality of human life, and with the opportunity to live a quality life. God's ministers are to

352

spread the faith, teach and practice morality, and affirm relentlessly that moral principles and ethical reasoning originate from God (first reading). Christians are God's eternal plan for the world, revealed in the life and actions of Jesus Christ.

The Prophet Malachi criticized the men of God for aligning themselves with the secular elite, misleading the People of God for their personal interests, being authoritative, and showing "partiality in your decisions." As baptized, we all share in the priesthood of Jesus and therefore Malachi's words apply to all God's people: whether on political platforms; in the judicial, educational, medical, and security services; or in the business or corporate world. The Christians of Thessalonica recognized all this as gifts from God and not as human philosophies or viewpoints (second reading).

The foundation stones for God's grand design are love, forgiveness, compassion, generosity, tolerance, and selfless service to God and humanity. God has proven his love for the world since creation. The ultimate proof that embraces all creation is the incarnation of his "Beloved Son," and his relentless intercession, as well as his instruction to all to live the "Christian Way." Again, like the Thessalonicans, our faith in God must define the meaning of life and control our lives each day. We must not become dependent on external trappings such as money, power, and pride. Rather, we all have one heavenly Father who calls us to live humbly and be at peace with one another as brothers and sisters. The Word of God teaches us that God dwells in each one of us and we must admonish one another to be "full of goodness" (Romans 15:14) and "love one another with brotherly affection" (Romans 12:10).

We must acknowledge God is in us, because he made us in his image. And that image includes admonishing one another to be better than what worldly ambitions push us to be. However, those admonitions should not be done by shaming and degrading each other or tearing each other apart so we can take pride in being right. They should be out of love for God and for neighbor. We want them to be better because God wants them to be better, not so we can better our own egos. We can be firm with each other, but still kind. That is how we can show the value in every life, by holding each other accountable to showing respect and compassion to all, especially those who stumble along the way.

Therefore, should you not learn to treat others the way you want them to treat you? Should you not bring love, compassion, and smiles to all children who may die like Little Yueyue?

Should you not learn to recognize Jesus Christ in the beggar's face, the body of the homeless person sleeping on the street, and in the gaze of the confused, unsettled, and disheveled person you see in your daily travels?

Should you not look for a clothing drive you can organize or donate to and collect slightly used clothing for distribution to the poor, or look for a "meals for those in need" program near you where you can serve the hungry and the refugee?

Every hour of every day, every minute and every second, we need to know that we are not primarily women and men of the free market forces, but human beings created in the image of God. Our loving God wishes us to live on earth as a "Family of God" under Jesus Christ with one Faith, a common life of love enlivened by the Spirit, and a common march towards heaven where we shall meet Little Yueyue welcoming us from the bosom of Abraham. For now, however, we say with our hearts, *"sileo in perficio pacis,"* Little Yueyue! Rest in Perfect Peace.

The Peace of the Lord be with you.

Prayer
Father, we mourn the untimely death of Little Yueyue, our daughter, granddaughter, and sister, now in your loving embrace. Touch the hearts of people to show love and compassion to all your children, young and old. Amen.

THIRTY-SECOND SUNDAY OF THE YEAR

Wisdom 6:12-16; 1 Thessalonians 4:13-18; Matthew 25:1-13

GOD IS LORD AND RULER OF THE UNIVERSE

How did you respond to last week's story about Little Yueyue who met her untimely death in a busy narrow street in the city of Foshan, Guangdong, in southern China, a street not packed with party revelers, but people apparently wholly changed and influenced by a new social and economic world system? This new emerging reality completely disregards the natural law of fraternal charity enjoined on us by our religions, teaching us to see ourselves as God's children, who must show love for one another; instead, this new world perspective focuses on fulfilling solely ourselves, regardless of the cost to other people in the world.

One of my friends receiving my weekly Sunday homilies was utterly shocked about the eerily dreadful fate of Little Yueyue and the cold-hearted perpetrators of such a heinous crime. He was so emotionally expressive writing back to me: "These reflections are becoming more and more attention-grabbing ... making in-roads into the very remote areas of our consciousness." Another friend wrote: "This is another touching piece, and I wish this was read in all churches, worldwide!!!" A third person expressed fear that what happened to the child occurs frequently in some way, shape, or form in countries throughout the world.

The manner of Little Yueyue's death stands as an ultimate rebuke of the emerging worldview, a major potential shift away from a way of life solely predicated on divine directives that have shaped and guarded humanity from the time of creation. Little Yueyue's death was a wake-up call to the world to acquiescence to the relevance of God, whose rejection could utterly damage society and project humans as market entities who must, therefore, compete for survival.

While strongly rejecting external moral values, the new norm also projects the individual's opinion, either good or bad, to be expressed and protected as a person's right. It seeks to wipe out religion, starting with government educational reforms and economic development programs. Wealthy financial institutions and developed countries demand similar educational reforms devoid of moral and religious content as a pre-condition to receiving economic aid. Again, poor countries must accept many so-called human rights before financial aid is considered. The poor countries are therefore being towed behind a system where moral virtues, communal character of society, and man's capacity for God are subtly being interchanged for "individual relevance."

The question about the purpose of life or why we are on the earth has always occupied the mind of the human being. It seems a general answer would be that our purpose on earth is to discover the right attitude to life and to make the right decisions. To fully recognize and accept this notion about life will be a great renaissance on earth for everyone. We discover in today's first reading that wisdom is easy to find because wisdom rather seeks us as part of the divine plan of salvation.

The Wisdom of Solomon, also known as the *Book of Wisdom*, is one of the seven books not included in the Protestant Bible. When Martin Luther (1483-1546) translated the Bible into the German language, he followed Saint Jerome by placing these books at the end of the Hebrew Old Testament. He used the term *Apocrypha* to show that they did not form part of the accepted canon of Scripture. Many Protestant communities have followed this tradition by not including the books in translating the Bible into other languages. The Council of Trent in 1546 declared the books to be "sacred and canonical" and referred to them as *deuterocanonical* to show that their acceptance as "sacred and canonical" came later after the *proto-canonical* books.

The title *Wisdom of Solomon* originated from the traditional belief that King Solomon composed it because Solomon is made to speak in certain instances. Scholars have established

356

the book was written in the Greek language in Alexandria, Egypt, towards the end of the first century B.C. The main theme of the book is that Wisdom, which is the conscience or essence of the human being and directs him to live righteously, is a gift from God who created everything and knows everything. The book reveals that Wisdom—personified as a wise woman—has been with God from eternity and is "a reflection of eternal light, a perfect mirror of God's activity and goodness" (Wisdom 7:26). The Book of Wisdom therefore inspires us to seek God's wisdom and righteousness so that we are not misled by earth's deceitful ideals.

The Book of Wisdom sought to inform the Jewish community in Alexandria about the faith of their ancestors in God. It assured the Jews, particularly the younger generation, of God's presence in their lives. This was when Jewish religious leaders were concerned about the Hellenistic/Greek culture, religion, and social life that seemed to undermine their own. They persuaded the youth to cherish the fact that God, who had always been on the side of their fathers, would continue to protect them. There was, therefore, the need for regular liturgical celebrations to read the Word of God and to remind them of God's filial affection.

The Book of Wisdom was very important to the Early Christians who saw Jesus as the Messiah and the Wisdom of God. He was the archetype of Moses, who has delivered the People of God from the slavery of sin to a New Promised Land where they become children of God through baptism. The course of human life changed, a dispensation defining a New People of God on an alternative path to God and living with unconditional faith and hope in him. The Church teaches God created us to know him, love him, and serve him and that we should develop a respectful attitude towards God. We show this attitude to life by how we know, love, and serve our neighbor. If the entire world would see the essence of life as an obligation imposed by God to love one another, people such as Little Yueyue would not be treated so heartlessly by fellow children of God.

357

The Parable of the Ten Virgins, also known as *the Parable of the Bridesmaid,* or *the Parable of the Bridegroom,* is about Jesus' prophecies regarding his future return and the salvation of those who find him as the Wisdom of God. The parable is about ten virgins, five of them described as foolish, for they did not take extra oil for their lamps as they awaited the bridegroom's arrival. When the bridegroom arrived, their lamps had gone out, and they did not have extra oil to join the procession and the ceremony. The wise virgins who carried extra oil kept their lights continuously burning and joined in the wedding feast because they were prepared and vigilant.

The customary marriage at the time of Jesus was in three phases. The first was the engagement, which was the agreement between the fathers of those to marry. The second was the betrothal when promises took place. The third was the actual wedding ceremony when the bridegroom, with family and friends, processed from his house to meet the bride and take her to her house for the final wedding ceremony and banquet. In the parable, it is presumed ten young girls—bridesmaids—were selected to meet the bridegroom and escort him and his entourage to the wedding.

Carrying special lighted lamps was a way of distinguishing invitees from "scammers" or thieves who might try to get into the wedding hall. Five of the girls exhibited wisdom by being fully prepared for any eventuality, while the other five were unconcerned about the unknown and did not adequately prepare. They could not attend as the procession shut the entrance door before they returned from their trip to find oil. We can imagine Jesus concluding with, "Let wisdom guide you because you do not know the day or the hour your Creator will come."

The Gospel is about the return of Jesus, the bridegroom, and the importance of our preparation when we suddenly hear the cry of his coming. It is all about the importance of staying vigilant, not only for the return of Jesus, but against the "scammers" in the darkness who try to detract us away from the real joy and happiness in our lives: that which we find through loving God and our neighbor, not materialism or money. Jesus is our oil lamp to be always kept lit as we journey through life. We must endeavor to always fill the lamp with the oil of faith, which is renewed by prayer, the Eucharist, reconciliation, and acts of love.

The parable is also for those who are rejecting God in their lives or those who are waiting to accept Jesus as the Wisdom of God. In a world becoming increasingly secular, Jesus makes an important point about the great divide between people of faith and the rest of the world. He also shows a divide between people who show a love of God by caring for the poor and downtrodden, such as Little Yueyue and those who deliberately ignore them, even when they are seen dying in a pool of blood. Again, in a world that denies God, the faith, hope, and love, which God's Spirit beams on us as our light or flame of life, may so easily be extinguished like the lamps of the foolish maidens in today's parable. Our hope in life is that the "wisdom and power of God," Jesus Christ, will give us peace and a glorious preparation to meet our Creator at the end of our life on earth. For believers, death is not the end, but heaven is when we rise with the "Wisdom of God, Jesus Christ" (second reading).

Today's liturgy focuses on two big themes, and both are heavy: Standing up for what is right by God's Wisdom, and being prepared, alert, and ready to leave the world. Of course, if you do the first, the second will fall into place!

What do you let rule your life: the various trends that are in vogue one day and gone the next, or God's commands to know him and help the poor and downtrodden?

As a person of faith, what are some ways you can show your love for God's children in this world?

The Peace of the Lord be with you.

Prayer
Father, let the world accept Your Son as Your Wisdom on earth. Let Your Spirit be a constant light, always directing all peoples to him to abide by what he teaches. Amen.

THIRTY-THIRD SUNDAY OF THE YEAR

Proverbs 31:10-13. 19-20. 30-31; 1 Thessalonians 5:1-6; Matthew 25:14-30

WE BEGIN, WE END, BUT WE HOPE

Typically, next Sunday is the end of the Church's Liturgical Year. We dedicate it to Jesus Christ as King and Lord of the Universe, and to the next life to come. He will wait to receive us after our life here on earth. As the Liturgical Year is drawing to an end, we remember the reality of all other beginnings and endings we experience as part and parcel of the vicissitudes of life.

According to Jan Layton (University of North Carolina), philosophers used the phrase "everything that has a beginning must have an end" in 1702, as a clarion call to people to "make peace with the fact that they must live without any attachments and need to understand that everything that has a beginning must have an end. People, pets, trees, buildings, and Earth will eventually be gone, and one must accept this." Archaeologists confound us with discoveries of ancient cities buried under land and sea, and ancient stone tools like those found on a site in Kenya dating to 3.3 million years (Nature, May 21, 2015), showing how even whole civilizations have a cycle of beginning and ending.

The life cycle of biological organisms, including humans, are the stages from when we begin with birth and when we end with death. We define the age of reason at age 6 or 7 when the child recognizes being part of a human ecosystem, appreciates societal norms, and develops decision-making initiatives and responsibilities. At college or university, for example, parental chaperoning decreases, and individuals attain adult perspectives while making independent choices regarding work, marriage, and other aspects of life. Again, they experience an enhancement of the human inclination to widen the aura of dreams, successes, and novelties.

Later in life, the signs of aging become more apparent with their inevitable physical defects and imminence of death. God created each person for a specific purpose and whether we accomplish one or not, one's life will end. We are born, we live, and we die. "Seventy years is all we have—eighty years, if we are strong; yet all they bring is trouble and sorrow; life is soon over, and we are gone" (Psalm 90:10), buried in the earth or gone with the wind after cremation. Nothing lasts forever and we soon run our course on earth and everything ends; family and friends, dreams, work, wealth, love, beauty, fame, tragedies, misery, tensions, disagreements, and all material things.

Beginnings are usually thrilling! The birth of a child enchants us. Newlyweds and their families show happiness. Ordination to the priesthood and religious life are moments of delight. The first days after graduation or at a new job are exciting. The first time one gets hands on the keys to a new car, or a new home, is a dream-come-true moment; in all this, beginnings are pleasant, joyful, and can fill one with confidence and hope.

Although one's life span may hold joyful moments, the endings can be sorrowful, frightening, and painful. In the *Book of Ecclesiastes*, the lilies of the valleys, the aesthetic beauty of the countryside, and the greatest delights, power, and influence we enjoy (including "all things" of the world) are called the vanity of vanities. *The Book of Ecclesiastes* is about Solomon, the great king—powerful, wealthy, and sagacious—reminiscing about his life on earth and asserting that all had been in vain. Indeed, all things are vanity, because everything or every event under the sun may have its moments of glory, but there will also be times for ending.

The Liturgical Year Calendar is about the birth, life, death, and resurrection of our Lord Jesus Christ. As the year ends, we welcome the Season of Advent, beginning the Church's Year, and a time of preparation for Jesus' birth. We wait in joyful anticipation, motivated by the oracle of Isaiah 11:1-10 about the Savior's "hoped-for reign of idyllic peace, justice and universal knowledge of God." The liturgy urges us to deepen our faith in God's promise.

The birth of Jesus Christ marks the dawn of the Incarnation—the Word made Flesh—when the cusp of light beams from heaven into a world of darkness. The entire world echoes the joyous songs of praise by the Angelic heavenly choir: "Glory to God in the Highest, and on Earth Peace to People of Good Will." God lives among his people, Emmanuel. Throughout the liturgical year, we follow Jesus' life from Bethlehem, until our praise of God among us, turns into grief on Calvary which shattered all hope for God's kingdom: "And we had hoped that he would be the one who was going to set Israel free" (Luke 24:21).

The ending of Jesus' life on earth was different. He rose from the dead! He will return! Each event of his life in relation to the world becomes significant as we look beyond his earthly life. He promises to come again to meet the faithful who live on earth loving God and neighbor. This the new way of life for the world. We must invest our time and talents to ensure a happy ending.

Jesus illustrates this path of life with the *Parable of the Talents* or the *Parable of the Bags of Gold* in today's Gospel. A talent (Greek, *talanton*) was the largest currency denomination, weighing from 25 to 40 kilos, different from a smaller and lesser valuable mina (Greek, *mna*). In the Gospel of Matthew, the third servant concealed his talent in the ground while in Luke's version he kept the gold coin hidden in a handkerchief (Luke 19:20). The third servant took no action, perhaps arguing that the master desired a good turnover and failing to generate one would incur the master's displeasure. The other beneficiaries of the master's generosity were hardworking and faithful, investing their allocations wisely, and making profits.

Jesus' return must see the faithful fully engaged in active and responsible service to him, and not merely professing faith in him. He expects "unquestioning and productive obedience to

362

his teaching," like a "worthy wife," who works hard for the family and takes care of the poor (first reading). The first reading recognizes the significant and carefully guarded role of the woman in the ancient Middle Eastern world when gender roles were strictly defined. She is the ideal wife, resourceful in using her talents wisely to manage her household and caring for the family and bringing joy. Her spiritual life brings honor to the family, and her generous heart reaches out to those around her, especially the poor and needy. However, the ultimate joy is the expectation of all the principal actors of the family—fathers, mothers, children and the extended family. Beauty, power, or charm are not what we will be judged on, but hard work, dedication, an open heart, and a sense of purpose.

The parable also shows how God provides his subjects with unique talents and sufficient grace (2 Corinthians 12:9), including wisdom, and creates a conducive environment with freedom to manage their own affairs; in the end, they become good stewards. It speaks to accountability on Judgment Day or the Day of the Lord, when those who lived up to the master's expectation are invited to "share your master's joy." God loathes unresponsive subjects who do not make use of their time and talent. He loves the hard-working and diligent, faithful one who doubles his assets by following the teaching of Jesus. God will reward him or her abundantly.

Indeed, it is not how much money one produces because there are different levels of competence. After all, the master is wealthy already, calling the money the servants made "a little amount." It is our faithfulness, inner dispositions, hard work, and good intentions that will be judged as the first two servants received the same reward of sharing the master's joy. This is a compelling call for preparedness as the master may return at any moment. Thus, like the first two servants, we shall meet our master because we made good use of our talents.

The second reading is best understood by the Early Christian belief that the return of Jesus was imminent. It would be the Day of the Lord, Judgment Day, when the present world would "die," and another be born. This urgency motivated the apostles and early missionaries to spread the news about repentance and change of life. It was a message that shaped the lives of the believers. Therefore, Saint Paul urges Christians not to be afraid of the Day of Judgment since they would be among the "children of the light" beaming from the sky and "children of the day" (second reading). When Jesus is the most dynamic influence in our lives, our ending in this world will not be emptiness, frightening, or distressing because of the hope of a new life beyond.

Have you really discovered the talents God has given you? Can you name some of them?

How do you make these talents grow? Or is there anything in your life holding back your talents?

The cycle of life is an opportunity for all of us to find our talents and use them through the different phases of our lives to help others come closer to Jesus Christ. We change through each phase, but the goal does not: sharing our love with God and with neighbor through acts of charity, kindness, and a distribution of our talents. We help others come closer to God, closer to family, closer to community. We must be relentless in this until it becomes second nature, as the "good wife" of the first reading. This is how we prepare ourselves for Judgment Day. This, in turn, hopefully inspires others to do the same, and the assets given to us by God will benefit society.

How do you earnestly seek to serve God with the gifts, talents, and graces he has given to you?

Are you content to rest on your laurels?

How do you look for new ways to serve those in need?

The Peace of the Lord be with you.

Prayer
Father, help all people to make good use of the gifts, talents, time, and resources you give to each of us to benefit your people, especially the poor and needy. Amen.

THIRTY-FOURTH SUNDAY OF THE YEAR
THE FEAST OF CHRIST THE KING
(Last Sunday of the Year)

Ezekiel 34: 11-12, 15-17; 1 Corinthians 15:20-26, 28;
Matthew 25:31-46

KING OF JUSTICE, PEACE, AND LOVE

The last Sunday of the Church's Liturgical year is designated as the Feast of Christ the King, also called Solemnity of Our Lord Jesus Christ, King of the Universe. The Feast was instituted by Pope Pius XI in 1925 to honor Jesus as King and Lord of all creation, who, after his ascension, assumed his rightful throne and crown at the right hand of God the Father. In 1969, Pope Paul VI moved the original date—the last Sunday in October—to the present (the end of the Church's Liturgical Year), to reflect the theme of Christ as King during his second coming. Anglicans, Presbyterians, some Lutherans, and Methodists also celebrate the Feast of Christ the King.

The Feast acknowledges Jesus Christ as king of the universe, who directs all aspects of human life and physical phenomena. Science has proven the planets, including our earth, revolve around the sun causing the seasons, and that the planets move on their axis, causing day and night. These natural cyclical phenomena of things put the universe in order.

Pope Pius XI indicated there would be chaos within nations if the world ignored "Jesus Christ and his holy law." World War I was between 1914 and 1918 in Europe. The war left millions of people dead, empires toppled, widespread starvation, diseases, deportations, and a continent destroyed. Atheism and agnosticism spread across Europe and many parts of the world. The rise of nationalism and secularism that started the war did not end when, amid unresolved political tensions coupled with more serious economic problems (Great Depression), individuals soon wielded power and influence, and craved large followings.

The declaration of the Feast of Christ the King occurred when Benito Mussolini seized power in Italy in 1922 and transformed the nation into a one-party dictatorship. Similarly, Adolf Hitler's Nazi Party in Germany wielded power that would make Germany a one-party state. Hitler invaded Poland in the latter part of 1939, resulting in the declarations of war by France and the United Kingdom, and that started World War II (September 1, 1939). Nazi Germany initiated the Holocaust that led to the killing of over six million European Jews between 1941 and 1945.

The declaration of the Solemnity of our Lord as King of the Universe was first aimed at ambitious leaders abusing political power and amassing economic influence. The Pope wanted them to envisage Jesus Christ as the ultimate power surpassing all earthly power. He recognized that "while governments come and go, Christ reigns as King forever." After fighting many controversial wars, Mussolini and his close companions were captured and executed. Their bodies were hung upside down in public at a gas station in Milan for public ridicule and confirmation of his deaths. Hitler committed suicide.

Second, in declaring Jesus as King of the Universe, the Holy Father wanted to encourage the faithful going through hardships to have faith in Jesus Christ, the king destined to ensure peace and happiness in the world. Third, the Feast, fixed at the last Sunday of the Christian Liturgical Year, reminded the faithful about the "End Times," "Judgment Day," or the *Parousia* —the second coming of Jesus Christ as King of the Universe who would rule over the Messianic Kingdom (Matthew 19:28; Revelation 20:1-6), bringing an end to evil and the suffering of the faithful (Luke 7:22-23). Other peoples and the faithful had to be aware that all things happening in the world shall end. Fourth, it gave the faithful the opportunity to honor Jesus Christ as King of the Universe. In other countries, they parade the Eucharist in a monstrance in streets for Jesus to receive praise and honor. Fifth, the Feast of Christ the King has its basis in Scripture and the Church's teaching on the Incarnation, the Divine becoming human.

Jesus had said that those associated with royalty are found in palatial households. They are "dressed up in fancy clothes" and "live in luxury." They get joy from a lot of fanfare (Luke 7:25). We associate kingship and royalty with power and majesty. We would therefore think about royalty when we celebrate Jesus as King. However, the Gospels take us down memory lane to Calvary, where many things happened that remind us of Jesus' suffering, crucifixion, and death. He was crowned with thorns and hung on a cross. We also meditate on the suffering and desolation of Mary at the foot of the cross as she encountered her son suffering the pangs of death. Again, we are reminded of the two criminals on either side of Jesus. We also picture John the Apostle and some disciples looking from a distance and lamenting their inability to salvage the situation.

In Christianity, the Cross is a symbol of the kingship of Jesus. He is the king who rules from the Cross, an inconceivable paradox in the secular world. It is on the Cross that we see his absolute obedience to the Heavenly Father and humility to accept death. Jesus completes his mission on the Cross, "as innocent as a lamb led to the slaughter."

Luke teaches a profound theology of the Cross vis-à-vis the kingship of Jesus. He recognizes as symbols of evil the Jewish religious leaders who orchestrated his crucifixion, the Roman soldiers who supervised it and mocked him, and the thief who taunted him. They did not recognize Jesus as God revealing himself to humanity (Incarnation). They jeered at him and demanded that he prove himself as God by descending from the Cross.

Luke contrasts this group with the other criminal (traditionally called Dismas) who was also crucified. He looked beyond the crucifixion and saw Jesus as Lord and Savior. He represents the group in need of God's grace like the sinner, the tax collector, the widow, and the broken-hearted. He also represents personalities and discerners like Nicodemus, people searching for the meaning of life. Dismas, the criminal, acknowledges Jesus' innocence and before his life ended proclaims faith in Jesus. This is a courageous act of faith which the disciples could not equal until after Jesus' resurrection. Again, he affirms Jesus' kingship and asks to be remembered in his *Kingdom,* a kingdom open to all who profess Jesus as Lord and Savior. Jesus hints about his own identity and authority by promising the repentant criminal a home in Paradise.

Jesus' enemies openly accused him of "misleading the people" with his teaching that led to "a riot among the people all through Judea" (Luke 23:5). They planned to accuse him of "telling them not to pay taxes to Caesar." They faulted him of "claiming that he is the Messiah, the King" (Luke 23:2). Ironically, the Roman governor, Pontius Pilate, would not change the inscription on the top of the Cross: "Jesus, King of the Jews," a claim punishable by death under the Mosaic Law. Jesus was innocent under the Roman law and the Governor was proclaiming him King of the Jews, maybe pun intended, yet the truth was being proclaimed.

The Feast of Christ the King honors Jesus as King who died for the love of humankind. We owe our existence to him since "all things were created through him and for him." Jesus is "the image of the invincible God." He is the "first born of all creation" (Colossians 1:15-29). Born in a stable, Jesus had no interest in political power. His supremacy surpasses any earthly power, and yet, he redefines the concept of leadership or kingship as humility and service, especially to the underprivileged in society due to poverty, ethnicity, and disease. Jesus' kingdom does not accept violence, revenge, envy, greed, or a desire for excessive power.

Today's feast, therefore, reminds political leaders, the Legislative, the Judicial, and Civil Societies, as well as religious leaders, to imbue in themselves the values of Jesus' kingdom based on service. Jesus prayed for peace in the world and called upon leaders to avoid hatred and evil. Authorities must not use power to enforce a culture of impunity and manipulation to feather their own nests. They must collaborate to extend Jesus' "Kingdom of truth and life, of holiness and grace, a kingdom of justice, love and peace" (Today's Preface). When we accept Jesus as king and savior and allow his values to direct our lives every day, we will be instruments of love and peace in the home, community, and the church.

Each passing day, however, the world is becoming more like in 1925: secularized, irreligious, unspiritual, nationalistic, prejudiced, hateful, with political unrest, economic quandary, dictatorships, threats of war, selfishness, desires for wealth and possessions, and desire to control. We all need to accept Jesus Christ as king in our lives. Our leaders must represent Jesus as the Shepherd-King (Isaiah 56:11); Jeremiah 2:8; Ezekiel 34:7) and the humbled king, bringing their people together instead of lording over them. They must not see themselves as royalty or better than others, but rather show the people respect, love, and care, since to care for the least is indeed to care for Jesus (Gospel reading). Every time the poor knocks at the door of our hearts, or someone does so on behalf of the desolate and the distressed, Jesus does the knocking, asking for the door of our hearts to be opened.

As the Liturgical Year ends, assess how you showed total allegiance to Jesus as King and Savior.

During this past year, have you become more the person Jesus wanted you to be—a person of faith, demonstrating true love for God by sincere love for neighbor?

We all have power and status either in business, politics, community, church, or home. Have you used your power and status in a disparaging way to control others instead of serving them or caused suffering to others instead of alleviating their pain?

The Peace of the Lord be with you.

Prayer
Father, Your Son portrays a new image of kingship as shepherd and servant of your people. We praise and thank you for this year. As we prepare for another liturgical year, we pray that Your Spirit enlightens us to follow the footsteps of our king and Lord. Amen.

Solemnities of the Lord
in Ordinary Time

THE FEAST OF THE PRESENTATION OF THE LORD IN THE TEMPLE

Malachi 3:1-4; Hebrews 2:14-18; Luke 2:22-40

THE LIGHT OF CHRIST IN US

Just as all religions revolve around a particular creed, Christianity orbits around Jesus Christ and the belief that he is the Son of God. The Liturgical Calendar sets out specific dates and seasons to celebrate important aspects of his life. The feasts and seasons in the Liturgical Calendar offer "a unique perspective to reflect and meditate on the Life of Christ, the glory of His saints, and the work of our salvation" (Good Catholic.com, 2024).

Today, February 2, observes and honors Jesus Christ on the day he was presented in the Temple in Jerusalem. This was a common Jewish custom under the Law of Moses. Forty days after the birth of a firstborn male, the parents brought him into the Temple to be dedicated or consecrated to the Lord. Today marks exactly forty days after Christmas, which would have been the day of the presentation of the Lord. Other rituals preceded the ceremony. The child was circumcised and named on the eighth day to signify his initiation into Judaism and acceptance into its covenant community. We can imagine how the ritual became a daily activity in the Temple, with many families visiting from all of Israel. The family of Joseph had traveled from Nazareth, in Galilee.

On the day of the presentation of the child in the Temple, the mother was also ritually purified after the birth of her son. Saint Luke combines the ceremony of the ritual purification of Mary forty days after her son's birth and the presentation or consecration of her son. In respect for Mary's purification on the same day as Jesus' presentation, today is also known as the Feast of the Purification of Mary. At the purification ceremony, the woman provided a year-old lamb as a burned offering and a dove or pigeon as a sin offering. If the woman could not afford a lamb, she brought two each of the birds as burned and sin offerings (Leviticus 12:1-8). The type of sacrifice offered by Joseph and Mary shows the couple was a poor family from humble beginnings, like Jesus being born in the shepherds' shed and placed in a manger. Luke also focuses on the presentation of Jesus in the Temple to show Jesus presented as sacred to God through his parents observing the traditional rituals.

Only the Gospel of Luke narrates the combined custom of the Presentation of the Lord and Purification of Mary, possibly because of converts to Christianity who might not know much of the Jewish custom. Luke underlines the fact that Mary and Joseph fulfilled the Law of Moses as dedicated Jews. Jesus was presented to God in accordance with the Law: "Dedicate all the firstborn males to me, for every firstborn male Israelite and every firstborn male animal belongs to me" (Exodus 13:2). Again, following Exodus 13: 13b-15, the presentation of a firstborn male was symbolically to redeem the son by offering a sacrifice: "a pair of turtledoves or two young pigeons."

It is clear Joseph and Mary raised Jesus to observe the Jewish Law. Later in life, he said he had not "come to abolish the law or the prophets" and that all the words of the law would be fulfilled (Matthew 5:17-18). As a dedicated rabbi, Jesus taught in the synagogues and every year went to celebrate the Passover and other Jewish festivals in Jerusalem.

Notably, Mary did not need purification since she was sinless from conception; nor did Jesus need to be redeemed because of being the son of God. However, the rituals the parents of Jesus performed were to fulfill their obligations regarding the Law.

In his narrative, Luke stresses that God's salvation through Jesus was universal, and that Jesus is the "light for revelation to the Gentiles," a dispensation designed for the salvation of all peoples. Hence, today is referred to as Candlemas Day to mark the blessing and procession of candles, a practice in the Church started in France.

The candles signify another "Epiphany" because the Holy Spirit prompted the Prophet Simeon and Prophetess Anna to present the divine mission of the Child, Jesus, as the Light of God and the Messiah designated to bring salvation to the world. The presence of Jesus was a source of peace to Simeon who implicitly admonished all people to acknowledge the child as God's presence or light in the world. Hence, Christians (particularly Catholics, Anglicans, Methodists, Lutherans, and the Orthodox) process with candles to commemorate the entrance of the Lord into the Temple and celebrate Jesus as Light to the world. Christians take blessed candles home as an expression of their faith. Symbolizing Jesus in their homes, the candles are lighted throughout the year or during family prayers.

Saint Luke seems to link Jesus' presentation in the Temple to the expectation of Israel during the time of Malachi. The people lamented the absence of God to stop injustice, greed, negligence of religion, and decadence perpetrated by the leaders, elite, and the priestly family (Levites). The Prophet Malachi responded on behalf of God, prophesying that "the messenger of the covenant" would soon appear in the Temple with authority to achieve justice for all in Israel.

In today's Gospel, Simeon, filled with the Holy Spirit, appears in the Temple at the presentation ceremony to confirm Jesus as the fulfillment of the expectation of Israel. Like the "messenger" in Malachi, the Spirit of God endowed Jesus to fight fierce opposition from the ungodly. The devout Simeon connects Mary to the redemptive work of Jesus, which would include suffering like the pain of a sword thrust into her Immaculate Heart. Luke envisages the sorrows of Mary, especially during the Passion of Jesus.

The devoted elderly widow, Anna, is likewise filled with the Holy Spirit to recognize the divine presence in Jesus and the blessings from him to God's people. Hence, today is also known as the "Feast of the Holy Encounter" or "Encounter Day" to show how Jesus (God) encountered Simeon and Anna in the Temple.

Ultimately, we commemorate the Church as the symbol of the Light or presence of Jesus in the world. Through the sacraments, we encounter Jesus in specific ways. In baptism, a child is consecrated to God and initiated into the community of the faith of "God's People." In Confirmation, the adult receives the Holy Spirit and its extraordinary spiritual gifts or graces: wisdom, understanding, counsel, fortitude, knowledge, piety, and the fear of the Lord (Isaiah 11:1-2). These gifts must manifest in one's adult life to produce the fruit of the Holy Spirit: love, joy, peace, patience, kindness, goodness, faithfulness, gentleness, and self-control (Galatians 5:22-23). While we celebrate the Eucharist today, we present ourselves to God gathered in love and unity, to hear the Word of God and be consecrated in his body and blood. In the Christian community, certain individuals are ordained to the Priesthood or choose consecrated life. Accordingly, today is known as "Consecrated Life Day" when the Church urges us to pray for those who have embraced the priesthood and consecrated life. In marriage, Jesus is at the center of the union between couples. In light of human imperfections, we encounter Jesus in the Sacrament of Reconciliation. Lastly, before our final breath on earth or when we are sick, the community, represented by the priest, invokes God's grace for healing or a happy death.

Evidently, from cradle to grave, the Church animates us to radiate the Light of Christ, which is made brighter each time we receive any of the sacraments. Each sacrament is a fountain of grace and an expression of faith in Christ Jesus. As we glow in His light and abound in His grace, we too become light and blessing to one another, particularly those who have not recognized Him as Lord and Savior. The Light of Christ shown from above, and his grace showered upon us, nurtures us to be productive in the fruits of the Holy Spirit to show love, mercy, and compassion for the poor, the sick and dying, those discriminated in society, and the powerless.

Other spiritual exercises recommended by the Church and adopted in certain traditions are ways of inviting Jesus into our lives. Pregnant women are blessed and after giving birth they go to church to give thanks to God. Families gather to pray, inviting Jesus to be part of their households during certain occasions such as gathering for meals, before and after traveling, etc. All this shows God working in us to bring meaning into our lives and the lives of others. However, we must be in the state of grace to receive God's love, mercy, and forgiveness. Saint Luke describes the elderly and holy Simeon and Anna as people of strong faith. Simeon was "righteous and devout" and believed in God's plan for the redemption of Israel. The Prophetess Anna "worshiped night and day in the Temple with fasting and prayer." Through their prayers and commitment to the Word of God, they could discern and recognize Jesus as the Light of God in the world and in their lives.

Let us aspire to be like these two holy personalities. Let us pray constantly to see Jesus in everyone and everything around us. It is by praying that we can appreciate that our own sufferings, weaknesses, and sinfulness tie to the suffering of Christ. It is by praying that we grow in Christ to become "strong, filled with wisdom, and the favor of God." It is by praying that we receive God's gift of grace to accept and respect our marriage partners, children, family members, and loved ones despite their human vulnerabilities.

Let us join the Psalmist in the Responsorial Psalm to sing: "It is the Lord, the King of Glory, the strong and mighty who comes to dwell in us."

The Peace of the Lord be with you.

Prayer
Father, we humbly invite Your Son into the temples of our hearts and beseech him to nurture in us your seeds of Wisdom, Peace, and Love. Amen.

THE FEAST OF THE ASCENSION OF THE LORD

Acts 1:1-11; Ephesians 1:17-23; Matthew 28:16-20 Year A

BE MY WITNESSES

The Resurrection, Ascension, and Pentecost are the three core tenets and feasts in Christianity. Like the doctrine of the Trinity, this trilogy of beliefs meshes to express one central profound creed and acknowledged truth in Christianity that *Jesus is God, the Son of God* (John 1:1,14). Any attempt to dismantle these manifestations or failure to recognize any of them and their theological inferences seriously cripples the Christian religion and renders it meaningless and inconsequential. The three events happened swiftly relative to history as mysteries beyond human experience. However, seen through the lens of faith, they reveal Jesus as God and master of atmospheric gravity and the supernatural world.

The observance of the *Feast of the Ascension of the Lord* dates to the fourth century. It is traditionally celebrated on a Thursday, exactly forty days after Easter Sunday, and ten days before Pentecost Day, to conform to Luke's account of the two events. Ascension officially marks the end of the Easter Season. Ecclesiastical provinces may move its observance to the following Sunday to emphasize its profound significance, and to encourage greater participation by the faithful in the celebration of the liturgy.

Saint Luke uses forty days as a metaphor for the Biblical number "forty." There are other times that the number 40 assumes great significance in the Bible. In Noah's time, "rain fell on the earth for 40 days and nights" (Genesis 7:12); Moses fasted for forty days and forty nights on the *Mountain of the Lord*, after which he received the Ten Commandments (Exodus 34:28). After many years of slavery in Egypt, the Israelites sojourned in many places traveling through hard times in the desert. Israel's disobedience delayed their entry into the Promised Land for 40 years. Jesus fasted for 40 days to overcome Satan (Luke 4:1-13). The *Resurrected Christ* lived on earth for 40 days to demonstrate his dominance over death. He used 40 days to establish a special and permanent connection with his disciples, appearing to them several times (John 20:19-29; 21:14), teaching them about the kingdom, and commissioned them as witnesses "to the ends of the world (first reading).

The description of Jesus' Ascension is reminiscent of the ascension of Elijah and the descent of the Spirit of God on Elisha (2 Kings 2:11). Jesus' Ascension (Acts 1:1-11) is soon followed by the outpouring of the Holy Spirit upon the disciples (Acts 2:1-4). Again, the Ascension of Jesus reminds us that the *Salvation Plan of God* is a process, perfect, detailed, and well-calculated (John 3:14-17). Jesus had descended to the earth as God-incarnate (God-becoming-man), suffered human humiliation, and died on the Cross for the atonement of the sins of the world (Philippians 2:6-11). After his resurrection, Jesus had to leave the earth to go to where he had come from: "In the beginning, the Word already existed; the Word was with God, and the Word was God" (John 1:1).

The Ascension of Jesus commemorates his victory regarding his mission on earth, ending in his suffering, crucifixion, and resurrection. Today, a great multitude of saints in heaven will welcome Jesus into his glory, the same glory from which he descended to the earth (John 1:1-5). Indeed, what sets Jesus apart from countless others alleging to be Messiah is his resurrection from the dead. The link between the ascended Jesus, the apostles, and the Church is the Holy Spirit, who now leads God's people. The Holy Spirit would now guide the course of witnessing to the entire world (John 14:16-17). A new life-experience directed by the Holy Spirit had begun which will reach its full completion at Jesus' second coming or descent from heaven (John 14:1-3).

Saint Luke concludes his Gospel with a brief description of Jesus "taken up into heaven" in the presence of the apostles (Luke 24:51). What appears as an eyewitness account to the event is narrated again in detail in Luke's second book, *The Acts of the Apostles*. On the *Mount of Olives* (or Olivet), traditionally called *The Mount of Ascension*, Jesus appears to his apostles. There is a brief dialogue. He repeats his most salient and compelling command, referred to in theological parlance as the *Great Commission*, directing them to be his witnesses "to the ends of the earth" and "to baptize in the name of the Father, the Son, and the Holy Spirit" (Matthew 28:18-20). After bonding with his apostles in a passionate final farewell and assuring them of the gift of the Holy Spirit, Jesus is taken up and disappears in the clouds. The apostles gaze into the sky in astonishment. They hear the message of two angels implying that Jesus is truly alive and will descend during his second coming, also called the *Parousia*, in a manner like his Ascension (Acts 1:10-11). As Paul explains in the second reading, the Christian goal and hope is to share the heavenly glory where Jesus is seated at the right hand of God the Father.

Jesus' Ascension and the prophecy regarding his return both happen on the *Mount of Olives*, regarded sacred in both the Old and New Testaments. A Jewish tradition showed the coming of the Lord and the resurrection of the dead would begin on the *Mount of Olives* (Zechariah 14:4), and so many Jews desired to be buried on the Mount or its premises. It is estimated that over 150,000 graves are on the Mount. Jesus frequented the *Mount of Olives* (Luke 22:39). The top of the Mount offers an aesthetic view of Old Jerusalem from where Jesus wept over the city (Luke 19:41). He preached and prophesied from the Mount (Matthew 24-25, Mark 13, and Luke 21); a series of sayings collectively known as the *Olivet Discourse*. After his daily preaching and teaching in the Temple, Jesus went to the Mount to rest or to spend the night (Luke 21:37; John 8:1). After the Last Supper, Jesus and his apostles went to the *Garden of Gethsemane*, which lay at the foot of the Mount (Matthew 26:30).

The decisive directive to the apostles to be witnesses "to the ends of the earth" was Jesus' declaration for missionary activity that continues unabated as a mandate for global evangelization. In the Early Church, martyrdom was the ultimate way of witnessing to Christ and the Gospel. Surprisingly, Christian persecutions continue today in some places in the world. However, Christians were also called to witness to the Word in the world by their way of life and not only with their lives. This is still true today. The Catechism of the Catholic Church teaches that we "attain salvation through faith, baptism, and the observance of the Commandments" (CCC 2068). This means holding on to the Gospel, and by works of charity (James 2:24,26). Actions demonstrate faith and show we are indeed justified by the faith we profess despite voices and actions of other people contradicting the Word.

For the three years Jesus moved with his disciples, they believed in him as the Messiah. The difficulty was how to accept he was not the kind of Messiah they and the people of Israel anticipated. Even on the day of his Ascension, the disciples asked him, "Lord, are you at this time going to restore the kingdom to Israel?" Jesus assured them the Advocate would guide them to all truth. (John 16:12-15).

The purpose of the Holy Spirit is to help the world see the truth about the nature of God as told in the famous passage from St. Augustine's *Confessions:* "You have made us for yourself, O Lord, and our heart is restless until it rests in you." The Holy Spirit guides us in discovering that the Lord is "exceedingly worthy of praise," his "power is immense," and "wisdom beyond reckoning." The knowledge about God and the praise accorded him, as St. Augustine notes, "brings us joy."

Again, the Holy Spirit guides us to know the truth about ourselves and to discover the limitations that can impede our spiritual growth. When we yield to our limitations, we wrongly make choices based upon the lies and deceits of selfishness, power, greed, intolerance, fanaticism, and violence. These may appear to us to bring peace and happiness but invariably result in our becoming fearful, despondent, and despairing. But most significantly, the Holy Spirit guides us to the truth that will enable us to focus our lives on justice, honesty, integrity, compassion, love, and charity.

Celebrating the Feast of the Ascension of Jesus today, we are also preparing like the apostles who waited ten days to receive the Holy Spirit and his seven gratuitous gifts on Pentecost Day: wisdom, understanding, counsel, fortitude, knowledge, piety, and the fear of the Lord. As Paul states, these gifts bear the fruit of love, joy, peace, patience, kindness, goodness, faithfulness, gentleness, and self-control (Galatians 5:22-23). It is appropriate on Pentecost Day that the Church administers the *Sacrament of Confirmation* to bring these and other virtues to the front of the adult mind to meditate deeply upon them and sharpen Christian attitudes in them. An adult Catholic parishioner commented elsewhere, stating: "I became a mature Catholic to realize the power of the Holy Spirit in my life. As a budding Christian, I spent most of my time and prayers directed to God the Father and God the Son. It truly is the Holy Spirit that is the love of the Father and Son, now poured upon me as God's greatest gift."

Today, we lift our eyes intently up toward the skies with the apostles, gazing with at the ascent of the Lord into heaven, and believing in his promise to send the Holy Spirit: "He is the Spirit who reveals the truth about God" (John 14:17). Jesus is always with us in his Spirit not leaving us orphans: "And I will be with you always, to the end of the age" (Matthew 28:20), words of inspiration regarding his omnipresence as God and spoken moments before his ascent into heaven. Jesus is always with us fully in his humanity and divinity. For example, whenever we gather around the *Altar of Grace*, we become extremely consciously aware of his presence: the Word is proclaimed and animated; at the "Consecration," the priest raises Jesus' Body and Blood in the form of Bread and Wine, for the *New People of God* to worship; we receive Jesus' Body and Blood to identify with him as our Lord and

Savior, the Light of the world, shining into the darkness in our hearts and around us to give us peace, joy, and meaning in life.

Jesus' presence and our profound experience of him at the Eucharist must manifest in our everyday lives: to love sincerely, hate what is evil, and hold on to what is good (Romans 12:9-16), clearly espoused in his New Commandment: love one another (John 13:34). Living the New Law of Love with the help of the Holy Spirit is the greatest way to becoming witnesses: "If you have love for one another, then everyone will know that you are my disciples" (John 13:35).

The *Great Commission* (Matthew 28:18-20) enjoins us to spread the message by providing testimony to the Word (1 John 1:1), but equally fundamental in the mission of witnessing is living out the Law of Love by projecting Jesus' love for us toward our neighbor.

Witnessing was the mandate for the disciples after the Ascension when Jesus handed the mantle to the disciples and the Holy Spirit.

How do you prove to yourself and others that you, too, are indeed a true witness of Jesus Christ?

Examine your thoughts, words, and deeds to see if you are true to the Word of God and Jesus' new Law of Love.

Can you share how you show Jesus' love to others?

What is in your life that you might call a detour, a roadblock, a traffic jam, a breakdown on the journey of life Jesus has beckoned you to take?

Do you rely on the Holy Spirit for a breakthrough?

The Peace of the Lord be with you.

Prayer
Father, we glorify your exalted Son Jesus Christ, now sitting at Your right hand in heaven. Let all your people live on earth in faith, hope, and love and one day be with him in eternal joy. Amen.

THE SOLEMNITY OF THE MOST HOLY BODY AND BLOOD OF JESUS CHRIST
(Thursday after Trinity Sunday)

Deuteronomy 7:6-11; 1 John 4:7-16; Matthew 11:25-30

CORPUS CHRISTI: THE BODY OF CHRIST

The story of how the *Feast of Corpus Christi*, also known as *the Solemnity of the Most Holy Body and Blood of Jesus Christ*, became institutionalized in the Church usually begins with the Eucharistic miracle in 1263, in Bolsena, Italy. The story is about a German priest, Peter of Prague, stopping in Bolsena en route to Rome on a pilgrimage. Like many people at the time, and even as of today, he expressed doubts about the real presence of Christ in the Eucharist. Celebrating the Holy Eucharist on an altar built on the tomb of St. Christina, he observed blood oozing out from the consecrated host and dripping over his hands onto the corporal and the altar cloth. The priest stopped the Mass and requested an audience with Pope Urban IV who was living in the city of Orvieto close to Bolsena.

After instituting an investigation into the alleged Eucharistic miracle, the Pope confirmed its authenticity. He commissioned St. Thomas Aquinas (1225-1274), one of the greatest Catholic Church philosophers and theologians and a staunch advocate of the Eucharistic Presence, to compose the *Proper for Mass and Office* in honor of the Holy Eucharist as the Body of Christ. In August 1264, Thomas Aquinas completed the composition and appealed to the Pope to create a feast "emphasizing the joy of the Eucharist being the Body and Blood, Soul and Divinity of Jesus Christ." His compositions are still used for Eucharistic adoration such as "Panis Angelicus," "Pange Lingua," "O Salutaris Hostia." The Pope accepted the request and instituted the *Feast of Corpus Christi* by a papal bull. The relics are still reverently preserved in the Cathedral of Orvieto, Italy, attracting many pilgrims and tourists. Many people also visit the altar of the miracle in the church of St. Christina in Bolsena, where the miracle took place. After his second visit to the grotto in Bolsena, Pope Paul VI went to address the 41st International Eucharistic Congress in Philadelphia, USA, and described the Eucharist as "a mystery great and inexhaustible."

It is accepted, however, that the institution of the *Feast of Corpus Christi* was due in part to the work of St. Juliana of Liège, a visionary and prioress of the convent of Mont Cornillon in Belgium (died in 1258). She had a fervent devotion to the Blessed Virgin Mary, the Passion of Jesus, and the Eucharist in her youthful years. Devotion to the Eucharist was a popular spiritual exercise among groups of women in the Diocese of Liège, where Juliana was born. In her visions for a period of about 20 years, she was directed to ask for an official celebration of the feast in the Church and a special devotion to the Blessed Sacrament. The Eucharistic miracle of Bolsena confirmed her visions, and several extant texts and vita show her influence. Soon after her death, and one year after the miracle, Pope Urban IV instituted the feast as *The Solemnity of the Most Holy Body and Blood of Christ.* It is popularly known by its Latin name as *Corpus Christi* (The Body of Christ) and celebrates the "real presence of Jesus Christ in the Holy Eucharist—Body, Blood, Soul, and Divinity." The Council of Vienna (1311-1312) endorsed the feast under Pope Clement V. In 1317, Pope John XXII re-instituted it for the universal Church.

On the Feast Day, Mass is celebrated, and in some countries, the faithful parade through the streets with the consecrated host in a monstrance. This shows that Jesus is King of the World, and his message of salvation is for the entire world. Processions in these countries end with Benediction of the Blessed Sacrament, comprising songs of praise in honor of Christ in the Blessed Sacrament, and a priest blessing the people with the monstrance.

Corpus Christi is observed as a public holiday in some countries with a large Catholic population dating back to when huge numbers participated in processions. The Feast was suppressed during the Reformation when many Protestants denied Jesus' presence in the Eucharist, upholding it as a "merely symbolic or spiritual exercise." The Anglican Church later restored the feast as *The Day of Thanksgiving for the Institution of Holy Communion.* Some Lutheran and Western Orthodox churches also observe the feast.

The feast falls on a Thursday after *Trinity Sunday*, but dioceses are permitted to transfer it to the following Sunday to allow greater participation in the procession of the Blessed Sacrament within the church premises or through the streets. In some places, procession of the Blessed Sacrament is transferred to the *Feast of Christ the King* that commemorates the *Kingship of Jesus Christ* on the last Sunday of the Church's Liturgical Year.

Thursday is associated with the day of Jesus' *Last Supper* with his apostles and focuses on what took place. Jesus blessed bread to become his Body, and wine his Blood; thus, instituting the Sacrament of the *Holy Eucharist.* Corpus Christi, therefore, observes a specific event in the life of Jesus, stressing his real presence in the Holy Eucharist: "Jesus Christ is present in the Eucharist in a unique and incomparable way. He is present in a true, real, and substantial way, with his Body and his Blood, with his Soul and his Divinity. In the Eucharist, therefore, Jesus is present in a sacramental way, that is, under the Eucharistic species of bread and wine, Christ whole and entire, God and Man" (Catechism of the Catholic Church, 282).

While we worship the Lord in the Eucharist, he "draws us towards him into his mystery in order to transform us as he transforms the bread and the wine" (Pope Benedict XVII). Pope Benedict added, "while we gaze at the Eucharist and meditate on Jesus' suffering and the cross as well as his resurrection, we also renew our faith in the real presence of Christ in the Eucharist and discover God's love." The Eucharist becomes "an inexhaustible source of holiness" (Pope John Paul II), reminding us of the greatest attribute of Jesus as *Emmanuel,* meaning "God is with us", (Matthew 1:23), as well as his promise to be present with us always until the end of time (Matthew 28:20). Indeed, the procession with the Eucharist is to celebrate "God with us," and for the community to thank God for his presence.

The Eucharist was instituted in the context of a meal with the apostles as the core of Christian life. God comes down as living bread from heaven, the prototype of manna in the desert: "I am the living bread that came down from heaven," and "unless you eat my Body and drink my Blood you will not have eternal life" (John 6:51). This is about a divine reality on earth that we can only understand with faith. While material food provides energy for the body, the Eucharist, as God's spiritual food, unites us to Christ and makes us live like him.

Again, at the Last Supper, Jesus instituted his *Commandment of Love*—symbolized by the washing of the disciples' feet. At the Eucharistic celebration, therefore, we experience the living presence of Jesus Christ in the community, uniting us to worship together, and urging us to live as brothers and sisters in love. Amazingly, the Eucharistic celebration brings different ethnic and social groups together to profess one faith that unites us in mind and heart to worship together. Again, at the Eucharistic celebration, we receive the Body and Blood of Jesus Christ in Holy Communion and must fully know his amazing divine presence. Indeed, the divine presence in me makes me recognize and accept the divine presence in my neighbor. The Eucharistic celebration is an assembly of friendship, love, peace, and understanding. Around the *Altar of Grace*, the community of believers is fed with the same *Loaf of Bread,* broken and shared, and drink from the same *Cup of Blessing,* which constitute the *One Body of Christ* (second reading).

The sharing of a meal or "eating from the same pot" with any family or at a gathering fosters unity and peace. We share

God's life, and therefore, must expunge divisive tendencies, selfish motives, and resentments, and show concern and tolerance for everyone. Furthermore, at the place of Eucharistic worship, we take our experience of God's love to our homes, families, friends, and workplaces. In these places, we must show how we understand Jesus' *Commandment of Love* and practice it with mind, heart, and soul. We are to share what we eat, drink and experience; show friendship and empathy; share a smile and give a helping hand; visit the sick and aged; give hope and assistance to the needy and helpless; and be disciples of justice, peace, and generosity.

At the Last Supper, Jesus Christ, the High Priest (Hebrews 2:17; 4:14-16), in his first Eucharistic celebration, ordained his first group of priests (the Apostles), as the Holy Priesthood to minister around the table of the Lord and give his body and blood—as spiritual food and drink to God's people. Jesus Christ, who offers himself in the bread and wine, is associated with the priesthood of Melchizedek (Hebrews 7:1-25). He is also linked to Abraham, who acknowledged the priesthood of Melchizedek (first reading) and was blessed by him. Additionally, Priests are called to proclaim the Word of God to ensure that everybody experiences the love and saving grace of God.

Holy Thursday also commemorates the agony in the *Garden of Gethsemane*, reminding us to embrace the life of Christian suffering and the duty to assist those undergoing pain and hardships.

There is a lot that we need to do for ourselves and our children on this Feast Day. Children like processions and should participate in parish processions to show them the meaning and the importance of the *Feast of Corpus Christi*.

The word *Eucharist* means thanksgiving for the sacrifice of Jesus Christ on the Cross. Attending Mass is the greatest way to give thanks to God for our salvation and to seek forgiveness for our failures.

We need to inculcate in the youth the importance of sacrifice, charity, selflessness, and gratitude. We must speak to them about vocation to the priesthood and religious life. We must educate and encourage them to support and pray for their priests and religious men and women who have dedicated their lives to the worship of God and the service of God's people.

We must visit the Blessed Sacrament and participate in Benedictions.

The People of God must appreciate the *Holy Eucharist* as the real Jesus Christ and be inspired to receive Holy Communion.

A recent *Pew Research Center* (August 8, 2019) survey showed that most Catholics (about 69%) do not believe in the *Eucharistic Presence.*

It is said St. Thomas Aquinas was so enamored by the Eucharist that he described the Eucharist as the "food of Angels." It is said that after his writings on the Eucharist as he was praying in front of a crucifix, his confreres saw him lifted into the air and heard a voice coming from the crucifix saying, "Thou has written well of me, Thomas, what reward will thou have?"

Thomas replies, "Nothing but you, Lord."

Can you envisage what Thomas Aquinas saw in the Eucharist?

Does this impact how you would approach the altar today to receive Holy Communion?

Do you see the Eucharist as just a part of a liturgical celebration or you believe Jesus' real presence?

The Peace of the Lord be with you.

Prayer
Father, today, we honor your Son in the Holy Eucharist, which is the bread that ensures eternal life, and given because of your bounteous love. Let your Spirit, Lord, teach us how to love and share our lives with one another. Amen.

THE FEAST OF THE SACRED HEART
OF THE LORD
(Friday after the Second Sunday of Pentecost)

Hosea 11:1, 3-4, 8-9; Ephesians 3:8-12, 14-19; John 19:31-37

O SACRED HEART OF JESUS, I PLACE ALL MY TRUST IN THEE

The feast of the Sacred Heart is another popular religious devotion to Jesus Christ in the Roman Catholic and some Anglican and Lutheran Churches. The feast was first observed in the monasteries of the Middle Ages with devotional prayers and spiritual exercises. However, its present form derives from visions received by a French nun, Saint Margaret Mary Alacoque, who died in 1690. There are no records to show she knew about devotions to the Sacred Heart before the revelations.

This feast honors and adores the wounded physical *Heart of Jesus*, symbol of his divine heart that loved the world enough to suffer and die on the cross to save it. Devotions are in the form of reparation or expiation to the Most Sacred Heart of Jesus, a point explicitly made by Pope Pius XI: "the spirit of expiation or reparation has always had the first and foremost place in the worship given to the Most Sacred Heart of Jesus." Pope Pius XII also declared that devotion to the Sacred Heart of Jesus was "the foundation on which to build the kingdom of God in the hearts of individuals, families and nations." It led to the practice of the image of the Sacred Heart being blessed and "enthroned" in homes of devotees for veneration and to remind them they were consecrated to the Sacred Heart of Jesus. Many institutions, including schools and colleges, churches, parishes, and hospitals, have been named after the Sacred Heart. Scapulars and medals depicting the portraits of the Sacred Heart on one side and the Immaculate Heart of Mary on the other are worn by people to show they are under the protection of the Sacred Heart.

The feast is celebrated 19 days after Pentecost Sunday, which falls on a Friday, the day of the week on which Jesus was crucified, and his heart was pierced with a lance. The object of veneration is his heart, which is usually presented in paintings, statues and sculptures as "a flaming heart shining with divine light, pierced by a lance-wound, surrounded by a crown of thorns, and surmounted by a cross and bleeding. Sometimes the image is over Jesus' body with his wounded hands pointing to his heart. The wounds and crown of thorns allude to the manner of Jesus' death, while the fire represents the transformative power of divine love."

The devotee feels partly responsible for Jesus' death because of human sins, hence the reparation to God. The gratuitous love of Jesus to die to save humankind overwhelms us and teaches us that true love gives life and is truly costly. The devotee prays for divine assistance to forgive, sacrifice, and show love in all circumstances. Our hearts must be moved to pity the poor and needy just as Jesus' heart was and is moved with pity for the people (Matthew 9:36).

The Sacred Heart, therefore, symbolizes several related ideals for the Christian: love, self-sacrifice, truthfulness, honesty, justice, and promotion of peace. All these are ideals for a humble and gentle heart, like the heart of Jesus (Matthew 11:29). Jesus stressed that a trustworthy follower must be like the good shepherd who puts his life at risk for his sheep. The good shepherd fights wild animals and thieves breaking into the sheepfold. Similarly, the true Christian is at risk in a world that portrays a new social order of individualism, hatred, injustice, dishonesty, and needless wars which the Christian must always fight. The three hearts that portray love are the Sacred Heart of Jesus, the Immaculate Heart of Mary, and the Chaste Heart of Joseph.

In her visions, St. Margaret Mary Alacoque received twelve promises to those who venerate the Sacred Heart:

1. *I will give them all the graces necessary for their state of life.*
2. *I will give peace in their families.*
3. *I will console them in all their troubles.*
4. *I will be their refuge in life and especially in death.*
5. *I will abundantly bless all their undertakings.*
6. *Sinners shall find in my Heart the source and Infinite Ocean of mercy.*
7. *Tepid souls shall become fervent.*
8. *Fervent souls shall rise speedily to great perfection.*
9. *I will bless those places wherein the image of My Sacred Heart shall be exposed and venerated.*
10. *I will give to priests the power to touch the most hardened hearts.*
11. *Persons who propagate this devotion shall have their names eternally written in my Heart.*
12. *In the excess of the mercy of my Heart, I promise you that my all-powerful love will grant to all those who will receive Communion on the First Fridays, for nine consecutive months, the grace of final repentance: they will not die in my displeasure, nor without receiving the sacraments; and my Heart will be their secure refuge in that last hour.*

The last promise has given rise to the Catholic practice of attending Mass and receiving Communion on the first Friday of each month.

The Peace of the Lord be with You.

Prayer
Father, in your goodness grant pardon to those who seek your mercy through the Sacred Heart of your beloved Son, whose amazing love has saved the world from the shackles of sin. Amen.

THE FEAST OF THE TRANSFIGURATION OF THE LORD

Daniel 7:9-10, 13-14; 2 Peter 1:16-19; Matthew 17:1-9

"LORD, IT IS GOOD THAT WE ARE HERE..."

Today, most Christian traditions are celebrating the Feast of the Transfiguration of Jesus, when Jesus was transfigured on the mountain (now referred to as the Mount of Transfiguration). In the presence of three apostles, Peter, James, and John, Jesus becomes radiant in glory on the mountain. Moses and Elijah appear to speak with him, and a voice from above confirms Jesus as Son of God, whom we must listen to. Christians believe Mount Tabor, a significant site in both the Old and New Testament times, to be the place where Jesus was transfigured. The Mount continues to be a site of religious importance, attracting pilgrims yearly from all over the world to the Church of the Transfiguration and the nearby Eastern Sanctuary of the Orthodox Church. The feast is so significant in the faith of the Church that it is always celebrated on a Sunday.

All the Synoptic Gospels, Matthew, Mark, and Luke, record the story about the *Transfiguration of the Lord*. The so-called synoptic problem seeks to resolve the actual literary question regarding the source of the striking similarities in the three Gospels regarding "structure, content, and wording." Although a clear solution is elusive, many scholars opine that Matthew and Luke used a Marcan source while **Matthew and Luke** shared additional material known as the Q-source. In the Transfiguration narrative, even the buildup to the time it took place is similar in the three Gospels. Jesus was heading towards Jerusalem with his apostles via Caesarea Philippi whose aesthetic landscape, copious water supply, and luxuriant vegetation made a booming commercial and cultural center. Because of its surreal environs, the city became the hub of pagan

393

religious worship with many "big and small" temples dedicated to local and family gods scattered around the surrounding area.

Being the center of many religious sites, Caesarea Philippi also had a large and deep cave which was known as the Underworld, or Hades, the abode of Satan and his cohort of evil spirits. The entrance was called the *Gate to the Underworld* or the *Gate to Hades.*

Jesus brought his apostles near the entrance of the Underworld, surrounded by pagan gods and idols in Caesarea Philippi, and he asked them a direct question about how the people perceived him. Then, he directed the same question to them. Peter's reply was spontaneous and surprising: "You are the Messiah, the Son of the living God." The direct response of Peter, and the profundity of the revelation, was powerful enough for Jesus to realize God the Father had made the striking proclamation through Peter. Again, for Jesus, it was beyond doubt that God the Father had chosen the *petros*, the dominant rock or foundation upon which to build the kingdom of God, the Church. Jesus confirmed this insightful truth, and pointing to the *Gate to the Underworld*, declared that the power of the spirits could not defeat the Church. Indeed, Peter's mission was couched by the declaration. He would be given the keys to the new world, the kingdom of God, with unhindered authority to direct the purpose of its people towards God in heaven. Thus, in pagan surroundings, the divinity of Jesus is proclaimed by one who acknowledges him as savior, and Jesus declares the prominence of Peter in the mission of the Church of Christ.

Possibly referring to Isaiah's discourse on the *Suffering Servant* (Isaiah 53), Jesus used some days to educate the disciples about the true meaning of the Messiah, his destiny to suffer human humiliation, and how the message referred to him (Luke 22:37). He would undergo similar trepidation in Jerusalem in the hands of the elders, the chief priests, and the teachers of the Law: "I will be put to death, but three days later I will be raised to life" (Matthew 16:21). Jesus acknowledged that God inspired Peter to declare him Messiah and Son of God, for which Peter received a bedrock function in the Church. And then, Jesus realized Satan tricked Peter into doubting what he had said regarding the Messiah's death and resurrection. Although we may profess staunch faith in Jesus, we must always know Satan's unrelenting war on our minds to deceive us into a state of disbelief. It was an opportune time for a divine plan to reveal the divine nature of Jesus to the disciples to clear their apparently discombobulated minds!

The Synoptic Gospels narrate that about a week after all this, Jesus invited three of his apostles, Peter, James, and John, to pray with him on a high mountain. Something remarkable happened: Jesus was praying a few feet from them when they noticed a transfigured Jesus becoming radiant in glory. According to Matthew's Gospel, "his face was shining like the sun, and his clothes were dazzling white." Then, the apostles saw the appearance of two Old Testament personalities: Moses and Elijah. The account of Luke specifies that Moses and Elijah were talking with Jesus about how "he would soon fulfill God's purpose by dying in Jerusalem" (Luke 9:31).

In a state of fear and absentmindedness, Peter requested to build three tents for them, since it was good to be in their presence, and Peter felt the three men needed to remain at the place for some time. A thick cloud covered them, reminiscent of the Old Testament times (Exodus 33:9-11), and a voice declared, "This is my own dear Son, with whom I am pleased—listen to him!" The cloud lifted Moses and Elijah away, leaving Jesus alone with the apostles, who were understandably even more terrified. Jesus touched them to assuage their fears but urged them to keep the incident silent until after his resurrection. This tells us that conforming to God's time of events in his salvation plan is important. The transfiguration was well-timed to reveal the identity of Jesus to the apostles and to strengthen their faith, especially to confront challenges in their future mission.

At long last, the apostles saw and heard it all and gained a considerable understanding about Jesus and his mission. Moses symbolized the Law because he received the Ten Commandments, which were the basis of the entire Mosaic Law that guided the lives of the people of Israel. Elijah, one of the most remarkable prophets of Israel, represented all the prophets who preached God's Word to the Jewish people. The presence of these prominent figures confirmed Jesus epitomized both the Law and the Prophets, giving credence to the Scripture verse in *The Letter to the Hebrews* that in the past God spoke through our ancestors and prophets but now he has spoken to us through his Son (Hebrews 1:1-2)

Moses went up Mount Sinai to meet the Lord and his face shone bright like the sun (Exodus 34). Similarly, Jesus went up the mountain to meet Moses and Elijah, and the glory of God shone around him. The holy mountain became a meeting place for the divine and human nature, and Jesus became the conduit or bridge between God and humankind. The voice of God the Father called Jesus "Son," showing Jesus was the primary personality at the scene and not Moses or Elijah. This was the same voice and message John the Baptist heard at the baptism of Jesus and told some of his own disciples (John 1:32-35). Again, the voice, "listen to him," indicates that Jesus is now the messenger of God (the new Moses) and the mouthpiece of God (the Elijah) (Malachi 4:5-6). Christians see in the transfiguration a proof that God is not "the God of the dead, but of the living," and Moses and Elijah appearing on the mountain is an example of eternal life.

The apostles would always remember this occasion and reminded the followers of Jesus about it: "We saw his glory, the glory which he received as the Father's only Son" (John 1:14). Peter would also acknowledge their presence on the mountain and the voice from above, confirming Jesus as the Messiah: "We ourselves heard this voice come down from heaven while we were with him on the holy mountain" (second reading).

Christians ascribe great significance to the transfiguration as one of the major moments in the life of Jesus, including his baptism, crucifixion, resurrection, and ascension. It is one of the miracles of Jesus, whose uniqueness lies in the fact that the miracle is about Jesus himself, transfigured before the apostles, shining like the sun, with his clothes became dazzlingly white.

Today, we are commemorating the transfiguration of Jesus on Mount Tabor near Jerusalem when the divinity of Jesus Christ was revealed to three of Jesus' apostles, Peter, James, and John. The appearance of Moses and Elijah confirmed Jesus as the continuation of God's Salvation plan, or redemptive history designed for humankind. The leading message was in the voice of God the Father: "This is my beloved Son, with whom I am pleased—listen to him." Christianity is not a concept but a way of life coded in the life of Jesus Christ, "the Way, the Truth, and the life" leading to the Father in Heaven (John 14:6).

I desire to be like the apostles and engrave this glorious experience at the deep end of my memory track.

I desire it to remain with me with the incredible power to influence and strengthen me to walk with the Lord Jesus for the rest of my life—trusting him, listening to him, and loving him because he is the Savior who died for my salvation.

Indeed, I desire to experience him uniquely at Mass today in his Word and when bread and wine are transformed before me into his precious Body and Blood.

In the privilege of listening to the Word and receiving him in the Communion, I will joyfully say in my heart, "Lord it is good that we are here."

The Peace of the Lord be with you.

Prayer
Father, You Son is transfigured each day before us in the Blessed Sacrament. His presence in our lives gives us hope and meaning in life. Help each of us to always acknowledge him as Lord and Savior. Amen.

Holy Days

THE ASSUMPTION OF THE BLESSED VIRGIN MARY
(August 15)

Revelation 11:19; 12:1-6. 10; 1 Corinthians 15:20-26; Luke 1:39-56

MARY FULL OF GRACE

The Book of Revelation, also known as *The Book of the Apocalypse*, is replete with symbolic language, imagery, and visions. Many of them were borrowed from the Old Testament prophetic books like the *Book of Daniel* (dated about 200 B.C.). These representations in the Old Testament deepened the faith of the Jews during persecutions, assuring them of the continual presence of the prevailing power of God to turn things in their favor. For example, the strange imagery of beasts represented evil foreign leaders who would be defeated by God. Similarly, the dragon in the *Book of Revelation* exemplified the cruelty of secular leaders towards Christians starting from the first century.

When Christianity reached Rome, many considered Christians a threat to the empire for proclaiming the coming of a new king and a new kingdom, and for condemning the religious practices in the empire. In the summer of 64 A.D., when fire burned a large part of Rome, Emperor Nero was blamed for intentionally causing the fire for his own amusement. He accused Christians, indicted them of treason, and set up a calculated scheme to obliterate Christianity in the empire. The author of *The Book of Revelation* intended to inspire Christians persecuted by Emperor Nero and subsequent emperors until the end of the fourth century. Emperor Constantine the Great and his co-emperor Licinius ended the persecution with the *Edict of Milan* in 313 A.D. that allowed the practice of Christianity in the empire. Christianity as the state church of the Roman Empire occurred later in A.D. 380 with the *Edict of Thessalonica* that endorsed the *Nicene Creed.*

In the first reading, the images and allegories reflect the threats of the power of evil—either Satan or human power—to thwart God's plan for salvation and frustrate human cooperation. The Evangelist recollects how on the eve of the new Messianic Era, "that ancient serpent, called the Devil, or Satan, that deceived the whole world" (Revelation 12:9), reappears with a vicious plan to prevent the survival of both the Messiah-child to be born and the mother. Michael and his angels render the terrifying dragon powerless. The dragon, Satan, is thrown down to the earth and heaven sings, praising God for victory over Satan (Revelation 12:10-12). The mother is also rescued, whisked away into the desert, but Satan stands ready to fight her descendants who are faithful to God (Revelation 12:17-18) and to destroy the *Kingdom of God* (Luke 8:12; 10:17-19; 11:20; John 13:27).

John's vision is about a woman in celestial glory adorned with the stars, sun, and moon (Genesis 37:9-10). She is the vessel or ark bearing the Messiah, but in painful labor. The woman is Mary. The child is Jesus. Jesus begins his reign over the whole world on God's throne. This is proven in 313 and 380 A.D. when Christianity is affirmed in the Roman Empire. The pain of the woman is the suffering of the fledging Church. The twelve stars stand for the twelve tribes of Israel, but now represent the twelve Apostles, the leaders of the New Israel, the new kingdom of God, or the Church to which we all belong. The woman has a role in God's Salvation Plan. She is chosen from eternity to bear a son (Luke 1:38). After this, she lives forever in a place prepared for her. This Grace in eternity will be shared by all persons who allow themselves to be guarded by God's holy will.

The reading also reminds us of the mischief spread by those representing Satan who sought to destroy Jesus at different times: after his birth, like King Herod; those who opposed his mission, like the Jewish religious leadership; those who were resolute to halt the spread of Christianity,

402

such as Paul, before his conversion; and the adherents of different schisms in the Early Church.

Today is the Feast of the Assumption of the Blessed Virgin Mary into heaven. The traditional belief in the Catholic Church, the Eastern Orthodox Churches, the Oriental Orthodox Churches, and the Anglican Communion is that the Blessed Virgin Mary was physically taken up into heaven at the end of her earthly life. The Eastern Orthodox and Eastern Catholics refer to the Feast as "Dormition of the Theotokos" (the falling asleep of the mother of God). This implies that there was "the real physical elevation of her sinless soul and incorrupt body into heaven." However, the Virgin Mary's death place is unknown, although Jerusalem and Ephesus have been suggested. Her tomb in Jerusalem dates to the 6th century.

The belief in the Assumption dates to the 7th century. Bishop Theoteknos of Livias (c. 550-650) wrote that although the "Assumption" does not appear in the Bible, it is as true as Enoch and Elijah, who did not experience death. He wrote about Mary's special character, for which the assumption could be deemed proper: Mary described as God's "highly favored," and as "the Lord is with you," as well as "blessed are you among women."

Early Church Fathers presented Mary as the "New Eve" who said "yes" to God when Eve said "no." The Council of Ephesus in 431 A.D. endorsed the devotion to the Virgin Mary, which was already widespread. While other Christians perceive the Bible as the Last Testament, the Roman Catholic considers the Church "as an instrument of God receiving new revelations from the Holy Spirit" (John 20:21-23). The Assumption which does not appear in the New Testament is one of these manifestations. Thus, there was no visible disagreement in the Church when on November 1, 1950, Pope Pius XII confirmed the Assumption of Mary as Church teaching before over 50,000 Faithful at St. Peter's Square in the Vatican. The document states in part: *"The Immaculate*

Mother of God, the ever-Virgin Mary, having completed the course of her earthly life, was assumed body and soul into heavenly glory."

The beliefs about the Virgin Mary include the doctrine recognizing her Immaculate Conception. This belief states that after original sin became a mark on humankind, only Mary was born free from sin. Again, there is the belief about her perpetual virginity.

St. Paul writes in the second reading that "Christ has been raised from the dead, as the first fruits of all who have fallen asleep." Mary is therefore the excellent proof that just as Jesus rose from the dead, those professing faith in him will be part of the resurrection.

Today's Gospel reading reminds us of the gifts received by Mary and Elizabeth. They rejoiced at their pregnancies and were moved by the grace they each received from God. They felt their babies move inside their wombs and rejoiced about the marvels of the Lord. Elizabeth confirmed Mary as "Mother of God" and Mary predicted her own blessedness: "All ages to come shall call me blessed."

Like the Blessed Virgin Mary, we have received grace as God's children in his kingdom. Mary is our model of faith who reveals to us how we must live in God's grace. We must, therefore, always feel God's presence in us, realizing that sin distances us from God. Therefore, we need to be more disciplined about how to control our free will. Mary was instrumental in God's Salvation Plan and fully cooperated. Let us ask for her intercession to be humble and submissive to do the will of God. She leads us to understand precisely where Jesus, her son, intends his faithful followers to reside after this earthly life. Mary was assumed into heaven, which is a reward promised to each one of us. We look at Mary and know where we shall be by following her son, loving him, and serving him in our neighbor in this life.

Like Mary, let our spiritual and devotional life bring a change in our lives and the lives of others to bring them closer to God. As a woman of compassion and care, Mary went in haste to assist her elderly cousin, Elizabeth. Like

Mary, let us be ready always to assist the elderly, the sick, the poor and needy, the jobless, the homeless, those overwhelmed by uncertainties and adversities, the depressed, people struggling to find meaning in life and looking for security, those struggling in married life, and those who lack faith. In all these ways, we shall prepare for our own assumption to meet God the Father, Jesus the Son, the Holy Spirit, Mary the Mother of God, the Angels, Saints, and all peoples from the corners of the world.

May the Lord bless you on this Glorious Feast Day of the Assumption of the Blessed Virgin Mary into heaven.

Let us recite the oldest recorded prayer to our Blessed Lady:

"Beneath your compassion,
we take refuge, O Mother of God:
do not despise our petitions in time of trouble:
but rescue us from dangers,
only pure, only Blessed One."
(Dated about 250 A.D.)

THE FEAST OF ALL SAINTS
(November 1)

Revelation 7:2-4, 9-14; 1 John 3:1-3); Matthew 51-12a

CALLED TO SAINTHOOD

Catholics and other Christian denominations commemorate All Saints' Day on November 1 to honor and venerate all the saints, known and unknown, who are in heaven. It is a holy day of obligation in the Roman Catholic Church. In the Eastern Orthodox, All Saints' Day is observed on the first Sunday after Pentecost.

It is a public holiday in some places such as Germany and France where some businesses are closed. Again, All Saints' Day has become a day when in some places like the Philippines families remember their deceased relatives and family friends and visit their graves, repair and clean their graves, and offer prayers, flowers and lighted candles.

According to some sources, the origins of All Saints' Day date back to the seventh century (609 or 610). On May 13 of that year, Pope Boniface IV consecrated the Roman Pantheon in Rome to the Blessed Virgin Mary and all the martyrs of the Church. It replaced a pre-Christian Feast of the Lemures when the dead were remembered. Later, Pope Gregory III (731-741) extended the feast to honor all the saints in heaven on November 1 when he dedicated a chapel in St. Peter's Basilica in Rome to honor all the saints. In the ninth century (837), Pope Gregory IV made the Feast universal.

There also developed the tradition of keeping vigil on the eve of All Saints Day when the saints were "hallowed" or revered, hence All Hallow Even (All Saints' Eve), which literally means, The Evening before All Hollows Day, or The Evening before All Saint's Day. Over the years, Hallow Even became known as Halloween and people dress up in disguise as saints or scary images and display lanterns showing frightening images. Trick-or-treat has become a common practice on Halloween when children wear costumes from door to door in a neighborhood for "treats" or might play tricks on people who refuse.

Later, November 2, All Souls Day, became connected to the Feast of All Saints to remember and pray for the dead in purgatory who have not made it to heaven. It is the belief that the living can pray for souls in purgatory for their sins to be forgiven, to enable them to go to heaven.

Like Christmas, Halloween is now a secular phenomenon and commercialized, but its origins from All Saints' Day connote a profound spiritual significance. Usually, photos of saints show halos crowning their heads depicting holiness and sometimes their presence among angels hanging over the clouds and playing harps praising God.

Sainthood is the goal, and the Book of Revelation shows how one day, at the end of time, the saints from all the corners of the world will gather around the throne of God and live a life of perpetual adoration and praise. Indeed, our catechism teaches that God creates us to know, love, and serve him, and live eternally with him in heaven after our lives on earth. Heaven is our goal and sainthood is the passport, living holy lives on earth to be crowned saints by God. Sainthood is therefore our goal, and we start our process for sainthood here on earth.

In the Beatitudes, our Savior Jesus gives the blueprint towards sainthood. Each one of them is a mark for "Blessedness" which, as we read do not seem difficult yet can be extremely challenging for us to follow. We believe the revelation to the Apostle Paul that God puts us on the path to sainthood: "My grace is sufficient for you, for my power is made perfect in weakness" (2 Corinthians 12:9).

The Beatitudes are about love and selflessness, mercy and generosity, patience and humility, and peace and justice. They are about kind words to a spouse, sister or brother, and a parent and sibling; help and comfort to the suffering; an open arm to the weary, refugee and stranger; care of the sick,

407

disheartened, and those seeking meaning in life; and support to the needy.

There are many saintly acts and ministries to give away time, talent, and treasure at home, workplace, street, within the community, and church. What ministry have you chosen? Simple deeds and gestures make a saint.

In 2009, I authored a novel entitled Stranded on Both Banks, in which I portrayed life in rural Africa. Towards the end of the book, the main character, the impressionable Juni, the "City Boy" gone to a rural environment for the first time, is now a grown-up, and reminisces about the elderly Nana Serwaa he met in the village:

"My childhood memories about Nana Serwaa's kindness when she visited us in Kumasi were so vivid. She possessed a peaceful aura and exuded gentleness and docile affability that attracted everybody. The people were simply fond of her. Children in the village found her extremely delightful. She knew each child by name and was grandma to all. There might have been just a few who had not eaten from her pot."

Another major character, Rev. Fr. Appiah Koduah, describes the saintly life of his aunt, the same Nana Serwaa, in a eulogy:

"We had a great mother, one who taught us to be kind and generous. If you ask me what the secret of her attraction was, it was simply that all who came to her received her undivided attention. Her story makes us feel that our mother is one of the people hidden away in the calendar of the saints. She had a terrific sense of humor that brightened our spirits and a sense of purpose that impacted greatly on our lives."

Many people are hurt and disappointed when their good deeds are not acknowledged and seem to fall by the wayside. They should continue their sacrificial deeds because good deeds never get lost. We sow a good deed in the minds of others and will always have a positive impact. Nana Serwaa's kindness and concern for others had been sown in the mind of Juni. We do not lose good deeds before God; they glorify God, who will reward us with crowns as his saints.

In the story, Fr. Appiah Koduah says his aunt "had a terrific sense of humor" suggesting that his aunt recognized the funny side of life. She shows us that simple and ordinary people become saints held up for inspiration and that saints are not only those formally recognized by the Church. We are all created to be saints, including people we pass by in the streets.

In the homily on the thirtieth Sunday, we carried a story about a homeless man, Richard Leroy Walters (1931-2007). He lived in Phoenix, Arizona, and died at the age of 76, leaving behind four million dollars for charities including the National Public Radio (NPR), a Catholic Mission of Mercy in Phoenix, and a volunteer nurse with the mission, Rita Belle, who took care of him when he was ill. Walters was a retired engineer and an atheist who gave up material comforts and lived as a happy person without a home or a car while sleeping on the grounds of a local senior center. Among his few belongings, it is reported, was a radio. It is also said that although he was a homeless man, he handed out flowers left over from the markets to people just to make them happy and smile. He became a Catholic on his deathbed with the aid of his nurse.

Yesterday, October 31, was the memorial of Blessed Irene Stefani (1891-1930) born in Italy as Aurelia Mercede Stefani. She took the name "Irene" when she professed as a Consolata Missionary Sister at the age of 20. She worked in Kenya (1920-1930) attending to the sick in hospitals and the wounded in Kenya and Tanzania during World War I (1915-1918). A medical colonel called her the "angel of charity," and in Kenya and Tanzania, children and adults called her Sister Nyaatha (translates, "Mother of Mercy"). That summed up her life as a nun. She died in Kenya of bubonic plague while working with the sick.

Sister Nyaatha was beatified on May 30, 2015. The miracle that initiated the way to her beatification was described as "multiplication of water." When about 270 people were taking refuge in a church during the civil war in Mozambique (1981-1992) for four days, water replenished for drinking inside the baptismal fount in the parish church of Nipepe,

Mozambique. On hearing about her death, one former student of hers is reported to have said, "Sr. Irene has not been killed by an illness; it is love that killed her!" (Consolata Missionary Sisters).

We are all called to be saints. Heaven is our goal. Our own limitations may mar the route, but Jesus Christ, our Lord and Savior, will always provide the grace to live up to the task so we can become saints in heaven.

The Peace of the Lord be with you.

Prayer
Father, Lord of compassion, be with us as we journey through life, guiding us to abide by the teachings of your Son so we can enter your kingdom. Amen.

COMMEMORATION OF ALL THE FAITHFUL DEPARTED
(All Souls' Day November 2)

Wisdom 3:1-9; Romans 5:5-11; John 6:37-40

EVERYONE'S JOURNEY

The Commemoration of All the Faithful Departed or All Souls Day is observed on November 2. On this day, Christians remember all the faithful departed, visit their graves with flowers and lighted candles, and make intercessory prayers to gain indulgences for them. In some areas, photographs of the dead placed on tables in the church with lighted candles are blessed.

Like the Feast of All Saints' Day, the Feast of All Souls Day, dates to the tenth century to Odilo, Abbot of Cluny (died 1048), France. The Cluny Abbey was the center of a monastic reform following the rule of Saint Benedict dedicated to the Western monastic traditions of peace, solitude, prayer, work, and charity to the poor. The names of the faithful departed who were not canonized were pasted in the church to be remembered. With over 10,000 monks (Cluniac Order) in over 1,500 monasteries at the time, the practice known as "Remembrance Day," was later extended throughout Europe. It was designated as All Souls Day when all the faithful departed, known and unknown, were remembered. It became universal during the papacy of Pope Benedict XIV.

While All Saints' Day focuses on the saints in heaven, All Souls Day has its emphasis on the dead who are yet to attain heaven. Where these souls dwell is known as Purgatory, which according to Church doctrine formulated at the Councils of Florence and Trent, is defined as a place of purification of the faithful who died with "stains of sin" before their final entry into Heaven.

The doctrine of Purgatory has been commonly interpreted to mean a kind of "mini hell" if one does not immediately qualify to go to heaven. According to the Catechism of the Catholic Church, however, purgatory prepares one to "achieve the holiness necessary to enter the joy of Heaven." (CCC 1030). It is the "final purification of the elect, which is entirely different from the punishment of the damned." Pope Benedict XVI, dismissing any human time duration, writes that "it is the time of 'passage' to communion with God in the Body of Christ." Indeed, it means that "the stain of sin and our impurities will be removed that we might be made ready for eternity."

Another aspect of the feast brings home the fact that human beings are created to journey to their maker. Therefore, we pray for those who, due to some "stain of sin," have not yet reached the place they can see their Creator face to face and see him as he is (1 John 3:1-3). We believe that God is all-loving and trust that all peoples will want to be in his presence, hence the need for our intercessory prayers.

The Akan people of Ghana have a saying that while a dead person is being buried, death is like a person rolling his eyes through the living to pick the next victim. It is significant, therefore, that as we commemorate the Day of the Dead (Día de los Muertos), we remind ourselves that death is a necessary end for all. It is everyone's destiny which cannot be avoided or predicted, the point of transition at the tunnel of life into an ideal world in the eternal presence of God. We must think about death, but our preparation toward sainthood is in the present where the kingdom of God is already in our midst and Jesus urges us to cast the Beatitudes into a solid general principle of life.

The Peace of the Lord be with you.

Prayer To Christ for Grace
O Lord Jesus,
Pour into us the spirit of your love,
That in the hour of our death,
We may be worthy to vanquish the enemy
And receive the heavenly crown. Amen.

THANKSGIVING DAY IN THE UNITED STATES
(Fourth Thursday of the month of November)

Sirach 50:22-24; 1 Corinthians 1:3-9; Luke 17:11-19

IN ALL THINGS, GIVE THANKS TO GOD

Many indigenous cultures and communities throughout the world have always observed and remembered Thanksgiving Festivals as a remarkable event in their history, beliefs, and other aspects of their social life. Usually a yearly affair, a *Thanksgiving* festival is celebrated for hours, a day, or weeks, and people travel from far and near to the places of their heritage. It is a period when ancestors are remembered, unity fostered within families and communities and acts of love and gratitude expressed. Most of the *Thanksgiving* festivals throughout the world are observed to give thanks to God whom the people believe is the creator and provider of all things. For example, the *Passover Festival* of Israel dating to the *Exodus* period and the ancient civilizations of the Egyptians, Greeks, and Romans honored their gods after the fall harvest each year.

Thanksgiving, Christmas Day, and New Year's Day are part of the broader fall and winter holiday seasons in the United States. Thanksgiving is a national holiday in the United States. The concept or origin of giving thanks to God for a good harvest in the United States is traced to both the cultures of indigenous Wampanoag people and the Pilgrims who came from England in 1620 on the ship *The Mayflower*. The native *Wampanoag* coached the settlers to grow native crops like maize, master hunting and fishing skills, and survival skills. The harvest in the following year (October 1621) was bountiful. The settlers invited the locals to celebrate their success with food and wild turkey and give thanks to God. Soon after the first Thanksgiving celebration in 1621 between the natives and first settlers, conflicts arose between

413

the two groups due to the ideals of colonialism and the "Great Dying" plague believed to have originated from Europe that killed tens of thousands of the native people. The refusal to tell the story from an indigenous perspective has made some Native Americans consider Thanksgiving as a "National Day of Mourning."

The settlers in New England regularly observed the Thanksgiving as "days of prayer, thanking God for blessings such as military victory or the end of a drought." Some historians, however, suggest that other earlier settlers arriving in the United States in 1565 celebrated Thanksgiving Mass as their thanks to God for arriving safely. Early documents show that on December 4, 1619, the land of Virginia observed Thanksgiving and designated the date as a holy day, "a day of thanksgiving to the Almighty God."

Thanksgiving in the United States received Congressional approval during the time of George Washington and Thursday, November 26, 1789, was designated as "Day of Public Thanksgiving." It became a federal holiday in 1863 when Abraham Lincoln designated the last Thursday in November as a National Thanksgiving holiday. He described it during the time of the American Civil War as a national day of "Thanksgiving and praise to our beneficent Father who dwelleth in the Heavens." President Franklin Roosevelt changed the date to the fourth Thursday of November.

Thanksgiving was therefore founded as a religious observance for all the members of the community to thank God for a common purpose — "for the civil and religious liberty," for "useful knowledge," and for "God's kind care," as well as "His Providence," (George Washington in 1789) for the United States as a nation and for the citizenry. The Congressional declaration of 1782 was specific about the "many instances of Divine goodness" in the life of the nation and the urgency to show "gratitude to God for His goodness by a cheerful obedience to His laws and by the practice of true and undefiled religion, which is the great foundation of public prosperity and national happiness."

Thanksgiving is observed nationwide in America on the fourth Thursday in November, while in Canada, it is the second Monday of October. Traditionally, it is a time when family members come together for a large thanksgiving meal or dinner with turkey playing a central role. According to statistics, about 46 million turkeys were consumed in the United States in 2024. It is a time to express gratitude for God's favors and blessings for families, and to share and give away. The poor and needy receive food, especially the traditional turkey, and most religious and charitable groups, corporations, and civil societies sponsor annual food drives.

Sadly, however, the profound religious meaning of the gracious celebration of Thanksgiving has toned down, and for many families, it is only at Thanksgiving that "Grace" (prayers before and after meal) is said. There are a lot of vacation and travel, fun-fares, parades, television and radio programs, and sports during the Thanksgiving weekend. Many students in college travel home to reunite with their families while those who remain on-campus and international students are fed Thanksgiving dinners. Thanksgiving Day is regarded as the start of the Season of Christmas, and the next day, famously called *Black Friday,* is a remarkable shopping day throughout the country.

Catholics attend Mass on Thanksgiving Day to gather as one family—the *People of God*—around the Eucharistic meal to express solidarity and show love of God and neighbor. At Mass, the Faithful listen to the memorable story of the ten lepers healed by Jesus. Only one returned to give thanks to God! The challenge leaps forth—do you give thanks to God? Do you acknowledge his relevance in your life? Do you teach your children about showing gratitude to God as a provider of all that the family has? As parents, will you ensure that your children in college will return home the next year for Thanksgiving Day still acknowledging the values taught at home, including belief in God?

The Gospel reading reminds us to return to the source of every gift, God who created us and has given us gratuitous love and blessings. Jesus underscores the importance of expressing gratitude for blessings we receive from God. Again, it signifies our invitation to give thanks as we gather as *Family of God* around the Eucharistic table where we express our love of God and for neighbor. As we acknowledge God in our lives and thank him for everything, we also need to recognize God in the many people around us, particularly the poor and needy, the sick, the elderly, migrants, refugees, and the suffering. Charity is the language and expression of faith. The more one loves and the more one gives, the more one demonstrates faith and receives more blessings from God. By expressing gratitude to God and recognizing neighbor, we cement relationships with God and each other.

Today, as you celebrate Thanksgiving, see the face of Jesus Christ on the face of each member of your family, especially those who need your forgiveness. One or two of them—or you—may not be alive next year to join in the Thanksgiving family gathering!

From hence, we are asked to return to the source of every life and gift, the God who created us and gives us his love and blessings. Our Lord and Savior, Jesus Christ, emphasizes the importance of always expressing gratitude to God.

Happy Thanksgiving Day.

The Peace of the Lord be with you.

Prayer
Father, each of us needs to return to you as the source of life and give you the praise due to you. Let us see one another as brother and sisters who must always live in peace. Amen.

THE SOLEMNITY OF THE IMMACULATE CONCEPTION OF THE BLESSED VIRGIN MARY
(December 8)

Genesis 3:9-15, 20; Ephesians 1:3-6, 11-12; Luke 1:26-38

LIFE LIVED IN THE SPIRIT OF GOD

The Solemnity of the Immaculate Conception of the Blessed Virgin Mary is celebrated on December 8. Also known as Immaculate Conception Day, this Catholic feast recognizes the Blessed Virgin Mary, mother of Jesus, was conceived without Original Sin and preserved from sin in all her life. Catholics observe December 8 as a day of obligation requiring attendance at Mass.

The Immaculate Conception of Mary many times misunderstood and confused with the Feast of the Annunciation of the Lord (March 25) which celebrates the conception of Jesus by Mary, exactly nine months before Christmas. The Annunciation of the Lord commemorates the visit of Archangel Gabriel to Mary to inform her she would conceive a son to be called Jesus. When Mary said "yes" to the angel, she conceived Jesus in her womb. Separately, the feast on December 8 is the commemoration of the Conception of the Blessed Virgin Mary by her mother St. Anne; and September 8, celebrates the Birthday of the Blessed Virgin Mary, nine months after her conception.

The Immaculate Conception of the Blessed Virgin Mary is the Patroness of the United States of America. The French Jesuit explorer, Father Jacques Marquette and his companion Louis Joliet, begun evangelizing in the Mississippi basin in 1673 entering the area from Canada. The name Father Marquette gave to this massive and long river was, "The River of the Immaculate Conception" intending to consecrate the river and the natives around it to the Blessed Mary. In 1846 the bishops of the United States declared Mary as the patroness of the country under the title of the Immaculate Conception. The Solemnity of the Immaculate Conception is a holy day of obligation in the United States.

The countries that observe Immaculate Conception as a national holiday include Argentina, Austria, Chile, Colombia, East Timor, Guam, Italy, Peru, Panama, Philippines, Portugal, Spain, and Vatican City. In some of these Catholic countries, the day is usually a family day marked by the celebration of the Eucharist, cultural processions and dancing, fireworks, and ethnic meals. In the Philippines, the day is observed as a public holiday in honor of the Blessed Virgin Mary and as Patroness of the country that was permanently signed into constitutional law in March 2017. In Panama, the Feast of the Immaculate Conception on December 8 is also celebrated as Mother's Day, and the people of Guam venerate Mary's statue on December 8.

The Church teaches that Jesus, the Son of God, could not be conceived in sin and hence God gave a special grace to Mary to be born free from sin. Mary's sinless status was in part a precondition for Jesus' conception and redemptive act. God had chosen Mary to be the mother of his son before the creation of the world. The Feast of the Immaculate Conception means that God filled the Blessed Virgin Mary with grace and love and that includes preserving her free from all stains of Original Sin. Mary's status as Immaculate is an act of God's love and grace announced by the Angel Gabriel, "Peace be with you! The Lord is with you and has greatly blessed you" and therefore "Your son will be called the son of the Most High." The message tells the world she was preserved to be the mother of God, a revelation that existed long before the expressed Catholic dogma. It is proper to conclude, therefore, that Mary was conceived without Original Sin and remained free of every personal sin in life. Through God's grace and merits of Jesus Christ, she was already redeemed from the moment of her conception.

In the Middle Ages, the doctrine of the Immaculate Conception was an issue of dispute, but did not receive particular attention from St. Bernard or St. Thomas Aquinas. Eadmer of Canterbury (1064-1124), who was the secretary of St. Anselm, argued Mary was free from Original Sin with the Latin axiom, "Potuit, decuit, ergo fecit" ("God was able to do it; it was appropriate; therefore, he did it"). The present doctrine seems to be based on the argument by John Duns Scotus (1265-1308). He purported that the flesh through whom the Son of God was to be born could not have been subjected to the influence of the Evil One.

At the third apparition of the Blessed Virgin Mary to St. Catherine Labouré in France on November 27, 1830, St. Catherine saw letters written in gold that read: "Oh Mary conceived without sin, pray for us who have recourse to thee."

The feast has been observed since the fifth century in the Eastern Church and the eighth century in the Western Church. Pope Clement XI designated the feast as a Holy Day of Obligation on December 6, 1708. In 1854 Pope Pius IX declared the feast as an essential dogma for the Roman Catholic Church: "The most Blessed Virgin Mary, in the first instant of her conception, by a singular grace and privilege granted by Almighty God, in view of the merits of Jesus Christ, the Savior of the human race, was preserved from all stain of sin." At the same time, the Pope commissioned a statue in Rome depicting Mary crushing the serpent's head under her feet to demonstrate the mystery of the Immaculate Conception. Every year, on December 8, the Holy Father presents a wreath in honor of Mary. An officer of the Roman Fire Brigade climbs a ladder to place the wreath of flowers on the arms of Mary's statue. In a vision in Lourdes (1858) four years after the declaration by Pope Pius IX, the Blessed Virgin Mary told Saint Marie-Bernadette Soubirous in a vision: "I am the Immaculate Conception."

The Church's doctrine and tradition continue to say that both Adam and Eve were created immaculate and without sin, but they fell from God's grace. Their sin corrupted the world, which is passed on to everyone. This is called Original Sin. It simply means that the nature of the human being was corrupted in such a way that we have a tendency to sin. Mary and Jesus were also created immaculate and remained faithful so that through them, humanity is redeemed. Jesus becomes the New Adam (1 Corinthians 15:45-49), and Mary the New Eve attested by Early Church Fathers like Saint Justin Martyr (born A.D. 103) and Saint Irenaeus of Lyons (A.D. 180).

The significance of Mary's conception is baptism cleanses us of our Original Sin. If we remain faithful to God like Jesus and Mary, we will be made immaculate in heaven. Again, it makes Mary a prophetic model possible for all to attain if we cooperate with the grace of God. When we see Mary as the first fruit of Jesus' redemption, we come to know fully that the message or mission of Jesus to save the world is true and has meaning. We can be saved, just as Mary was.

Another Catholic tradition is that three people were born without Original Sin. They are Mary, Jesus, and John the Baptist. Mary's birth and infancy is not in the Bible, but Early Christians held the belief that her birth also had to be miraculous. Hence, the story that the Archangel Gabriel appeared to Anne and her husband Joachim, a childless couple, to announce Anne would give birth to a child who would be honored by the world. The difference with John the Baptist is that he was conceived with Original Sin like anybody but not born with it! He was cleansed of Original Sin at the visitation of Mary to Elizabeth when the "infant leaped in her (Elizabeth's) womb." It was a spiritual baptism received from Christ that cleansed him of Original Sin before he was born. The tradition says that John the Baptist was, however, subject to the effects of Original Sin after his birth, unlike Jesus and Mary. He was not free from sin in his life. But he lived a decent life filled with the Spirit of God.

What does today's feast mean to us? Just as John the Baptist received baptism by Jesus through Mary to remove his Original Sin, in the same way Jesus Christ, through Mary, was born to transform our human nature into a closer relationship with God. Through baptism, we renounce sin with unequivocal affirmation to do God's will with spirit-filled faith, humility, and obedience, like Mary. Again, like John the Baptist, we are subject to the effects of Original Sin, and we can either cooperate with God's grace to nurture our relationship with him or live without him.

Many people in the world go their own way. They do not allow the Word of God to touch them. They cultivate a passion for things in the world. Let us use the grace of the gift of faith to overcome the effects of sin so that our lives center on Jesus through the intercession of the Immaculate and Blessed Virgin Mary.

The Peace of the Lord be with you.

Prayer
O Mary, conceived without sin, pray for us who have recourse to Thee. Amen.

EPILOGUE

Religion may not completely explain the meaning of life, but makes us conscious of the fact that humans are at the center of life's concept. This is true especially looking at the saying attributed to one of the greatest ancient philosophers, Socrates (c.470-399 B.C), that "the unexamined life is not worth living."

The book you have used for reflections for almost a year now, I am sure, has helped you to examine and understand the purpose of your life, beliefs—essentially, as a Christian—and actions as related to other human beings. Hopefully, this noble pursuit has helped you to realize definitively you have common goals and aspirations with your fellow neighbors, those both next door and across the globe, culminating in a grand pursuit of security, goodness, and happiness.

The Catholic Catechism (1721) echoes the well-known Baltimore Catechism, clearly stating that "God made me to know Him, to love Him, and to Serve him in this world and to be happy with Him forever in heaven." This, I believe, expands and underscores the profound idea in the laconic assertion attributed to Socrates that we must seek wisdom to understand the meaning of life. Such knowledge, Socrates attests, will teach us that our duty to God is to make ourselves and all others content.

According to the Book of Hebrews, God revealed himself partially through the prophets in the past, but now, He has done so through His gift, a Son (Hebrews 1:1-2), because of His gratuitous love for us (John 3:16). The Christian Church's yearly liturgical calendar commemorates the major events in salvation history, highlighting each stage of the life of Jesus Christ. Each public or private celebration comprises prayers, worship, and readings from the Old and New Testaments. In the Catholic Church, the major events in salvation history spread across a three-year cycle as Year A, Year B, and Year C.

I have endeavored in this book to lead reflections on the Sunday readings of the Liturgical Year A or Cycle A. It is my fervent hope that through these reflections, you will arrive at a better understanding of the wisdom and knowledge of the Word of God, renew your faith in the Incarnate Son, Jesus Christ, and commit more fully to Walking in the Footsteps of JESUS.

The Peace of the Lord be with you.

COMMON CATHOLIC PRAYERS

Prayer of Saint Francis of Assisi

Lord, make me an instrument of your peace.
Where there is hatred, let me sow love; where there is injury, pardon;
where there is doubt, faith;
where there is despair, hope;
where there is darkness, light;
and where there is sadness, joy.
O Divine Master,
grant that I may not so much seek
to be consoled as to console;
to be understood as to understand;
to be loved as to love.
For it is in giving that we receive;
it is in pardoning that we are pardoned;
and it is in dying that we are born to eternal life. Amen.

A Father's Prayer to St. Joseph

Hail, Guardian of the Redeemer,
Spouse of the Blessed Virgin Mary.
To you, God entrusted his only Son;
In you, Mary placed her trust;
With you, Christ became man.
Blessed Joseph, to us, too,
show yourself a father
and guide us in the path of life.
Obtain for us grace, mercy, and courage,
and defend us from every evil. Amen.

From: Patris corde

A Mother's Prayer

Father in Heaven,
grant me the grace to appreciate the dignity
which you have conferred on me.
Let me realize that not even the Angels
have been blessed with such a privilege,
to share in your creative miracle
and bring new Saints to Heaven.
Make me a good mother to all my children
after the example of Mary, the Mother of your Son.
Through the intercession of Jesus and Mary
I ask your continued blessings on my family.
Let us all be dedicated to your service on earth
and attain the eternal happiness of your Kingdom in Heaven. Amen.

God, Hear My Prayer

(A Child's Prayer for Protection)
God in Heaven hear my prayer,
keep me in thy loving care.
Be my guide in all I do,
Bless all those who love me too. Amen.

Thank You Prayer

Thank You, Lord.
I am grateful to you
for all the blessings in my life,
for my family and friends,
for my health and my safety,
for my food and my clothing,
for my shelter and protection.
I am grateful for the joys
that I experienced today.
But I am most grateful
for my struggles,
because they bring me to you.
Through the pain and sorrow,
I know you are with me,
even when I forget you are there.
And only through sorrows,
can I truly embrace the joys.
So, thank you for everything,
the ease and the difficulty,
the wins and the losses,
the light and the dark,
that always lead me home to you.
Thank You, Lord.

BIBLIOGRAPHY

Carroll Stuhimueller, C.P., Biblical Meditations For Ordinary Time-Weeks 1-9 (New York/Ramsey: Paulist Press, 1984)

Carroll Stuhimueller, C.P., Biblical Meditations For Ordinary Time-Weeks 10-22 (New York/Ramsey: Paulist Press, 1984)

Carroll Stuhimueller, C.P., Biblical Meditations For Ordinary Time-Weeks 23-34 (New York/Ramsey: Paulist Press, 1984)

Fernando Armellini, SCI, Celebrating The Word. Year B (Nairobi: Paulines Publications Africa, 1994)

Good News Bible. With The Deuterocanonical Books (The United Bible Societies)

Joseph G. Donders, Praying and Preaching the Sunday Gospel (Maryknoll, New York: Orbis Books, 1990)

Kevin O'Sullivan, O.F.M., The Sunday Readings, "Cycle B" 2 (Nagasandra, Bangalore: St. Paul Press, 2002)

Peter Coughlan & Peter Purdue, Commentary On The Sunday Lectionary. Cycle C (Collegeville: The Liturgical Press, 1970)

Robin Duckworth, ed., This Is The Word Of The Lord: The Year Of Mark, Year B (London: Oxford University Press, 1980)

Sunday & Daily Homilies (Dallas: Gold Label Publications)

MSGR. RAPHAEL A. OWUSU PEPRAH

Monsignor Raphael Owusu Peprah is a priest of the Catholic Archdiocese of Kumasi, Ghana, now assigned to the Diocese of Richmond, Virginia, USA.

He is a product of St. Peter's Major Seminary, Cape Coast, Ghana. He obtained BA and MA (Status) from Oxford University, UK, specializing in Geography. He has a Diploma in Educational Planning and Management from London University, Institute of Education, UK.

He has held positions as Executive Director of the Ghana Diocesan Catholic Priests Association, Rector of St. Peter's Basilica, Kumasi, Director of Pastoral Center, Kumasi, Chaplain and tutor at Opoku Ware Senior High School, Kumasi, Vice Rector at St. Hubert's Seminary, Kumasi, and Vocations Director. Currently, he is the Pastor of St. Luke Catholic Church, Virginia Beach, Virginia, USA.

He has authored the books, *Stranded on Both Banks,* and *Walking in the Footsteps of JESUS,* Year A, Year B, and Year C.